The Wedding Feast of the Lamb

Wolsey; a butcher's boy
from Ipswich

animals are saved p. 32

John D. Caputo, *series editor*

PERSPECTIVES IN
CONTINENTAL
PHILOSOPHY

EMMANUEL FALQUE

The Wedding Feast of the Lamb
Eros, the Body, and the Eucharist

TRANSLATED BY GEORGE HUGHES

FORDHAM UNIVERSITY PRESS
New York ■ 2016

This book was first published in French as *Les noces de l'agneau: Essai philosophique sur le corps et l'eucharistie*, by Emmanuel Falque © Les Éditions du Cerf, 2011.

Fordham University Press has no responsibility for the persistence or accuracy of URLs for external or third-party Internet websites referred to in this publication and does not guarantee that any content on such websites is, or will remain, accurate or appropriate.

Fordham University Press also publishes its books in a variety of electronic formats. Some content that appears in print may not be available in electronic books.

Visit us online at www.fordhampress.com.

Library of Congress Cataloging-in-Publication Data

Names: Falque, Emmanuel, 1963– author.
Title: The wedding feast of the Lamb : eros, the body, and the Eucharist / Emmanuel Falque ; translated by George Hughes.
Other titles: Noces de l'agneau. English
Description: First edition. | New York, NY : Fordham University Press, 2016. | Series: Perspectives in Continental philosophy | Includes bibliographical references and index.
Identifiers: LCCN 2015050568 (print) | LCCN 2016019976 (ebook) | ISBN 9780823270408 (cloth : alk. paper) | ISBN 9780823270415 (pbk. : alk. paper) | ISBN 9780823270422 (ePub)
Subjects: LCSH: Human body (Philosophy) | Human body—Religious aspects—Catholic Church. | Lord's Supper—Real presence.
Classification: LCC B105.B64 F3513 2016 (print) | LCC B105.B64 (ebook) | DDC 128/.6—dc23
LC record available at https://lccn.loc.gov/2015050568

Printed in the United States of America

18 17 16   5 4 3 2 1

First edition

Contents

Translator's Note

In Emmanuel Falque's work we encounter one of liveliest and most challenging voices in contemporary French philosophy and theology. Falque is a key figure in the "theological turn" that has transformed recent phenomenology in France.[1] It has been suggested that he is part of the new generation of philosophers who have been rethinking phenomenology, along with Claude Romano and Jocelyn Benoist—and he aligns himself directly with philosophers such as Natalie Depraz and Jérôme de Gramont. But what gives Falque's work its distinctive style is that he "dares" to do philosophy and theology at the same time. *The Wedding Feast of the Lamb* provides an important synthesis of his views, as well as a demonstration of the method that Falque believes to be the best way forward in philosophy and theology.[2]

The phenomenological tradition remains important to Falque—as it does in most modern French philosophy. He insists, however, that what theology can and must do is transform phenomenology. The passive approach of so much contemporary phenomenology and its concern with its own abstractions does not interest Falque; he believes strongly that philosophy must deal with real problems such as those we confront in our own bodies and our own lives. He looks back in this respect to a much earlier generation of phenomenologists, to figures such as Max Scheler, Edith Stein, and Hannah Arendt, whose ethical approach directly reflected their own actual situation. And if Falque thinks that phenomenology must change in such a way, the same goes for his theology. He likes to cite

Pope John XXIII, at the opening of the Second Vatican Council, insisting that the Christian mystery today "should be studied and expounded through the methods of research and through the literary forms of modern thought."[3] Paul Ricœur has reminded us that philosophy does not speak from a "placeless place," and Falque's view of his own situation is that it lies within a tradition of reason and discourse derived historically from the Christian community. We never, he insists, think alone.[4] Moving to the limits of the territory that stretches between philosophy and theology, he is thus able to analyze experience and its ramifications ("experience" being one of Falque's key words). The experience of suffering in relation to the deaths of two people he loved, for example, provided the motivation for his earlier book, *Le Passeur de Gethsémani* [The guide to Gethsemane].[5]

Falque teaches in the faculty of philosophy of the French Catholic Institute, and he does not disguise his commitment to the Catholic faith. At the same time he asserts firmly that he does not write Catholic apologetics; rather, his focus on experience leads him to ask difficult questions that many Catholics would prefer to gloss over. He refuses to shy away from the problem of how we can understand the Resurrection (the central topic of his book *The Metamorphosis of Finitude*[6]), and he is constantly aware of the problems posed by Catholic views on sexuality, sexual difference, and the body. He pays homage to the way that phenomenology has reopened questions of meaning, but thinks that when it comes to considering the body we need to progress further and more widely. In *The Wedding Feast of the Lamb*, Falque emphasizes that, in trying to understand the body, we cannot ignore the life of our organs and our own interior chaos. If he draws on Nietzsche and Deleuze, he also makes plain that his thought has been shaped by discussions with practicing surgeons and anesthetists, as well as psychoanalysts. It is vital also to be aware of the discursive traditions within which we hold opinions—so Falque uses a reading of Genesis to reexamine the basis of male-female relations and the topic of difference. His biblical readings and his treatment of incarnation allow him to consider our fundamental animality in the context of Christian life and thought.

The central problem of *The Wedding Feast of the Lamb,* however, is that of the eucharist. We attend this ceremony, we see it as an essential part of Christian life in the world, but what does it really mean? How on earth can it be that Christians still claim to eat Christ's body? Is it a form of religious cannibalism? How have we carried over the tradition of the Passover meal into the ritual of the modern Mass? Why should the Mass be connected with wedding feasts, or the erotic? Is there any possible modern way of making sense of transubstantiation?

Such questions are explored by Falque as a philosopher—one who wishes to ensure that our concepts for dealing with them are well founded—and they are also dealt with through witty divagations into ancient debate on the subject. As Falque points out, "today's questions always derive from those of yesterday, indeed also from their answers."[7] It is perhaps his most fascinating talent to be able to exploit what he has called the "reciprocal fecundity" of modern and medieval philosophy. He quotes with ease and familiarity from a vast corpus of medieval philosophy and from the Fathers of the Church—material that is brought into play because, although our views may have moved in a different direction, our arguments are still shaped by the residue of earlier discourse. Falque relates Bonaventure's view of the eucharist to performativity and speech acts. He explores the revulsion that St. Augustine suggests as a possible response to being given flesh to eat and blood to drink in the act of communion. We find him citing Canon Law and the decisions of Pope Alexander III (1159–1181), as well as the arguments of Yves de Chartres or Anselm of Laon, in order to discuss sexual difference. In a particularly rich and fascinating passage, Falque looks at John Chrysostom's speculation that the tongue becomes red with the blood of Christ in drinking the wine of the eucharist, and he ponders Bonaventure's problem as to whether our teeth risk breaking the flesh of Christ in chewing the Host. Falque's eye for a good example is remarkable. He seems to have taken on board what Ricœur calls the "most significant difficulty that a phenomenology of religion must confront": the necessity of adding "cultural and historical mediation" to linguistic analysis.[8]

If he is not a Catholic apologist, however, he is also not simply a medievalist. Falque may have a talent for picking out plums from arguments of the past, but he is also thoroughly modern in his "expressivist" focus—taking art to be a key expressive activity that offers a clarification of what man is.[9] His discussion of the eucharist draws in an illuminating way on the butcher-shop paintings of Francis Bacon, the nudes of Lucian Freud, and the studies of bodies in an anatomy demonstration by Lydie Arickx. Art provides for him another aspect of what we experience and need to understand.

"Exploration" might then sum up the intellectual approach Falque favors. He explores what looks promising. There is no single way offered here around the dilemmas facing the Christian in the modern world. One could apply to Falque the famous distinction made by Karl Jaspers between "system" and "systematization."[10] Falque's approach is systematized (philosophical and theological), but he does not attempt to push things into the straightjacket of a single (and unconvincing) world-system. Philosophy and theology shed light on experience, and Falque insists that it is possible to "cross the Rubicon between the two disciplines."[11] Translating his work is not easy; his extraordinary erudition poses almost as many problems for the translator as does the rigour of his philosophical thought. I hope, however, that this translation communicates Falque's ideas along with some of the vitality and inventiveness of his style, and I should like to salute his courage in facing real problems of Catholic doctrine. Participating in the Mass can never be quite the same after one has worked one's way through the topics in this book. *The Wedding Feast of the Lamb* forms part of what Falque calls his "triptych" of works on similar themes, but I think it is here that we encounter some of the most attractive aspects of his work. We meet a Catholic philosopher who makes his faith—and his experience—work for us in a compelling fashion.

Opening

Moving forward in the world of ideas means shifting the frontiers and thwarting people's expectations, because to think is to decide. Dogma, of course, would just stick to the essentials. And dogma has to be deployed at times by the philosopher, as by the theologian—even when these two are effectively the same person. But the Christian mystery today, as in the past, "should be studied and expounded through the methods of research and through the literary forms of modern thought."[1] I attempted this in previous publications by employing the narrative of the Passion, in the philosophical exploration of anguish and death (*Le Passeur de Gethsémani* [The guide to Gethsemane]). The project was more difficult with the Resurrection, where I had to deal with what is existential in birth and in the resurrected flesh (*The Metamorphosis of Finitude*). When it comes to the eucharist—where we need to consider what this "body" that we eat consists of ("this is my body"), and the "animality" in us that we often hide (the figure of the lamb), as well as the modality of the "eros" through which we come to celebrate the eucharist (the wedding feast)—then we are bound to find it even more difficult to push our inquiry forward, because there is an interior Chaos that remains truly hidden and it is something with which we need to come to terms (*The Wedding Feast of the Lamb*[2]).

I have tried, however, to construct a triptych based on these three topics. And, even if it means leaving many things for others to explore, I have tried to take a route whose itinerary is shaped by its end—one that privileges humankind as the site where God comes to us. Aquinas ascribes to St. Augustine the saying, "Walk like this human being [Christ] and you will come to God. It is better to limp along on the way than to walk briskly off the way." And Aquinas then comments, "For one who limps on the way, even though he makes just a little progress, is approaching his destination; but if one walks off the way, the faster he goes the further he gets from his destination."[3]

and "remains"

Preface

The Ghent Altarpiece, or, The Adoration of the Mystic Lamb

It is only a step—but what an important step—from the altarpiece of the Last Judgment (c.1446–1452), by Rogier van der Weyden in the Hospices de Beaune, to the Ghent altarpiece in Saint Bavo Cathedral (c.1430–1432), with its depiction of the Adoration of the Mystic Lamb, by the brothers Hubert and Jan van Eyck.[1] The first of these altarpieces is addressed to the sick and dying, and shows them the hope of resurrection, as the crust of the Earth is broken open by the bodies of the resurrected rising from the dead. A weighty topic is made even more serious here, as I tried first to describe in one book (*Le Passeur de Gethsémani* [The guide to Gethsemane])[2] and then to develop in another (*The Metamorphosis of Finitude*). The Resurrected One, taking on the form of a *passeur*, or guide, and showing a way or a "passage through," assumes responsibility for the blocked horizon of our existence, which he then transforms. That is what the polyptych of the Last Judgment taught us: what remained was to conceptualize it. And so in the introduction to *Metamorphosis* I discussed the "Beaune altarpiece or the germination of the resurrected."

The second altarpiece (Figure 1), that of the Van Eyck brothers at Ghent (the Adoration of the Mystic Lamb), is addressed to the faithful and to communicants. It draws the eye of the spectator to a sacrificial lamb, a kind of setting for the consecrated Host, which is waiting to appear. As the last book of the Bible proclaims in a kind of beatitude echoed through the liturgy, "Blessed are those who are called to the supper of the Lamb [*Beati, qui ad coenam nuptiarum Agni vocati sunt*]" (Rev. 19:9).[3]

Figure 1

The Lamb in its "apocalypse" or its "revelation" (*apokalyptô*) brings people together and gathers them like "a great multitude that no one could count. . . . They cried out in a loud voice 'Salvation belongs to our God who is seated *on the throne*, and *to the Lamb*.'" (Rev. 7:9–10) Like a monstrance on its base, the animal in the altarpiece stands there on the altar (Figure 2), taking the form of a mystic body and a eucharist for contemplation: the Adoration of the Mystic Lamb.

It is as though a groom has prepared Easter wedding celebrations for the great holy feast: "Then I saw between the throne and the four living creatures and among the elders a Lamb standing as if it had been slaughtered," says St. John, writing on his island of Patmos. "Let us rejoice and exult and give him glory, for the marriage of the Lamb has come, and his bride has made herself ready; to her it has been granted to be clothed with fine linen, bright and pure. . . . Come gather for the great supper of God" (Rev. 5:6, 19:7–8, 19:17).

Everything that this book tries to show in its discussion of eros, the body, and the eucharist, is already implied in the revelation to St. John or in the Ghent altarpiece. And the images that have constantly been with me as I write are (1) of *animality* (a sheep waiting to be sacrificed); (2) of the body, of *corporality* (Adam and Eve framing the polyptych); and (3) of

Figure 2

eros or sexual difference (from the distance between John the Baptist and Mary, to the separated troops of men and women surrounding the sacrificial lamb).

(1) When the prophet Micah, right at the top of the altarpiece, leans over a balcony—above the world, as it were—to have a look at what is happening below (right upper panel), or when Zechariah seems to read in his book of what is about to happen there with the lamb (left upper panel), what do they actually see in the center of a *scene* (*scène*) that is, as we shall see, a kind of *Last Supper* (*Cène*)[4]? What is there that still speaks to us when we look at the altarpiece today in the Cathedral of Saint Bavo in Ghent?

First of all there is the animal, or animal(ity), in the figure of the lamb—or perhaps we should talk of a sacrificial sheep.[5] We notice (a) that blood is gushing out; (b) that the animal is standing up; (c) that its gaze is staring and contemplative; and (d) that the lamb, which is animal rather than beast, unites in itself what is necessary for an incarnation—which, by way of the eucharistic viaticum, the sustenance for our journey, will continue to be manifest—and will give of itself to be eaten.

(a) The blood that spurts and flows from the pierced aorta of the lamb makes "real" for us the presence of the body in a monstrance designed for adoration: the Adoration of the Mystic Lamb. It is almost as if there is something avowedly divine in the gaze of an animal that takes humanity in its view but rejects all hint of bestiality along with all the excesses of sin. The blood, gathered in the chalice placed there to receive it, runs out of the fleece of the lamb on its side ("The river of the water of life . . . flowing from the throne of God and of the Lamb" [Rev. 22:1]). It flows as the water of life will flow, from the heart of Christ, whose side has been run through with a spear ("One of the soldiers pierced his side with a spear, and at once blood and water came out" [John 19:34]). In the work of the Van Eyck brothers there is not just mysticism and symbolism, but also realism, almost a biological realism. The sheep takes on the shape of an animal, sign of a total assumption of the cosmos, just as Christ takes on the shape of a man substantially and totally united with the divine.

John Wycliffe and Jan Hus, precursors of the Protestant Reformation, had maintained, shortly before the altarpiece was painted, that "Christ is not in the sacrament of the altar identically, truly and really in his proper corporeal presence."[6] Hubert and Jan van Eyck, as if recalling these reformers, who were condemned by the Council of Constance (1415), represent here, according to their own lights, what is unimaginable, pushing to its extreme the "reality" of the eucharistic bread. This reality is substantially present, there on the altar, through the image of the lamb sacrificed. The blood that streams out of the side of the animal, like the blood drawn from the side of Christ, figures for us the union of the divine and the human. It is a union that goes so far as to take charge of and change sin, but it also, perhaps, leads us toward our own animality.

(b) That the lamb is standing up recalls to us the One who is already resurrected and who is thus *raised* (*anistêmi*) from his descent and sojourn with the dead (Acts 2:24). We read on the altar: *Ecce Agnus Dei qui tollit peccata mundi* ("Here is the Lamb of God who takes away the sin of the world" [John 1:29]); and we should add: *IHES, Via, Veritas, Vita* ("I am the way, and the truth, and the life" [John 14:6]). Many representations of the Last Supper quite rightly show us the sacrificial lamb, going so far as to include it in the food that is to be eaten.[7] But with the Van Eyck brothers we are already given the Resurrected One to contemplate: "a Lamb standing (*estêkos*) as if it had been slaughtered" (Rev. 5:6). The Lamb is not only sacrificed through its death; it is here shown in its Life—and not simply any Life: it shows itself as "the one who *lives* for ever and ever" (Rev. 4:10). That which is called Life (*zôê*) extends so far that *all* life participates in this one who lives (*tô zônti*), and no life, not even animal life, can be foreign to it. The mystic life becomes curiously zoological—not, of course, in that God becomes (the) animal, but in that God also takes on *our* part of animality, by espousing humanity. The viaticum of the eucharist gives Life to our life solely insofar as it carries, almost maternally, *all* our humanity and is metamorphosed.

(c) There is something astonishing about the fixed and contemplative gaze of this "sheep," at least for those who dare to submit themselves to it and let themselves be gazed at. Pictorially and literally present in the altarpiece, the lamb perched on its altar stares out at the crowd gathered to view him at the same time as he contemplates them. He stares out because he is not (of) humankind, nor (of) God, but (of) the animal, iconically placed there, as though waiting for us and offering himself in the form of a sacrifice. Certainly the Resurrected One is only symbolically present in the figure of the sacrificial lamb, and perhaps less present here than in the bread of the eucharist. All the same, the animal gaze is there in place of a monstrance, showing us the body of Christ in the ceremony of adoration of the Blessed Sacrament. In the world of the Van Eyck brothers, that which gives itself to be seen (on the altar), to be drunk (as the blood), and to be eaten (in the flesh or by the body) takes the form of animality. Necessarily, of course, this is symbolically figured for us and is, as it were, to be transubstantiated. For a long time, philosophy—and, in particular, phenomenology—has made the animal a metaphysical object of inquiry (for example, in the writings of Uexküll, Husserl, Heidegger, Deleuze,

Derrida, Bataille, Jonas, and Agamben). Theology has been left behind in this respect, but we must hope that it can now catch up.

The lamb contemplates us, because it is *at us* that the figure is directed, placed as we are somewhere in the four-part procession with the women (upper right), or the ecclesiastics (upper left), or the Jews and pagans (lower left), or with the apostles and the huge crowd of Christians (lower left). An undeniable sweetness is inscribed in the way the lamb looks out on us. Sometimes this seems to distance us (the animal), and sometimes it brings us very close (the human being). The halo in the form of a cross behind this "animal face" shows us not that God is incarnate here (in the animal), nor even that God is manifest—a misapprehension that I shall contest throughout the book—but that all the universe is called here into a kind of recapitulation and sanctification. We need to avoid taking what would be a laughably condescending stance, and it should be emphasized that it is not through *animality* that the Word comes to be incarnate, but *exclusively in our humanity*. In coming to be incarnate in our humanity, then, the Word takes on—through us and no doubt for us—that part of animality that is undoubtedly in us. The Council in Trullo held in 692 tried to forestall potential problems here, insisting on the representation of God in human form. They were not opposing animal symbolism, but attempting to avoid possible misconstructions in a largely pagan world. "On the cross the human image of the Saviour should be substituted for that of the lamb."[8]

(d) And so, animality and bestiality should not be muddled up. The latter is precisely a drift from the former into sin. There is nothing as "beastly" as humankind, capable of blaming the animal (or the animal in oneself) simply for existing. Humankind is drawn from the animal, but not reducible to the animal (in an evolutionism that still awaits its metaphysic as well as its theology). And it is the bestiality in itself that humankind fears, rather than its animality. As the extreme limit of the human in relation to the divine project, sin remains certainly like "a crouching beast hungering for you, which you must master" (Gen. 4:7 [JB]). And far from discrediting the whole collection of animals that Adam is called upon to name (Gen. 2:19–20), the Beast of the Apocalypse (Rev. 19:20), like the beast in our inner selves, is exactly a denunciation of that "ancestral fault" that the "Lamb who takes away the sins of the world" has come to remove from us. The bestial, then, as we shall see later, is not the animal (§13).

Paradoxically, it is by taking on and transforming animality into a humanity that recognizes its filiation that bestiality or sin will be eradicated. (We must avoid flight into an "angelism" that totally neglects our humanity, or indeed our own origin in a certain form of animality.) Pascal reminds us that "Man is neither angel nor beast, and it is unfortunately the case that anyone trying to act the angel acts the beast."[9]

What we see in the Ghent altarpiece—how "Salvation belongs to our God who is seated on the throne, and to the Lamb" (Rev. 7:10) is unlike the golden "image of a calf" at the foot of Mount Sinai (Exod. 32:1–6). The latter is simply a kind of travesty, transforming into sin and bestiality what should have been divinity ("He took the gold . . . formed it in a mold, and cast an image of a calf" [Exod. 32:4]). Divinity would have been the total assumption of *our* animality, the vocation of which is to be transformed into humanity and called to be incorporated in God ("the Lamb of God" [John 1:36]).

(b) However, the recognition and conversion of animality into humanity is not the final word on the Ghent altarpiece, nor on our perspective here (§28). We could say that Adam fails in his task of naming the animals in Genesis—at least it is at this point that his lack of a partner becomes apparent. Moreover, he does not recognize himself immediately in the animality that is summoned up for him, even if it is from the same dust from which he was formed ("The Lord God formed man from the dust of the ground" [Gen. 2:7]). Eve appears, then, in the first book of the Bible, as in the altarpiece, as a kind of limit of Adam—a limit that she will teach Adam to recognize and love. The bodies of Adam and Eve surprise us on the Ghent altarpiece (Figure 3).

The discreet appearance of pubic hair, evidently a reminder first of all for men and women of where they come from (the dust we have in common with animals), led to these panels being sold by the clergy to the Brussels Museum in 1871. Certainly the couple are both there, at the far sides of the polyptych, after the Fall: Eve holds the fruit tightly in her hand. Adam has one foot forward, ready to flee, and the scenes of jealousy between Cain and Abel show a desire that needs to be brought under control. But the look on the faces of Adam and Eve speak to us of more than simple regret over the Fall. We see something of the true burden of our humanity. We see nostalgia, certainly, but above all we see their entry into an open future and a sense of waiting to be transformed. There are two bodies—fallen, assuredly, but also close to our own corporality. Adam's hand is turned aside to point at his chest and at his own rib. It draws our attention to the rib, or rather to a kind of boundary line—the place of a limit—from which Eve, his wife, was taken. Man and woman are marked irremediably here by a lack, or perhaps we should say, by a difference. It is always in being different, one from the other, and in differentiating themselves, that the couple are able to love. The world is a boundary or limit for God, woman is a limit for man, and the animal is a

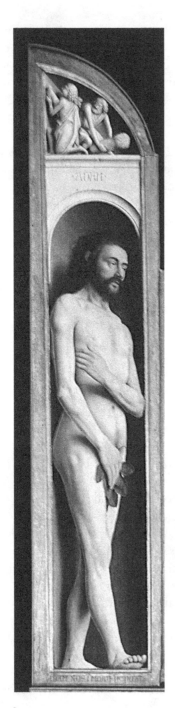

Figure 3

limit for both humankind and God. It is an attachment to these limits that must conquer our supposed desire for what is unbounded or unlimited (§22).

As I have tried to show elsewhere, it is not in our nature to go beyond our condition as creatures. God created us in "difference"—men (*ish*) and women (*ishah*)—and wished that we should never cease to "differ" (§23). This separation is good in Christianity (where Eve is taken from Adam's rib), in contrast with Platonism (where we find an ideal of fusion in the myth of the androgyne or of the lost half). We need, then, to live through our humanity and our difference, if only to make the splendor of divinity shine out. The distance of the naked bodies of Adam and Eve from one another on the Ghent altarpiece speaks of what is in the eucharistic offering. Not only does the eucharist involve taking charge of animality (the sacrificial lamb), but also, and above all, it involves the exposed bodies called to their differentiation in conjugality, as in this ecclesiastical context (*this is my body*).

(c) Eros, or sexual difference, appears thus to be constitutive of the erotic scene, as it is also of the eucharistic scene of the Last Supper (*Cène*). The conjunction of these two scenes (*scène* and *Cène*) will come as a shock only to those who have been involved in neither of them. All the same, we must take care: eros as a form of eucharistizing (see Luke 22:19, *eucharizomai*) does not reintroduce the dionysiac into the act of celebration, nor does the taking charge of animality signify that God will come directly to be incarnate in it—rather, the contrary. It is precisely because the holy Last Supper (*Cène divine*) tells exactly what the *human scene* (*scène humaine*) is that we must start from the eucharistic Last Supper to fully understand the erotic scene, and not the other way around.

God in his agape does not imitate the amorous lovemaking of humankind. Rather, it is humankind that learns precisely from the agape of God, in eros, how to love a body that is offered in difference: "'This is my body, which is given for you'" (Luke 22:19). I am not suggesting here that eros and agape are the same (univocal). But we shall see later (§10) how the eucharistic act can serve as a model, a place of integration as much as of transformation, where our human *eros* becomes the divine *agape*. That is the true meaning of the *erotic scene*, to be taken and included with the eucharistic Last Supper.

It is not simply a question of the difference of bodies (*this is my body*), but of a body given or offered, going so far as a total giving up of the self (given for you—for *you* in the intimate and familiar sense). The Van Eyck brothers tried to show this symbolically, in the Ghent altarpiece above all, but also elsewhere. John the Baptist and Mary are shown at the right and left of the Father (or the Son?) on the throne of glory: "The two images on either side echo the divine image, and their symmetry symbolically restates the distinction between masculine and feminine."[10] Mary's halo shows how she is "more beautiful than the sun" and "most blessed among women." And John the Baptist, "sovereign holiness of the law of the Gospel, the voice of the apostles," is also shown with his halo of light, "so great a man."[11]

Woman *and* man—man *and* woman: the difference here is not simply that of the human and the divine (Mary and John the Baptist are both shown as belonging to humanity); it is also of femininity and masculinity. Mary, turned toward her inner self (and there is so much within that inner self), is shown reading a book, mouth slightly open as if ready to take communion. John the Baptist, looking outward (and so much is in the outside world), points with his finger announcing the Lamb of God figured in the altarpiece. With bare head and feet, he is ready to set off on his evangelical mission. As Aristotle tells us, the female "is that which generates in itself" (immanence), and the male is "that which generates in another."[12] The division is clearly shown here, so that we may well believe it was portrayed knowingly by the Van Eyck brothers. They agree with the Church, which acknowledges and assures that there is *heteros* in *eros*, or an other in difference. They follow the Church in respecting the gifts accorded to each. "The man generates outside himself: is he who sows the seeds of souls as priest and preacher (John the Baptist). The woman generates in her own breast: it is she who makes grace germinate through her prayers and through listening to people (Mary)."[13]

Apart from the separation of Mary and John the Baptist, eros is emphasized in the altarpiece through the separate crowds of men and women who have come to contemplate the Mystic Lamb. It is not a question here of difference through abstinence, as we go from the virgin martyr to the repentant prostitute, from the religious figures to the laypeople drawn toward the Lamb. Rather, it is a question of a unity differentiated, but within the same desire for communion: "I have eagerly desired to eat this Passover with you" (Luke 22:14). Everything yearns toward and gathers itself together in the crowd assembled here. The sacrificial lamb lovingly draws toward him those who are not yet in place or have only just arrived. At the outskirts of the central panel we see soldiers, judges, hermits, and pilgrims, under the direction of a giant-sized St. Christopher, approaching the sacrificial lamb. The sacramental act is not only performed as something that is moved through (from animality to divinity passing through humanity); it is also an act of assuming, or taking on (Adam and Eve in the difference of their corporality), and one of learning about desire (the

ascent toward the lamb sacrificed in an eros registering appropriate dif-
ferentiations).

In the Ghent altarpiece, as in this philosophical study of the body and
the eucharist, we find the sacrifice of the Mass, a sacrifice that locates for
us—today, as always—a *content* (the body in the formula "this is my
body"), a *tradition* (in the sacrificial lamb), and a *modality*, or form (the
eros, or the body delivered to you).

There is much of existential philosophy here (the body, the animal,
eros). These topics are taken on and changed by theology as it recapitulates
them (*this is my body*, the sacrificial lamb, the conversion of *eros* by *agape*).
In the mystery of the consecrated Host we find all this encapsulated; it is
there that God becomes the one who takes on and recapitulates our materiality and transforms it in his divinity. "I do not worship matter," St. John
of Damascus quite rightly says, arguing against the iconoclasm of the
eighth century AD. "I worship the God of matter, who became matter for
my sake, and deigned to inhabit matter, who worked out my salvation
through matter. I will not cease from honouring that matter which works
my salvation. I venerate it, though not as God. How could God be born
out of lifeless things? And if God's body is God by union (*kaq upostasin*),
it is immutable."[14]

The Wedding Feast of the Lamb

Introduction

The Swerve of the Flesh

The traditional dualism of body and soul is now considered dated, but we have put a new binary structure in its place: that of flesh and body. Certainly this is an important step forward and one that has proved fruitful. When we talk of the "flesh" we describe the *lived experience* of our bodies, and we bring into view what we actually do, while we also bracket off the *organic* quality of the "body," seeing it as an obstacle to the body's subjectivity. But there are some questions that we still need to consider: Hasn't philosophy forgotten the *material* and *organic* body in coming to speak of flesh as lived experience of the body? And hasn't theology become blocked in its discussion of the organic or the living body of Christ? Hasn't it overdone spiritualizing the mystical, offering us a quasi-spiritual angelic flesh?

It would be useless to denounce a supposed drift into Gnosticism by theology and philosophy if a consensus had not been established, in phenomenology, on the one hand, and in a certain reinterpretation of doctrinal statements, or dogmatic theology, on the other. It is found in phenomenology where there is the notion of "flesh without body," or the primacy of the lived flesh (*Leib*) over the organically composed or objective body (*Körper*), providing a theme that runs right through contemporary philosophy (from Husserl up to and including Michel Henry).[1]

The consensus is also found in doctrinal or dogmatic statements because of the difficulty we have nowadays in believing that bodies step out of coffins, as we sometimes see represented in sculpture in the doorways of cathedrals. Our difficulty in that respect makes it almost impossible to think seriously about the organic at the heart of the Resurrection. The "body" is forgotten and buried in the "flesh" in phenomenology (where flesh has priority over the body) and also in theology (where an objectivity for the resurrected body becomes difficult). What seemed like a step forward only yesterday (the taking into account of the subjective aspect of the body) has today become exactly the opposite: a step backward (an absence of discussion of the objective body).

I am not suggesting—it goes almost without saying—that we reintroduce a simple concept of the materiality of the body, or its "extension," as though this extension were a device through which we could examine all corporality. The time for that is past, and space imagined in a "geometrical manner" (Spinoza) is also out of date, as is the Cartesian reduction of the body to artificial machines moved by springs.

All the same, the question abides with us: when we speak of the lived experience of the body, aren't we losing sight of the materiality of the body that also makes up its existence? My body has its weight, which I have to carry. It shows its wounds, which I cannot ignore and which sometimes cause me to suffer. It digests and secretes without me needing to think. It grows larger and grows older without being told to do so by me. There's not much point in a protest from "the despisers of the body": the Great Self of corporality, even if anonymous, dominates the "I" of my thoughts. Our "I" has no option but to bend its knee before corporality. Nietzsche laughs at us: "'I' you say, and are proud of the word. But the greater thing— in which you do not want to believe—is *your body* and its *great reason*: it does not say I, but does I." The Self of your body is what, in reality, makes your true I. "The Self says to the I: 'Feel pain here!' And then it suffers and thinks about how it might suffer no more. . . . The Self says to the I: 'Feel pleasure here!' Then it is happy and thinks about how it might be happy again."[2] Trying to deny the body, even if just by shifting the center stealthily and phenomenologically toward lived experience (flesh), is in reality denying the body's organic nature. And we know full well to what extent "organicity" is able to dominate us: "When our stomachs are 'out of sorts' they can cast a pall over all things," Heidegger says. Paradoxically, it is in his reading of Nietzsche that Heidegger finds a possible organic origin for the basic affections: "We live in what we are embodied [*leiben*]."[3]

There have been some objections to the effect that I have proposed, in previous writings, a "flesh without body"; to this, there has been a reaction that starts with quite appropriate questions. But I hope to put the record straight in this book and perhaps even to reorient my own thought where necessary.[4] Challenges always catch one slightly off guard, but what follows from them is at least a development in one's thought; otherwise, there is a risk of slow death by repetition, or a kind of self-prolongation into inanity. One takes one's side in an argument—because thinking is also a matter of decision-making: phenomenology is perhaps not the last word in the ambitions of philosophy (something that up to now I have not suggested). And neither "flesh" nor the "lived experience of the body" are ultimate terms in all theology (as I underlined in *The Metamorphosis of Finitude*). I don't wish to deny or go back on what I have put forward elsewhere; rather, I think it will be affirmed in finding something of a counterbalance—a counterbalance that is best adjusted when it is closest to equilibrium. So, where phenomenology uses "flesh" of the "lived experience of the body" unilaterally (see Edmund Husserl, Maurice Merleau-Ponty, Emmanuel Levinas, Jean-Louis Chrétien, Jean-Luc Marion, Jean-Yves Lacoste), I give more weight to a "philosophy of the organic," one that does not forget or neglect our own proper animality (like Nietzsche certainly, but also like Francis Bacon or Lucian Freud). And when theology—or perhaps I should say "my theology"—defines suffering and death phenomenologically as the "breaking up and exposure of the flesh," and resurrection as the "raising of the flesh" or the metamorphosis of our manner of being through our bodies, I want to offset this now with a consideration of the eucharist, taking fully on board this time the gift of the organic to the organic (*hoc est enim corpus meum*—this is my body).[5]

The *shifts of the flesh*, or a journey ahead toward the lived experience of the body that forgets its organic nature (as in the primacy given to the flesh over the body in phenomenology, and resurrection of the flesh as the lived experience of the body in theology), would leave aside an important reminder—in other words, would defer consideration of the "body" as such. Like a physiologist, one has to sound out the body, to "auscultate" it, to observe it. One has to extend one's view of the body and intensify what one says about it. Philosophically, first of all, in this book we descend into the abyss, to discover there the Chaos of our existence as well as its embodiment, until we come to read the figure of the sacrificial lamb (Part I). Next, we stay with man to uncover his animality, to recognize his organic nature, and to differentiate his sexuality (Part II). Then, theologically, we see the Son of God, as "embodied God" transforming our animality at Easter, giving his own body to be eaten, and giving himself up to eros while awaiting "*agape*" [the Christian "love-feast"] (Part III). Thus we can make our dwelling place in him, gather together in a "common flesh," or *Ecclesia*, and entirely live there (Conclusion). The route I have chosen can certainly seem hard, because (in Heidegger's terms) it probes the ground, it unearths (*ergründen*), more than it tries to ground, or found (*begründen*): it plunges into the depths more than it surfaces into the light. As a thinker, I am trying to explore my own humanity. I am like an explorer of caves who will not draw back in case he endangers an enterprise whose end he himself does not know. What I do know is that to take on this enterprise is to advance further along a precipitous road. It is a route to which I have already, for some considerable time, been committed.

PART I

Descent into the Abyss

Grande profundum est ipse homo
Man himself is a great deep.
　　　　　　　　　　　—St. Augustine, *Confessions* 4.14.22[1]

We descend ever deeper into the abyss, because the chasm that opens before us is so profound. As we lose ourselves there we find also an extraordinary sensation of proximity. Those who plunge beneath the surface of the Earth are witness to this effect. From the stagnant pool (*"la souille"*) in Michel Tournier's *Friday, or, The Other Island* to the explorations of subterranean caves (at Padirac, in France, for example), submerging in the depths of the Earth is a way of reuniting with an "underground" self, or perhaps a "mezzanine" self, that we cannot ignore.[2] Some people call this the "unconscious." I call it Chaos, Tohu-Bohu,[3] or the mass of sensations. I don't mean to deny what psychoanalysis has revealed to us here, but rather the contrary; what I wish to explore is not exactly psychological, nor symptomatic, nor a matter of affect. It is not pathological or historic (features that have contributed to the significance of psychoanalysis). It is quite simply cognitive—indeed, existential and universal.

The abyss makes humankind. It is what humankind is constructed upon: It is what we can never destroy, even if we never recover from it. To borrow a term from the Jewish tradition, there is a *Shéol* (the grave, the pit, the underworld) in humanity. It is not simply a version of the Greek Hades (hell or the abode of the dead), but the etymology of its name points to a "corruption," a "place of questioning, of interrogation" (*cheôl*).[4] Chaos, the abyss, the gap, the opening—what Jackson Pollock paints in his work *The Deep*: "A break in the middle of a field of force, something bottomless under the cover of a cloud that immobilizes it."[5] That is what we must now philosophically or, quite simply, humanly try to rediscover.

In our descent we strive to reach an abyss. Descent will substitute for programmatic or existential development, setting itself up instead as a series of problems. Thus, I have found it necessary in this book to question, first of all, by way of exploration, the limits of phenomenology (Part I). I go on to the problem of the sacrificial lamb (Chapter 2) and the meaning of the eucharistic eros (Chapter 3) before looking philosophically (Part II), and then theologically (Part III), at our animal nature (Chapters 4 to 7), our organic nature (Chapters 5 to 7), and our erotic nature (Chapters 6 to 9), as they are all engaged in the eucharistic act. Everything is there, or perhaps is just implied, in the "first moment" by way of an "expansive introduction," or a "great crossing," of what will later be deployed theologically and philosophically. Discussion of these issues has often been a matter of special pleading, directed in such a way as to not burden itself with fine details (Part I). But it remains true that, in the eyes of both author and reader, development of thought is a necessary condition for the recognition of its truth (Parts I and II). Development is important also in order to counter objections that a humble but inevitably bold inquiry may raise.

The abyss certainly ensures that we feel bad about it, seeing that we become formless there: We break up. We are first of all ruined there, spoiled, like objects that fall and collide. But then there is more and better in the abyss, which takes the place and role of finitude, once there is a question of the eucharist (*Wedding Feast of the Lamb*) and not simply of resurrection (*Metamorphosis of Finitude*).[6]

According to nautical terminology, abyss (or abysm) refers to the depths of the ocean, to places that humankind can almost never reach, inhabited by the "abysmal protozoan fauna, medusae and other marine monsters."[7] The abyss is etymologically "bottomless" (*a-bussos*). It points to a region—unexplored, no doubt, and perhaps also inexplorable. As for those *abysmes* that, according to Aristide Quillet's encyclopedic dictionary, are "subterranean cavities, fissures resulting from a collapse, or excavations hollowed out by waters," they denote the profound depths of that which faces us, and sometimes engulfs us, impenetrable and without limits.[8] They are there for better and for worse: for better, in the abyss of science and the meditations that are opened up on the trail of astronomy or by the mysteries of religion; for worse, in the fathomless abyss that loss and oblivion may sometimes cause us, as when ships are "swallowed up" by the sea.

To be swallowed up in this way in the abyss is not simply to collide or to lose one's shape. It is, rather, to be lost, to fall—to collapse. It is to disappear into a bottomless pit and into impenetrable water from which nothing can retrieve us. To go down there—"Descent into the Maelstrom," or descent into the abyss—means accepting that one will not draw back or, at the very least, that there will be no quick exit.[9] There is in humankind, as also in the world, something dark that can hold onto us, whether we call it Chaos, Tohu-Bohu, or the "bottomless." It makes of us more than we know. It makes us lose our way. "In the beginning, there was first a yawning gap," Jean-Pierre Vernant explains.

> The Greeks called it Chaos. What was this gap? An emptiness. A dark emptiness where nothing can be distinguished. A place of falling, of vertigo, of confusion—without end, bottomless. We are caught up into this gap as though by the opening of an immense mouth where all will be swallowed up in the same indistinct night. . . . Then the Earth appears. The Greeks call this Gaïa. . . . On the Earth everything feels shaped, visible, solid. We can define Gaïa as that on which the gods, humankind and the animals can confidently walk. It is the floor of the world.[10]

I shall brave this challenge and suggest that the abyss, this *Shéol*, the Chaos or Tohu-Bohu—a dimension of the *cosmos* as well as of *anthropos*—is precisely what the *This is my body* of the eucharist comes to explore, comes to take on, the better to transform.

I don't mean to deny in this book a dimension of sin in the "sacrificial lamb" (§13); I do, however, hope to do it more justice in a forthcoming book.[11] But salvation is not simply a matter of redemption; it is also solidarity or fellowship. It is through the fellowship of God and humankind, which goes into the furthest depths of the obscurity that makes up our created being (our passions, impulses—our animality), that humankind will be saved. We need to admit, then, that "descending into the abyss" is not simply sounding out the depths of sin, something that would be more appropriate to consider under the heading of bestiality (§13). Just as the unconscious in psychoanalysis cannot or should not be labelled in terms of moral worth or value, so Chaos in philosophy, or Tohu-Bohu in theology, do not fall simply within the domain of sin or error. Beyond Good or Evil—or, better, on this side of Good and Evil—Christ plunges into the abyss of humankind and the world, and rejoins Adam on the day of Holy Saturday. Christ does this not just to save Adam from the Fall but also to espouse the bottomless in its own depths, to rejoin the "originary Earth" (*Urgrund*), and to sojourn there before drawing from it. The Orthodox icons of the great Resurrection show this scene to those who know how to read it: Christ stands above the cross and pulls Adam from the grave that has also been his. As the famous ancient homily for Holy Saturday on the Lord's descent into Hell recounts for the enlightened listener, "He [the Lord] took him [Adam] by the hand and raised him up, saying; 'Awake, O sleeper, and rise from the dead, and Christ will give you light.'"[12]

I want to emphasize here—not to narrow down the field of inquiry, but rather so as not to judge matters too hastily—that the descent into the abyss inaugurated by *hoc est corpus meum* on the day of the Last Supper is not simply because of our exploration of humanity. Certainly it can and must be taken that way, and indeed leads us in that direction. Philosophically speaking, we need to follow the heuristic path rather than the didactic one and to explore the laborious passage in terms of humankind, rather than directly moving to the revelation of God. But then theologically we shall discover that we are not alone in this place, with humankind and in philosophy. And this is precisely because God has always already traversed the route in order to find us there and go along with us. A plunge to the depths of our Chaos is not, for believers, something undertaken completely alone, even though companionship cannot exempt us from the solitude of all humanity, nor even simply reassure us. It is in the form of one of humankind that we "limp along on the way" (see end of Opening). And this is so whether we go with or without the Son of Man—though the Son of Man is always there to escort us and, as it were in advance, committed to his resurrection. "The descent of a *single person into the abyss* becomes the *ascension of all*, out of that same abyss," we must remember, following Hans-Urs von Balthasar's commentary on the great Holy Saturday (*La Dramatique divine*). It has been suggested that "what makes possible this dialectical reversal derives on the one hand from the 'for all' of the descent, and on the other from the *prototypical resurrection* mentioned here: *Without this resurrection the Son would certainly sink into the abyss, but all would not be resurrected.*"[13]

A descent like this into the abyss is thus, in a sense, programmed and at the same time a kind of preliminary guide. "This is my body" is not like "I am my suffering body" (*Passeur de Gethsémani* [The guide to Gethsemane]) or "he is the resurrected body" (*Metamorphosis of Finitude*). In suffering, as in resurrection, the philosophically existential is directly given in equivalent doctrinal terms and then transformed. It becomes "anguish" in Gethsemane (*Passeur de Gethsémani*) or "birth" in the Resurrection (*Metamorphosis of Finitude*). But in the case of the eucharist (*Wedding Feast of the Lamb*) the associated experience awaits its formulation. The words *this is my body* are, of course, also those of a bridegroom to his bride, before they signify the union of Christ with his apostles, or that of the Church with all humanity. But it would be unsatisfactory to reduce them to this, because if on the one hand the eucharist is *eros* converted into *agape* in the gift of embodiedness (see Chapters 2, 6, and 9), it also questions, more paradoxically, what belongs to the space of animality, through the figure of the sacrificial lamb (Chapters 2, 4, and 7), as well as the role of the organic body in that which is given to us to eat (Chapters 1, 5, and 8).

I hope that my reader will bear with me, or at least give me some leeway, especially in the first part of this book, and risk being surprised by what later becomes explicit. I must emphasize again here that to speak of the animality in humankind is not to reduce Christ to animal, and that is so even though the question will arise of Christ taking on animality in order to transform it into the humanity that is acknowledged in his filiation within the Trinity. To return to the erotic character of the eucharistic agape is not to identify it with a dionysiac form of carnal love, nor to reduce it to a kind of disproportionate rapture, though rapture plays its part in the folly that it proposes. If we expect a great deal from the "power of the body," we don't need to go overboard with enthusiasm for a force that is impossible to control. All the same, it has been the constant admission of weakness in Christianity that has only too rapidly led us to disregard the power of the Holy Spirit that is capable of bringing about our metamorphosis. As far as I can see, even more here than elsewhere, we don't need to force our understanding to read our situation fully, but rather must allow ourselves to be divested of preconceptions. These ideas may become radical, certainly, but the objects (the body and the eucharist) are so difficult to describe because the reality is so extraordinary: "'Take, eat; this is my body'" (Matt. 26:26).

Some readers—undoubtedly those philosophically inclined—will be surprised to see theological perspectives so directly engaged from the start of this book. I talk of the figure of the lamb (Chapter 2), or the eroticized body as the eucharisticized body (Chapter 3), even before I undertake a long philosophical analysis of animality (Chapter 4) or organic corporality (Chapter 5). Other readers—theologians, especially—may wonder why there are so many quibbles at the start of the book about the limits of phenomenology. And they must wonder why this is necessary when what is up for analysis is a question of *the body of Christ given to us* rather than just "bodying life" (Chapter 1). I know I am asking a great deal, and asking it of philosophers as well as theologians, but it is only problematic if the cut-and-dried separation of their respective disciplines has made interpenetration impossible from the start, preventing a mutually beneficial approach.

I should like to make this clear. An appropriate distinction between disciplines does not bar a certain unity of thought, particularly as far as the person who comes to use them is concerned.[14] The reversal or recovery of frontiers between the two disciplines in Part I of the book is thus intentional and, at the same time, a practical necessity. A long detour helps us arrive at a point of junction in the problematic, to show that there are three dimensions in the act of the eucharist: embodiedness, animality, and eros. This first moment of descent into the abyss—in the form of a large-scale introduction to and synthesis of the whole of the movement proposed—in a sense says all, and yet nothing, of the proposition that I wish to express here. It says *all* because the whole of its scope is contained in its first premises, and it says *nothing* in that this cannot really be seen until the argument has been run through in its entirety, and also recapitulated. One can't judge a book or an author by what has to be said in the opening statements, but only by the full course of the argument once it has been wholly made. If philosophers are disappointed by too much theology, I would suggest that they push on, at least as far as Part II, where I aim at another mode of doing philosophy. And to theologians uneasy about the uphill struggles into philosophy, I would ask that they hang on until the end of the journey—at least waiting until the power of transformation of the eucharist is fully shown (Part III).

The eucharist is not in this sense something that "could be believed." It is also, and above all, credible. It is incumbent on each one of us to decide on this, and it is also a matter for all humanity, at least in the doctrine and tradition of Western culture that we inherit. The point is not, first of all, nor simply, whether we take communion. It is not just a matter of insisting that everyone come up to the table of the wedding feast, or the act of eucharist. My basic argument, insofar as there is one basic argument, is not put forward so as to convert or transform others. It comes down to an acceptance or recognition that Christianity has the cultural means, as well as the conceptual means, to touch the depths of our humanity, as that humanity is constituted in the twenty-first century—albeit through an *interior Chaos* that was taken on board and metamorphosed by God himself. What at first may seem surprising to us (the erotic, the animal, or the organic appearing in a discussion of the mystery of the eucharist) can show in this sense an exceptional fruitfulness, as we pose questions here "in a way that responds to the needs of our time" (Vatican II) concerning the Wedding Feast of the Lamb, or the invitation to the banquet table. "'Take, eat; this is my body.' . . . 'Drink from it, all of you; for this is my blood'" (Matt. 26:26–28). The "wine of the absurd," or the "bread of indifference," so disparaged by Camus and many moderns (and yet still called upon when they have to make vows and promises), will also have to be considered—in wine that has been transubstantiated and bread consecrated on the eucharistic altar—even though we risk the loss of all our humanity that is still to be transformed and risk the loss of God, who comes precisely to us in order to incorporate us there.[15]

Philosophy to Its Limit

To do philosophy *to its limit* is probably to reach the limits of doing philosophy. One can philosophize to its limit, in the sense of a limit to what remains to be done, because no other solution seems possible (as when I have to miss a rendezvous even *at the very limit* of the deadline because something more important has come up). More significantly, philosophers have been trying recently to do philosophy *at its limit*, precisely because they would then reach the limit of philosophy (rejecting the ascendancy of a predicative discourse, in phenomenology, as in analytic philosophy). Going to the "margins" of philosophy (Derrida) or relying on the "creation of concepts" such as rhizomes, extraterritoriality, or other invented conceptual monsters (Deleuze) is, however, not a possible solution to the problem of how to do philosophy, and it entails leaving the ordinary modes of thought in which Western philosophy—as inheritor of the Western tradition—was engendered.

Thus, although I may turn here from time to time to those thinkers who have looked for another way of doing philosophy (Deleuze or Derrida, for example), I do not intend to abandon ordinary modes of reason. There is certainly a "logic of feeling" that we can find within the act of thinking, with the help of the painter Francis Bacon (see Deleuze), and there is an "animal in us" found in the strange experience of nudity (see Derrida). But we can talk about these things without doing philosophy at its limits and without transgressing the fixed bounds of rationality. To do philosophy *to its limit* does not come back, then, either to philosophizing as a worst case scenario or to doing philosophy beyond philosophy. Quite simply, it entails touching on the limits of doing philosophy, in particular when these limits are in what is called phenomenology. Without giving up on what engendered us (phenomenology), we shall come back here to its *limits*. That is to say, we shall come back to the impossibility of formulating, starting from phenomenology, what it is that *lies beneath signification*—when that is precisely what we have come today to consider.[1]

It is the *this is my body* of the eucharist that takes on exactly a mode of non-signifying of organic embodiedness—something that simply the lived experience of the flesh in the Resurrection could not express or even envisage (see *Metamorphosis of Finitude*). The distinction of these doctrines (on resurrection and the eucharist) reaches out to the diversity of experience (birth and eros), as well as to the difference in what the doctrines concern (flesh and the body). This is the way thought moves and takes a step forward, not by going two steps backward, but by shifting toward what has not yet been seen and taking what has been seen in another light. Moving or shifting is not going back on what one has thought, but rather the contrary (after all, philosophers have their epochs just as artists do): It may open up a spectrum that has previously been too narrow. In "philosophy to its limit" there will always be, then, the residue of the body (§1) as there will be a Chaos and Tohu-Bohu (§2). So, we can head toward the limit of the phenomenon (§3) as we make our way to the threshold of a bodying life (§4) capable of engendering what is in our true humanity. Paul Ricœur underlines that "each work responds to a determinate challenge"—a notion that could very well describe the relation to my previous books of what I undertake here. "And what connects it to its predecessors seems to me less the steady development of a unique project than the acknowledgement of a residue left over by the previous work, a residue which gives rise in turn to a new challenge."[2]

§1. The Residue of the Body

Probably we can no longer be satisfied, as far as philosophy is concerned, with the simple charms of the "toucher-touched"—a notion that derives from the episode of the woman with a hemorrhage in the Gospel of St. Mark, which I have used and discussed extensively elsewhere.[3] But the body remains. Or rather a "residue" remains (of the body) that is still always subjectivized. Embodiedness is, if not extended (*étendue*), at least spread out (*épandue*). It cannot be reduced to subjectivity nor declared purely objective. It is in fact a body—perhaps we should describe it as "intermediate," or a frontier zone? And this residue is between the *subjec-*

tive flesh of the phenomenologist and the *objective body* of the scientist. It is that of the organic matter to deal with or operate on, which is not totally objective because it cannot be reduced to a geometric form. Nor is it totally subjective, because it does not fully correspond to the ego when we examine it in terms of consciousness. We can take as an example the body under anesthetic, something most of us have experienced ourselves and seen in others, both animals and human beings.[4] A doctor, or rather a surgeon, works with or cuts open the body as bodily objectivity (*Körper*). He or she knows that another subject is there, at least as far as they share a hypothetical humanity. And he or she shows respect for the body lying on the operating table, if not as a matter of experience, at least through a professional ethic (isolation of the part to be operated on; prohibition of completely stripping the body to the nude). Nonetheless, the body that doctors work with, and do something to, cannot be called a purely subjectivized flesh (*Leib*). Nor does the encounter with the lived experience of the medical staff constitute intersubjectivity, or a mode of empathy, of the kind that is so often falsely sought.

Only if one had never visited an operating theater in which the body was to be operated on, or if one had been taken in by the kind of philosophical discourse that doctors themselves do not heed, would one believe that the lived experience of the body, or the "flesh," was the site of a lived intercorporality. In the operating theater, the silence of "anaesthetized matter" no longer lets through any cries of pain from a particular subjectivity. The body extended on the operating table is not there in length, breadth, and depth—as we might describe a Cartesian geometric space. It is there in heartbeats, respiration, and intestinal rumbles—qualitative attributes of biological life. We may be surprised to have to claim these attributes here, but they also are part of our living corporality in its proper qualities, even though we quite often, and quite wrongly, try to ignore them. The geometric rigour of the objectified body must give place to the biological copiousness of a flesh that is profuse and also impossible to subjectify. Extended, the anesthetized body is, as it were, spread out onto the operating table; it is fleshly matter that has often been offered and given and over which the doctor would be able, in the absence of regulation, to exercise an unlimited power. It is the "unconscious of the body" (Nietzsche), as we shall see later, that makes our corporality—rather than the psychic that waits on the organic, or the simply physical—lost in its own objectivity.[5]

In philosophy, or at least in phenomenology, we come across the notion of flesh (*Leib*), used to speak of the lived experience of the body or of the body itself: "Husserl suggests that the sphere of what is proper to the individual, [or 'ownness,'] sends us back to that first experience where the lived experience of the consciousness is constituted or engendered. It has the status of something that originates, in so far as it is the originating matrix of our corporality. The notion of 'flesh' suggests that this problem area is irreducible to objective spatiality." [6] There is also the body (*Körper*), which, according to Husserl, remains purely objective: "The inertia of the *Körper* which can indicate the body in the physical sciences just as well as the celestial bodies in the Aristotelian cosmology, or the corpuscles in quantum physics." Husserl maintains that "in a human context the 'body' signifies a simply organic structure in its static, functional and quantifiable configuration."[7] But what do we find in, and what can we say about, the relation *between* the flesh and the body? Between the subjective lived experience of corporality (*Leib*) and objective reduction into its entity (*étantité*) (*Körper*)? Phenomenology does not tell us, yet ordinary experience is able to help us. There is a biological aspect to myself that is not quantifiable (not extended in geometric fashion in the body) but that nonetheless cannot simply be reduced to subjective qualities (how the ego copes with the flesh). The body spread out—on the operating table, certainly, but also dozing on a bed or even crucified on a cross—is more than the simple extension of matter (the objectivity of the body) and more than pure selfhood of the flesh (subjectivity of the flesh). Between the objective body and the subjective flesh, between the *Körper* and the *Leib*, stands the flesh in the current sense of the term: *Fleisch* in German, *flesh* in English, and *chair* in French. In every case the flesh as commonly understood is "linked to blood, to meat, to that soft substance of the body which is opposed to the bones. It is unstable, fluid and soft in character and reduces the structural stature of the body."[8] It is surprising to note here that phenomenology does not know how the body is material, unless it is made objective. To appear "in flesh and bone" (*leibhaft gegeben*), in phenomenology, is paradoxically to have neither flesh nor bone. And, as we shall see later (§19), when phenomenology speaks of "self-givenness" (*Selbsgegebenheit*), we find that in reality there is no-body much there. In Husserl, as also in the swerve of the flesh in phenomenology, and in theology, there is a kind of docetism (i.e., belief that Jesus's physical body was an illusion) with regard to the flesh. We could call this an idealism of the perceptible, or a theoreticization of the flesh (Romano)—something from which even Merleau-Ponty was not exempt. A concern with clarity overrides the inevitable confusion of these fleshes, as also of bodies, so that no obscurity or chaotic version of reality remains where the pure transparency of intentionality, even if always reversed, overrides the impossibility of signifying or of structuring. As Gilles

Deleuze points out, commenting on the work of Francis Bacon and using Bacon's work as his leitmotif, "the *phenomenological hypothesis* is perhaps *insufficient*, because it merely invokes the lived body. But the lived body is still a paltry thing in comparison with a more profound and almost unliveable Power [*Puissance*]."[9]

The in-between of the spread-out body—neither flesh nor body, neither purely subjective nor exclusively objective—is then, as I see it, what philosophy needs to recover and what theology needs to deal with. It is a part of the darkness in humankind, made up of passions and drives, which the mirages deriving from *signifying* in phenomenology are wrong to evacuate. One phenomenologist at least saw this: Heidegger reading Nietzsche— but he saw it only to pass over the problem. And one philosopher has formulated it as a reading of a certain kind of contemporary painting: Deleuze interpreting the work of Bacon—though outside the context of Christian thought. To return to Chaos and to Tohu-Bohu in the form of the depths of the world, as of our humanity, opens up a road to the obscure, when *this is my body* will encounter and will metamorphose, as Zeno of Citium, the Stoic, suggested (with a certain verve): "The Deity will manifestly be the author of evil, dwelling in sewers and worms." Christianity, and Tertullian, in particular, try to correct this stance, in order to avoid materialism, but at the same time go back over it without hesitation—at least in order to avoid too much Platonizing, or to avoid a falling off into the mistakes of angelism, a tendency that is only too frequently present in Gnosticism.[10]

§2. Chaos and Tohu-Bohu

What is meant by "to know"? Probably—as Heidegger suggests, discussing Nietzsche—it means "to impose upon chaos as much regularity and as many forms as our practical needs require."[11] I shall not revisit here the genesis of the concept of Chaos, as it has already been discussed elsewhere (J.-P. Vernant). Heidegger touches only briefly on this aspect of his subject. Still, we can say—at least in order to recapture and deal with the force and content of *this is my body*—that (1) in ancient Greece, Chaos is "originary," and (2) this is also true of its equivalent in the Semitic tradition, the Tohu-Bohu.

(1) *In ancient Greece.* "First of all Chaos came into being; but next wide-breasted Gaia, always-safe foundation of all . . . and Eros [Love] more beautiful among the immortal gods."[12] This stanza from Hesiod's *Theogony*, which has been much discussed, gives us Chaos as abyss, or as the yawning gap, in reality never covered over; it is something that the

philosopher, or at least the theologian, must accept or even exhibit to us. Not just disorder or confusion, Chaos has to reach as far back as this third term of the abyss as its origin. According to Heidegger, "Chaos, *khaos*, *khainô*, means 'to yawn'; it signifies something that opens wide or gapes. We conceive of *khaos* in most intimate connection with an original inter- pretation of the essence of *alêtheia* as the self-opening abyss: 'From Chaos were born Erebos and black Nyx.'"[13]

We must take care here concerning the different interpretations of Chaos (the open, the confused, disorder) that try falsely to swallow it up into the cosmos, its opposite (the world, order, beauty—even cosmetic products [see §18]). Hesiod's ancient poem does not suggest that the nights of love between Chaos and the Earth bring forth darkness. It does not say that Chaos and the Earth, which along with love are the primordial pow- ers, mate together and engender Erebos and night. It says, more simply and more radically, that "first of all Chaos came into being," then—or next (*gai*)—came Earth (Gaia) and Love (Eros). Chaos in ancient Greece is where we come from (*originaire*), not simply what is there (*original*). It engenders nothing but nonetheless remains as the base on which all will be engendered.[14]

Because we are rooted in Greek culture, Chaos remains as a fissure, or gap, in the abyss of all existence. Deriving both from *chaïnô* (to open oneself or gape) and from *cheïn* (to pour out or spread), Chaos designated at once yawning gap and opening (*chaïnô*) and mixture and confusion (*cheïn*). This is almost certainly what the eucharistic communion of *this is my body* takes on and transforms, without ever concealing or repudiat- ing—whether it is a question of the Chaos of the world (yawning gap and confusion in the annihilation of the living, up to and including our own bodies) or of that of our own lives (abyss and mixture of passions and drives that our biological flesh retains in itself as the strongest form of their expression).[15]

(2) *In the Semitic tradition.* "In the beginning when God created the heavens and the earth, the earth was a formless void [*tohu wabohu*] and darkness covered the face of the deep" (Gen. 1:1–2). There was, then, an "Earth" (formless void) and even an abyss (the deep [*tehôm*]) before the creation of the firmament or the vault of the heavens, on the second day of the creation of the *Hexaemeron* (i.e., the six days' work of creation). The Earth and abyss were before the creation of our "Earth" on the third day. We know about this because it has been the subject of extensive com- mentary. The idea of a creation *ex nihilo* does not appear until much later in the biblical exegesis, in the Second Book of the Maccabees: "I beseech thee, my son, look upon the heavens and the earth, and all that is therein,

and consider that God made them of *things that were not*; and so was mankind made likewise" (2 Macc. 7:28). Similarly in theology we have to wait until the end of the third century before this idea is explicitly formulated by Tertullian: "There will be a doubt, perchance, about the power of God, who formed the great body of this world from that which was not, no less than from a deathlike vacuity and emptiness."[16] Tertullian's "that which was not" is not so much pointing negatively to the nothingness that a God will dominate as pointing positively to the all-powerful nature of he whose role is to start things. "In the seven days of the creation (in effect) God does not overcome, through his word, the confusion that is anterior to the creation. . . . It is not God and chaos that are face to face here, but the cosmos and chaos. And God, the Creator, is in command of both."[17] Moreover, in the final analysis, to say that God creates "out of nothing" (*de nihilo*) according to St. Augustine's formula—*fecisti aliquid et de nihilo* ("[you did] create something, and that out of nothing")[18]—signifies, because of the ambiguity of *de nihilo* in Latin, not simply that "God created starting from (*ex*) nothing, leaving it and substituting the existent for it ('after nothing becomes being')"; it suggests also that "God created *with* (*de*) the nothingness, to make the existent, in the form of matter, from nothingness itself."[19]

Following this interpretation, and returning now to my particular perspective, we can conclude that the original opening or yawning gap *is always there*, at the heart of Hellenism (Chaos), or Judaism (Tohu-Bohu), or Christianity (*de nihilo* or *ex nihilo*). The Earth "formless and void" is not easily covered, and God's prerogative in starting creation does not preclude in fact that something will remain of the opening and the yawning gap, and even of a confusion and jumble that is not easily assimilated.

It is precisely this that confronts God himself, at the moment of creation—of creating us. And it is what we ourselves are confronted with, so far as our own passions are concerned, and what we still confront. "The beginning has been made," Bonhoeffer tells us, with profound insight,

> But still our view remains focused upon one event, on the Free God. . . . It is dark before him, and that is the fame of his glory as Creator. His work is beneath him in the deep. Just as we look down, dizzy, from a high mountain into a chasm and the night of the abyss lies beneath us, so is the earth under his feet: distant strange, dark, deep, but [it is] his work. . . . *The Spirit of God was moving over the face of the waters.* . . . God reflects upon the work. The simultaneous release and joining of formless force into form, of existence into formed being, is the moment of the *hesitation of God.*[20]

Whether one was Greek (Chaos), Jewish (Tohu-Bohu), or Christian (creation *ex nihilo/de nihilo*)—but also if one were Sumerian (the primeval sea [*apsu*]), Chinese (the primordial chaos), or Egyptian (the primeval ocean)[21]—a "jumble," "confusion," "disorder"—or rather the "wide open," the "yawning gap"—remained, and no act of recognition or of giving of meaning (or, for that matter, of creation) could assimilate without necessarily negating it. My thesis is that "what we wish to recognize is the following—surely some terrible, savage, and lawless form of desires" is in every man—to follow Plato and his famous "tyrannic man" in Book IX of *The Republic* (where moreover we find, long before Freud, the explicit root of these desires in dreams). Plato sees these desires "even in some of us who seem to be ever so measured."[22]

If we go along with this supposition—and it is difficult to refute it, since it is found in philosophy, in psychoanalysis, and quite simply in the most ordinary experience of life—have we, however, somehow forgotten the body and the eucharist? As far as I can see, we have not. For the "body" given at the Last Supper, and offered once more at the heart of the liturgy, goes far beyond the circle of the disciples, whether they were gathered together just a little while earlier in that "large room upstairs, already furnished" (Luke 22:12), or whether it is we who today turn toward the altar of a sanctuary. Not only the formula *hoc est enim corpus meum* but also, and above all, the inevitable solidity of the body so paradoxically "given to eat" precisely accommodates this world and the whole of our humanity, up to and including its abyss (*kaïnô*), its jumble, and its formless void (*tohu wabohu*). So that is what we must attempt to do here, or else we shall lose the true substance of the eucharistic bread. It is certainly this "chaotic-there" that the Last Supper took over on Holy Thursday, whether in us (passions, drives, animality) or beyond us (the wide open, the yawning gap, disorder, confusion). And the Sunday liturgy, in the words of the deacon in particular, celebrate this and to an extent live it through, the better to transform it: "By the mystery of this water and wine, may we come to share in the *divinity* of Christ, who humbled himself to share in our *humanity*."[23] The liturgy reaches up to and includes the Chaos of the world and our humanity—going, we might dare to add, as far as our animality.

§3. The Limit of the Phenomenon

We have undertaken a detour (toward Chaos and Tohu-Bohu), and to bring us back (toward a truly *bodied* sense of the eucharistic mystery), we need now to examine as promised—and to establish a certain distance from—phenomenology. When we conceptualize the "chaotic" as the abyss or the gap that we have seen from Hesiod to Nietzsche, couldn't it be said that phenomenology tries to do too much with its concept of the phenomenon? Isn't it just covering up this overflowing obscurity with the transparence of intentionality, whether or not the phenomenon is "saturated"?[24] Such a harsh criticism might have been attacked as pointless if Heidegger had not himself already made it in passing, in the search for a fresh start when he was discussing Nietzschean Chaos in a series of lectures at Freiburg: "Must we not also *take back* this invasion by what we encounter?" Heidegger asks, stealthily pushing phenomenology to its limit. He talks of taking back what we encounter through "the words in which we have taken hold of what was encountered, in order to possess what is *purely* encountered, to let it be encountered. . . . Or does the region of what can no longer be said, the region of renunciation, begin here where we can no longer or not yet decide upon what is in being, in nonbeing, or not in being?"[25]

Making something seen, if it involves reaching the "region of what can no longer be said" (the Chaos where the eucharistic *this is my body* will come if we take it on), entails going through an experience, as in the detour by the simple "cognition of . . . a blackboard," where for once Heidegger demonstrated through his own cognition the limit of the phenomenon in phenomenology—or, in other words, a "beyond phenomenology" (Didier Franck).[26] He addresses the need to go beyond phenomenology once one has undertaken to enter into the abyss, and to signify it otherwise.[27]

Heidegger describes, as a "familiar example" during his lectures, what is there in front of his eyes: "We enter this room—let us say for the first time—and ascertain that this blackboard has been covered with Greek letters. In the case of such knowledge we do not first encounter a chaos, we see the blackboard and the letters."[28] We have to be careful here. The philosopher of Freiburg, at the University of Freiburg and in front of the Freiburg students (probably in or around 1938), does not mean to indicate that a knowledge of Greek is sufficient in itself to obliterate the chaotic, the open and the obscure of the blackboard.

> Perhaps not everyone is able to ascertain that these are Greek letters, but even then we are not confronted with a chaos: rather we confront something visible, something written, that we cannot read. We need to radicalize this reflection on, or rather this apprehension of, the blackboard. It is not a question of whether or not we can decipher these Greek letters: we see them "as characters" in the same way as we see this thing "as a blackboard": "*This blackboard*"—what does that mean? Does it not already mean the knowledge attained: the thing as blackboard?[29]

Doesn't the being of the thing—or the being *as* being and the being *as* thing—already determine the thing in the horizon of being? To put it another way, when we start from our own existence in the form of the beings that we are to ourselves, don't we always have to presuppose the being-in-the-human-world as a *cosmos*? Don't we have to evacuate ourselves of Chaos and of our own animality in order to signify something? In his radical approach, Heidegger paradoxically calls into question the intentionality of the phenomenon. Even the *phenomenon of intentionality* is questioned. It is as though intentionality, whichever way we take it, whether saturated or not, always manages to escape the invasion of Chaos, which is always bodied and not intentional. Heidegger, leaving phenomenology here, in a sense under the pressure of Nietzschean Chaos (the open and yawning gap), and leaving Kant also (the "mass of sensations"), affirms that "to know this thing as a blackboard, we must already have ascertained what we encounter as a 'thing' as such, and not, say, as a fleeting occurrence." And he adds, as if to hammer home that he is leaving the lived experience of the phenomenon to return to the thing itself (*Sache*), that

> we must have perceived in our first meeting up with it what is taken in advance as a thing in general, what we encounter, what we confront and what strikes and concerns us in *what and how it is*. We encounter black things, gray, white, brown, hard, rough things, things resonant (when struck), extended, flat, movable things—thus a manifold of what is given. Yet is what is given what gives itself? Is it not *also* already something *taken*, already taken up by the words *black, gray, hard, rough, extended, flat*? Must we not also *take back* this invasion by what we encounter through the words . . . Or does the region of what can no longer be said, the region of renunciation, begin here?[30]

When phenomenology perceives something, in reality it has always already been perceived that it perceives. We can certainly bring in death as the horizon of life (Heidegger), or intentionality as the inverse of the face (Levinas), the thickness of the flesh (Merleau-Ponty), the saturation of the sign (Jean-Luc Marion), the "event of an intimate call" (Jean-Louis Chrétien), the auto-affection of the self (Michel Henry), or the experience and the absolute (Jean-Yves Lacoste). But in each case, "apperception" is based on perception, in the sense that to perceive what one perceives in the return to things themselves determines in advance the apprehension of these phenomena, defining them as phenomena, on the one hand, and reducing them always to the Kantian "mass of sensations," on the other. Heidegger suggests, in what was probably one of his most fascinating lectures (because he was insidiously leaving phenomenology), "Behind, so to speak, what appears so harmlessly and conclusively to us as an object, we do meet up with the mass of sensations—Chaos."[31] (The investigation of the "mass of sensations" brings in Chaos here; I will consider this further in §4.)[32]

We need to concede, then, as certain Nietzsche scholars familiar with phenomenology have quite rightly pointed out, that the borders of Chaos are inaccessible through a phenomenological approach. This is due (1) to the constant recourse to the lived experience of consciousness (or of the flesh), as opposed to the solidity of the body in its biological dimension and drives, and (2) to the constant recourse to the ideal of passivity as against force, so that the subject no longer tries to be made flesh, or rather to be embodied, in the initial Chaos with which he is confronted.

(1) *The ideal of lived experience, or* Erlebnis. A phenomenalism of the inner world in fact runs through all philosophies of consciousness, even those that borrow their terms from Nietzsche. It is an illusion, or a chronological reversal of cause and effect, that one has to wait for things to appear in consciousness before they exist, or before they take on meaning. When we say, "I feel unwell," we go directly to "this or that (that) makes me feel bad." If the phenomenon in phenomenology is not just a question of looking for causes, what it demands from being is first that it can be signified, and put into the framework of a subjectivity by which it takes on meaning (for me): "*I* feel unwell." The neutrality of evil, its chaos, and its virtual anonymity, which reach into my physiology (*that* makes me ill: *there is* something bad in me that bothers me, *a* virus or *a* cancer that is eating up my body, though I do not know exactly where or how it is), mean that the statements of the suffering subject, like the identification of the *one* who suffers with the *that* which is suffered, do not bring much to this suffering—rather, the contrary.[33] In me *there is* suffering, but it is not a question here of donation or "givenness" (Husserl), nor even of the absurd or non-sense (Sartre); instead, it is the absence of meaning (*sens*) or, better, of a kind of blank in the very idea of meaning or non-sense.

As far as insomnia, for example, is concerned—relying here on Levinas, who distanced himself here from phenomenology—the "fact that there is [*il y a*]" is "precisely the absence of all self, a '*without-self*' [*sans-soi*]."[34] And this invasion of myself by something that I do not recognize as myself—that is "the physiology of my flesh" that encumbers me (Nietzsche) or "the impersonal 'field of forces' of existing" (Levinas)— certainly makes my existence a matter of existing, but *existing without existents*; that is, it is without an ego (*moi*) (as consciousness takes account of what is happening).[35] And yet it is still me (in this physiological flesh, for example, that weighs me down and drives me to distraction as it refuses to fall into sleep). Chaos is not vacancy or nothingness, in a kind of escape, or at a boundary that one always knows will somehow make sense, as in the existential fall (Heidegger) or the existential absurd (Sartre). Rather, Chaos is invasion. It is the impossibility of coming to terms with the "mass of sensations"—not simply in that it breaks open the framework of what we can come to terms with, to signify in another way (the saturated phenomenon), but, inversely, because it shows us that it is not able to formulate itself (the limited phenomenon).[36]

The limit to the phenomenon does not come, or does not solely come, because the phenomenon cannot be constituted by consciousness. On the contrary, it comes from accepting a limit that Chaos overflows, without ever being received or transformed into consciousness: "The only way to preserve meaning for the concept of constitution would consist in recognizing it as the work of the drive-body [*corps pulsionnel*] and not that of intentional consciousness. . . . To become-conscious of lived experiences means to constitute them as identical cases . . . [and] that reflection falsifies everything, because it logicizes everything."[37] It does so in a kind of "Phenomeno-Mania" (Nietzsche's term), which is characteristic of phenomenology today. Thus Nietzsche's "fundamental thought" quite rightly develops—"in anticipation"—"critical tools against certain tendencies of phenomenology."[38] We need such tools when we come to examine the *this is my body* of the eucharist in this context. It is not "I *have* a body" (a statement of ownership that contemporary philosophy has thankfully denounced); nor is it "*I am* my body" (an identification that is frequent today). The "*this* of his body that *is*" reaches out simply to the anonymity of the "there is" [*il y a*] of corporality, descending in a unique way into the depths of the abyss, the Chaos of the world, as also of myself, and thus making it possible to show this body and to transform it.

(2) *An ideal of passivity opposed to that of force.* This is what we find when subjects no longer make an effort to be "embodied" in the Chaos that confronts them. It is something we find in phenomenology as well as in theology.

(a) From the point of view of phenomenology, first of all, the spirited attacks against Heidegger's authentic being-there (Dasein) and his ambition to overcome everything, including the agony of death, are well known.[39] But still, with all this enthusiasm for the "dismantling" or "dismissal" of the subject, we cannot help asking if the subject does not lose its active quality, its identity, at least insofar as it describes a carefully chosen truth, such as *liberty*, where decision and not simply openness is demonstrated. Certainly, according to Nietzsche, truth is not, or is no longer, simply what is suitable or "adequate." But that does not mean that it has to be *alêtheia*, or an unveiling, as Heidegger implies. As it is creative, it is also, and above all, an *acte libre*—a freely performed action; it is the courage to exist within a subject capable of self-affirmation. In 1883, Nietzsche talks about "truth and courage only among those who are *free*. (Truth, a *sort* of courage)."[40] I shall be taking this line, and I am not alone here. Didier Franck writes, "An analysis which takes account of the operative forces would perhaps be more convincing. But has phenomenology ever given us the means to think about these forces?"[41]

(2) From the point of view of theology, we should note that theological discussions of power and force (Chaos) are equally unsatisfactory. Saint Paul's view is well known: "My power is made perfect in weakness" (2 Cor. 12:9). So is Nietzsche's critique: "*Deus, qualem Paulus creavit, dei negatio* [God, as Paul created him, is a denial of God]."[42] Modern Christianity has followed the path of phenomenology, espousing in its ideal of "weakness" and "vulnerability" the philosophical outlook of pure "reception" and the "passivity" of the subject. (It is only necessary here, by way of example, to cite the celebration of the human face in the context of Christianity—although in the work of Levinas, the subject is without a face.)[43] The God of Christians, and in particular in his person of the Holy Spirit, is referred to and refers to himself as a God of power: "You were also raised with him through faith in the power of God" (Col. 2:12). Certainly the disciple remains weak if it is only up to *him* to live. As I have argued elsewhere, there is "Force against force": "The *Holy Spirit*, as metamorphosis of the Son by the Father, and of mankind in him, thus paradoxically connects with what Nietzsche despaired of finding in Christianity—the separation '*of strength from the manifestation of strength*' [paralogism of force]."[44]

The limit to the phenomenon because of its abstract and purified character suggests to us that the phenomenon reaches its limit, abandoning Chaos—or "the area of what cannot be spoken"—as unthinkable. We confront here the swerve of the flesh to the body (§1); the over-development of the intentionally lived, as opposed to the non-signifying Chaos (§2); and the unchecked primacy of passivity over activity (§3). These three stumbling blocks are "limits" that a philosophy of the body (and of the eucharist?) must accommodate. We must take them over and transform them. A new and different starting point is necessary, and not just for Heidegger, who brushed all this aside early on—even if he made some attempt to reactivate the topic in the Zollikon Seminars.[45] The need for a new starting point applies to Nietzsche, and even more to us—as well as to Heidegger commenting on Nietzsche, reaching out to the limit of the phenomenon and opening the field to what is on this side in phenomenology. Here he opens the field toward that which cannot be spoken, in terms that simple signification offers us—toward the Chaos that only our human biological body encounters: the animal and instinctual.

I do not wish to say more here of flesh, nor of body—nor of "flesh" (*Leib*) insofar as the retroactive effect of the Kantian mass of sensations and Nietzschean Chaos in all phenomenology has rejected in advance the idea of a lived space, or intuition, made conscious as such (*Erlebnis*, insight). Nor will I speak about "body" (*Körper*), because the reduction of embodiedness to its extension does not do justice to its character of spreading out—that is, its "expansion" rather than its "extension" in the simple fact of being there, tangible, visible, and open to change, in its own eyes as well as in the eyes of others. Only painters such as Francis Bacon or Lucian Freud have been able to show this in their work—in contrast to theorization on the matter.[46] It remains simply to embody (*leiben*, in the Nietzschean sense of the term), or in other words, to see what *biological life* achieves in us and almost without us. Only this life helps us arrive at our true animality and at the Chaos that comes to meet it there. "Nothing else is 'given' as real but our world of desires and passions . . . as a kind of *instinctive life* in which all organic functions, including self-regulation, assimilation, nutrition, secretion, and change of matter, are still synthetically united with one another—as a *primary form* of life."[47] It is then to the guiding thread of the body, and to the terrible original text *homo natura*, that we come this time, on the edges of Chaos. And by taking this direction we give a real content (fleshly, human, even cosmic and animal) to *this is my body* in Christianity, because, for Nietzsche as for us, it is primarily a question of "the body and the body alone that philosophizes [*der Leib philosophiert*]."[48]

§4. Bodying Life

To return to Chaos—that is, to the openness and the obscurity of the world and of myself—comes down then, according to my way of thinking (and I share Nietzsche's viewpoint here), to living as one who is bodied. This is probably where we can reach toward the strength and profundity of the *hoc est corpus meum* at the time of the celebration of the Last Supper. To be bodied, or "to body" (*leiben*), points first of all to a surge or impetus, something both alive and vast: intoxication (or rapture) as "the feeling of plenitude and increased energy," a dionysiac dimension of the Life, in the face of which the "life" of St. John—not to mention the eucharistic Last Supper—cannot remain indifferent (see §35).[49]

This impetus, or this feeling—which is also a physiological condition as we experience it in a moment of rapture, or intoxication, or drunkenness—is not just an interior mental-event taking place, as though a simple change of tone in affectivity, not directly drawn from the body, could be enough to make us what we are. The mood experienced here is not affect, but a kind of biological thrust of our body that raises us beyond ourselves (e.g., anger), or lets us tie ourselves up in ourselves and dulls us (e.g., shame). I hope we can agree on this. The point is not simply to deploy some kind of physiology of passions, like a contemporary neurology—one that privileges the somatic over the psychic;[50] it is important simply to understand, and to seek, what is at the foundation of our embodiedness, where the "mass of sensations" escapes all signification and thus also escapes from phenomenology, which is caught up in the mysteries of the *signifier*. As Kant explained, in his masterly fashion, "Unity of synthesis in accordance with empirical concepts would be entirely contingent, and, were it not grounded on a transcendental ground of unity, it would be possible for a swarm of appearances ["a mass of sensations"] to fill up our soul without experience ever being able to rise from it."[51]

What can we say, then, about this mass of phenomena, or rather this "mass of sensations," that the consciousness can never manage to synthesize? What would a "picture" be if we had not *beforehand* set our sights on it as a picture? Or perhaps we should talk about the phenomenon of a picture, be it black, gray, harsh, rough, extended, or flat. Why does the part of us that is our drives, or our own animality, prevent us in some way, apparently in advance, from signifying the picture by adjectives like these, that are somehow too rational or commonsense? Moreover, if we are confronted, as in the celebrated account by Husserl in *Cartesian Meditations*, with "the pure—and, so to speak, still dumb—psychological experience, which now must be made to utter its own sense," how can we live in such a silence without having already designated it as part of our lifeworld, or surrounding lifeworld (to use his terms)?[52] Is there a world before predication that has to wait for our words before it can be *predicated* (Merleau-Ponty)? As the biologist Jakob von Uexküll has demonstrated and the philosopher Martin Heidegger has shown conceptually, the dog, the cat, the tortoise, the fly—even the mollusc—can be part of the picture along with the rest of the "mass of sensations" (see §16).[53] But is signifying what really counts for them, or for us in our relationship with our own animality? If we presuppose that the animal lacks a world, aren't we always looking at the animal and imposing on it our own abundance? Aren't we merely seeing its significations in terms of our own signifying? Aren't we conceptualizing what the animal embodies it its body and drives in terms of consciousness and the human? Heidegger, discussing the problem of the philosopher as solitary, says, "Nietzsche declares often enough in his later years that the body must be the *guideline* of observation not only of human beings but of the *world*: the projection of world from the perspective of animal and animality. The fundamental experience of the world as 'chaos' has its roots here."[54]

If we move to the problem of our own animality, Chaos can then be the name we give to *bodying life*: Life seen overall as bodied. We cross a threshold here and move from the major confusion of the chaotic (the mass of sensations) to Chaos itself, as an opening up of the biological body, or the thrust of our drives toward what remains creative in their relationship with the world (*pulsio* from *pellere*; pushing-repulsing). Chaos here does not point to "a turbulent jumble" nor to the "unordered, arising from the removal of all order," but to "what urges, flows and is animated, whose order is concealed, whose law we do not descry straightaway."[55] An irresistible biological approach is at work here, representing the world as "bodying," as "a gigantic 'body,'" as it were, whose bodying and living constitutes beings as a whole."[56] One "bodies" then in Nietzsche—as in the intransitive verb *leiben* that comes up in phrases such as "to be empty" (*nichts im Leibe haben*) or "to be pregnant" (*gesegneten Leibes sein*)—when the drive or the "thrust" (*pulsio*) emerges, and nothing holds it back. If I suggest that health or illness provide the point of view from which we start here, as well as the starting point of our thought processes, I am not reducing the psychic to the biological in the neurological sense of the term. Rather, I wish to note, or to clarify, how our well-being (or our ill-being) is rooted in life at the level of our most basic corporality. "Every time an event enters into the consciousness," Nietzsche says, indicating how living is first of all being embodied, "it is the expression of the ill-being [*malaise*] of the organism."[57] Chaos then goes deep down into our emotions as well as into our drives and into our physiological and instinctive bodies. It starts as a kind of bottomless descent into our own animality; in that way it ensures that our embodiment, or our drives, reach into what we live without ever being able to signify what it is that we live (and thus the famous and appropriate resemblance between *Trieb* [drive] and *Tier* [animal] in the German language).[58] Simply to spiritualize all of this is not convincing. Nor is it enough to point out that a drive is not an "instinct," or to suggest that a drive simply unites and traces out "the frontier between the mental and the physical."[59] This again tries to signify too much, and attempts to humanize things too directly at the exact place where we must stop doing so. I shall come back later to the topic (§17), to show that Freudianism does not work as well as Nietzsche's approach here because it fixes drives to some particular end, whether they are repressed or disguised (sublimation). In the end, the sphere of the consciousness determines the aims of the unconscious, whether these aims are unimportant or only part of what the unconscious expresses (the sunken part of an iceberg, so to speak). As long as sense determines non-sense—or, rather, as long as beyond-sense or non-sense is not brought out into the open, or somehow thought to be there—the descent into the abyss has not really been attempted, and a signifying base will, after all, always try to give structure to everything. Gilles Deleuze, in an interview, risks surprising those who want to see ethics (bestiality or sin) where in reality it is a question of metaphysics (animality or Chaos): "the problem is not that of being *this or that within man*, but rather of *a becoming inhuman*, of *becoming the universal animal*: not to see oneself as a beast, but *to deconstruct the human organization of the body*, to cross this or that zone of intensity of the body, each one discovering which zones are his or her own, and the groups, the populations, the species that inhabit them."[60]

As far as the unspoken is concerned—or rather, "the region of what can no longer be said, the region of renunciation"[61]—we might ask whether we are really able to throw light on the topic in a philosophical work on the body? The question may seem incongruous, even ridiculous—or at the very least presumptuous. After all, the specter of the rapture or intoxication of the gods hangs over the topic of banquets, particularly those "agape" where a "good wine" is served and there is "good bread" to eat. From the paradoxical proximity of dionysiac drives and eucharistic embodiment (§35) we can derive a conception of the action of grace (*eucharis*) that is, to say the least, ambiguous: a mad drunken bout as opposed to a meal shared in the agape; human bestiality as opposed to the humanization of the animal in us; a reduction to the biological rather than a renewal of the Christly. St. Paul himself gave warning, to Greeks who were first of all and above all dionysiac: "When you come together, it is not really to eat the Lord's Supper. For when the time comes to eat, each of you goes ahead with your own supper, and one goes hungry and another becomes drunk" (1 Cor. 11:20). Some three centuries later, Tertullian, distancing himself from the Montanist movement, attacked those Christians who were permissive toward paganism—those, according to St. Paul, whose "god is the belly" (Phil. 3:19). Tertullian thought that in taking too literally the idea of the flesh to be eaten (*this is my body*), they were vying with drunken orgies. His warning to them was not without a certain humor:

You are more irreligious, in proportion as a heathen is more conformable. He, in short, sacrifices his appetite to an idol-god; you to (the true) God will not. For to you your belly is god, and your lungs a temple, and your paunch a sacrificial altar, and your cook the priest, and your fragrant smell the Holy Spirit, and your condiment spiritual gifts, and your belching prophecy. . . . If I offer you a paltry lentil dyed red with must well boiled down, immediately you will sell all your "primacies"; with you "love" shows its fervour in saucepans, "faith" its warmth in kitchens, "hope" its anchorage in waters; but of greater account is "love," because that is the means whereby your young men sleep with their sisters! Appendages, as we all know, of appetite are lasciviousness and voluptuousness. . . . On the other hand, an over-fed Christian will be more necessary to bears and lions, perchance, than to God; only that, even to encounter beasts, it will be his duty to practise emaciation.[62]

In spite of these appropriate counsels of vigilance, in particular from the period when the dionysiac was dominant (St. Paul, or Tertullian), we can still encounter this problem today—despite the fact that everything has been done to formalize the episode that is, to say the least, *strange* of the "body given to eat," or the eucharistic body. Thus we constantly come up against this question: Is it necessary and will it always be necessary to spiritualize everything here? Must we lessen the scandal of the body given to us literally to chew (*trôgon*) as real foodstuff and the blood given to drink as true beverage?—"for my flesh is true food and my blood is true drink" (John 6:55). Certainly, as I aim to show in this book (see especially §26), neither "body" nor "blood" had the same meaning in Palestine as they did in ancient Greece or Rome. Moreover, to eat and to drink in terms of a filiation with one's ancestors or in reference to rites of passage would not have had the same signification in Athens (dionysiac banquet) and in Jerusalem (Passover). The question, however, remains—at least for us, as in the past—"how can this man give us his flesh to eat?" This is what the Capernaites (the Jews of the Synagogue of Capernaum) ask, and it appears that we are not talking about something that was inevitable, even when "his hour had come," that is, at the Passover (John 6:52, 13:1) (see §25). What we need in Christianity, first of all, is "bodying life" (*leiben*). We need this when biology makes a body with the body, as it does in the world, just as we need it when Chaos is married to the "mass of sensations" with which we cannot come to terms. The incorporation in the eucharist, as we shall see later (§30), demands that our bodies make body with the body of Christ ("You are the body of Christ and individually members of it" [1 Cor. 12:27]) and thus that we are also *bodied*—because our life is, above all, organic, and we need to start from the body and physiology. The *this is my body* then becomes a gift of the organic to the organic, rather than simply spiritualization in the mystical context. Appetites, emotions, drives, and all that make up our instinctive life with all its organic functions conjoined are taken into the eucharistic bread, reaching also into the abyss or the chaotic base of our humanity: "It is because our *bodies* are *driven* that subjectivity can be so truly a constituent element, and it is consequently in such bodies that we have to look for the ultimate source of phenomenality."[63]

A journey has already started here, and we will not stop midway, even if carrying on requires a certain boldness. I will return to and lay claim to matters of dogma, but precisely to show them "in a way that responds to the needs of our era"—that is, "in following the methods of research and presentation that are used in modern thought."[64] Examining Chaos or corporality (Chapters 1, 6, and 7); that part of us that is animality and that will be changed to humanity (Chapters 2, 4, and 7); and eros always already included in agape (Chapters 3, 6, and 9)—and claiming the contemporaniety of these topics today—is not simply a question of following fashion or rhetorical tricks, because these topics have been neglected in philosophy and even more so in theology. It is rather a question of yielding to necessity—that which arises from the thing itself being studied and not from the categories we impose on it. It is a question, as we have already seen, of "the projection of the world from the perspective of the animal and animality. The fundamental experience of the world as 'chaos' has its roots here."[65] Christ himself seems to have taken this way, a way that is so difficult to articulate and to come to terms with. He took the place of the animal (of animality) that was biblical, and he did so in a way that is not often questioned because it is so astonishing. That is not to say that he was incarnate in or through the animal (a pagan notion justly condemned at the Council in Trullo, in 692 AD). Rather, in taking on our humanity, he also took on and took into his care our animal origins. For a start, we find his icon, or his representation, in a certain form of animality: in the figure of the sacrificial lamb.[66]

Presented (*mise en scène*) in the form of a sacrifice in Judaism, the lamb is presented to the Last Supper (*mise en Cène*) through Christ in a Christian Passover. Going from the sacred (*sacer*) to the shared meal (*Cena*), the sacrificed lamb comes to be entirely eaten (flesh and blood), which marks the important seal of animality in the great Passage undertaken by God. This is not *bestial*—a form of animality that would precisely mark the dimension of sin (§13)—but it is nonetheless the *animal* in humankind that God takes on, and metamorphoses, in a kind of staging of the Last Supper (a *mise en Cène*) on the great day of Holy Thursday. The philosophical gives way for the first time to the theological here, not to juxtapose the two, and even less to muddle them together, but to let them be seen on the stage of our humanity, inhabited by Chaos and animality. What is staged at the Last Supper is a God embodied with the lineaments of a God sacrificed, ready to accept responsibility for all and ready to transubstantiate all.

2

The Staging of the Last Supper

Ever since Vatican II, public discussions of the eucharist (not to mention library shelves devoted to the topic) have been dominated, quite appropriately, by reflections on the eucharist either as a meal (a "repast") or an "action of grace" (*eu-charis*): the food that gives us strength; the sharing with fellow guests; the one who presides, and so on. A curtain has been drawn, however, over the meaning of what is to be eaten—probably because the significance of transubstantiation, something inherited from medieval categories, is not simple to explain. If the eucharistic Passover is certainly *bread broken for a new world*, or if the wine is *fruit of the vine and work of human hands*, that is what is given to us first of all to eat and drink: "For I tell you, I will not eat it [this Passover] until it is fulfilled in the kingdom of God [*ou mê phagô to pascha*]. . . . From now on I will not drink [*ou mê piô*] of the fruit of the vine until the kingdom of God comes" (Luke 22:16–18).

In the Christian version of the Passover, bread (the body) is certainly eaten, and wine (the blood) drunk—but as substitutes for the flesh of the lamb and the sacrificial blood of the Jewish Passover. In short, for the bread to become the body and the wine to become the blood, in the Christian staging of consecration during the repast of the Last Supper, we need to connect with and transform the flesh sacrificed and the blood offered in the Jewish staging of the sacrificial lamb (on the altar of the Temple). The Last Supper of Holy Thursday takes on and transforms the setting of the day of the Great Shabbat (*Shabbat Hagadol*). In both there is the animal:

sacrificed in one case (Judaism: the sacrificial lamb), accepted and transformed in the other (Christianity: the Lamb of God). In eating the body—*this is my body*—the disciple receives, in fact and paradoxically, *all* of divinity, including all of creation, which is concentrated there and which we share in our animality. The incarnation is an assumption and recapitulation of *all*—nothing slips away from God except sin (and thus bestiality, as opposed here to animality [see §13]). In the image of humanity resurrected we find also our animality transformed and oriented toward the full humanization and filiation of the whole cosmos (§28). The paschal lamb sacrificed for us is thus certainly for our salvation (he who takes away the sins of the world) but also an assumption of our Chaos, the Chaos of our emotions and our drives, in the form of a building block and substructure of our humanity (a conversion of animality into humanity through filiation as recognized by the eucharist). "We cannot hold it to be unimportant that the Word of God was incarnate and would save in effect *only human nature*," the ninth-century Irish theologian Johannes Scotus Eriugena, would bravely point out.

> But we should believe very strongly and understand with the greatest exactitude that it is by the incarnation of the Word that all creatures living in the sky and on the earth *have been saved*. . . . All *creatures* (animals without understanding, as well as the trees and plants and all that make up the world) which have been created as far as their cause is concerned (though not their bodily mass) like man, will be resurrected with man, and in man, at the time of the resurrection of man. . . . If, in taking on human nature, the Word took on all creatures, then the Word has saved all creatures, and all creatures shall be saved for eternity.[1]

§5. The Figure of the Lamb

As we turn from Chaos to bodying life, we need to take account of our animality. We might recall here that the picture Martin Heidegger glimpsed in the classroom at his lectures, as part of the "mass of sensations," was not directly related to the physiological body unless it had ceased to be a phenomenon, or at least ceased to signify (§4). Christ, however, offers his "body"—occupying the place of that animality by which we are constituted, but of course without falling off into any kind of bestiality that might be synonymous with sin (§13). He offers his "body," daring this substitution, putting himself in the place of the sacrificial lamb. Certainly what the Book of the Apocalypse describes is not really familiar to us: the triumph of the Messiah over the dragon, and his wedding feast with the Church and humanity:

"Let us rejoice and exult
        and give him the glory,
for the marriage of the Lamb
        has come [*gamos tou arniou-nuptiae Agni*],
and his bride has made
        herself ready;
to her it has been granted to
        be clothed
with fine linen, bright and pure" . . .

"Blessed are those who are invited to the marriage supper of the Lamb." . . . The beast was captured. And with it the false prophet who had performed in its presence the signs by which he deceived those who had received the mark of the beast and those who worshipped its image. (Rev 19:7–9, 20)

We can just stick to symbolism, ignoring any form of naturalism, but then the "lamb" becomes so unlike an animal that it seems to bear on itself the weight of sins rather than that of animality—like the "lamb led to the slaughter" in the Song of the Suffering Servant (Isa. 53:7), or the "Lamb of God who takes away the sin of the world" in the words of John the Baptist (John 1:29), or the "slaughtered" Lamb in the Book of the Apocalypse (Rev. 5:6). We could argue at length, as has been done in the past, over the choice of the lamb as the image of he who comes to save us; in the impact of its figure it serves as a special offering because it is "without blemish, as a burnt offering to the Lord" (Lev. 23:12). In its innocence it lives in an ideal way, along with the the ox and the goat (Deut. 14:4), not to mention "the wolf [that] shall live with the lamb" (Isa. 11:6). In its docility it is "like a gentle lamb led to the slaughter" (Jer. 11:19), and in its humility it is "like a sheep that before its shearers is silent" (Isa. 53:7). I should add that we need to distinguish between the sacrificial lamb that is a sacrifice due to God—and that must not on any account be eaten—and the paschal lamb that one *must* eat, when it is "roasted over the fire," or "eaten in one house . . . and you shall not break any of its bones" (Exod. 12:8, 46); moreover, concerning its meat, Exodus tells us "you shall eat it hurriedly" (12:11) and the "blood shall be a sign" (12:13)—the "congregation of Israel" shall "take some of the blood and put it on the two doorposts and the lintel of the houses in which they eat" (12:6–7).[2] In short, the Wedding Feast of the Lamb, at least as it is classically understood, celebrates the Passover of God with his people (Judaism) and of Christ with the Church and with humanity (Christianity), rather than the *Passover*, or the passage from animality to humanity recognized in its filiation (from Chaos to cosmos), that *this is my body* comes originally to celebrate.[3]

It has not been sufficiently emphasized, perhaps because it seems obvious, that, as Marcel Jousse tells us, "the history—the Palestinian history— of man is the history of his *mouth*. In the Palestinian ethnic habitat two human actions are constantly emphasized, the act of eating and the act of drinking. . . . 'Pastor' has its place as a word speaking of someone who *makes eat* (grazing the sheep and also preparing for them to go to the butcher as food)."[4] We shall return then to what was apparent at the start: the sheep, living biologically, to be fed by a people of shepherds, is also meat that can and must be eaten (at least on the day of Passover), and it is this that provides the rationale for breeding the animal. The meat can be used at the wedding feast, in accord with rules that designate the animals whose meat is to be eaten as those that have "cloven hoofs" and that chew the cud (are "ruminant"): the sheep, certainly, but also the ox, the goat, the deer, the gazelle, the roebuck, the wild goat, the ibex, the antelope, and the mountain sheep. On the other hand, there are animals that chew the cud but do not have a cloven hoof (the camel, the hare, the rock badger, and the rabbit) and those that do not do not chew the cud but have a cloven hoof (the pig). These latter animals will be considered unclean ("You shall not eat their meat, and you shall not touch their carcasses" [Deut. 14:8]). Only the lamb—or more or less only the lamb—has the privilege of being sacrificed and eaten.

The paschal lamb, even with the stipulation to "eat it hurriedly," is thus first of all something *that is eaten*—something that helps us understand how in the case of the unleavened bread of the Host, as with the sacrificial lamb, there is a necessary precipitation for the believer to eat it and then pass straight into the world. And the lamb sacrificed by the priest in the Jewish Passover—certainly not eaten, but destined to be sacrificed—will take on the image of the Resurrected Christ that the Book of the Apocalypse comes to celebrate precisely in the Wedding Feast of the Lamb: "then I saw between the throne and the four living creatures and among the elders, a Lamb standing as if it had been slaughtered. . . . Worthy is the Lamb that was slaughtered to receive power and wealth and wisdom and might and honour and glory and blessing" (Rev. 5:6–12). The Second (New) Testament thus continues to insist, taking its support from the First (Old Testament), that Christ has taken the place of the sacrificial lamb and is also given to eat, as one shares and eats the paschal lamb at the heart of Judaism. And so we find the many allegorical readings that come from the relationship between the one Testament and the other: "He was oppressed and he was afflicted yet he did not open his mouth; like a lamb that is led to the slaughter" (Isa. 53:7). Similarly, "Jesus was silent" in front of the high priest (Matt. 26:63), or as regards Pilate, "Jesus gave him no answer" (John 19:9). As noted earlier, the blood of the lamb is put "on the two doorposts and the lintel of the houses" of the families of Israelites and they are safeguarded from the plagues that afflict the Egyptians (Exod. 12:5, 7). And humanity is saved by the blood of Jesus that "came out" when "one of the soldiers pierced his side with a spear" (John 19:34). The Lord tells the Israelites "you shall not break any of its [the lamb's] bones" on the day when it is eaten in the Passover feast (Exod. 12:46), just as the soldiers "did not break his legs" when they saw that the crucified Jesus was already dead (John 19:33). We can understand, then, Philip's response to the Ethiopian eunuch who has been reading about "the lamb that is led to the slaughter" (Isa. 53:7): "The eunuch asked Philip, 'About whom, may I ask you, does the prophet say this, about himself, or about someone else?' Then Philip began to speak, and starting with this scripture, he proclaimed to him the good news about Jesus" (Acts 8:34–35).

In short there is a perfect consonance here—between Christ given to eat and the paschal lamb as sacrificial lamb. The consonance is fully justified and formalized in the first Letter of St. Peter: "You were ransomed . . . with the precious blood of Christ, like that of a lamb without defect or blemish" (1 Pet. 1:18–19). And it is constantly repeated in the *Gloria* in celebrations of the eucharist ("Lord God, Lamb of God [*Agnus Dei*], Son of the Father"), earnestly spoken in the first eucharistic preface for Easter: "For he is the true Lamb [*verus est Agnus*] who has taken away the sins of the world." And it is explicitly formulated on the day of the celebration of the Last Supper: "As we eat his flesh that was sacrificed for us, we are made strong."[5] The identity of Christ-the-Lamb must become again for us today the site of a renewed philosophical and theological examination, of which the potential sorrow and misery cannot disguise the triple depths—divine, human, even animal—that are contained within it. As Pope Benedict XVI has justly said, "The paschal lamb and all the sacrifices of the Old Covenant are replaced by the gift of his Body and his Blood, the gift of himself."[6] So we eat the "body" of Christ in the Christian Easter as the paschal lamb, the symbol of the sacrificial lamb in the Jewish Passover, was eaten, and moreover, as the fact of being "laid . . . in a manger" (Luke 2:7)—where all that is placed must be eaten—prefigures the other fact that he who is "lying in the manger" (Luke 2:16) will give in the Last Supper "his flesh to eat" (John 6:52). Our paschal lamb, Christ, has been sacrificed and is God (1 Cor. 5:7). To understand this perfect coincidence of the Lamb and Christ is the necessary condition that gives sense to *this is my body* and that can thus point to the animality in the tradition from which this eating is drawn.[7]

We can, of course, suppose a double objection. (1) First of all, the Son of Man takes bread and wine, and not the flesh and the blood of the lamb (which were present at the Passover feast) to provide the gift of his body. The paschal lamb, like the sacrificial lamb, provides only the *framework* in which the bread and wine are employed in the eucharist, but without any process of assimilation.[8] (2) Second, if there is an identity with, or perhaps better identification of, the body and the lamb in the consecrated bread, this will concern humankind, and thus Christ—only in relation to our salvation from sin, and certainly not in relation to our animality. The lamb is not, or is no longer, an animal in the sacrifice, precisely in that it is no longer a question of consumption (eating) but of consuming (immolation or sacrifice). These above objections are powerful ones, and they provide what is probably one of the reasons for the massive rejection of animality that is found, with a few notable exceptions, in the context of Christian culture (§15).

(1) To the first objection—the Passover simply as *framework*—I would respond that to dissociate the bread on the altar from the flesh of the lamb, and the wine on the table from the sacrificial blood, does not fit the tradition within which the Passover is celebrated. For the disciples themselves, the preparations for Passover would have included both the unleavened bread and the sacrifice of the lamb (Mark 14:12). And it is here precisely that the question of a body to be eaten comes up: "Take: this is my body" (Mark 14:22). If the flesh and the blood of the paschal lamb had not been first of all in the Jewish tradition—according to the great passage out of Egypt in Exodus, to be consumed as well as to be celebrated (Exod. 12:14)—neither the "bread" would have become the "body," nor the "wine" would change to "blood." It is not shocking that there is flesh to eat or blood to drink in the Christian Passover—these are inherited precisely from the Jewish tradition. What shocks, on the contrary, is that the "flesh" and "blood" are literally *my body* (*to soma mou*) and *my blood* (*to aïma mou*) (Mark 14:22–24). The mine-ness of the body to be eaten and the blood to drink, to use the phenomenological term (*Jeimeinigkeit*), is what makes things very difficult. If we no longer eat the animal (the lamb), are we—in a cannibalistic hypothesis that we shall return to later—eating the man (*this is my body*)? (See §25.) Or perhaps we could say that we need to find the animal in humankind, to understand that we do not give up animality (the lamb) in the sacrifice, even though the sacrifice is that of

humanity (*this is my body*). Doesn't the Son take on and transform it, passing through that animality into a humanity recognizable in its affiliation by means of the eucharistic bread?

(2) To the second objection—the lamb as symbol of innocence in contrast to sin, and not animality in contrast to humanity—we could again reply in terms of the culture in which the sacrifice is expiated. I have emphasized already, following Marcel Jousse, that "the history—Palestinian—of man is the history of his mouth."[9] Better, we can consider that the shepherd who leads his sheep (John 10:4) is identified as one who brings them to eat and gives them to be eaten. The sheep is then an animal that one eats, and not simply a sacrifice that is celebrated. We must emphasize also, relying this time on Moses Maimonides and his *Guide for the Perplexed*, that the sacrificial lamb and the paschal lamb are originally different. The first is "consumed" (without being eaten by the priest), and the second "consumed" in a different sense (eaten by the guests who celebrate Passover). But gradually these two are identified. In the history of Judaism, the *exterior* sacrifice of the immolate lamb is gradually replaced by the *interior* offering of the broken spirit:

Sacrifice and offering you do not desire
. . . Burnt-offering and sin-offering
　　　you have not required.
Then I said, "Here I am;
In the scroll of the book it is written of me.
　　　I delight to do your will, O my God."

(Ps. 40:6–7)

For you have no delight in sacrifice;
　　　if I were to give a burnt-offering,
　　　you would not be pleased.
The sacrifice acceptable to God is a
　　　broken spirit;
A broken and contrite heart, O God,
　　　you will not despise.

(Ps. 51:16–17)

Certainly in ancient Judaism lambs were sacrificed, but progressively less frequently. There were other ways to celebrate the God who had sometimes been celebrated with too much idolatry. Maimonides, the controversial twelfth-century Jewish scholar, says, "The commandment that sacrifices shall be brought and that the temple shall be visited has for its object the success of that principle among you: 'Know me, and serve no other being; I will be your God, and ye shall be my people'" (Lev. 26:12). And that is why "for its sake I have transferred these modes of worship to my name; idolatry shall thereby be utterly destroyed, and Jewish faith firmly established."[10]

Does the purely pedagogic role of the sacrificial lamb definitively remove all traces of animality from it, so that once established the animality can be overlooked (when the *broken spirit* comes to be substituted for the sacrificial lamb, and the burnt offering of the animal is suppressed)? In fact, this is far from what happens. Because the sacrificial lamb rapidly rejoins the paschal lamb in the celebration of the day of the Great Passover, and what remains of the animal—even if "just a bone with a little roasted meat"[11]—is still eaten today in remembrance both of the lamb of the burnt offering (Lev. 23:12) and of the paschal lamb (Exod. 12:6–11). The Christian Passover, on Holy or Maundy Thursday, will recall and will also search for the lamb to be eaten "when the Passover lamb is sacrificed" (Mark 14:12)—that is, at the precise hour when, according to the prescriptions of the Law, the sheep are sacrificed at the Temple—on the night at the start of the Feast of Unleavened Bread (John 18:28), and on the noon of the day of preparation for the Passover (John 19:14).[12]

What remains, then, is the identity of Christ and the lamb, whether paschal or sacrificial, but both are fused into an animal that is eaten in the context of Judaism and taken in another way in the portion of bread at the heart of Christianity. "He [Christ] abolished the first to establish the second," Paul explains firmly in the Letter to the Hebrews. "And it is by God's will that we have been sanctified through the *offering of the body* of Jesus Christ once for all" (Heb. 10:9–10). The identity—or perhaps we should say, the identification—is not simply in relation to sin (a theme that has been frequently and justly developed) but also in relation to animality—at least in order to take as null and void, and as exclusively symbolic, the Jewish image of the Lamb through which the Christ is also sacrificed.

Before propensity to sin there is a more original animality, and we need also to consider it despite its incongruity. The "substitution," if there is one, derives certainly first of all from putting divinity in place of, or instead of, our humanity. God who was made man was not made animal—unless we fall into the paganism that the Council in Trullo (692 AD) roundly and soundly condemned.[13] It is true nonetheless that he takes on himself our share of animality (Chaos, passions, drives, and embodiedness), without which his humanity would not have been fully incarnate. If *the animal* remains in us—as science certainly leads us to think (Darwin), and according to an evolutionism that happily the

Church now forbids us to deny (Congregation of the Doctrine of the Faith)—it is important nowadays to think this through metaphysically, even theologically. Heidegger points out that "the animality of man has a deeper metaphysical ground than could ever be inferred biologically and scientifically by referring man to an existent animal species."[14] He does not deny evolutionary theories, but definitively privileges the philosophical approach rather than a naive approach to the results of biology. He quotes Nietzsche, from *Thus Spoke Zarathustra* (1884): "The apes are too good-natured for man to have originated from them."[15] This is the genesis—metaphysical and not simply scientific, that Christ first came to bring us in the eucharistic bread. He ran the risk of remaining a total stranger to our humanity, as also perhaps to our animality and to the interior Chaos that it comes to show. As Gregory of Nazianzus tells us, "that which He [God] has not assumed He has not healed; but that which is united to His Godhead is also saved."[16]

§6. From the Mystic Lamb to the Flayed Ox

Do we find traces of our rather bold project elsewhere? Certainly we do in the Early Church Fathers, as we shall see later (§14), and particularly in the writings of Irenaeus, who identifies the "dust" from which Adam is formed (Gen. 2:7) as the "(same) ground" from which the animals were made (Gen. 2:16). Tertullian also, in contrast to the Gnostics, sees in the muscles, bones, nerves, veins, hair, and even the "down" of Christ the "almost biological and animal truth of his flesh (*De carne Christi*), as well as his 'origin of earth' (*Adamâ*)."[17] And as some philosophers—those who are not Christian but who open the way to a reading of the eucharistic body that is not simply philosophical but also Christ-centered (such as Deleuze, reading Bacon)—show us, in art above all we can find what we are looking for in the figure of the lamb or of the "flayed ox."

Believers are then more or less accustomed to the aesthetic representation of the lamb. According to recent analysis, Andrei Roblev's *Icon of the Trinity* shows a "head of the Lamb" with/or the "image of the Holy Face" that can be seen in the blood of the chalice at the center of the altar, depending on whether one looks at it at it from the left or the right.[18] Again, as outlined in the Preface, the reredos of the Adoration of the Mystic Lamb, by the Van Eyck brothers in the Saint Bavo Cathedral at Ghent, shows the lamb in the form of the proud animal upright on the altar, adored by the elect and by a cohort of angels, enthroned in place of and instead of the eucharistic bread and of the Resurrected Christ. But, at the risk of surprising any reader or art lover who has not come across them, we should also point to the several versions of the seventeenth-century artist Francisco de Zurbarán's painting *Carnero con las patas atadas* [The bound lamb].[19] The lone animal lies on the block, ready for the slaughterhouse or for sacrifice. Emerging from a subdued background, its body is so luminous that a portion of divinity seems to appear in the thick wool, ready for shearing, and in the flesh waiting to be worked on. The head of the lamb, or ram, that is offered rests here like a carcass, which brings to mind a surrender rather than simply resignation. Above all, the bound feet recall not only the room with the sacrificial offerings hanging on hooks at the Temple, but also Christ bound, a theme often evoked and represented in seventeenth-century spirituality (for example, the bound Christ described a century later by Ignatius Loyola). It is then he—the Christ led to the cross as "a lamb that is led to the slaughter" (Isa. 53:7)—that the animal represents in the eyes of the Spanish Christian artist. Not in that it becomes animal(ity), but, by taking on our humanity, it also takes part in the sacrifice and receives, in a very striking touch of realism, that which is also our true portion of animality. God is not an animal, and humankind is not only animal, but in becoming human, God encounters the "animal part of ourselves," which he had to inhabit in order to metamorphose.[20]

The "flayed ox" (or "carcass of beef"), for those who know how to read it and decipher it, takes us back to a residue of embodiedness and animality that we can never totally suppress. Rembrandt, in his painting *Flayed Ox* (1655), now in the collection of the Louvre Museum in Paris, reminds us in reality of the image of Christ crucified: a butcher's carcass, a body or *meat* extended or, rather, spread out, because it is also hooked up. "True animal crucifixion, this flayed ox shows us the expressionist realism of Rembrandt. . . . The pathos of the scene invites the spectator to consider the civilized cannibalism of the Dutch Golden Age."[21] The artist Chaim Soutine tried to paint his own flayed ox (c.1924); we know this not only because he did so, but also because he spoke about it. His picture, with an almost gory sensuality coming through its open flesh, shows us humanity, as well as divinity—both of which take on animality when shown in this way.[22] But, finally, we have to wait for Francis Bacon and the comments that he made on his own work to see what there is of the religious and the Christ-like in the theme of the flayed ox, even though Bacon situates himself outside any Christian convictions. The religious and Christ-like theme emerges in the form of animality, or of flesh and the biological life of humankind, an animality that is crucified. In his paintings he gives us images of a man called the "Pope," and he gives a *Crucifixion*, as well as *Painting* in which the reference to the crucifixion is explicit.[23] In the upper part of *Painting*, the carcass of an animal is stretched out and the flesh is spread forth so that we can see the "carcass of meat." When he was asked whether these works were "painted as part of Christian culture and . . . made for believers," Bacon replied, "Yes, that is true." But the image of the Crucifixion is, he says, "a magnificent armature on which you can hang all types of feeling and sensation," rather than just one particular set of beliefs.[24] In other words, in showing the crucified divinity, Bacon certainly meant to find humanity (the Man-God), but also animality (the Man-God in the image of the flayed ox, or even of *meat*), insofar as this arrives at a "Chaos," the "flesh spread out," or the "mass of sensations," which we continue to search for and even to incorporate. The painter talks about this in a way that contemporary believers might find quite difficult to understand: "I've always been very moved by pictures about slaughter-houses and meat, and to me they belong very much to the whole thing of the Crucifixion. . . . Well, of course, we are meat, we are potential car-casses. If I go into a butcher's shop I always think it's surprising that I wasn't there instead of the animal."[25]

§7. Toward Another Metamorphosis

Gilles Deleuze devoted his book *Francis Bacon: The Logic of Sensation* (which is probably better known to philosophers than to theologians) to Bacon's ideas and paintings, taking as fundamental the assertion that "Bacon is a religious painter only in butchers' shops."[26] One could cer-tainly be shocked, even scandalized, by such declarations, which seem to be based on contradictions. On the one hand, there is carnage (*carne*, "flesh"), and on the other, the spiritual or spirituality (*spiritus*, "spirit"). But Bacon, this religious painter—even though a nonbeliever—offers us a way forward into unity, for those who make an effort to understand and who do not take immediate offence at his work.

(1) *First, the philosophical unity*—of humanity with its appropriate ani-mality that exists in the meat, as it does also in that limit-zone that ulti-mately we shall all fully share. The philosopher (who could also be talking here about the paradoxical features of resurrected flesh, as we see it in *The Incredulity of Saint Thomas* by Caravaggio, based on John 20:24–29) says, "Meat is not dead flesh; it retains all the sufferings and assumes all the colours of living flesh. . . . Meat is the common zone of man and the beast, their zone of indiscernibility." Further, Deleuze says: "This objec-tive zone of indiscernibility is the entire body, but the body insofar as it is flesh or meat."[27]

I explored, in the first chapter, the notion of flesh in the current usage of the term (§1); I have avoided the over-spiritualized lived experience

(*Leib*), as well as the reified material body (*Körper*). And perhaps it could be said that here we have what I was looking for, in this "meat" which is something the surgeon fully understands (§1), because it is also what surgeons are concerned with, even though most often they do not dare admit it even to themselves.

(2) *Second, the theological unity.* The meat is certainly what the flesh is destined to become after it is dead: it is what remains of our biological body. Perhaps it is also this that Christ at the Last Supper, and on the evening of his Passion, will take on in *this is my body*. If the *my body* is a *this*, then we can accept that the *this* can (even must) become "meat," or "cadaver"—certainly when it is given over to butchery in what are, according to Bacon, true crucifixions, but also when it is flesh to eat, which is not simply meat to be chewed (something about which even the early Christians, in particular Tertullian and St. Augustine, asked themselves [§25]).

We can suggest, even though it may sound too bold or paradoxical, that the *becoming-animal* of humankind, starting from human aspirations that are too immediate to spiritualize, as well as the *becoming-meat*, starting from flesh that is biological but also lived, mark two different stages of a human immersion in Chaos or the Tohu-Bohu, to which God cannot remain indifferent. "Pity the meat!"[28] Or rather, as Gilles Deleuze cries in commiseration with Francis Bacon, pity our biological flesh (*Fleisch*). And it is this that can be reiterated in every eucharist through *this is my body*, when it is totally accepted and at the same time transformed.

As far as the proposals offered here are concerned, above all in relation to the eucharist, we can reassure the reader—if not theologically (Chapter 7), then at least philosophically and aesthetically. We must agree with Deleuze that "Bacon is Cézannean"[29] The *trans-substantiation* of the body in painting (Cézanne) implies in effect the theological truth of the *transsubstantiation* of the animality in humanity recognized here in its filiation—Christ himself, like the painter, "lending his body to the world" (Merleau-Ponty) fully taking on our humanity and along with that our part of animality.[30]

In terms of a believer's relationship to contemporary art, Christians can't simply be satisfied with goodwill, can't simply accept a kind of condescending neutrality when they have not actually experienced any kind of transformation. We expect also a performance (to "perform"), or that capacity in which, through action (the "performative"), we come to be modified by what arrives from the outside, disturbing the conventional framework of our lives and demanding that we rethink for ourselves.[31] We can make the connection here between the fourteenth-century icon of the Crucifixion in Moscow's Andrei Rublev museum of art, Rogier Van der

Weyden's lamb, Rembrandt's and Soutine's flayed oxen, and Bacon's *Painting* (with its reference to the Crucifixion). So much depends on the way everything holds together, as we see in Cézanne's attempt simply to capture the secret of Mount Saint-Victoire and the way in which it could be "incorporated": "I cannot attain the intensity that is unfolded before my senses," Cézanne complains to his son. "I have not the magnificent richness of colouring that animates nature."[32] We could say that Cézanne is not a phenomenologist but a "figurologist,"[33] and in this respect he can clarify some of the meaning of the eucharist for us. He helps us see that it is not simply a question of giving up the lived experience of the flesh (*Leib*), but rather of conceding that what is *figural* in some of the most contemporary art (the meat, for example) says more than the *abstraction* of that older modern art upon which phenomenologists in general have focused (for example, Martineau on Malevich; Marion on Rothko; Henry on Kandinsky).[34]

The place of the animal, or rather, the place of animal(ity) in us, is that which the Emmanuel ("God with us") has to take upon himself, along with us and for us, to transform us, if we believe that the *this is my body* of the Wedding Feast of the Lamb is really capable of such an espousal. There is, then, in philosophy as in theology, an omission even more fundamental than the neglect of being: it is the neglect of our animality that tries to conceal the chaotic abyss of our humanity, but also tries to shoulder responsibility for it and transform it. The metamorphosis of the body in flesh in the Resurrection necessitates, as a kind of return toward an "other metamorphosis" of the flesh in the body, that the "spiritual" (the *pneuma*) of the body always responds in the first place to the "flesh" of the psychic or animal body (1 Cor. 15:45). Pope Benedict XVI is quite right to say (although he does not draw from this statement all the consequences that a philosophical treatment might attempt) that if humanity aspires "to be pure spirit and to reject the flesh as pertaining to his animal nature alone, then spirit and body would both lose their dignity."[35]

§8. A Matter of Culture

If we come, then, to a certain form of confessionalism, we must take care to ensure that *hoc est corpus meum* is not simply the prerogative of Christianity. The dogma of the eucharist is not just something for the believer (in giving us faith); it is also "credible" (with a universal rationality). And thus in the present book I hope to address *all* readers. The formula *this is my body* is not simply one of conviction, but also one of "culture," or of pure and simple humanity. Jean-Luc Nancy points out, despite his leanings toward a deconstruction of Christianity, "We come from a *culture* in which this cult phrase [*hoc est enim corpus meum*] will have been tirelessly uttered by millions of people officiating in millions of rites. Everyone in this culture, Christian or otherwise, (re)cognizes it. . . . It is our *Om mani padne* . . . our *Allah ill'allah*, our *Schema Israel*."[36] Rather than the *cogito (ergo) sum* of Descartes or of Heidegger's *moribundus sum* [I am in dying], the *hoc est enim corpus meum* is what founds Western culture, attempting to convince me, Nancy suggests, that "this (*hoc*)" "is/has" become my body; it thus reifies at the same time as it predicates. The named body, which since the Last Supper has been philosophically interpreted, takes what happened on Holy Thursday as its bed, so to speak—where it *rests* and also where it *flows*. And this *event* of the Last Supper feeds the whole of Western thought, so that perhaps the eucharistic body becomes the model of all corporality. In this process, then, have we found or lost the body? The question cannot be dealt with simply, but it is the philosophical ambition of the present essay to try at least to contribute to the discussion and, if possible, provide some answers. I quite simply reject the arguments of those who accuse Christianity of being the principal force in the "objectification" of the body in Western culture through transubstantiation (*this is my body*) and who suggest that we need to deconstruct the body to reconstruct it in another way. As far as I see it, to transubstantiate is not at all to reify (or "object-ify") but to let a (quasi-organic?) *force* express itself. Nancy, in a philosophical dispute that I should like to join, says, "The anxiety, the desire to see, touch, and eat the body of God, to *be* that body and *be nothing but that*, forms the principle of Western (un)reason. That's why the body, bodily, *never happens, least of all when it's named and convoked*. For us the body is always sacrificed: eucharist."[37]

To reply to this, we must look again at the route we have covered: the body, whether seen in terms of its drives or its organic nature, characterizes what is offered in the eucharistic bread (§1 and §4). The animality in us— in the effigy of the lamb as that which must be taken on and transformed (§5) and the region of "what can no longer be said" (§3)—touching, on the other hand, the "part of the darkness" in us (open, mix, and disorder), reaches toward this *basis* that only God is to encounter and initiate (§2). The eucharistic sacrifice, treated philosophically, holds, in what it contains, the body (§1 and §4) as well as its legacy, animality (§5 and §6) and its extension, our own Chaos (§2 and §3). It remains for us to define its *modality*, eros changed into agape (§9 and §10), and its *finality*, abiding, dwelling (§11), and to discover its *habitus* (§12). In fact, it is a question of going from the wedding feast to the sacrifice of the lamb. The *this is my body* speaks first, at least in human experience, of the given as conjugal, before it is ecclesiastical. If to eat the flesh and to drink the blood has no other end than to abide in Christ (or "to live continually" [Knox translation])— "Those who eat my flesh and drink my blood abide in me, and I in them" (John 6:56)—perhaps we have to find or invent a form of *carnal fidelity* in which the bond with the body takes precedence over pledges in the form of language, or at least confirms them.[38] This is what happens certainly for married partners (in the way they lead their erotic life), but also, perhaps paradoxically, for the priest (in his way of celebrating the eucharist) and also for all human beings whether or not they are consecrated (in the intimacy of their own corporality). "The central words of the Last Supper are 'This is my body and I give it to you'," Timothy Radcliffe writes in an article on affectivity and the eucharist that is bold but gives us much food for thought. "The eucharist, like the eros (sex), is based on the gift of the body. . . . We understand the *eucharist* in the light of the *eros* (sexuality), and eros in the light of the eucharist."[39]

3

Eros Eucharisticized

§9. The Body Eucharisticized and the Body Eroticized

We can find confirmation in the tradition of the Church for what has been suggested here—relating the banquet and the *consumption* of the eucharistic body at that banquet with the *consummation* between spouses through the body ("consummation" being the term used to confirm the sacrament of marriage).[1] We could cite in this connection one of many examples in the commentary on the Song of Solomon (or Song of Songs) written by St. Bernard, along with his brother Guillaume de Saint-Thierry, for the Abbey of Clairvaux, when the two shared a sick-room in 1124. "I must ask you to try to give your whole attention here," says the Abbot, commenting on the opening of the Song. "'Let him kiss me with the kisses of his mouth'" (Song of Sol. 1:1). "The mouth that kisses signifies the Word who assumes human nature; the nature assumed receives the kiss; the kiss however, that takes its being both from the giver and the receiver, is a person that is formed by both, none other than 'the one mediator between God and mankind, himself a man, Christ Jesus.'"[2]

Certainly this is not, or not directly, a question of the eucharist (*this is my body*), but rather of the incarnation (the person of Jesus Christ). But the references to the erotic in the Song of Solomon are extensive. To water down this fact would be to make light of a tradition of mysticism that was able to explore eroticism, even at the risk of shocking readers or of leading to the suppression of books devoted to it. I shall hold to the idea that we have, in the Bible, "fragments" of "a lover's discourse" and maintain that the *this is my body* of the eucharisticized body has analogies with the *this is my body* of the eroticized body.[3] Benedict XVI underlines, by way of paradigm, how "the mutual consent that husband and wife exchange in Christ, and which establishes them as a community of life and love, also has a eucharistic dimension."[4]

The text of the New Testament confirms both this analogy and the direction our argument has taken so far—the writings of St. Paul, in particular. It is worth pointing out that the great *theological* discussion of the institution of the eucharist in the first Letter to the Corinthians (1 Cor. 10–11)—the sacrifice (10:23–33), man and woman before God (11:1–16), and the Lord's Supper (11:17–34)—retraces exactly the *philosophical* route that we have been following in preparation for (1) the animal and meat, (2) eros, or the difference between man and woman, and (3) the body and bodily life. As we shall see in what follows:

(1) To insist first of all that "'All things are lawful,' but not all things are beneficial" is to give a ruling on what has been "offered in sacrifice" (1 Cor. 10:23, 28).

(2) To say that "woman came from man, so man comes through woman; but all things come from God" (1 Cor. 11:12) is to make sexual difference originary and willed by God for humanity (see §21).

(3) To institute the *this is my body* that is "given for you" as *the* message of God that was handed on to us (1 Cor. 11:23–24), is profoundly and definitively to implant the human eros previously expressed in the bodies of sexuality into the divine agape that is now celebrated (the body of the eucharisticized bread). The wedding feast or the "nuptials" of the Lamb are not *just* a question of the animality that has to be accepted in humankind (§5). They are also, and indeed above all, the nuptials of God with humanity, which perhaps bring the human out of simple animality. "'For the marriage of the Lamb has come, and his bride has made herself ready: to her it has been granted to be clothed with fine linen, bright and pure'— for the fine linen is the righteous deed of the saints" (Rev. 19:7–8).

§10. Charitable God

The modality of eros—*this is my body*—is then the *modality* of the eucharisticized body insofar as it can also be an exchange of speech in the act of sexuality. But I would not want to suggest a complete "univocity" (Marion) between eros and agape (i.e., that the words are used with the same meaning and in the same sense), nor that there is a complete "equivocity" (Nygren) (i.e., that the words are used with different meaning and in different senses). I do not agree with the latter (equivocity) because it risks separating divine charity and human love to such an extent that nothing remains in common between them. On the other hand, univocity reduces the form of divine love so thoroughly to its model of human love that nothing remains in it that is specific to God. The danger in the past was that of equivocity: "The difference between them [agape and eros] is not of degree but of kind."[5] The danger today is that of univocity: "God loves like we love."[6] We need then to substitute, or counterbalance, the erotic phenomenon, which certainly describes and is founded upon a true experience of the body (see Marion, as well as Bataille or Artaud), with that of a charitable phenomenon (§33).

It is not simply that eros can be identified with agape (a first practical movement where experience of the body serves as a model for the encounter with Christ and the Church in the eucharistic bread). Eros is also transformed, or metamorphosed, by the divine agape that gives it meaning (a second didactic initiative where the encounter between God and humanity in the eucharist is established in reality, transforming the simple human meaning of the bodies bound together). An encyclical of Benedict XVI underlines this even in its title: *Deus Caritas Est* [God is love]—*agape* and not *amor* (*eros*) or *dilectio* (*philia*). Although the term "love" is said, quite appropriately, in the text to be one of the most "frequently used and misused of words" (§2), the reciprocal transformation of eros by agape is what is principally considered: "*eros* and *agape*—ascending love and descending love—can never be completely separated. . . . the element of *agape* thus enters into this love, for otherwise *eros* is impoverished and even loses its nature [§7]. *Eros* is thus supremely ennobled, yet at the same time it is so purified as to become one with *agape*" (§10). The phrase "unity of love" (as agape) (*unitas caritas*), used in the title of the first part of the ecclesiastical document, does not refer to a single meaning of the term "love" (as eros): *univocitas amoris*. Recent analyses have used a double substitution—from the univocal to unity, from charity to love—that a consideration of eros and agape cannot in reality support.[7]

A philosophical reading of the famous recommendation of St. Paul to the Ephesians is more convincing (see §23). St. Paul says, "Husbands, love your wives, just as Christ loved the church and gave himself up for her" (Eph. 5:25). The thought is more radical here, authorizing not simply an analogy between the erotic *this is my body* of the espoused couple and the charitable *this is my body* of God and humanity. Paradoxically, it makes the second (the charitable body) the model for the first (the erotic body), a move that indicates, moreover, how it is an analogy—of attribution, not simply of proportionality.[8] Certainly in heuristic terms, for research purposes, we had better go from *eros* to *agape*; conjugal experience and the erotic experience of a couple through their bodies can and must serve as the "existential" of the eucharistic that makes sense of "Take, this is my body given for you." But from a didactic point of view, or in terms of teaching that respects the order of things, agape may be said to integrate and transform eros. In this way, the integration of the bodies of the spouses, united with the body of God in an act of love (eucharist: this is my body [of God] given for you), precedes and also integrates the exotic interplay of humans among themselves (sexuality: this is my body [of man or woman] given for you). To love one's wife as Christ loved the Church, and gave himself for the Church, reminds us precisely of the precedence of God's bodily love for humanity over man's fleshly love for woman, rather than the inverse. Whether it is a question of encountering Chaos (§2) or accepting bodily drives (§4) or taking responsibility for animality (§5), the eucharistic associated with the altar linen is the basis for, and encompasses, the erotic we associate with our bed linen—such that there is not in reality a fulfillment of the erotic for a couple except within the "hand" of he who contains and transforms them in his *agape*.[9] An artist who understood this—or at least brought it into view so that others could consider its implications—was Auguste Rodin, in his work *The Hand of God*. In this sculpture, the entwined couple is contained within the hand of God, which holds them together.[10] The eros is thus eucharisticized in that it is transformed—from animality to humanity in its filiation, as well as from the erotic to love, or charity, in a transubstantiation. Benedict XVI tells us, in *Sacramentum Caritatis* [The sacrament of charity], "The substantial conversion of bread and wine into his body and blood introduces within Creation the principle of a radical change." He talks of the transforming power of the eucharist that we need to think of as "a sort of 'nuclear fission,' to use an image familiar to us today, which penetrates to the heart of all being—a change meant to set off a process that transforms reality, a process leading ultimately to the transfiguration of the entire world, to the point where God will be all in all" (cf. 1 Cor. 15:28).[11]

§11. From Birth to Abiding

The eucharistic sacrifice—philosophically interpreted—possesses, then, its content (bodily life; §1 and §4), its inheritance (animality; §9), and above all, its form (eros, or *this is my body*; §6). But we need still to consider its finality, apart from its habitus (i.e., customs unconsciously associated with it by those who participate) (§12). We need to think of it in terms of *abiding here*: "Those who eat my flesh and drink my blood abide in me [*en emoï*], and I in them [*kagô in autô*]" (John 6:56) (§11). Looking at what it is to "abide" is in a sense the ultimate goal of my triptych of books, and I should perhaps explain my overall plan here. (1) First, in *Passeur de Gethsémani* [The guide to Gethsemane], I examine the bodily form of what awaits us, or the anxiety of death that is reflected back onto the present. The Son of Man is he who "suffers" the world in his own corporeality and takes on the burden of its finitude, as both suffering and mortality. "His hour had come to depart from this world and go to the Father" (John 13:1). (2) Next, in *The Metamorphosis of Finitude*, I look at the bodily form of our past, or rather, the "birth" that has taken place. I examine how the philosophical birth from below (phenomenology of birth) clarifies and is transformed by the theological renaissance from on high (theology of the resurrection). Here I take the road that leads from "suffering" to "passage": "'How can anyone be born after having grown old? Can one enter a second time into the mother's womb and be born?'" (John 3:4). (3) Now, in *The Wedding Feast of the Lamb*, I finally come to our bodily form in the present, with *this is my body* as viaticum, as proposed today to the believer in espousals where we take full responsibility for our humanity, but where we are waiting still to be asked "'How can this man give us his flesh to eat?'" (John 6:52).

Past, future, present (dimensions of time); suffering, birth, flesh (existentials); dereliction, resurrection, eucharist (theological statements from the individual point of view, not dogma); suffering, passage, the act of eating (transformations)—these are modalities in a triptych where suffering is found along with birth and living or abiding here. In this triptych we are always returning to the same story: "come into the world" (John 6:14); "come in the flesh" (1 John 4:2).[12]

What I have in my sights is to *abide* [Gr. *menein*][13] instead of the *hoc est corpus meum* that we still consume today. I do not want to be reductive, even if that entails certain breaks, sometimes arbitrary, with phenomenology. I want to avoid interpreting *bodily substance* as a simple condensation of the "metaphysics of presence" (Derrida), or as what has been called the pure "reification" and "objectification" of corporeality (Nancy).[14] Perhaps, as we shall see later (§36), we have philosophically narrowed down *abiding* or *remaining* too far, to an *objectifying* or *reifying*, as though all abiding were a kind of substantializing that was decidedly impossible to inhabit. Stanislas Breton warns severely, "There is in this attitude (which only sees in Aquinas' notion of substance [or transubstantiation] a simple 'thing') not just a sign of ingratitude, but a lack in their culture, which is expressed in the enthusiasm of our young philosophers, after the arrival of phenomenology, first for Husserl and then for Heidegger."[15] We cannot tar all phenomenology with this brush; far from it. In particular, the corpus of theology resists very directly the objectifying of substance found in phenomenology.[16] But it remains important to ask if the eucharisticized bread really does give access to an "abiding" place where we can live ("Those who eat my flesh and drink my blood abide in me, and I in them" [John 6:56]). And we might ask whether it is really necessary to indict all "abiding" as a form of "substantializing"? The question "Where do you abide?" is relevant, (1) certainly and philosophically, to phenomenology (Husserl, Heidegger, Merleau-Ponty, and others), but also (2) theologically, to the gospels (John 1:38).

(1) We may answer the question ("Where do you abide?") by saying that the Earth can become habitable for us: "The Originary Ark, the Earth, Does Not Move."[17] Or we may answer that we live "as poets" to cope with the intrusions of technology: we live in the quadripartite (of the Earth and sky, divinities and mortals).[18] Either way, the challenge for humanity now is that of dwelling, or abiding (as ecology tells us today), rather than withdrawing from or dominating (as in the conquest of space proposed in the recent past). Heidegger tells us, "*ich bin, du bist* mean: I dwell, you dwell. The way in which you are and I am, the manner in which we humans *are* on the earth is *Bauen* dwelling. To be a human being means to be on the earth as a mortal. It means to dwell [*bauen*]."[19]

So, is Christianity first of all a way of dwelling here? Or rather, if it is a *way* of dwelling here, is it also where we *can dwell*, in these times when many people denounce Christianity as having lost itself in the process of modernizing? To reply, we don't have to hold forth on the pseudo-topic of the end of Christianity, or evoke the cliché of passing from one millennium to another, or develop all the worries that arise from quibbles over a Western faith that is always trying to establish its identity. The habitable depends not upon adaptability, but upon its foundations. It holds within itself its own establishment and its abode: the eucharistic viaticum as a place to "abide" (§34).

(2) Moreover, the question "Where do you abide?" (Or "Where are you staying?") is one that can be addressed—theologically this time—to he whom John the Baptist describes simply as "the Lamb" (John 1:36) without any reference this time to sin ("who takes away the sin of the world" [John 1:29]). Posing the question helps us see the dimensions of *our* animality in the Son, the one who recapitulates, as he comes to convert and transform. John starts by saying, "Look, here is the Lamb of God" (*Ecce agnus Dei*). We might recall Pontius Pilate: "Here is the man!" (*Ecce homo* [John 19:5])—the phrase taken up by Nietzsche.[20] The whole of the narrative of the Gospel of John is in reality consecrated to this question of

abiding; it is as though it were, right from the start, his leading concern. The eucharist, as I have already pointed out, gives us the response in its discourse on the bread of life: to eat "my flesh" and drink "my blood," to dwell (*menein*) in him and he in us (John 6:56). What abides (*menein*), rather than what merely subsists (*subsistere*) (see §36), is what truly gives meaning to presence. The descent into the abyss—Chaos and Tohu-Bohu rejoined in the bodily life of the eucharistic bread and exhibited through the animality of the sacrificial lamb—does not reach either "substance" or "subsistence," because they would be *sure* and *stable*, simply to protect us from danger. The house "built . . . on rock" (Matt. 7:24), the heritage of those who "stand firm in faith" (Isa. 7:9), is often wrongly interpreted as a search for something firm and constant, as in the *cogito* of Descartes (Second Meditation), as though one could distance thought as well as faith from the attacks of doubt that can provoke and that question us.[21] In theology, then, even more than in philosophy, we cannot expect reassurance, or even simple security, from "abiding in his presence" ("abide in me, and I in them" [John 6:56]). That is not at all what is envisaged in the act of the eucharist. It does not, in its viaticum, disguise any of the dangers of existence—nor even see them in another way. We need not simply to abide there, me in him and him in me; we need to strive together to abide. The dwelling has no substance as "subsistence," but is "an effort to sojourn in the presence."[22]

What should be apparent, although not yet fully developed, is that the eucharistic bread—if it becomes part of my embodiedness, encounters my animality and descent into the depths of Chaos—reaches and expects its "dwelling." This is not by a door opened to paradise, in flight into the distance. It is, as I see it, in the true sense of *abiding*, that the viaticum keeps us in our humanity in God incorporate. We could say that every day that passes we not only make our way through our animality (Chaos, drives, the passions that make up the eros), but also make an effort to take on our animality and to transform it into a humanity recognized in its *filiation* (Chaos, drives, passions lived and transformed by the agape). "Wisdom, (including that of God toward man)," according to the remarkable humanist Charles de Bovelles, Canon of Noyon, "is the virtue capable of setting man on his feet [*hominem sistit*], of sustaining him and consolidating him in his humanity [*continet figitque in Homine*] or, if you like, of stopping him going beyond the bounds of the human [*vetat ex liminibus excedere humanis*]."[23] God does not call us to angelism, as if we were illicitly to go beyond the limits of our created being, but invites us to a new kind of humanism: a humanism that was finally lived and changed by divinity, as far as and including the transformation of our own animality

(§28). We should not expect mistakenly to become "angels" in heaven, but simply "*like* angels [*ôs angellos*]" (Matt. 22:30). The attractions of angelism do not stop us being part of humankind, or rather, "husbands and wives at the Resurrection." On the contrary, we have to acknowledge ourselves *as such* before God, in an irreducible sexual difference that the angelic attitude of praise comes simply to indicate as well as to respect (§21).[24] *Abiding in Christ*—such then is "the fundamental act of Christian being" that the philosophical approach finds in the theological abode of the eucharisticized bread. It is its proper end, and it is in the form of a viaticum, such that we do not have to quit the common humanity that we share.[25]

§12. The Reason for Eating

If we have covered the action of the eucharist philosophically with regard to its content (the body or bodily life), its inheritance (animality), its expansion (Chaos), its form (eros), and its finality (abiding here), it remains now for us to look at its habitus, at how it is disposed: to "discern." We cannot escape a diacritical position at the moment when we communicate. St. Paul tells us, "Examine yourselves [*dokimazetô eauton*], and only then eat of the bread and drink of the cup. For all who eat and drink without discerning [*diakrinôn*] the body, or the Lord's body, eat and drink judgment against themselves" (1 Cor. 11:28–29). I shall be discussing later the transubstantiation of the bread into body, its "real" presence, which is also "real" in the consciousness in another sense (§19). It is not simply a question of something that we *eat* in order that the sacrament is operative. In fact, it is necessary for us—for us also—to *cooperate*, as is the case with any meal duly shared. Thomas Aquinas says, very seriously, "Even though a mouse or a dog were to eat the consecrated host, the substance of Christ's body would not cease to be under the species, so long as those species remain." But, he adds, "it must not be said that the irrational animal eats the body of Christ sacramentally; since it is incapable of using it as a sacrament. Hence it eats Christ's body 'accidentally,' and not sacramentally, just as if anyone not knowing a host to be consecrated were to consume it."[26]

Eating the "bread" sacramentally or drinking the "wine" sacramentally—in other words, recognizing that they are "body" and "blood"—is then something that necessitates a judgment, or at least an act of discernment. Does this mean that one has to prove one's "understanding" in order to take communion? Certainly not, if that implies an act of reasoning; however, necessarily yes it if is a question of heartfelt participation and a belief stemming from faith. St. Matthew tells us, "When you are offering your gift at the altar, if you remember that your brother or sister has something against you, leave your gift there before the altar and go: first be reconciled to your brother or sister, and then come and offer your gift" (Matt. 5:23–24). Against all tendencies toward Gnosticism, and whatever the level of comprehension, *all* Christians are invited to the eucharistic table. The Christian's approach to the altar, no matter the degree of rationality involved, nonetheless requires a discernment in faith, a "belief" that definitively distances us from the mouse (*mus*) or dog, or the person who is ignorant of what he or she eats (*nesciens*)—in other words, from those who never see anything but bread (when it is also a question of the "body") or wine (when it is also a question of "blood"). But is that to say—taking another tack, starting all over again—that the Host is not in itself consecrated, and that it is through us that the transubstantiation takes place? Certainly we cannot think that. Because the bread may not necessarily be seen as "body" from the point of view of the one eating, but is necessarily so, Aquinas tells us, in terms of "the thing eaten."[27]

The situation, then, should be clear. There is a habitus (i.e., a custom unconsciously associated with it by those who participate), or, we could say, there are *reasons to eat* in the act of the eucharist. As St. Paul says, you must "examine yourselves [*dokimazetô eauton*]" before eating and drinking, while "discerning [*diakrinôn*]" what you eat and drink (1 Cor. 11:28, 29). There are no shortcuts here, and this participation in the eucharist is not something that can be defined in isolation. Everything depends on the angle from which we look: (1) in subjective terms, or (2) in terms of objective reality.

(1) *From the subjective point of view.* To communicate with the body and blood of Christ is not simply to eat them. The believer aspires to, or discerns, exactly the body of the Lord, when communicating with the bread, and aspires to, or discerns, the blood of the Lord when communicating with wine. To eat and drink one's own condemnation—"judgment against themselves [*crima eautô*]," as St. Paul puts it (1 Cor. 11:29)—is not simply to confuse the eucharistic bread with the other parts of a meal, as might have wrongly been done in the early agape, or communal meals; rather, it is "not to appreciate what is necessary for the reception of the body of Christ."[28]

St. Augustine was right when, like Aquinas later (in his example of the mouse and the dog), he was not satisfied that the full meaning of the communion was given simply by talking of the *reality* of the conversion of the eucharistic bread into body or wine into blood. He tells us "there is a certain manner of eating that Flesh and drinking that Blood, in which whosoever eats and drinks, 'he dwells in Christ and Christ in him.'" And, as a kind of warning, he says that "he does not 'dwell in Christ and Christ in him,' who 'eats the Flesh and drinks the Blood of Christ' in any manner whatsoever, but only in some certain manner, to which He doubtless had regard when He spoke these words."[29]

The habitus, or the subjective disposition, of the communicant—that of discerning—counts above all in the act of the eucharist, but not more (in the Protestant point of view) than the objective reality of he who is present when we communicate (a necessary condition for Catholics). The way or the manner in which the believer approaches the table of the communion meal is part of the act of communion ("examine yourselves" and "discern"), as much as that which is its objective (the aforementioned transubstantiation): "Whoever, therefore, eats the bread or drinks the cup of the Lord in an unworthy manner will be answerable for the body and blood of the Lord. . . . If we judged ourselves, we would not be judged. But when we are judged by the Lord, we are disciplined so that we may not be condemned along with the world" (1 Cor. 11: 27, 31–32).

We ought to make things plain here, once and for all, because unless we accept it we are lying to ourselves: the cultural formula (Nancy), as much as the Christian formula (Magisterium of the Catholic Church)—of "the body of Christ" (*Corpus Christi*)—when we go up to the table every week, says nothing, or says remarkably little, to the believer or unbeliever today, unless that formula is based on a contemporary anthropology of the body. We will always be haunted by "avatars of cannibalism," which we do also need to confront (§25).[30] "Eating the body" does not simply sound for us today like something from the world of ancient Palestine (I shall return to this subject later, discussing the *flesh* taken as the whole human being); first of all, it is within the framework of our inheritance of Greek or Hellenic culture that we already find the Capharnaite world suspect (the meat). "How can this man give us his flesh to eat?" (John 6:52). Certainly some people will respond that it is part of the "mystery" and that it is better not to think too much about it; perhaps some will say that such questions only cause confusion.

The ancients were not, however, taken in by this. All of them, from the greatest to the not so great, confronted the question, with a courage that nobody dares to imitate today. St. Augustine did so (talking of the crime and the horror that the Savior seems to demand), and Thomas Aquinas certainly did (talking of the permanence of the species—bread and wine—that they are "commonly used by men" because "it is not customary, but horrible, for men to eat human flesh, and to drink blood"—"lest this sacrament might be derided by unbelievers, if we were to eat our Lord under his own species" [see §25]).[31] We find even more of this in the Venerable Bede, the eighth-century monk, where the cruelty borders on a kind of carnage that one cannot, however, avoid imagining: "The Jews thought that our Lord would divide his flesh into pieces [*particulatim carnem suam divideret*], and give it to them to eat: and so mistaking him, strove."[32]

In short, the *musterion* of the eucharist is not a question of something "mysterious" or "numinous"—a kind of Gnostic secret revealed only to initiates, or that we can never approach head on. This "Christian mystery," like all the Christian mysteries, is in large part already revealed, and we are all called to enter into it. We cannot, of course, cease looking into its depths. But we need our intelligence once again to dare to enter into it. Without that, we are renouncing what is purely and simply our humanity, in a kind of blind faith.[33] The hypothesis of the eucharist containing bodying life (§4) might in this sense shock us, as might equally that of the inheritance of our animality (§3), or the conversion of animality into a humanity that recognizes its filiation (§7), or the extension of Chaos (§2), or the form of eros (§9). All of these philosophical approaches, however, seen in existential terms, clarify the contemporary for us as well as pointing to what there is in it of our humanity. They show us the possibility of its conversion and accommodation of divinity—as far as and including the viaticum of the eucharist. We still need terms like "conversion," "transubstantiation," "manducation," "operation," "species," "substance," and "accidents"—terms that have been found necessary and will continue to be used—but their use now is meant to integrate them in a reformulation through which doctrine becomes philosophically "actualized." It is not simply a question of adjusting to the tastes of our times (actualizing), but of deploying the terms in all of their potential (*actualitas*). Apart from the essential address by the organic to the organic in the *this is my body* of the eucharist (§1), there remains a reason for us in "eating" it whereby faith ensures at least that we are already transformed or have understood. Berengarius of Tours says, in his letter to Adelmann, that St. Augustine "did not say 'into the hand, into the mouth, into the teeth, into the belly,' but 'into one's thought' [*Non ait 'In manum, in os, in dentem, in ventrem,' sed 'in cogitationem'*]."[34]

(2) *In terms of objective reality* of the body subsequently consumed here, I am very far from suggesting that the act of the eucharist depends solely on the subjective disposition of the communicant (see §29). Nor do I suggest that we should deny the reality of the eucharistic conversion and attribute everything to communal symbolism. The way that the sacrificial lamb takes on our animality and humanity—which it will be important

to look at again in detail (Chapter 7)—comes precisely to show the *real* presence of the body of Christ in the act of transubstantiation. It is not simply a figurative intention that is signified. The mouse or the dog, as we have already seen, going toward the sacrament from the point of view of "the one who eats" (*ex parte manducantis*), but not from the point of view of "the one who is eaten" (*ex parte manducanti*). There is thus a kind of eating that does not depend solely on chewing, or "manducation," but that also brings in transubstantiation. Abiding in the act of the eucharist does not, as we have seen (§11), stem from the metaphysic of presence that has so often been rejected, but from the act of being, newly interpreted (by Thomas Aquinas) as an "effort this time to abide" and not as an "enclosure, or reification, in the thing."[35]

Is the presence then *real*, as the traditional expression has it? We can certainly argue this insofar as the presence here is the act of making present and not simply a reduction to the thing. The distance of God apart from me, remaining *there* when I am not (in the tabernacle of the so-called reserved sacrament), has less to do with its being there than with the donation or gratuitous transfer always active in its charity. We can then go along with tradition. The doctrine of transubstantiation does not imply the subjectivization of the present of humanity as its condition. Rather, it implies the objectivization of the charity of God as a movement of donation or transfer: "In the eucharistic present, all presence is deduced from the charity of the gift: all the rest in it becomes appearance of a gaze without charity: the perceptible species, the metaphysical conception of time, the reduction to consciousness, all are degraded to one figure (or caricature) of charity."[36]

If we take account now of the absolute gift—not regarding the consecrated bread simply as thing (objective reality)—and we put this along with the examination of the self, or discernment, at the time of communicating (subjective disposition), then in the transubstantiation of the bread into body, and the wine into blood, there will be a "real presence," in the two senses of presence as the body of Christ and as presence in the consciousness of humanity. It is real insofar as it does not depend upon humankind that the body of Christ is here converted and made present. It is also real in that the thing transformed becomes here for us "the thing itself" (*Sache selbst*), this time truly in "flesh and bone" (*leibhaft gegeben*), as organic calls to organic and takes on itself each day the Chaos of our animality to convert it into humanity. It makes of, and with, him an eternal offering, so that we may obtain our inheritance. This is done not through angelism or a kind of otherworldliness (something we should definitively renounce) but through a new mode of what is human—and both filial and Christian. It is an appropriate way of living in the world, in which an other takes on Chaos and is also metamorphosed by it.

All the same, we are left with questions that threaten to nullify what is here proposed: Is there no humankind if we are not eucharisticized? Is animality so important that nothing remains of the human if we are not saved in this particular way? Obviously, it would be wrong to suggest that. For the *eu-charis*, or the *action of grace*, is not simply restricted to the agape. We can put forward two reasons here: First, the human being is always already humanized, once created, although nonetheless never dissociated from that animality that Adam had to name (Gen. 2: 18–20). Second, the whole of humanity is included in the *hoc est corpus meum* of the Holy Thursday, and this is the dynamic of humanization in filiation as well as hominization in our genesis (Teilhard de Chardin) to which all humanity is called from our origin (§28). Christians, in this sense, cannot simply be content with loving one another, even though it is the golden rule of Christianity that was expressed in that way (John 13:34). They must also, and particularly when it is a question of the eucharist, look forward with one another—certainly to eat, but also, above all, to be incorporated in the resurrected Word. It is neither an individual nor a community that is called upon to be humanized in the resurrected Son, but the whole of humanity—to go, in other words, from that Chaos that is rightly brought to light in the eros, to the cosmos that is also lived by the agape. Paul tells the community at Corinth, "So then, my brothers and sisters, when you come together to eat, wait for one another [*allê-lous ekdechesthe*]" (1 Cor. 11:33). The reason for eating, or the act of discernment, operates less on our reason per se (where there is always a problem about dictating everything) as on that which is actually given in the act of the eucharist. As Irenaeus says so impressively at the heart of *Against Heresies*, "Our opinion is in accordance with the Eucharist, and the Eucharist in turn establishes our opinion."[37]

The Sojourn of Humankind

Homo sum, humani a me nihil alienum puto
I am a human being, I consider nothing that is human alien to me.
—Terence, *Heauton Timorumenos* 1.1.25

Apocalypse, in the Book of Revelation, opens with a vast introductory program of the nuptial festivities of the Lamb (Rev. 19:7) (see Part I). God takes part with humankind in the Apocalypse—they are to sojourn with him—in a sense to dwell here: "'See the home of God is among mortals. He will dwell with them; they will be his peoples, and God himself will be with them'" (Rev. 21:3). It is not enough to call on us to dwell with God, nor even to participate in the act of the eucharist as an appropriate place for remaining or "manence" (§11, §36). The sojourn of humankind in God through manducation (the eucharist) is still the necessary response to the sojourn of God in the human by incarnation (the nativity). We eat *his* flesh only because he took on *our* flesh. And in this sharing of flesh he exposes our humanity, just as he did by his assumption of it in his divinity. The risk, or sin, is that of fleeing this—either in raising oneself up into angelism, or in sinking into the bestial.[1] We must try, with the aid of grace, to stay or dwell in our created humanity, rather than always wanting to abandon it. God is *with them*—or we could talk of Emmanuel *with us* (*immânû él*)—when he comes to espouse the "us" that ensures we are also "with him." God can always be there without us, but we cannot, for our part, dwell without him; at least, he makes his dwelling in us and makes every effort to sojourn there. In short, it is not appropriate for a man to be made divine (the Greek perspective; see Irenaeus), except, and only, when God himself is humanized and calls us to our true humanity (the Latin perspective of St. Augustine or Aquinas). It is in reality more difficult to "be man" and to "dwell in man," and thus to respond to our condition as a creature, than to wish to break those limits and go beyond our nature. A love for limits is thus necessary for the sojourn of God in humankind (see §22), insofar as his life does not take us outside our own humanity, but rather consolidates it and demands of us that we come to love it.

Certainly we are not up to the measure of God, and we cannot there-fore reduce God anthropologically to our humanity (as Hans-Urs von Balthasar presciently warns us). All the same, God made himself the "measure of man" in his incarnation (see Karl Rahner) and it is thus through humanity that we go to God.[2] God has chosen that we go through our humanity to discover his divinity. As Aquinas says in a familiar axiom, "whatever is received in a thing exists there according to the *manner of that which receives it* and not according to its own manner."[3] We hope then that we can receive God, especially in the act of the eucharist, so that he can reside in humankind as far as our proper limits allow (Thomist perspec-tive). We expect this rather than always waiting for a revelation or an Apocalypse that would somehow assimilate our condition as creatures into a general bedazzlement, when nothing or almost nothing would remain of our nature (Dionysian perspective). To put it another way, the phenomenon is not *saturated* except insofar as its receptor or devotee recognizes himself as *limited*. This is probably the necessary condition for him to be metamor-phosed—or at least truly metamorphosed—here.

We can then set out in praise of *difference*, to show that nothing is to be feared more than uniformity, whether we are speaking of reducing every-thing to sameness, or of making all identical. Nonetheless, we must be on our guard. It is not enough simply to reject *sameness* so as to reach out for the act of differentiating, and thus to differentiate oneself (a naive inter-pretation of the reduction of the other to the same that we find in Levinas). It is quite possible to denounce the flight from, and evasion of, fusion and identity, while still continuing in that direction. The male who is lured by and searches for the female as his better half arrives from the Greek world (see the myth of Aristophanes in Plato's *Banquet*), not the Jewish world (the myth of the creation of Eve from Adam in Genesis). I have tried elsewhere to show that *separation*—between, for example, the light and the darkness, the waters and the firmament, the sky and the Earth, the animals and inert things, human being and animal, Adam and Eve—as an act of *creation* is seen as a good in the Bible. In the Platonic myth, separation is an act of *punishment* and thus is bad or depreciatory (e.g., separation of male and female because of the jealousy of Zeus, the myth of the androgyne in the *Banquet*).[4] Wrongly refusing a difference from the start, we try eagerly at first to unify and merge one thing into another, whether the human being and God or man and woman. In reality, it is there that to be created comes down to differentiating oneself, or rather to accepting and receiving difference—indeed, to receiving in oneself some-thing of this difference. Hegel showed us this, and we need to grasp it if we hope to renounce the illusions of identification. God *is love*, not in that he participates in love or would be love, but in that he is love itself. And love itself, or in person, is not unification, but rather is *differentiation*— differences even if they are ultimately overtaken and reconciled. Hegel, in his *Lectures on the Philosophy of Religion*, tells us: "When we say, 'God is love,' we are saying something very great and true. But it would be sense-less to grasp this saying in a simple-minded way as a simple definition, without analyzing what love is. For love is a distinguishing of two, who nevertheless are absolutely not distinguished for each other."[5]

To put it another way, and to suggest an analysis that is well known, there are three persons in the Trinity because to love, for God, is to differ-entiate oneself; being "love," God is differentiation, engendering the other in order to love: Father, Son, and Holy Spirit. There is also, and for the same reason, a created world that "is not" God; through love or differentia-tion, it is different from God—that is, from the world wished for and desired by God. Also, there are aspects of men that "are not" of women, and aspects of women that "are not" of men, since to love within a shared humanity is not to renounce differentiation. On the contrary, it is to encounter one another all the more through the resistance of the heteroge-neity of identities.

In short, it is here that our common erotic experience is confirmed: to love is not to identify with, nor simply to unify with, but to differentiate the more that one unifies. The erotic embrace makes "one flesh" (Gen. 2:24), according to an important thesis that I shall look at later (§23). It does this not by the loss or the fusion of flesh, but through bodily resistance to the difference of the other, which ensures that the husband's experience of his wife is experience *as a man* and the wife's experience of her husband is experience *as a woman*. To make *one flesh* is not to renounce one's own flesh—far from it. The flesh of the other sends me back to my own flesh, as my flesh in relation to the other's flesh, such that we can never truly dissolve ourselves in a *unity of the flesh*, or into what has not been differentiated. This is a psychological question, certainly, but also and above all a somatic one—one that makes sexual difference not simply a cultural matter (gen-der theory) but also a matter of nature (taking a new and necessary look at the basic concepts of natural theology). We need to recall this when we are trying to establish the metaphysical basis of the man-woman difference, rather than simply being satisfied with ethical principles that await their true anthropological substructures (Chapter 6).

The love of difference is, then, what defines difference as love. And one could add that difference sends us back both to the act of differing as a form of temporization and to what differentiates as polemic. In short, dif-ferentiation is also *temporizing* and *combat*. But in this case (what Derrida named "*différance*"), as in the other (the division as transformation in Hegel), "'*Différance*' would be said to designate a constitutive, productive, and originary causality, the process of scission and division which would produce or constitute different things or differences."[6] Or, we could say, the myth of the Golden Age, or original unity—whether a question of the fusion of humanity with God, or of unity without differentiation in eroticized flesh—remains always a myth or a delusion. This is the case in philosophy (the erotic unity of the male and female species in Plato's *Banquet*), as in theology (the mythic fusion of flesh almost always misunderstood in the "one flesh" of the book of Genesis). The differences sometimes produce disputes, but they are also, in this case, signs of the act of differing rather than vain attempts at a false fusion.

The overriding necessity of differing is what makes love—it is not the result of love—and this is true even though we may come not to understand ourselves because of differentiating ourselves. Our relationship to difference and to the act of differing is *of our origins*, and everything stems from that rather than working in the opposite direction. We do not go from unity to difference, but from the original act of differentiation as creation or love to the differences in our acts of loving, those differences that consecrate our unions as *differentiated communion* and not as some kind of supposed *rediscovered unity*. Taking difference on board, in the best sense of its underlying support rather than its trial, I should like to sing its praises, especially since the act of love comes back above all through our bodies to differentiate us. We shall see how this is reflected in our relationship with animality (Chapter 5), and with the organic (Chapter 6), and finally with sexuality (Chapter 7). In these three fields, our true selves speak—not against animality, embodiedness, or sexual difference, but through them, in that we take responsibility for them and are transformed. The scheme of this book (Part I) finds here its philosophical extension (Part II) and finds later its theological fulfillment (Part III). The sojourn of God in humankind opens a new start: one that, following the figure of the first psychological Adam, converts him into the second spiritual Adam, without denying or withdrawing anything of the former. Irenaeus tells us, "This, therefore, the Word of God was made, recapitulating in himself his own handiwork."[7]

4

The Animal That Therefore I Am

The *scriptural* figure of the sacrificial lamb, on the site of the animality in us that is taken on and transformed by God (Chapter 2), leads us now to *philosophical* consideration of our own metaphysical animality and to our biological roots. The question of the animal origin of humankind is not simply scientific, nor even simply ethical. We can certainly celebrate quite a few anniversaries related to the topic (e.g., publication of *The Origin of Species* by Darwin). Heidegger points out, "The animality of man has a deeper metaphysical ground than could ever be inferred biologically and scientifically by referring man to an existent animal species that appears to be similar to him in certain external respects."[1]

Certainly the biological must also be a prop for metaphysics, and to descend the genealogical tree on which we stand (*homo habilis, homo ergaster, homo erectus, homo neanderthalensis, homo sapiens*) is unimportant as far as making sense of our own animality is concerned. But philosophy is only interested in the animal, as theology is only interested in the Lamb, insofar as it sends us back to one image: animality. We need to recognize our dependence upon, and our origins in, that image. St. Paul writing to the Corinthians gives us our leitmotif here, without having to turn to philosophy or Darwinism: "It is not the spiritual that is first, but the physical [*psuchikon*], and then the spiritual [*pneumatikon*]." (1 Cor. 15:46).

What counts in philosophy as in theology is the question of essence, and not simply the physiological species, as in biology. That humans are of the *animal species* tells us in reality nothing about their features, nor of their nature and destiny. At most it tells us about an origin that we would certainly be wrong to forget. Animality in humankind, on the other hand, reminds us of a tie, or link, and necessitates that we give it metaphysical meaning. To do this we have to explore the deepest levels of our Chaos, of our passions and drives—something that, as we have noted, certain philosophical approaches, particularly that of phenomenology, have wrongly put on one side, by dint of wanting to signify too much (§3). There is nothing in reality telling us that we must definitively leave this animality behind or get rid of it, precisely because we are constituted by it. But also, nothing stops us from thinking that it is on the basis of this animality that we are given to see and to think our humanity, and that our bodies themselves (biped, fine-skinned, sensitive to touch, sexual in relation to one another) are, if not the actual proof of this, at least the sign of it.[2]

The way in which a human being depends upon a characteristic animality rather than just the animal is, then, such that it reveals the human being precisely through a capacity to transform animality into humanity. That is to say, the human being need not deny the Chaos—the drives and the passions that make up corporality—but, on the contrary, offer them in a *this is my body* (to man, to woman, to God, to humanity), consecrating the human in an offering of the body to otherness, even to divinity. Not, as we have seen, that God becomes animal, even though God can take on our characteristic animality (consider the condemnation of the Council in Trullo). And it is not that the human identifies totally with what there is *of* the animal, in laying bare a kinship with the animal or the first primates. We do not have to reject the theory of evolution—which both John Paul II and Benedict XVI have recognized in its scientific aspect—but the true "mutation" is not that of the animal into human (evolution), so much as that of the human into the Son of Man, integrated and incorporated in the Son of God (resurrection). Pope Benedict writes, "Christ's Resurrection . . . If we may borrow the language of the theory of evolution . . . [was] the greatest 'mutation,' absolutely the most crucial leap into a totally new dimension that there has ever been in the long history of life and its developments."[3]

I think we need to emphasize strongly—even at the risk of drifting off into propositions of the kind that the Council in Trullo (692 AD) justly condemned (see Preface)—that bringing together divinity and animality in the figure of the sacrificial lamb (§5) does not make the divine into animal, any more than it makes the human into animal. *Neither God nor humankind are animals*: the first because God takes on *uniquely* our humanity (God-made-man), and the second because humankind find themselves always already metaphysically humanized—and even belong theologically to the divine rather than to the animal kingdom: "God created humankind in his image, in the image of God he created them, male and female[4] he created them" (Gen. 1:27). He created man, in his gender ("he created *him*"), with a significance that has been so much discussed today that there is no need to consider it here. Humankind discovers difference, then, in the otherness of masculine and feminine that constitutes the one and the other ("he created *them*").[5] It remains—seemingly inconsequential, but important for us if we want to consider the eucharistic act in cosmic terms[6]—that God himself, in his incarnation, takes on our part of animality and transforms it into a humanity recognized in its filiation, in that nothing of that which is human must or can be strange to him in his incarnation, apart from sin. This is frequently, though unjustly, misunderstood. If we are to rethink the eucharist, dedicating "ourselves with an earnest will and without fear to that work which our era demands of us,"[7] then we should also take into account reflections on animality that philosophers have long been committed to (see, for example, Nietzsche, Husserl, Heidegger, Scheler, Derrida, Deleuze). And this is the case even though *theology* could stand independently here, especially while these philosophers remain for the moment fixed upon the biological or anthropological (accepting and celebrating Darwinism) but without taking note of the metaphysical or theological consequences. The animal in humanity actually tells us nothing about humankind if it is not philosophically experienced (Chaos, passions, drives . . .); it also remains insignificant for the believer if it is not taken on and accepted theologically (incarnation and eucharist). "The Animal That Therefore I Am"—a phrase taken from the title of a posthumously published work by Derrida[8]—does not suggest that I am *only* animal, and even less does it suggest that I am bestial (§13), but there is *in me* a part that is animality, and that the Son, in becoming exclusively incarnate in man, comes so as to "gather up all things in him" (Eph. 1:10) and to transform, when "we will be changed, in a moment, in the twinkling of an eye, at the last trumpet" (1 Cor. 15:51–52). Animal then I am, and to return now to philosophy, we can define this in the following ways: (1) a submission or an avowal, certainly, but also (2) an expression of identity—even (3) a face-to-face.

(1) We cannot but recognize (and without any loss of prestige) that *therefore* I am an animal marks a fact that is absolutely undeniable, unless we want to deny both the flux of passion and drives that makes up our characteristic Chaos, and that the act of the eucharist will come to take on and metamorphose (Part I). I am *therefore* an animal because it is something I cannot deny without in some sense trying to abstract myself from the biological life of which I am constituted. What could here be seen as

resignation or submission (there is really no other choice than to recognize in myself my animality) ought nonetheless to be transformed into an avowal (I grant that there is in me something of animality from which I cannot be exempt). There is even a recognition (what there is of the animal in me is not in opposition to my humanity, nor in opposition to my aspiration to be dwelt in and transformed by divinity; rather, it calls on me to give meaning where I find first of all the openness or insignificance of my existence). It does not make sense to go against the animality in ourselves, any more than one can hope to master one's passions or drives. Animal therefore I am, although I am not reducible to my animality, and on this impregnable basis I construct my humanity.

(2) We can also find in "the animal that therefore I am" an expression of identity. It is not "I think therefore I am" (*cogito ergo sum* [Descartes]), nor "I am in dying" (*sum moribundus* [Heidegger]), but "the animal that therefore *I am*" constitutes one of the strongest certitudes for humanity. Although philosophy has probably forgotten this, as we shall see later (§15), the first definitions of humankind as "featherless two-footed animal" (Plato, in *The Statesman*), or as "rational animal" (Aristotle, in *Metaphysics*), are based on an *animal life*, or a *zoôn*, that Western thought has progressively veiled. The unquestionable fact about the human being is perhaps not that of the certitude of the being's thought (Descartes), or of death (Heidegger), but rather of the life the human being enjoys without needing to think about it—to the extent that humans actually just do not think about it.

Because of the animal or animality in all of us, it is not as conscious humankind that we feel distress at the prospect of death. Rather, as humans with bodies, we live so as to forget, or just not to know, that biological life will come to enfeeble us; we move forward toward an eventual death that the principle of entropy will not, under any circumstances, be able to conceal.

We are of humankind certainly in thinking about death and the anguish of death, whether it be in the Garden of Gethsemane or on Mount Golgotha (*Le Passeur de Gethsémani* [The guide to Gethsemane]). And we are still of humankind, though transformed and offered divinity, when we accept that finitude can be integrated into God, that we are metamorphosed through birth and resurrection (*Metamorphosis of Finitude*). Again we are of humankind, but taking on our characteristic animality, when, in the act of the eucharist, we communicate through he who recapitulates all in himself, including the Chaos, the passions and drives that also make up our humanity. The true free human, "who thinks of death least of all things; and his wisdom is a meditation not of death but of life," certainly owes a lot to his reason, but only in that it connects nature and his nature. It reconciles here a certain form of the immediate in the divine, as well as a certain form of animality in the human.[9] Living one's life so that one forgets sometimes that one is living it, or even living *in* it, is the sign of animality that we find apart from anything else in humankind and that we often wrongly forget. The Kingdom of God brings this home, paradoxically and in its immediacy; Michel Henry, speaking in the tradition of Spinoza, but also holding to an auto-allocation of God in humankind, tells us, "What the animals say to us, is that it is possible to live uniquely *in life* and *through life*."[10]

(3) As for the face-to-face between human and animal, we need to make reference to the Bible here, and also to look at our experience.

(a) *Reference to the Bible.* Adam in the Garden of Eden is happily in a face-to-face with the animal: "The Lord God formed every animal of the field and every bird of the air, and brought them to the man to see what he would call them" (Gen. 2:19). We see a challenge here for Adam rather than for the animals. The Lord God is concerned less with the names or the concepts given by Adam to the animals (Hegel) than he is with the manner in which Adam remains open and available to welcome the entire creation in the act of speaking, or the "ark of speech."[11] But the act of naming ends in a setback, and an explanation has to be given, to establish the shift—necessary, in our view—from the "ark of speech" to the "ark of the flesh": "But for the man there was not found a helper as his partner. So the Lord God caused a deep sleep to fall upon the man, and he slept: then he took one of his ribs and closed up its place with flesh" (Gen. 2:20–21). In other words, the linguistic face-to-face between human and animal was not sufficient, even if it did trigger the act of speaking and the possibility of becoming inheritors of the word in the Word. The other face-to-face, more basic because probably more intimate, remains fleshly—or perhaps we should say never becomes verbal, even though it expresses itself, and is expressed on awakening, as lived experience of the flesh: "'This at last is bone of my bones and flesh of my flesh'" (Gen. 2:23). Speech backs up the flesh but can never substitute for it. It proffers itself when the flesh on its own cannot speak for itself, or needs to speak for itself differently. That is what happens in the conjugal relationship, as we shall see later, where the act of speaking crops up in the "failings of the flesh." It is always constitutionally impossible to feel what the other feels, and so speaking signifies to the other what one is feeling or is much affected by, and which cannot be expressed otherwise (§24). This also is the case with the incarnate Word, as we shall see later, where the eucharistic body shows us a bodily act, offering itself up (see the eucharistic realism of Lanfranc, where the gift of the body is a gift of its proper substance). It is not just that the eucharistic act has verbal meaning through the way it is expressed (see the eucharistic symbolism according to Berengarius, the identification of the *this* with the body [§27]).[12] In the act of communion with the body, in the conjugal act just as in the eucharist, the erotic coming together of body with body takes precedence over the conceptual exchange of word for word. Speaking in Genesis ("God said . . . and there was light" [Gen. 1:3]) cannot be fully understood except in the light of the incarnation in the prologue to John's gospel ("And the Word became flesh" [John 1:14]). Adam is not satisfied with merely welcoming Eve into the "ark of speech" (or welcoming her to the Son as Word); he makes his dwelling with her and in her, in the "ark of the flesh" (or in the Son as body). The face-to-face of human and animal that is not completely accomplished ("for the man there was not found a helper as his partner" [Gen. 2:20]) is transformed into a face-to-face between man and woman—this time fully accomplished ("bone of my bones and flesh of my flesh" [Gen. 2:23]). And it is only in the New Testament that this will be integrated into the act of the eucharist: "in him all things in heaven and earth were created. . . . In him [Christ] the whole fullness of deity dwells bodily" (Col. 1:16, 2:9).

(b) *Experience.* It is enough, as far as experience is concerned, to show the face-to-face of human and animal that we know from our most ordinary everyday life. We cannot deny the reality of this without rejecting what is commonplace in our own humanity, and in our own kinship with animality. "I often ask myself," Derrida says, curious and appropriately, "just to see *who I am*—and who I am (following) at the moment when, caught naked, in silence, by the gaze of an animal, for example, the eyes of a cat, I have trouble, yes, a bad time overcoming my embarrassment."[13]

Derrida's question might surprise us, or unsettle us, because animals are so often seen by human beings simply as things. However, the experience is there—even if philosophically, and in fact generally, it is most often unquestioned. The potential embarrassment of human nudity in a face-to-face with animal(ity) is the sign of a proximity and also of a radical strangeness: "It is as if I were ashamed, therefore, naked in front of this cat, but also ashamed for being ashamed."[14]

What happens is as though, in front of the animal, my humanity could not accept either its own humanity or its own animality. It cannot accept its humanity insofar as I should not be suffused with this shame when face to face with what I would usually be able to treat as a thing. And it cannot accept its animality because the proximity I find here has the effect of pushing me away: "Before the cat that looks at me naked, would I be ashamed *like* a beast that no longer has the sense of its nudity? Or, on the contrary *like* a man who retains the sense of his nudity? Who am I, therefore? Who is it that I am (following)? Whom should this be asked of if not of the other? And perhaps of the cat itself?" [15]

One cannot deny what happens here, even if the experience is disturbing. The way the animal looks at me sends me back to my own animality at the same time as it questions my humanity. Who am I? Who is the "I" in this experience of a face-to-face and of nudity, made both uncomfortable by being an animal, like the animal in front of me (sent back to my own corporality), and also uncomfortable as a human, so different from the animal before me (in my consciousness and shame at my own nudity that I do not share with the animal)? Ashamed to be an animal, or to be like an animal (in corporality or physiology), I am also ashamed, or at least very surprised, to find that I am not entirely one (here is an appropriate sense of modesty). In this discomfort so characteristic of humankind, we find something of humankind's humanity—something that does not strip us definitively of our animality, but that allows us to see at the same time the possibility of our own bestiality. It is a possibility of an animality gone astray (sin), though this applies only to humankind.

What can we say, then, as far as this experience of the face-to-face is concerned, about Adam and Eve disguised before God, ashamed of their nudity after sin: "'I was afraid, because I was naked, and I hid myself'" (Gen. 3:10)? It is a crucial question because this knowledge of nudity—which has nothing to do with their animality—was exactly what could not have been assumed before their transgression: "'Who told you that you were naked?'" (Gen. 3:11). Is it that they discover their humanity after their transgression, at the same time as they reject their animality? In fact, that is an absurd hypothesis, since having been created humans, they are also *animals*, or formed out of the same "ground" (Gen. 2:7, 2:19). And the revelation of their humanity does not come with and by sin, but, on the contrary, is there from the start in the project of divinity: "The Lord God took the man and put him in the Garden of Eden to till it and keep it" (Gen. 2:15). Adam and Even do not suffer *also* from being animal before or after the sin, even if both draw upon a man-woman difference (Gen. 2:23), and from the image of God in humankind (Gen. 1:27). Their true danger, or temptation, comes rather from bestiality, from the possibility that humanity will be led astray from fidelity to its face-to-face with the other: "This one shall be called Woman, for out of Man this one was taken" (Gen. 2:23) (see §13).

The Lord God looks after Adam from the start, giving him a helpmeet who is not simply animal (Eve). He takes care of the one and the other, even after the transgression: "The Lord God made garments of skins for the man and for his wife, and clothed them" (Gen. 3:21). We find proof here, or at least strong indication, that God shares their concern over nudity once it is revealed. Because if nudity had remained as it was before the transgression, it could be distorted by sin, so that certain human sexual behavior could even come to "pervert" animality as such. It could drop in an exclusive fashion into a bestiality that is unknown to animals themselves (e.g., prostitution, pornography, sadomasochism, initiation rites). What happened then was that, paradoxically, human beings also lived naked, without knowing it, in Eden—closer in that respect to the innocence of animality than to the learned knowledge of humanity. When sin intervenes, the human being loses exactly that wonderful lack of consciousness or lack of understanding associated with the animal, even if characteristically human, foundering in a bestiality that (I will emphasize again) has nothing to do with animality and that confines humankind to the bestiality of sin. Animal, but not bestial, humans can discover in themselves a true animality (male-female) willed by God and by the vocation of humanity (man-woman), but only when the other face-to-face, that of bestiality, has been renounced, as in the Wedding Feast of the Lamb in the Apocalypse, which will deliver us from it: "And I saw . . . those who had conquered the beast and its image and the number of its name standing beside the sea of glass. . . . And they sing the song of Moses, the servant of God, and the song of the Lamb" (Rev. 15:2–3).

§13. The Other Side of the Angel

Philosophy and theology, throughout their long history, have concerned themselves precisely and at length with the question of a consciousness without a body. Aquinas, discussing the innate self-consciousness of the angel, anticipates the immediate consciousness of the self in the Cartesian cogito.[16] In both cases, as so often where it is a question of "ab-straction," there is no need for the medium of the body to access the self, and thus philosophy leans in the direction of angelism, valuing the *cogitatio* over *affectio*, *agape* over *eros*, and *noûs* over *pathos*.[17] The hypothesis of a mind without body, or the temptation of angelism, is a feature of theology (surpassing human limits) as it is of philosophy (denial of the body in the name of the totality of consciousness). The *mind without body* of the angel is the other side of the coin of the *body without mind* of the animal. One can certainly discuss the possible consciousness of animals at length, and there is much debate on the subject in both philosophy and literature (Epicurus, Rabelais, Montaigne). But it is still the case that the question here is not simply a matter of being-ness, nor of differences of nature or degree, but rather a matter of the metaphysical access of humankind to our own animality.

Whether or not we are animal remains an oppositional discourse that has no counterpart in a propositional discourse today, particularly in the context of phenomenology (Husserl, Heidegger, Deleuze, Derrida, Henry, Jonas, Agamben). The only thing that really matters here is our access to the animal and to our own animality (see §16), where the "animal world" and the "human world" meet on the same philosophical ground. The work of the biologist and naturalist Jakob von Uexküll has been available for some time to feed the totality of our thought on this subject. Von Uexküll writes,

> Whoever wants to hold on to the conviction that all living things are only machines should abandon all hope of glimpsing their environments. . . . [Here we shall] not see in animals simply a mechanical assemblage; [but] . . . will also discover the *machine operator* who is built into the organs just as we are into our body. [We shall] address [ourselves] to animals not merely as objects but also as subjects, whose essential activities consist in perception and production of effects. But then, one has discovered the gateways to the life-world, for everything a subject perceives belongs to its *perception world* [*Merkwelt*], and everything it produces, to its *effect world* [*Werkwelt*].[18]

We are concerned with a *limit hypothesis*—one not of existence as difference, but rather of experience in a lived world. Certainly nobody could really say that they had definitely encountered a *mind without body* (the angel), any more than we encounter a *body without mind* (the animal). In both cases, it is not that we have really encountered them—at most it is that our paths have crossed and we haven't understood what it is to be like them (something that would be true for the animal and, of course, rather hypothetical in the case of the angel). Since we are mind *and* body, we are neither all one nor all the other; so, it becomes troublesome to try and believe ourselves simply one or the other. However, the impossible reduction of the mind to a blank sheet (*tabula rasa*), simply to its significations, aimed precisely at introducing this dimension. It also relied on the hypothesis of a pure corporality without mind, a quasi-animal access to the world through the body (*Körper*), or the organic flesh (*Fleisch*), without subsuming it into a signifying flesh (*Leib*); in other words, this is Kant's "mass of sensations," or the "region of what can no longer be said" in Heidegger, or the "fact that there is [*il y a*]" and "existing without existents" in Levinas (see §3). There the Chaos and the Tohu-Bohu of our own existence open up, reaching to the *Urgrund* or the *original basis* of our life, made up of our instincts, passions, and drives (§4). This is a long way away from psycho-analytic considerations, though no doubt they have their own validity (Part I). But we see here that the existential is universal. It does not need the support of the psychological or the pathological. It expresses itself in a language in which nothing indicates that orientation toward mind is the last word. It doesn't rely upon a psychic process otherwise directed elsewhere. The "unconscious of the body" (Nietzsche), as we shall see (§17), is not attached to the mind or simply enclosed in the unconscious (Freud).

It comes down simply to recognizing that "I am my body," or "There is a body." All the rest, including the mind, depends first of all upon the benchmark (*repère*) of original corporality. "I exist," Gabriel Marcel emphasizes;

> that is to say I have something that makes me known or recognized whether by others or by myself . . . and all that is inseparable from the fact that there is my body. . . . My body is the benchmark through which what is existent for me is placed. . . . There is between the existence of others (including, for example, that of Caesar, who existed in the past) and my own existence, that is to say my organo-psychical presence to myself, an objectively determinable temporal continuity. . . . All existence can be brought back to this benchmark (of the body) and cannot be thought of outside this reference except in terms of pure abstraction.[19]

As Pascal says, we are neither angels nor beasts, and thus, "anyone trying to act the angel acts the beast." We can add now, also from Pascal, that the "further one falls, the more wretched one is." Knowing both angels and beasts, in fact, we fear the one (beasts) more than we search for the other (angels).[20] What is said here in philosophical terms—in other words, viewing the temptations of angelism as a form of bestiality, or as a similar way of going beyond frontiers—was actually expressed right from the start in theology. Incarnation made it necessary! This problem was anticipated by Tertullian, and afterwards in the first Christian writings (third century after Christ), when they expressed opposition to an important Gnostic tendency that has in fact come back into contemporary docetism: "Both in Christ's case and that of the angels . . . they came in the flesh. Never did any angel descend for the purpose of being crucified, or tasting death, and of rising from the dead. Now, since there never was such a reason for angels becoming embodied, you have the cause why they assumed flesh without undergoing birth."[21] What is substantial in the body of Christ, and is perhaps his most profound aspiration, is not that he resembles the angels (the theme of *Christos angelos*), nor even that he leads us to take up a form of angelism (the addition of the theme of making man divine in a certain interpretation of Dionysius, for example). The Son, in becoming incarnate, has in reality no other wish, no other aim, than to resemble us, or rather to be *like us*—not angel but human, not through pure spirit but made into a body that is first of all material and inhabited also by the spiritual. "He was looked on as man, for no other reason whatever than because He existed in the corporeal substance of a man," Tertullian writes. He goes on to speak "of the muscles as clods; of the bones as stones; the mammillary glands as a kind of pebbles. Look upon the close junctions of the nerves as propagations of roots, and the branching courses of the veins as winding rivulets, and the down (which covers us) as moss, and the hair as grass, and the very treasures of marrow within our bones as ores of flesh."[22]

Our perspective then leads us back to the first origins of the Fathers of the Church. It is not the animal, or our animality, that is to be feared most, but the angel, or rather the Gnostic tendency, which always leads to distancing us from our materiality as well as from our humanity. The *body without consciousness* (the animal) is not the other side of the *consciousness without body* (the angel), except insofar as the hypothesis at the limits we associate with the second (the angel) also sends us back to the reality in ourselves of the first (the animal). We are left with an open question—at the limit of the thinkable, perhaps, but nonetheless central—as to the borders and thresholds of bestiality. Because if there is nothing to fear in our animality—in that, as we have seen, the sum total of our passions and drives, as of our Chaos, is offered and transformed by God in the act of the eucharist (Chapter 2)—there is, on the other hand, everything to fear in bestiality. Because the beast is not the animal, and bestiality marks precisely the descent of animality below the animal—a descent of which, paradoxically, only human beings show themselves capable. Only the human being is in fact "beast," or capable of becoming so, in all senses of the term: the imbecile as well as the brutal beast.

Knowing that human beings can raise themselves—not to the ranks of angels, but to a true spiritual assumption of the incarnate body—humankind can also fall. They can fall not into the animality of which they are already constituted, but into bestiality, where it is uniquely possible to veer off course from nature itself, and to founder below one's own nature. Nothing is beastly except that which humankind describes in such a way—in reality describing ourselves: namely, an animality that human beings come to reject, going so far as to indict it completely. This is where the symbolic dimension of the Beast as a measure of sin comes from. It has no need of the animal as such and gives another meaning, necessary and complementary to the act of the eucharist.

At the start, as at the end, of the biblical narrative—as I have already stressed but not fully developed (§5)—the Beast takes on the shape of the figurehead of sin and will make the eucharisticized body into an act of redemption (from bestiality to human), not simply one of solidarity (with the animality of humankind). From the "sin at the door like a crouching beast hungering for you" (Gen. 4:7 [JB]), according to God's words to Cain in Genesis, to the "scarlet Beast that was full of blasphemous names, and . . . had seven head and ten horns" (Rev. 17:3), the Beast (*therion*) sends us back to the savage and fearful world that menaces the human and could well make him fall below a humanity rooted in the model of the Earth and in a certain form of animality. Like the animality in us, the Beast also has to "ascend from the bottomless pit" (Rev. 17:8), but it is to "go to destruction"—unlike the Lamb, who "will conquer them" (Rev. 17:14) and who will sum up in itself the totality of humanity (Eph. 1:10). A double opposition marks the difference between animality and bestiality.

(1) First is the opposition of the Beast and the Lamb. On the one side, bestiality is the image of sin, and on the other, we find the symbolism of a divinity that can take on all our humanity. In fact, we never leave the basis of a certain animality, being liable either to drop into bestiality (sin) or to raise ourselves into a humanity that awaits its filiation (salvation). To be and to remain human in the recognition of our created being remains the aim of the act of the eucharist, not simply in taking on and transforming our particular animality (Part I), but also in preserving us from the danger of sin and from our own bestiality.

(2) Thus we arrive at the second opposition, or rather, distinction: salvation by *solidarity* that is so much a part of the eucharistic act—"here is the Lamb of God" (John 1:36)—simply as the image of a divinity capable of taking on our animality and transforming it (Chaos, passions, drives; see Part I). This gives way to salvation by *redemption*, classically and correctly required for us in order to undo our falling away and our sin: "Here is the Lamb of God *who takes away the sin of the world*" (John 1:29) (see Part II). The "blood of the Lamb" (Rev. 7:14) that flows from the side of the animal in the Ghent altarpiece, as we have seen (Preface), redeems the whole of humanity in the form of the blood poured onto the cross (John 19:34). So the problem is less that of recognizing in ourselves a certain form of animality than of falling into a bestiality that may go so far as to ruin the aspect of the animal in ourselves.

Neither angel nor beast, the question then is not, or is no longer, how to know what this "Animal That Therefore I Am" (Derrida) is; rather, we must ask ourselves what becomes of animality that is necessarily taken on once there is humanity—either falling into bestiality (human behavior mimicking an animal world that in reality it has never shared: pornography, prostitution, perversion of the self, and so on) or going beyond our humanity (the temptation of angelism, this time denying animality as though we were totally disincarnate, without passions or drives, without darkness or Chaos). The mystery of the Word incarnate (salvation through solidarity) stands as it were in front of the constitutive animality of our humanity, as the mystery of the blood that is spilt (salvation through redemption) stands before the potential fall of humankind into bestiality. In both cases the Beast threatens, but not the animal. We leave the *anima* or the breath that constitutes us (*psuchê*) as we wait for the *animus* or the spirit (*pneuma*), the "supplement of the soul" that permits us not to fall.

The animal in fact is *anima* rather than *animus*—thus we have the term "anima-lity." And it is this animality that is taken on and transformed in the act of the eucharist, and rescued, where there has been a fall into bestiality. As the etymologist R. B. Onians famously shows in *The Origins of European Thought*, "Animus . . . was overwhelmingly, throughout Latin literature, not the vital principle but the principle of consciousness. . . . As the early tragedian Accius tersely says, *sapimus animo, fruimur anima* [We discern with the rational mind, enjoy with the soul]; introducing which several centuries later the grammarian Nonius says, *animus est quo sapimus, anima qua vivimus* [It is the rational mind by which we know, the soul by which we live]."[23] We can distinguish, not especially to place them in opposition, but at least to point out their distinctive characters, the *anima* as breath and "life-soul" from the *animus* as "consciousness with all the variation of emotion and thought," or "the breath that was consciousness in the chest," or breath in words. Accius, a near-contemporary of Christ (first century before Christ), thus sees in the *animus* an essence of life (breath) in the same way that the Jewish tradition sees in Adam the figure of an "earthly one" (*adâmah*) in which the breath of life (*neshama*) is blown through the nostrils. "The Lord God formed man from the dust of the ground, and breathed into his nostrils the breath of life; and the man became a living being" (Gen. 2:7). The "rite of breath" makes life, as Marcel Jousse tells us, and restores us to life. The theology of the breath (life) responds to the anthropology of the dust (body)— instead of the substance of thought (soul) responding to the extension of a machine (body).

There is not, then, a soul separated from the body in the Greek conception of origins, or in the Jewish world, but rather a living breath (*anima-nèfèsh*) through which Adam becomes alive. The loss of this breath is precisely what indicates death, or a dismantling, rather than the disappearance of thought, or the stopping of the heart, or a flat encephalogram. The narrative of the "mystery of death," as recounted by the anthropologist Jousse, is so poignant that it deserves to be cited here at length. It helps us see that what *this is my body* offers in the act of the eucharist cannot be reduced to material terms. It is the offering of a body eaten and a life breathed into an earthly Adam waiting to be renewed:

> Country people are so accustomed to be tight-lipped that they cannot conceive how all of life and all of the understanding of life can be irradiated and manifest through the breath that goes in and out of the nostrils. Before the mystery of death you may be confronted by a spectacle—or it might be better to call it a kind of mime-show—that I have witnessed very often in the countryside. Death enters the farm. The farmer takes down the sole mirror in his poor house. He balances it on his mother's bed. She lies there totally immobile, having become cold as earth. He will delicately, religiously, liturgically, place the mirror against the cold nostrils of the one who has worked so hard and who is now lying there, inert. He waits several seconds to complete, for himself, the primordial ritual that I would call the "rite of breath." And with the suffering that comes from inexplicable things, perhaps because these things are inexplicable to us, he will turn the mirror around and will look at it to see if the clouding breath has passed onto it or died away.[24]

The *anima* as "respiratory breath" in the occidental tradition (Onians), or the "breath of life" animating a being made of Earth and dust in the Semitic tradition (Jousse), are what consecrated man, or Adam, as "living": "And the man became a living being [*hâyâh*]" (Gen. 2:7). Nonetheless, we must be careful here. To say of *anthropos,* or the *Adâmâ,* that he becomes a living being does not subtract from his animality; on the contrary, it inscribes him in it. We can point to how, even before Adam names the animals, the author of Genesis is careful to note that "whatever the man called each *living creature*, that was its name" (Gen. 2:19). The living creature who is man, in the insufflation or the breathing of the breath starting off "from the dust" (Gen. 2:7), joins here other living creatures, those animals who also await their names or their welcome into the ark of speech (Gen. 2:19). "The animal is qualified as *living creature* (literally breath of life) like man. . . . The Yahwist author, before showing the superiority of man over the animals wishes to recall that they have respiration in common."[25] Or, as we have already seen (§5), if the breath is the same as the breath that gives life to all living creatures, and thus inscribes us biblically in the great sphere of animality, the dust or clay is of a similar nature, or of the same texture: the clay with which "the Lord God formed man from the dust of the ground" (Gen. 2:7). The identity of the breath and of the clay does not take us beyond animality, as though Adam and Eve (Semitic tradition), or the rational human being (Greek tradition), had first been thought of independently from animals and their own animality. On the contrary, it brings us back to a common base, something we may see differently and from which we may eventually depart, but without ever denying this community of the *psuchê*.

This common texture of the clay and the breath, or of the body and the soul in Graeco-Latin terms (*soma-psuchê—corpus-anima*), thus precedes and makes possible the inspiration of the spiritual breath of God. God breathes his strength into matter that has been created by him, taking account of the density of the matter as well as difference. Irenaeus tells us, "our substance, that is, the union of flesh and spirit [*animae et carnis*], receiving the Spirit of God [*spiritus Dei*], makes up the spiritual man."[26] The trilogy of the Epistle to the Thessalonians cannot really be read in any other way: "May the God of peace himself sanctify you entirely; and may your spirit and soul and body [*pneuma, psuchê, sôma*] be kept sound and blameless at the coming of our Lord Jesus Christ" (1 Thes. 5:23). I can only repeat here what I have said elsewhere with regard to the correct interpretation of Irenaeus: "The mixture 'soul-body' [*psûche-sôma*] of the Old Testament (Gen. 2:7) receives the 'spirit-breath' [*pneuma*] of the New Testament (1 Thes. 5:23). This takes the form of a *prefiguration* in the Old Testament, after the initial mixture forms a properly constituted whole, capable of receiving such power from God."[27] The *anima*-lity in us is not an accident of our constitution that can be forgotten or that is simply overcome. We find this from the start in Indo-European culture (*anima* and *animus*), as at the origin of Semitic culture (the clay and the breath). It is also constitutive of our humanity, and it is in this respect that the eucharistic tradition also cannot hide it, in the ambivalence of the sacrificial lamb (the animal first of all in taking charge of our humanity and the deliverance from bestiality through the blood that frees us from sin).[28]

Certainly, Adam was not fully satisfied by his kinship with the animal, and thus it is also his belonging to Chaos and Tohu-Bohu that keeps him under the command of the *anima* (see §21). When he is called on to name the animals, in the eyes of God he has to confront his own animality as well as the strong passions and drives that he alone could not control. The difficulty he encounters in naming the animals is, as we shall see, a quite extraordinary indication in the biblical narrative of his human incapacity to live through interior Chaos until another—a female other— is given to him.

Eve shows us a limit for humanity and for man. She will help Adam to love his own limits as well as carry with him the Chaos and the animality by which she also is constituted (§22). It is in discovering Eve as "bone of my bones and flesh of my flesh" (Gen. 2:23) that Adam becomes other than his animality—in calling her "woman" (*ishah*) and not "female." And it is in differentiating herself from Adam and in recognizing him as "man" (*ish*), and not as "male," that Eve also comes to belong to his community of a differentiated humanity that cannot be reduced to a simple animality (Gen. 2:23) (§23). The *anima*-lity is thus preserved, not simply in biblical terms, but also as it becomes metaphysically constitutive of our humanity and of our belonging to the created world—even though that world will come to be, if not surpassed, at least seen in other ways.

However, and it is the least one can say, this question of animality and thus also of Chaos, of passions and drives, will be forgotten. Or rather, the process of history and philosophy as well as that of theology does every-thing not simply to detach us from the question, but also to make us think that nothing like that can, or ever could, happen to us. The difference in nature between human and animal (e.g., reason, liberty, work, laughter) or, even more, the constant spiritualization, at least in artworks, of Adam and Eve before the Fall (without passions, without emotions, almost with-out heart or body, apart from the paintings of Michelangelo on the ceiling of the Sistine Chapel)—all of that has not simply taken humankind away from our basic animality, but hidden what is suggested in the Bible of our human origins (identity of the same breath and the same clay), and this has been done to the extent of suggesting that those origins do not belong to the created being. How has this come about? And how has such neglect been maintained? What basic shared history has determined this? These questions are all the more meaningful because the *this is my body*, as I have emphasized throughout this book, comes in the form of the conse-crated Host, to take on and to transform, in particular, the unspoken of the animal in us, that "disembodied consciousness" (Chaos, passion, drives . . .) that we of course do everything to forget and stoically try to master.

§14. The Animal in Common

It would be wrong to accuse Hellenism and a certain form of Christianity of being at the origin of this neglect of animality. It would also be wrong to suggest that the turn was simply the avowal of a superiority that we keep on affirming—in terms either of reason (Hellenism) or of vocation (Christianity). In fact, for Hellenism, as for Christianity, the kinship with an animal outside us, and even more with the animal within us, exists from the start. The "animal in common" ensures that there is a community of animality between animals and human beings, through Chaos—passions and drives that we cannot deny without also cutting off some part of our humanity. Moreover, this animal in common is a part of the ordinary or communal of all living things, something that we also certainly need to share. We have thus a great deal in common with the animal, both in our community and in our daily lives, even though both of these will be taken on and surpassed in the context of humanity, in particular, as regards the difference man-woman (§23). If we were to reject the animality of humankind out of hand, if we were to go in such a direction—one whose limitations have not been sufficiently remarked upon—then we should encounter at once the objection of Paul Broca, a disciple in this respect of Charles Darwin. Broca (1824–1880), a French surgeon and anthropologist whose philosophical tone and caustic humor go beyond the limits of evolutionary theology, famously pointed out that "man is not the only animal who thinks, but he is the only animal who thinks that he is not an animal."

From the start, then, and even though the formula of the "reasonable animal" could serve as a weapon in the turn toward animality (§15), Aristotle anticipated all those who might be unwilling to undertake, might even be repulsed by, the study of animals and our own animality. We can try to raise ourselves toward the "ungenerated, imperishable, and eternal," he tells us in *On the Parts of Animals*, but they are "less accessible to knowledge." On the other hand, "respecting perishable plants and animals we have abundant information, living as we do in their midst." So from the point of view of "certitude and . . . completeness our knowledge of terrestrial things has the advantage." They are familiar to us and we can reach conclusions about them through induction. Certain beings "have no graces to charm the sense" (the earthworm, the mollusc, the slug), Aristotle says, in pre-Kantian tones; however, they "give immense pleasure to all who can trace links of causation, and are inclined to philosophy"—an interest taken in the ends of things. The aim is clear and it is enough to decide upon it, even if certain people, including a number of philosophers, come to doubt it. "We therefore must not recoil with childish aversion from the examination of the humbler animals."[29]

Perhaps, then, we do not need to reinterpret that famous citation of Heraclitus by Aristotle in the same chapter of *On the Parts of Animals*: "Heraclitus, when the strangers who came to visit him found him warming himself at the furnace in the kitchen and hesitated to go in, [is] reported to have bidden them not to be afraid to enter, as even in that kitchen divinities were present."[30] Heidegger's interpretation of this, in his "Letter on 'Humanism,'" is that "Heraclitus is not even busy baking at the stove. He stands there merely to warm himself. . . . [This] phrase places the abode of the thinker and his deed in another light. . . . Heraclitus himself says, 'the (familiar) abode for humans is the open region for the presencing of god (the unfamiliar one)'"[31] It is thus as "shepherd of being," Heidegger specifies, that the physician welcomes his guests to his stove.[32] But this is saying too much, or perhaps saying nothing at all, because it is not the deity to which Aristotle's anecdote about the visitor to Heraclitus's culinary den refers; he has just distanced himself from them, turning toward the "perception of animals," as being for us the most "familiar." By contrast, Heraclitus may be inviting us to consider animality, as animals. And because nothing is said in the text that would suggest they are not cooked here, we are brought down to Earth and reminded of our own nature.

Heraclitus, according to Aristotle, is "reported to have bidden them [the strangers] not to be afraid to enter." And straight away he adds, "So we should venture on the study of every kind of animal without distaste."[33] This is so clear that it cannot be gainsaid. The Heraclitian anecdote, as it is seen and commented on by Aristotle, does not hallow the deity (Heidegger); on the contrary, it invites us to look at our own animality, even if that means turning us away from a divinity who would tend to take us away from animality as well as from our own humanity. The analogy between the "divinities" and "every kind of animal" certainly does not make gods into animals—an absurdity as important in Hellenism as in Christianity. It simply confirms the search into animality as a search into our proper selves and not simply a physiological or biological study of animals and their parts that would not seem to involve us. "If any person thinks the examination of the rest of the animal kingdom an unworthy task," says Aristotle, in accents that recall those of Tertullian, "he must hold in like disesteem the study of man. For no one can look at the primordia of the human frame—blood, flesh, bones, vessels, and the like—without much repugnance."[34]

A kinship of this kind with the form of the "common animal," established with the animal in the context of Hellenism, can also be found in Christianity. There will certainly and rightly be a consensus to reject the notion of a direct salvation of the animals, without passing through humanity. It is not a question of considering the salvation of the animal independently from human salvation, in a kind of animism that Christianity has always rejected, but the prophecy of Isaiah does merit consideration here. Isaiah sticks to the hypothesis of a cosmic salvation for all living things, even when they are adversaries, going as far as to include all in the frame of animality:

> The wolf shall live with the lamb,
> the leopard shall lie down with the kid,
> the calf and the lion and the fatling together,
> and a little child shall lead them.
> The cow and the bear shall graze,
> their young shall lie down together;
> and the lion shall eat straw like the ox.
>
> (Isa. 11:6–9; see also Isa. 65:25)

Irenaeus, first among the Fathers of the Church, does not hesitate to affirm this in the most literal sense: "I am quite aware that some persons endeavour to refer these words to the case of savage men, both of different nations and various habits, who come to believe, and when they have believed, act in harmony with the righteous. . . . [The words shall also apply] to those animals mentioned. For God is rich in all things. And it is right that when the creation is restored, all the animals should obey and be in subjection to man . . . for they had been originally subjected in obedience to Adam."[35] Clearly this suggests that the appropriate refusal of a direct salvation for animals is not in contradiction with the recapitulation of the animal in humankind in the movement of the Resurrection and thus also—and this is my own hypothesis—with the animality of human beings taken on and transformed by the Man-God (not that God is animal any more than we are solely animal).

We could go on until kingdom come providing examples in the Christian tradition to show this pattern of the "animal in common" (in community and ordinarily), of humankind with the animal, certainly, but also and above all of humanity with its own characteristic animality. Numerous and recent anthologies show how well founded this is.[36] Perhaps the most incisive and clear formulation is to be found in the work of the Irish theologian Johannes Scotus Eriugena, who translated the Greek idea of recapitulation (*anakephalaiôsis*) for the Latin world, emphasizing how in the totality of the cosmos we find the plan of God "that he would bring everything together under Christ, as head" (Eph. 1:10 [JB]) and how this applies to all living things. Salvation reaches out to all created beings, in particular to their animality, insofar as they are part of humanity taken into, and part of, the mystery of the incarnate Word. Eriugena wrote,

> But we should believe very strongly and understand with the greatest exactitude that it is by the incarnation of the Word that all creatures living in the sky and on the earth have been saved. . . . All creatures (animals without understanding, as well as the trees, the plants, and all that make up the world) that have been created so far as their cause is concerned (though not their bodily mass), like man, will be restored to life with man, and in man, at the resurrection of man. . . . If, in taking on human nature, the Word took on all the creatures, then the Word has saved all creatures and all creatures shall be saved for eternity.[37]

All that has traditionally been said, and all that will be said in this book and elsewhere, has great difficulty in escaping one important and frequent cliché. Christianity of "election" (which sets itself up against Irenaeus or Origen, for example) and rationalist Hellenism (which sets itself up against Aristotle or misreads him) have had no other goal but that of dismissing animality by means of instrumentalizing it, both in themselves and outside themselves: "For Christianity, animals are instruments animated by the will of *God to serve man*, who commits no sin in causing them to be *destroyed*."[38] So, one can certainly accuse St. Paul, as has become commonplace, of leading humanity away from animals—specifically, of leading humanity from animality, (1) as far as caring for animals is concerned, and (2) from the point of view of the prohibition of certain meats. But these arguments are not convincing once examined within the contexts that have engendered them.

(1) *Caring for animals.* One could interpret the declarations of Paul to the community of Corinthians, which really are concerned with respect for, or deviation from, the law, as a rejection of animality. "Is it for oxen that God is concerned? Or does he not speak entirely for our sake? It was indeed written for our sake" (1 Cor. 9:9–10). One could consider this, as I hope to make clear, with philosophical integrity, as *God does not worry about cattle*—another missed opportunity for the New Testament to take on board the question of animality.[39]

The problem here, however, is not that of denial of the animal but that of giving priority to the salvation of humankind, if it is "entirely for our sake" that God speaks. This is not St. Paul *against* animality, but it is through the human that the animal is not simply animal. There is no denial of animality; rather, there is authorization to go beyond animality. As was mentioned earlier, the Apostle to the Gentiles himself always stressed (and I have tried in this book to make the same point) that "it is not the spiritual that is first, but the physical [*psuchikon*], and then the spiritual [*pneumatikon*]" (1 Cor. 15:46). Humankind being saved, this brings afterwards (and inversely also within humankind) the salvation of the entire universe—not in a total neglect of cattle (or oxen), as has been misunderstood, but in the assumption of these animals in us as we are taken into the Word. There is no salvation of animals, or of our own animality, independently of the will of God to save them, or to safeguard them in and through humankind. Only human beings, in fact, have some kind of custody over them and are constituted to be in some way the shepherds (of animality), especially when it is a question of the necessary salvation of living things. The Lord says to Noah, "You shall come into the ark, you, your sons, your wife, and your sons' wives with you" (Gen. 6:18). Noah, as pioneer of that covenant of a total alliance that will be preserved: "of every living thing, of all flesh, you shall bring two of every kind into the ark, to keep them alive with you; they shall be male and female. . . . Two of every kind shall come in to you, to keep them alive" (Gen. 6:19–20). The true "concern" is not for the cattle, but for humankind. But in being concerned for humankind, God is also concerned about cattle—not simply in that they are useful and necessary for food and work (the animal) but insofar as there is also life and the animal in humankind (animality), and in that nothing human, apart from sin, is completely strange to God, who has decided to take on responsibility in its totality.

(2) *Prohibition of certain meats.* The point of transgression of these rules was to open things up toward animality, rather than to obstruct animality. Peter's vision in the Acts of the Apostles is certainly astonishing in this respect: "He saw the heaven opened and something like a large sheet coming down, being lowered to the ground by its four corners. In it were all kinds of four-footed creatures and reptiles and birds of the air. Then he heard a voice saying, 'Get up, Peter; kill and eat'" (Acts 10:11–13). All the animals are here to be eaten—not, however, simply as a matter of opening up the rules as to what is permitted, but to universalize the message, to transgress the frontiers placed in the heart of animality as well as of humanity. The detour by way of animals (previously declared

pure or impure on a seemingly arbitrary basis) has no other sense than to make us see the community of human beings (falsely divided into the circumcised and uncircumcised): "'God has shown me that I should not call anyone profane or unclean'" (Acts 10:28). As when there was a question as to whether it was "for oxen that God is concerned," the point here is that St. Peter is called on to eat everything. It is not that he fights against the prohibitions of Judaism, but that he opens up animality, and humanity, to a new universality. Nobody is to be excluded from a salvation that aims to be inclusive, even if there is religious conflict over the flesh of meat. We should underline here how Christianity and Hellenism, in their origins as in their source texts, do not deny the "animal in common," but rather integrate it into a project of humanity, which can take it on board and need never deny it. "To speak of a Judeo-Christian mentality which would plunder the planet and tend more and more to destroy it is then a complete misunderstanding, at least if one means to define the plan that God proposes to man in the Bible. Rather it is exactly the opposite."[40]

§15. From the Turn to the Forgetting

If the common base of animality is so very much *there* right from the start—as from the point of view of the sacred texts (from Genesis to the Book of Revelations, passing by the epistles of Paul) as well as that of philosophy (*On the Parts of Animals* by Aristotle) and theology (in Irenaeus and Eriugena, for example), how is it that a real turn took place and that the question of the animal came to be forgotten, if not completely rejected, or at least always denied? The topic is all the more crucial because at the start, thought moved in another direction, privileging community over specificity and unity over diversity: "All that lives is one," says Empedocles (according to Nietzsche, quoting a letter by Goethe), "the gods, mankind and the animals."[41]

Plato himself is faithful to this tradition in his unique "definition of man," where he does everything to connect the human first to the animal, not to mention animality: the human being is a "featherless two-footed animal." These requisites raise a smile today as in the past, and Diogenes Laërtius, with barely disguised irony, couldn't resist recounting how "Diogenes [the Cynic] plucked a cock and brought it into this school, and said, 'this is Plato's man.' On which account, this addition was made to the definition, 'With broad flat nails.'"[42] We could add, moreover, that this original kinship with animality, which leaves its trace in Plato, is also claimed by a whole mythology, not to say a religion, which has not forgotten it—and which perhaps for this reason still finds its followers in our modern world. We do not need to endorse such views to note that the need for metempsychosis or reincarnation, a tentative or temptation for quite a few of our contemporaries, can also teach us something about our own animality that Christian tradition has often forgotten. It is not the return to Earth of the deceased being (concerning which, resurrection differs in every respect from reincarnation), but the filiation of humanity with a chain of living beings in which we are also constituted. Again, it is Diogenes Laërtius who recounts what Pythagoras said: "He had once been Aethalides and was accounted to be Hermes' son. . . . Afterwards in the course of time his soul entered into Euphorbus and he was wounded by Menelaus. Now Euphorbus used to say that he had once been Aethalides. . . . When Euphorbus died, his soul passed into Hermotimus. . . . But when Pyrrhus died, he became Pythagoras, and still remembered all the facts mentioned."[43] Certainly the transmission is made here from human to human, and not from human to animal. But passage by animality is possible, though some try to avoid it completely and others at times want it. As Plato recalls in his famous myth of Er, Orpheus chose to exist as a swan because of his abhorrence of women; Ajax preferred to live as a lion, which refused to be born as a man; and Agamemnon exchanged his like for that of an eagle. And, in Plato's *Republic*, Socrates tells Glaucon, "Not only did men pass into animals, but I must also mention that there were animals tame and wild who changed into one another and into corresponding human natures—the good into the gentle and the evil into the savage, in all sorts of combinations."[44]

I see it thus: if a chain of animality of this kind cannot exactly be claimed in the context of Christianity, it has at least the merit of reminding us how much we continue to share with animals and how we have a sympathy with them from our origins, as also we probably have with our own animality—something that it would be wrong to disregard. I would repeat our question—indeed, insist upon it—as to where the break comes from. When does the turn come, so that evidence of our community at this point becomes hidden? It is as though animals and, above all, the animality in humankind (Chaos, passions, drives . . .) were something about which we had to keep quiet, or at least bring under control, so that they would never get out of hand.

It is Aristotle (after Plato) who takes the turn or marks the break—not because it was his ambition or intention to repudiate the study of animals and the animality of humankind, as we have seen, but because he opened a track along which the history of philosophy as well as much of theology has continued to proceed: that of the human being as a rational animal.[45]

It is not that Aristotle leads us astray here; he simply decides that it is possible to follow such a path in another direction. Bearing in mind the rational animal, Aristotle further suggests that man is a "political animal" (*zôon politikon*). It is as though, freshly, all specific characteristics can be constructed only on the basis of a community. "Man is *by nature* a political animal."[46] The *zôon politikon*, we should note, appears here first of all from animality: zoology is not, as it was to be for Heidegger, "privative" (leading to loss or negation) (§16); here, for Aristotle, it is positive. It is simply and primarily as animal that the human shows himself to be a "political animal." This observation derives from nature in general and belongs also to the human's nature *as* human, even if it is evident "that man is more of a political animal than bees or any other gregarious animals."[47] The difference here is one not of essence but solely of degree. In short, there is no special privilege as far as political matters are concerned, unless it is for us to be able to govern ourselves more justly and in different ways—even, this time, by reason.

With the concept of the human as rational animal, Aristotle and those who come after him (the Stoics) introduce a rupture or break—one that is to have importance for Aristotle's own text as well as in the history of philosophy. "Man is the only animal whom she [Nature] has endowed with the gift of speech."[48] We still say this. Even in the formulation *zôon logikon*, the human is not divided off from a "positive zoology" but continues to belong to it. Described as a rational animal, a human being is no less conscripted as "animal" even in the definition. But the question does now arise that sets off the process of forgetting human animality. If man is "the only animal" that possesses speech (whether a question of the *logos* as reason or of the *logos* as discourse), does this possession still and always pertain to the world or the sphere of the animal? Or, to put it another way, according to the Aristotelian logic that lies behind the definition: Doesn't the determination of the species (human) by the *genus* (animal) and the specific *differentia* (rationality or politics) definitively destroy and annihilate the genus itself? If we attribute the *logos* exclusively to humankind, assuming that all discourse is first of all spoken, do we not exclude humans from the common lot of living creatures, making our rationality in some way contradictory with our animality ("the only animal")? In short, doesn't the phrase "rational animal" beg the question? Doesn't it somehow extract the rationality from animality and attempt as far as possible to forget animality?

In the final analysis, the Aristotelian notion just does not hold. On the one hand, discrimination in terms of rationality does not in the least mark the human among the animals, insofar as humankind remains animal.

On the other hand, the requisite of *logos* declined here as discourse does not exclude *phonê*, defined as "voice." In fact the *logos* is superimposed on the *phonê*—the discourse of the voice—in such a way that the most basic of the two (the voice, or the faculty of producing sounds) relies on the product that derives from it (speech, or the capacity to articulate thought). What makes our community in animality, here and always, is certainly not speech, or the kind of discourse that requires a shared rationality (judgment as to what is "useful" or "harmful," the "just" and the "unjust," and other moral notions); it is the "voice" that "is but an indication of pleasure or pain, and is therefore found in other animals." Recognizing that "man alone has any sense of good and evil, or just and unjust, and the like," does not mean that humankind has to deny the shared animality in our nature that "attains to the perception of pleasure and pain and the intimation of them to one another."[49]

We can certainly go this far. The decision made in philosophy and sustained throughout its history consisted of a pursuit of the route of pure humanity, and thus of rationality, as opposed to that of shared animality and affectivity. But in the eyes of Aristotle, the "shared feelings"[50] would always remain important, and it would be right to suggest, as we have already seen (Chapter 2), that Christ's mystery of the Passion, as well as of the eucharist or Resurrection, traces out a route of *pathos* that, without being obviously animal, nonetheless takes on our animality to convert it into a humanity that can be recognized this time in its filiation. Humankind find their role here where Christ himself rejoins them, but not as non-animal in a denial that could destroy the human by a process of disincarnation—a Gnostic tendency that should be avoided at all costs. Christ joins humankind obviously not so much to become animal—an incarnation as animal that would be as absurd for humankind as for God—but in an assumption and transformation of all our created nature, apart from sin or bestiality that is never directly given (§13). The descent into the abyss (Part I) moves here to the sojourn of humankind (Part 2) in that God, in the form of Emmanuel, lives and transforms our share of animality (Chaos, passions, drives; difference between male and female) to raise it into a humanity (desire, recognition, fecundity; difference between man and woman) that itself desires to be incorporated into God (Trinity and filiation). The poet Terence, a century before Christ, says, "*Homo sum, humani nihil a me alienum puto*" (I am a man: I consider nothing human alien to me).[51] It is an adage that Christ himself could have appreciated, passing over divinity this time.

One wonders if it is the case that voice affects certain depths of feeling and intimacy that reason tends rather to deny, or to distance itself from.

Isn't the mystery of the voice (*phonê*) superior, first of all and above all in the gospels, to the clarity of reason (*logos*)? Certainly the Son is the Word (*logos*) become flesh. But what he is in himself expresses itself differently for us. As with those whom one loves, we recognize him less through his discourse and his arguments than through his style and his voice—from the "voice from heaven" at the baptism in the Jordan (Matt. 3:17), to the voice of the shepherd whose "sheep follow him because they know his voice" (John 10:4), to the cry "with a loud voice" on Golgotha at the hour of the rending of the temple veil at Jerusalem (Mark 15:34). When we speak of voice, it is not a question of reason; perhaps it is even that the voice is the token of the innermost aspect of the ego, in that it "is part of the phenomenological essence of this operation in that *I hear myself during the time* that I speak."[52] The proximity of the voice is far from the possible distance of reason, or the *logos*, which remains the same even if it is not uttered. The voice, or the *phonê*, is instead a token of the presence of the self to the self, at least while one is speaking, and thus has a life that is always individualized and properly constituted. The voice, like the body, precisely because it is corporal, does not lie—but discourse can quickly go astray while imitating the truth. "The voice," Aristotle underlines, "is the sound made by an animal." And those among animals, including human-kind, who use the voice, produce "a sound with meaning" and not a simple phoneme or a noise that lacks contextualization. The voice does not say nothing. On the contrary, it is in that respect, according to Aristotle, that we distinguish it from "coughing up" or simple movement of the "tongue."[53] Whoever raises this voice, whether human (in a cry, a groan, a moan, a whimper, a howl) or animal (barking, mewing, cawing, roaring), it is "but an indication of pleasure or pain" in which there is also, as we have seen, "the intimation of them [pleasure and pain] to one another."[54]

Voice is always addressed or directed (cry, groan, moan), even when the possibilities of speech are exhausted (reason and articulate discourse). One becomes without speech, or "illogical" (*a-logos*), before becoming without voice, or voiceless (*a-phonê*). The voice, or *phonê*, is that which remains hidden under the *logos* because it has not, or has no longer, the strength to express itself otherwise—when it is hidden in a flesh in which it has become exhausted: "Then Jesus gave a loud cry and breathed his last" (Mark 15:37). With the voice they hold in common, animals seem to have direct contact and feeling, while human beings always retain distance and reason—and that difference is not without its implications, since eucha-ristic communion pertains to taste and to touch (changes in the senses), which are also the first two senses of animality. "Taste also must be a sort of touch, because it is the sense for what is tangible and nutritious. Both these senses, then, are indispensable to the animal, and it is clear that without touch it is impossible for an animal to be."[55] We need it, then—as far as animality is concerned, certainly, but also, and paradoxically, in the doctrine of spiritual sense. I shall return to the problem of the conversion of senses (§32), which is the basis of the Franciscan view of the eucharist (as developed by Bonaventure), according to which sensation is transformed and in a sense spiritualized. In a famous passage from Bonaventure's *Breviloquium*, we read, "The greatest delight is embraced, insofar as he is the Incarnate Word, who dwells bodily among us and gives himself to be touched, to be kissed, to be embraced, through a most fiery love that lets our mind pass over from this world through ecstasy and rapture to the Father."[56]

If man alone of the animals possesses speech, then his animality can be quickly forgotten or denied, in order to concentrate exclusively on his humanity or his absolute superiority. The turn is taken, or rather, the choice is made, or going to be made, if not by Aristotle then by those who follow him (the Stoics). The steps to this neglect are multiple and take us along a well-trodden route. We can point to Cicero first of all, who says explicitly, "animals have been created with a view to man." He asks, "What other end do sheep serve except that of clothing men with their wool? . . . The faithful watch that is kept by dogs . . . —what do these indicate if not that dogs were created for the convenience of men? Of oxen it is unnecessary to speak . . . their necks were meant for the yoke."[57] Next we turn to St. Augustine, who, at least in certain passages, makes the image of God in man the site of a definitive separation of the human from all other living creatures: "Where man is said to have been made to the image of God, it is said with reference to the inner man, where reason is to be found and intelligence, and it is from this that he gets 'authority over other [living things].'" Further, "It is above all as regards the spirit that man was made to the image and likeness of God."[58] Then there is Descartes, according to whom the absence of speech among the animals differentiates them from the deaf and dumb (who develop sign language): "And this does not merely show that the brutes have less reason than men, but that they have none at all."[59] But it cannot be denied that extreme oblivion—or rather, denial—will arrive with Malebranche, in a unification (we might even say a conspiracy) between philosophy and theology that subsequent generations would not hesitate to follow (at least until Husserl and Nietzsche). Malebranche considered that animals could not be said to feel at all, "because they only suffer mechanically." "Suffering is a penalty, and the punishment for some sin." Animals do not sin—not because they are exempted from sin, but because "under a just God those who have not merited it cannot be so unfortunate"—and so cannot truly suffer, as would be the consequence and punishment for sin. True suffering is thus restricted to humanity. The apparent suffering of animals is only the "reaction of the machine of the body," and not a true ordeal of an affected self."[60] In Malebranche's dialogue on death, Théotime explains to Ariste that when a dog whines and pulls back its paw because it has been pricked, this is not the "proof that it feels pain," but simply that "it has lungs and that the air is released from them violently by the movement of the diaphragm."[61] In short, the reduction of the animal to what we might call machine-ism, in terms of not only the anti-rational (Descartes) but also the anti-sensitive (Malebranche), goes so far as to separate humankind totally from animality. Its roots are in a certain kind of philosophical Christianity, but they draw on the classical tradition of metaphysics rather than the gospels themselves or the experience of the Fathers of the Church and the medievals. It was only with the emergence of a certain romanticism, or even of phenomenology in that form, that sensation and then also animality would come to be newly accepted (§16). The neglect of the animal becomes on the whole less concealed, although the density of the body, not simply as extended, nor simply as lived, but as "spread out," would then be veritably rediscovered (§17).

§16. The Metaphysical Animal

"With the exception of man, no being wonders at its existence; but it is to them all so much a matter of course that they do not observe it," says Schopenhauer, in a new definition of the human. "With this reflection and this wonder there arises for man alone, the *need for a metaphysic*; he is accordingly an *animal metaphysicum*."[62] The transition here from the "reasonable animal" (Aristotle) to the "metaphysical animal" (Schopenhauer) is famous. Going from one to the other, there is certainly a difference of formulation and conception, but also, and above all, a different way of thinking about both. While one (Aristotle) opens the way for a distinction between beings—in terms of reason, but also later in terms of language (Descartes), liberty (Rousseau), work (Marx), or laughter (Bergson)—the other (Schopenhauer) opens up a way of being human that gives us access to a world newly placed for discovery. "Without doubt it is the knowledge of death and along with this the consideration of the suffering and misery of life, which gives the strongest impulse to philosophical reflection and metaphysical explanation of the world. If our life were endless and painless, it would perhaps occur to no one to ask why the world exists, and is just the kind of world it is; but everything would just be taken as a matter of course." "I remind the reader of [the] origin [of philosophy] . . . in a *wonder* concerning the world and our own existence, inasmuch as these press upon the intellect as a riddle."[63]

We can question, and certainly be surprised by, the pessimism of this author (Schopenhauer), who has sometimes been considered as a representative of nihilism, even of decadence (Nietzsche). But the novelty in his thought remains important, and it opens up toward another way of doing philosophy: that is, an unprecedented unmasking of humanity not simply in terms of argument about what is really there (a breach between beings), but according to an ontological mode (a new dimension of being). What is human is not, or is no longer, the possession of an organ or a faculty (reason, work, laughter, or liberty) but a kind of wonder (*thaumazein*), which derives this time not from contemplation of the splendor of the world (finality in Aristotle), but from surprise as amazement (knowledge of the fact of death and the shock or pain and the misery of life in Schopenhauer). This is not a simple difference in the vision of the world: optimism and wonder on one side, pessimism and desolation on the other; there is a distance in the manner and forms of seeing the world. "Only to the brutes, who are without thought, does the world and existence appear as a matter of course." For human beings, by contrast, "it is a problem, of which even the most uneducated and narrow-minded becomes vividly conscious in certain brighter moments."[64] The question here is no longer whether one understands, which would be going back simply to rational differentiation, but whether things are understandable "as a matter of course": in short, if the access that has been opened to the world works in the same way for both humans and animals. It is not enough to suggest that a human can be more distressed than an animal, caught as we are when "life swings like a pendulum, backwards and forwards between pain and ennui."[65] But, as I hope to show later, the *metaphysical* route for humans distinguishes them from animal(ity), in that they enter into a mode particularly suited for questioning.

One could believe once again in a leap from, and in a neglect of, animality—as though the metaphysical need, whether satisfied or not, emerged yet again, specifically ready to cloud all issues. If it is not like this, that is not solely because the status of *metaphysician* for human beings is not one to be coveted (as a source of suffering and ennui), but also, and above all, because in this way human beings question themselves about the meaning of the loss of their share of animality, and not simply about their humanity. The gain is also a loss. And that is something we have to suggest, or to bear in mind, at least since Rousseau.

I am in accordance here with Michel Henry who insists that "what animals can say to us is that it is possible to live uniquely in life and through life"—a possibility of life that the contemporary penning of animals into natural reserves (animality), like the desertion of churches (religion), or the placing of artworks in museums (art), has effectively brought to an end. It is "the unspoken presence of pure Affectivity which alone, among realities contains its own revelation."[66] Rousseau's *Reveries of the Solitary Walker*, although it does not share the sense of desolation that we find in the work of the pessimistic philosopher (Schopenhauer), does show in a sense the same metaphysical momentum, even if it comes this time not from suffering or the awareness of death, but from what arises necessarily in life, in a coincidence of self with self in a kind of immediacy, and also animality. The animal is not necessarily bad, and neither is our own animality—to such a degree that animality seems to suggest a rather daring conjunction for Rousseau, where animal pleasure borders on divinity—at least in a conception of the world as infancy and immediacy. "As evening approached, I would come down from the heights of the island," Rousseau says, thinking himself alone,

> and I liked to go and sit at the lakeside in some secluded spot on the shingle; there, the sound of the waves and the movement of the water, gripping my senses and ridding my soul of all other agitation, plunged it into a delicious reverie, in the course of which night often fell without my noticing and took me by surprise. The ebb and flow of the water and its continuous yet constantly varying sound, ever breaking against my ears and my eyes, took the place of the movements inside me that reverie did away with and were enough to make me pleasurably aware of my existence, without my having the trouble to think . . . what does one enjoy in such a situation? Nothing external to the self, nothing but oneself and one's own existence: as long as this state lasts, one is self-sufficient like God. The feeling of existence stripped of all other affections is in itself a precious feeling of contentment and peace which alone would be enough to make this existence prized and cherished by anyone who could banish all the sensual and earthly impressions which constantly distract us from it and upset the joy of it in this world.[67]

It should, then, be plain. As metaphysical animal, one can go so far as to question one's own humanity in a radical fashion and ontologically— either recognizing there "the consideration of the suffering and misery of life" that starts us off (Schopenhauer), or to praise the "feeling of existence" that we live through (Rousseau). One could certainly, along with Heidegger, suggest that such a metaphysic "thinks of man on the basis of *animalitas* and does not think in the direction of his *humanitas*," and one could underline bluntly that "the human being in his essence is ek-sistent."[68] But to go on from there and deduce that in Schopenhauer, as well as in Nietzsche or Rilke, we find simply a "monstrous anthropomor-phization of the animal and a corresponding animalization of man" (course of 1929–1930, cited by Derrida), is to propose a reading that can-not be supported without losing hold of what makes up the substance of our humanity. To base everything on *Dasein* as "the privilege of speech" is to forget that we are *first of all* fleshly—made of flesh as the lived experi-ence of the body certainly, but also of the *body* in its objectivity (*Körper*), even of an ensemble or a pile of tissues and organs (*Fleisch*). Language only comes after the fact, to express the body and its different layers (see §24). And in any event, it cannot and should not override our corporality. If, then, it has been allowed to sink into oblivion and needs to be recuper-ated, according to the Heideggerian analysis, I insist on the need to look at the forgotten question of animality instead of the forgotten question of being. The latter is the result of an implicit decision to obscure and not consider the former. It derives from a restrictive zoology that continues to make the being-there of the human (rich in world) its norm—a viewpoint from which all animality is considered (poor in world)—though this animality is seen as lacking our being-there, which would determine everything. We should perhaps be courageous enough to affirm against Heidegger—along with Didier Franck, and initiating, as it were, a new point of departure—that, "The *ekstatic* determination of the essence of man (in Heidegger) implies the *total exclusion of his living animality*, and never in the history of metaphysics, has the being of man been so pro-foundly made *dis-incarnate*. . . . The *disappearance of the flesh, of the body*, is the price that is paid for the appearance of being."[69]

The other, or the new start, will not be based on being, or the *ekstatic* dimension of this being that is referred to as *Dasein*, but rather on the pathos and the flesh that we share with the animal, which imply that the animal is above all and always itself, but nevertheless make it possible for me to recover my animality. If the mode of empathy (*Einfühlung*) marks out first the characteristic limit of the phenomenology of *pathos* shared between one human being and another, its place can nonetheless be taken, at least for Husserl, by a possible animal-anthropological empathy, allow-ing the world of animal encounter to meet up with the human world, and vice versa (the dog's nose as an extension of the huntsman's nose, for example).

I want to move forward from this point, following a hypothesis that I will not abandon: The act of the eucharist will come precisely to dwell in such a mode of empathy on the part of Christ. The empathy, of course, is not with the animal but with humankind—going as far as the lower region of his Chaos, his passions and his drives. But it is not uniquely in the sublime parts of his consciousness and of his privileged being (we become "brother" and "sister" of our drives and passions, just as St. Francis would call the wolf of Gubbio "brother" no matter how difficult it was to tame). And empathy between humans and animals sends us back here to consider the empathy between humans and their own animality, as well as the possibility for God to dwell here; in doing so, God arrives at the totality of humankind precisely in order to metamorphose humanity. "It is not the spiritual [*pneumatikon*] that is first, but the phsyical [*psuchikon*], and then the spiritual," as we have already seen in relation to the first Adam (1 Cor. 15:46). But "It is sown a physical body [*soma psuchikon*], it is raised a spiritual body [*soma pneumatikon*]," as we must now add, given this impetus by the second Adam (1Cor. 15:44).

Along with Husserl, and this side of Heidegger—according to studies recently edited and translated that phenomenology, not to speak of theology, has not yet fully taken on board—the question shifts and can be posed in terms that the eucharistic act is able to recover, even if such different contextual worlds—those of the human, the animal, and the divine—can also interpenetrate here. It is appropriate to return to this here because I have so far simply adumbrated how the animals possess a world specific to themselves in which we are complete strangers, even if we know for certain that *their* world never integrally includes *ours* (§13). The example of the tick, as Uexküll explored it in the nineteenth century and as so many phenomenologists have taken it up in the twentieth century, is paradigmatic. Subject of its own world, and not simply object of the world of humankind, as we have seen in relation to the animal in general, the tick in its own milieu has a lived experience that is its own experience as tick and that we have difficulty in imagining. At the "tip of a protruding branch," the female, once having copulated, waits perhaps as long as a month for a "small mammal" to pass by at the right height, to make her repast upon the mammal and to nest in the mammal. But how did she get there? How did she get to this post of observation where she waits for her dinner? In reality blind and deaf, this "bandit" sees nothing and *understands* nothing. The tick "finds the way to its lookout with the help of a *general sensitivity to light*," and "becomes aware of the approach of its prey through the sense of smell." The butyric acid given off by the mammal is enough to persuade the tick of the appropriate moment at which to leave its post and leap off. If it falls onto a cold-blooded animal (e.g., lizard, frog) it will have to start all over again. But if it lands on a warm-blooded animal (e.g., dog, rabbit, scalp of a little boy) it has found its repast, and it uses its tactile sense "to find a spot as free of hair as possible in order to bore past its own head into the skin tissue of the prey. Now the tick pumps a stream of warm blood slowly into itself."[70] This description may provoke a smile, but in reality it translates an experiment that has been scientifically tested, and reiterated many times by Uexküll himself (in the cases of the snail and the fly, for example).

Uexküll's point of view is radically new. Far from a denial of animals, and of our characteristic animality, of the reduction of the body to a machine (Descartes), or of the animal philosophically and theologically instrumentalized (Malebranche), the object studied here changes for the biologist into a "subject that lives its own world, and of which it is the centre." It is from itself that it moves, indeed that it feels and suffers, and it is not simply from me—a me who thinks and observes that it is appropriate to consider this subject. Unlike those Walt Disney productions that never really put animals on stage, but simply show people projected into the forms of animality (Bambi, Bernard, Bianca, Scar, Moufassa, and others of the same type), the attitude that consists of seeing and understanding that the animal possesses its own proper world (to which we have only partial access) is not, or is no longer, strange to us. There are documentary films that try to show this to us: *Microcosmos*, on the population of grassland; *March of the Penguins*, on the migration of the emperor penguins.[71]

But what does it mean, then, for the tick—or simply for an animal in general—to apprehend the world in another way, at least from a human point of view, without sight and without hearing, but simply with a sensitivity of the skin to the light, a highly developed sense of smell, and a delicate sense of touch that allows movement from one place to another? Certainly, we can neither say what it would be like nor understand it, in that at the very least we would not be in that state ourselves except through *privation* or *projection* (of our own organs of sense), while the tick itself lives through that state by *negation* and according to *what belongs to it* (its own organs of sense). To see means nothing from its standpoint—we at least know this—because the tick does not have eyes, nor is it supposed to have them or to use them. There is an immeasurable difference between not seeing (privation) and not ever being able to see, nor knowing what it means to see (negation). The animal thus defines its world, a world whose radicality Kafka showed so wonderfully through his monstrous insect—cockroach, or black beetle, perhaps—in *Metamorphosis*. This world will always have a certain foreignness compared with every other sphere of animality and especially humanity: "When Gregor Samsa woke up one morning from unsettling dreams, he found himself changed in his bed into a monstrous vermin. . . . 'What's happened to me?' he thought. It was no dream. . . . [The] alarm clock had just struck a quarter to seven—he heard a cautious knock at the door next to the head of his bed. . . . Gregor was shocked to hear his own voice answering, unmistakably his own voice, true, but in which, as if from below, an insistent distressed chirping intruded."[72]

Different worlds—the worlds between animals, the animal world and the human world, and even the world of humans and the world of God—only meet one another sometimes, and it is that precisely, and paradoxically, that our humanity also shows, when we are talking about our capacity somehow to recover those worlds (animal worlds or the world of the divine), rather than setting up a frontal shock between them (animality and humanity, humanity and divinity). "The animal in his species does not feel 'exactly like me,'" Husserl says, in a remarkable unpublished sketch, "but it is however the *same things* that the animals perceive *in their own way*. . . . The beasts, the animal beings *are like us subject of a conscious life* in which the 'life-world' insofar as it is their own, is also in a certain way given to them as a certainty of being. . . . We *find the beasts in our world* thanks to an *empathy* which is an integrated modification of the empathy between men."[73] One knows, or at least one senses here, that the language has changed, as there is also a change in the approach to animality. The animal is no longer something to be disparaged, or even to exalt, but the site of another opening onto the world. Of course, the word "conscious" applied to an animal, in the writings of a phenomenologist, does not suggest that the animal has reflexive thought, like a human being, or that "it does not know itself and does not live in a culture" (which would, moreover, be the greatest difference between human and animal according to Husserl). Nonetheless, the usage of the term indicates that the animal relates also to a world, even if it be merely that of the flesh, where the forms of intentionality deriving from it can also, and sometimes are, those that we share (anticipation, memory, fear, desire, pleasure).

In short, there is certainly sensation and pathos among animals, Chaos made by passions, and strong drives that are also constitutive of us. They are such that the human paradoxically achieves self-discovery in his face-to-face with the animal, in the "the dog's nose as an extension of the huntsman's nose," or "the lion in its most savage state" (examples from Husserl). "All eyes, the creatures of the world look out into the open," Rilke proclaims in the eighth Duino Elegy. And, from a perspective radically different from what Heidegger would later write, he says, "What lies outside, their faces plainly show us."[74]

One could then believe that it would be necessary to wait for the start of the twentieth century for animal(ity) to be seen as a possible access to the world, even if an "impoverished" one. It was necessary to wait and to infer from our animality the thesis of the interpenetration of worlds—a thesis so new to us today that we can hardly articulate it. As far as the history of philosophy is concerned, or rather, one particular history, it has brought this thesis to light at times, embedding the animal in a corporality that probably also comprises *our* humanity—this last being taken on in an exemplary way and transformed in the *this is my body* or in the act of the eucharist. Seneca, the exact contemporary of St. Paul, underlines it in a way that has never been fully understood, or heard, in a letter to his disciple Lucillus—proof, if proof were needed, that the animal was not yet technicized when Christianity was born: "Therefore all animals have an awareness of their constitution and that is the reason why they are so ready at managing their limbs. [I am not] saying that all animals understand the definition of their constitution rather than the constitution itself. Nature is more easily understood than explained. And so [the newborn] does not know what a constitution is[,] yet knows its own constitution; and it does not know what an animal is[,] yet is aware of being an animal. . . . [An animal] is aware that it is constituted of flesh."[75]

These are the most remarkable lines by Seneca; they describe for us today also the openness of the world brought about by animality and our participation in this mode of being from which nothing must make us recoil. The animal does not "know," certainly, but there is nothing to say that it does not possess any knowledge; rather the contrary. What it knows is not the reflective consciousness of its own body, and this is what places it most often at a distance from ourselves. The animal experiences or knows simply—but importantly, even essentially—the immediate sensation of its own constitution, its fleshly mode of being by which it feels what is appropriate for its own preservation. Most often, natural catastrophes (e.g., great floods and tsunamis, volcanic eruption, collapse of walls) affect humans before animals. And if this is so, it indicates that it is the body's knowledge that counts rather the conscious certitudes of thought. It is thus paradoxically through "interpreting" that humankind no longer knows what it means "to feel" (*sentire, intellegere*). What the newborn needs, according to Seneca, and in this analysis the most up-to-date paediatrics would corroborate his thought, is not to know what an animal "is," but to share the feeling of "being an animal"—not in the sense that it might be below humans, but insofar as it is "aware that it is constituted of flesh [*sentit se carne constare*]." The *knowledge of the flesh* is not a knowledge that knows itself; it is one that feels itself—from the cry of hunger to the tears of the abandoned. There is in the animal (even in the newborn child, which can progressively forget it as it comes to reason) an affinity with itself, or a familiarity with its body. It is there that we live as our proper dwelling (*oikeiôsis*) and nature has given us each thing "as what is fitting [*homologia*]": sucking for feeding at the breast, crying for demanding attention, groaning for our complaints, excitement for rejoicing.[76] In short, the body that is given to me belongs first of all to the sphere of animality, and we forget this too quickly in proclaiming that "the human body is something essentially other than an animal organism," for the simple reason that he knows he *is*, not simply that he *lives*.[77]

Humankind as metaphysical animals—or the metaphysics of the human animal—do not then (or do not only) spring from "knowledge of death and along with this the consideration of the suffering and misery of life,"[78] nor the "ecstatic projection" into "the Da-sein."[79] Instead, humankind finds its meaning, its *raison d'être*, in the possibility for man of being in the world through his flesh, of enjoying the "precious feeling" of being-there, and of nourishing ourselves on an "empathy" and "interpenetration" of different worlds, by which we enlarge our communal space to all living creatures.[80]

All this will be readily understood by anyone who has grasped what the act of communion with the eucharisticized body signifies mystically. In making himself flesh, the Word certainly espoused *our* flesh, and exclusively ours, risking on the other hand that we might fall into those errors that we have always wished to denounce (see the just condemnation of the Council in Trullo). But it is still the case that this flesh—our flesh—brings out our animality, not in the sense of bestiality (§13), but in the closeness to our own bodies that the words with which we speak (language), and the multiplication of the meanings of the signifier (hermeneutics), have often made us forget. The immediacy of self to self, or indeed to the other or to God, is not something to be feared, nor even to be avoided, if it comes from, and is established in, the empathy of an encounter between the living creatures whom we expect to share their different worlds. The *intentional animal* in this encounter of worlds is also a *driven animal* in the closeness of animality and drive that we find in Husserl.[81] The terminological connivance in the German language of drive (*Trieb*) and animal (*Tier*), as we have already seen (§4), is at the very least an indication that we should proceed in this direction.[82] If Chaos or Tohu-Bohu are the names of the opening to (as well as the darkness of) that part of ourselves that we find difficult to accept (§2), we need to think, or believe, that the Word incarnate descended as far as that great opening of *our* passions and *our* drives to the Paschal Triduum (the three days of Easter)—not to wip. them out, but to convert them to a new mode of being that satisfies our filiation, or that is the solemn offering of our creative being. Such is, as I see it, the deeper sense of the wedding feast, in this eucharistic body-to-body of the Wedding Feast of the Lamb, in which the espousals require our acceptance while we transcend the lonely space of our singularity: "We must create a space for the eucharistic Saviour in our lives, so that he can convert our life into his life," writes Edith Stein, the inheritor in this respect of Husserlian empathy. "To live the eucharist means imperceptibly to leave the *narrowness* of one's own life to be born to the *immensity* of the love of Christ."[83]

5

Return to the Organic

From "The Animal That Thus I Am" (Chapter 4), or rather from the animality in myself that is called upon to be subsumed and converted in the
act of the eucharist, we return to the organic, to this *bodying life* that we
have already seen in the Kantian "mass of sensations" and in organs of the
body as the site of drives (§4).[1] The organic, however, this time does not
point simply to the *manner*, but to the *matter*, the organicity (or ensemble
of phenomena associated with the organ), as well as the materiality (organic
matter). It is not enough to account for the organic by saying that bodily
organs derive from the necessities of life (the hand as the effect of the need
to take something, for instance); rather, we could say that life derives from
the organ (the hand as cause of our prehensile grasping or seizing). Our
animality, as I have already suggested, is not primarily this organicity, this
ensemble of phenomena, or the organization of a machine. On the contrary, animality is the mark of our interior Chaos of feelings, that accumu-
lation of passions and drives that ensures we open up the world by the
body rather than by the consciousness—by the animal (far from being
beast) rather than by the angel (which could then seem foolish). The organicity of the animal, as of our own bodies, comes first from its materiality
as subject to decay (putrefaction), even though, while living, it is nourished
by breath, or by "thrust" (*poussée*) (§13).

    Der Leib Christi—"the body of Christ" in German (as the *soma Chris-
tou* in Greek, or the *Corpus Christi* in Latin) sends us back in this sense
also, but not solely in this sense, to the organic *flesh*, and to the indigna-

tion that it excites in being given us to eat, indeed to chew (*trôgon*) (§25). "Take and eat; this is my body"; *Nehmet und esset, das ist main Leib.* As we have seen from the start of this book (§1), the *Leib* here points to the origin, at least in contemporary German, in an "intermediary flesh"—not simply objective (positivist interpretation of *Körper*), nor simply subjective (phenomenological interpretation of *Leib*). The belly (*nichts in Leibe haben* [to be starving, have nothing in the belly]); the breast, or womb (*gesegneten Leibes sein* [to be pregnant, to be great with child]); to be "burned alive" (*bei lebendigem Leiber verbrannt*): all of these start off etymologically from *life* (*vie* in French, *lip* in Middle High German), which means that in giving us "his flesh to eat" (John 6:52), or rather his "body" (Mark 14:22), everything is given—up to and including the biological part of his being: "What we call *flesh* (*chair*) in French describes exactly the same phenomenon as *Leib* in German (but not this time simply in the orbit of the phenomenological lived experience): the astonishing enigma of the interaction of the vital organs, the tissues, the skin, the epidermis and the environment—that is to say: the circles of reaction which bring together all these layers as one flesh, soluble and separable only after death."[2]

Such a concept of "flesh"—if we continue to translate *Leib* in this way, sending us back first of all and essentially to the organic, as in Nietzsche, and in opposition to phenomenology at its most radical (Michel Henry, in particular)—could have little bearing on what is suggested to us by the Bible. This is often argued in order to underline that the body we eat—"The body of Christ. *Amen*"—is *not finally the body*, or at least not the body as we understand it; this argument is justified in part, but it does not exempt us from reflection on what the body is, today as in the past, when we say, understand, and indeed *chew* and digest what we do nonetheless call the "body of Christ" (§26). The "flesh" (*basar*), which becomes *sarx* in the Septuagint and *caro* in the Vulgate ("bone of my bones and flesh of my flesh" [Gen. 2:23]), sends us back, first of all in scriptural terms, to the biological aspect of human existence, even if it does not reduce things to this aspect. Thus we read of (1) the prophet Ezekiel, who sees humanity as "dry bones" (Ezek. 37:4); (2) the prophet Isaiah, who sees such decay in the flesh (Isa. 40); and (3) the Teacher (or Qoheleth) of Ecclesiastes, who recognizes in the vanity of the corruptible the site of community between humanity and animality (Eccl. 3).

(1) The apocalyptic scene of the Valley of Dry Bones described by the prophet Ezekiel is enough to rival all other scenarios of days without a tomorrow promising an auto-destruction of humanity: "The hand of the Lord came upon me, and he brought me out by the spirit of the Lord, and set me down in the middle of a valley; it was full of bones. He led me all

around them; there were very many lying in the valley, and they were very dry" (Ezek. 37:1–3). We must, however, be careful here. This is a long way from those myths of the great cemeteries of Pachydermata and valleys of tears that can be found (at least in imagination) in many regions of the world. It is rather the misery of a whole people that has struck Israel, since they have neglected to bury "with their fathers" those who have been entrusted to them by God. But the *life-less* here speak to us (we can say at the same time, and as a kind of aftershock) of what is also alive, at least when understood in terms of the organic, or organicity: "I will lay sinews upon you, and will cause flesh to come upon you, and cover you with skin, and put breath in you, and you shall live" (Ezek. 37:6). It has repeatedly been claimed, according to a formulaic exegesis that is, while not entirely incorrect at least inadequate, that "flesh" in the Hebrew world designates the whole of a human being in our corporal and spiritual being (*basar*). But this leads us to forget how much, in the Jewish world at least, the materiality of the body precedes and gives sense to the breathing in—the insufflation—so that the biological cannot be forgotten in the raising up, mystical and political, of the whole army of Israel. The Bible does not aspire to be a treatise on anatomy, but corporality is defined as an ensemble of organic tissues given life (bones, nerves, flesh, skin). And the destiny of decay or putrescence will be seen as the most common end (a perspective of death as, first of all, natural and, moreover, never denied at the height of the Jewish tradition.)[3]

(2) Thus we find a notorious vulnerability of the body and the flesh that is only too often repeated. Again, we must be cautious here. The "flesh" in the Bible (*basar*) is not simply a source of weakness or the exposure of the self to another, despite what seems to be affirmed in a certain naive reading of the biblical corpus and is found also in certain phenomenological texts (Levinas's *Totality and Infinity*, for example). The flesh, if it is to appear, is also and above all bound to disappear. There, again, the organic takes the leading role. According to the history of the people of Israel, and at least for the Jewish mentality, nothing can ensure that a human being will be an "empire in an empire" (Spinoza) and will escape into the *conatus* (the innate inclination to continue to exist and enhance oneself) apart from the divine *logos*. Nothing apart from the divine *logos* will ratify our efforts to persevere in our being, according to the most ordinary law of entropy: "The grass withers, the flower fades; but the word of our God will stand forever" (Isa. 40:8).

(3) The sharing of the organic, indeed the communality of organicity, is paradoxically the basis of the communality of animality that the Bible in reality never denies. It is precisely because of this organicity that the

man of the book Ecclesiastes, Qoheleth, in one of the most astonishing passages in the whole biblical corpus, comes to doubt his own advantages over animals, albeit in the context of the reward of sin: "I said in my heart with regard to human beings that God is testing them to show that they are but animals. For the fate of humans and the fate of animals is the same; as one dies, so dies the other. They all have the same breath, and humans have no advantage over the animals; for all is vanity. All go to one place; all are from the dust, and all turn to dust again" (Eccl. 3:18–20).

I cannot overemphasize how much this text of Qoheleth, or the Book of Ecclesiastes, supports and confirms the perspective that I aim to develop in this book. Certainly human beings have the advantage—or, as the French translation says, "a superiority"—over animals that the Bible quite rightly never contests, at least insofar as the face-to-face in sexual relations (*ish-ishah*). However, human and beast, or rather human and animal, are equal *in via* [in this life] with regard to vanity or worthlessness. Death is a destiny before being "a possibility-of-Being that Dasein itself has to take over in every case."[4] Coming in fact from a "foreign sphere," an obvious limit that is in opposition to authentic *Dasein*, death appears "as it were introduced from outside our existence." The dust of which humankind is made is also the dust of the animal, and the "death of man is originally parallel to the death of a beast."[5] It is difficult to reduce ourselves to this, particularly because the final message of the Teacher, or Qoheleth, in Ecclesiastes (formerly supposed to represent the Wisdom of Solomon) is not easy to grasp. If God gives the Sons of Adam a task at which to labor, he also judges or differentiates them. And if he differentiates them, he sees what they are, or have become: "Brute beasts they are to each other" (Eccl. 3:18 [JB]). This is entirely ambiguous, joining together what has importantly been distinguished as animality and bestiality (§13). Qoheleth the Teacher does not lament being animal, but laments the possibility for him of simply remaining in the animal state: "In showing that man, by his death has no 'advantages' over the beasts, because all is vanity, Qoheleth sees the dramatic gravity of the human condition. The perspective of death, seen as a return of all to dust and a silencing of breath, brings us back to the beginning, there where the meaning of humankind was decided, there also where the human condition was marked out as what appeared to be a condition with meaning. Qoheleth's discourse seems to point to a moment where one cannot come to terms with such a death."[6]

In short, what appears as a test for a human being when someone becomes conscious of this state of affairs—when one is indistinguishable in the face of death from the animal, even from the beast—becomes suddenly a test for God, in that humankind is more, and is worth more, than the animal. But this value only resides, as far as Christianity under-stands it, in the *this is my body* of the Son of Man tied up with the *this is our body* of ourselves, sons of humankind, taking it and changing it into a full humanity that recognizes itself this time in its creation and its filia-tion. Flesh is certainly organic, but its matter (organic) and its organicity (functional) are in some way called upon to be saved, according to a form of incarnation that this time (against all Gnostic tendencies) does not scorn the materiality of which we are universally constituted. "To provide a *theology of matter*," Marie-Dominique Chenu pointed out after Vatican II (*Gaudium et spes*), and following Henri de Lubac (*Corpus mysticum*), "we need to envisage even before the substantial place of matter in mankind, the cosmic and ontologic density of matter in the total project of the cre-ative emanation. It is not possible to construct a theology of man without a theology of nature, just as it is impossible to separate a theology of the Word incarnate from a theology of the Word as creator."[7]

If birth, then, or the Resurrection, can consecrate the passage of the body to the flesh, or the materiality of the corpse to lived bodily experi-ence, in that we live "waiting for bodies to arise" (*Metamorphosis of Fini-tude*), reflection on the body or the eucharist leads us in an opposite direction, climbing again from the flesh to the body. Reflection in this direction leads us to implant or root the whole of bodily lived experience in the organic body and the Chaos of our passions and drives. This bodily lived experience is summoned to be accepted and transformed in the act of the eucharist. And so, we come back, philosophically and theologically, in contrast to a contemporary trend that tends to flee the organic body in the name of the supremacy of the aesthetic body, to that organic nature of which we are also constituted and that makes for the density—so often denied—of our humanity.[8]

§17. What the Body Can Do

Human in our corporality, organic and thus mortal, we cannot however be satisfied with such inconsequence—with the inconsequence that leads toward our own destruction and putrefaction. If the compost of our exis-tences is a destiny that none of us will be able to avoid, all living flesh, and thus all humankind insofar as we are corporal and living, wants and can find more than death: humankind fights against death. In line with ordi-nary biological law, humankind also *struggles for life*, not simply in our social relations (the hierarchy of class and individuals), but also and most obviously in an internal struggle with our own corporality (viruses, microbes, infections, secretions, digestion, and so on). All living beings pose their strength against an admission of the weakness of their bodies, although this will finally be conquered from the outside, even in its willingness to endure or its power to stay in place. "Everything, insofar as it is in itself, endeavours to persist in its own being [*in suo ess persevare conatur*]."[9] The innate inclination to continue to exist (*conatus*) does not come from the order of the spirit supposed to dominate the body; that would indicate a certain dualism of mind and body that we now need to avoid definitively. The inclination derives from the mind and the body at the same time, but in a privileged way from the body, once we mention what Spinoza calls the "Affections" (*Affectus*): "The *modifications of the body*, whereby the active power of the said body is increased or diminished, aided or constrained, and also the idea of such modifications."[10]

The relevant question is not whether or not I experience these affections, because I always do (feelings of joy and sadness, for example). It is, rather, one of the *origin* of affect (mind or body). We can experience joy or sadness, for example, but nothing tells us that such a feeling is psychic before being bodily, without reducing it to a simple biochemical process (neurobiology). The original contribution of Spinoza here—that of attributing the origin of the "affections" to the body rather than to the mind—does not entail a denial of mind, or of thought, but shows instead that by *the process of my body* I can also enlarge the range of my thought. In other words, and according to a fundamental choice as far as the meaning and solidity of my own incarnation is concerned, the multiplication of intercorporal relations (society, love, friendship, travel . . .) will make the sphere of my thought grow larger (the field of possibilities): "The mind is not at all times equally fit for thinking on a given subject, but according as the body is more or less fitted."[11]

It is thus actively and not simply passively that one experiences the emotions—not in controlling them, but in understanding; that is to say, in accompanying them, with thoughts that follow from their nature and their truth: "Besides pleasure and desire, which are passivities or passions, there are other emotions [affections] derived from pleasure and desire, which are attributable to us insofar as we are *active*."[12] Despite the well-known complexity of Spinoza's system, the aim is clear: the enlarged treatment of the body, and of the relation of one's body to other bodies, produces a veritable *community of bodies,* which becomes at the same time a *community of thought* (doctrine of the parallelism of mind and body). We should not neglect the important "Nietzsche-Spinoza identity," though at the same time, the two perspectives are not to be totally confused (the bliss of the sage on the one hand, the overcoming of self of the Overhuman on the other). What "makes us stronger as far as Nietzsche is concerned" is also

"that which develops our power to affect and to be affected for Spinoza."
And "all those things that give joy to Spinoza" can be identified with "all
those things that make us dance in Nietzsche."[13]

Starting from Spinoza, a line of thought based on the *strength of the
body* was born, and it is one that theology needs to take into account. The
this is my body of the eucharistic act demonstrates in fact a power of the
body (of Christ) offered to one's own body (of a disciple) that the believer
receives at the moment of communicating and being integrated into the
body of a community, otherwise known as the Church, or *Ecclesia* (§30).
We would reach a dead end if we reduced "transubstantiation" simply to a
form of reification and forgot the "nuclear fission" produced by the consecration and the eating of the eucharistic body, as a "change meant to set
off a process which transforms reality."[14]

But what is it that the body we have so thoroughly forgotten can do?
This is a question both for the philosopher concerned with the human
body and for the theologian of the body of Christ, at least as far as God
was made man. In reality, we hardly know: "*No one has hitherto laid down
the limits [of what the body can do].* . . . No one hitherto has gained such an
accurate knowledge of the bodily mechanism, that he can explain all its
functions, nor need I call attention to the fact that many actions are
observed in the lower animals, which far transcend human sagacity."[15] As
far as corporality is concerned, Spinoza moves in the same way back toward
animality. It is probably Spinoza who has best understood the basis of all
organic living things: that the animal is precisely a *body without consciousness* (§13), that the animal holds on to that pure condition in order to
persist in its own being (*conatus*). Spinoza's ideal project was not simply to
acknowledge the part played by passions and drives, but also to understand them. What the body can do concerns human beings first of all and
above all, in that to understand is not to abstract or detach oneself from
the problem, but precisely to undo the Platonic or the mistaken Christian
perspective, which has become so customary. The example of the som-
nambulist is important in Spinoza's demonstration, allowing us to see the
power we can often have by our body alone. We see from it that we cannot
grasp with the mind alone, or with the mind simply accompanied by the
body. Spinoza points out that "somnambulists do many things in their
sleep, which they would not venture to do when awake: these instances are
enough to show, that the body can by the sole law of its nature do many
things which the mind wonders at" (e.g., keeping their balance when they
might otherwise suffer from vertigo, clambering over immense obstacles,
covering vast distances).[16] In short, it is useful here to turn around our
aim, to change our point of view. What is most wonderful "is the body,"

Nietzsche comments. Not the consciousness; that "is only an instrument and nothing more." The body in Spinoza (corpus), and the flesh in Nietzsche (*Leib*, in the sense of the vibration of the organic rather than the simple phenomenological lived experience), are seen as truly "marvellous." They are the "miracle of miracles" in coherence as well as in prominence: "The splendid cohesion of living things, the way in which their superior and inferior activities adjust and integrate one with another, the multiform conformity, not in a blind way and even less in a mechanical way, but critically, prudently, carefully even in a rebellious fashion—all this phenomenon of the body [*Leib*] is, from the intellectual point of view, superior to our consciousness, our spirit, our conscious ways of thinking, feeling and willing, as algebra is superior to the multiplication tables."[17]

There is, then, an "unknown of the body" (Spinoza), even an "unconscious of the body" (Nietzsche), that in reality goes far beyond the "psychic unconscious" (Freud). What our bodies "can do" is better than our consciousness. "The great principal activity (that of organisms) is unconscious," Nietzsche, the precursor here, insists. "Consciousness of myself is superfluous. . . . Wherever the adaptation of means to ends is excellent, we no longer have consciousness of means and ends. The artist and the work of art, the mother and child—and likewise if I observe myself chewing, digesting, walking etc., the economy of my forces during a day etc.,—And all that is *unconscious*."[18] It couldn't be said better. It is an error, or at least an incorrect view, to (1) understand this "unconscious of the body" as a simple *inversion* of the couple that make up mind and body (Heidegger) and (2) try still, and always, to *orient* things toward the conscious (Freud).

(1) According to Heidegger, "Nietzsche adopts Descartes' fundamental position completely," simply putting the mind in the place of the body.[19] This is a misinterpretation that silences any philosopher who hopes to do justice to the power of the body as it is envisaged by the thinker of Chaos and the Overhuman. The body in Nietzsche (in contrast to Spinoza at this point) is no longer substance—or substance instead of, or to be identified with, another substance (*Deus sive natura*). The Nietzschean concept of "flesh" (*Leib*) introduces a concept differentiated from the "living body" or the "organic body" that definitively escapes duality, even that of the terms themselves (mind-body), and recovers the power of a biological life that had been laid aside. My body is then *unconscious*. We could even say that it is principally so. But all our "body to body" contact, and the truth of all fleshly or corporal expressivity, is based on the form of this unconscious of the body: the "artist and the work of art," the "mother and child," certainly—but perhaps also (and especially) for the believer, the *this is my body* of Christ in the eucharist. In this case, as in all of these cases, it is a

question not of introducing a new preeminence (of the body over the mind, for example), but of thinking in *corporal terms,* and almost in organic terms, of the nexus, or the bonds, among the whole of living beings, by which they are constituted in their bodies and deploy their corporality.[20]

(2) Moreover, the philosophy of a "power deployed by the body" cannot simply turn to the psychic unconscious; that would be tantamount to forgetting its somatic roots (Freud). The following are three reasons that we need not develop such an approach:

(a) There is no doubt that Nietzsche is concerned with the psychosomatic, whether he is talking about bodily symptoms in the psyche or the influx of the corporal over the spiritual. The psychic is second and the somatic first. It is not that the psychic can be reduced to chemical processes (neurobiology), but that the somatic actually and truly distinguishes our activities, whether or not the "unconscious of the body" shifts to the sphere of consciousness.

(b) No particular topos, no fixed point of origin, can be attributed to the somatic. To do so would risk an arbitrary substantializing of the various disorganized drives at the center of a libido. The power of the body has no center and is organized independently of the self—almost without the self. Paradoxically, as far as I am concerned, I myself am often the greatest obstacle to the deployment of the differentiated power of my own body.

(c) There is no orientation fixed *a priori* to the body so that it is not at the mercy of an unconscious life that necessarily finds its completion in consciousness (even when the unconscious has been repressed). Certain topics can destroy what they were supposed to be looking at if we try to schematize or fix them too thoroughly—not simply for the well-being of the conscious life, but also for the expression of unconscious activity.[21]

Not psychic then, but essentially somatic: the Nietzschean "unconscious of the body" is not a seeking to know, nor even a seeking to know itself. By dint of speaking of the bodily unconscious, one can in fact silence through excess of consciousness that which lives in its own way, and convert into the language of causality that which is actually only something carried out: "Mastication, digestion, walking, the economy of my forces during the day etc." A learned ignorance supports and nourishes such an "unconscious of the body." We must be very careful not to subsume it into something else, in case we destroy through consciousness that body-to-body in which we are engaged. "It is not enough for you to recognize in what state of ignorance animals and men live," Nietzsche says. "You need to will to ignore it and learn more. You need to understand that without this kind of special ignorance life itself would be impossible, that it is a condition without which the living would not be able to preserve themselves or to prosper."[22]

Not knowing what the body can do—to return to Spinoza—we do not even try to find out, because we can never truly know, and because knowing it could lead to the destruction of its power. There is no choice but to live it and to let it express itself as such, even if sometimes this just means letting it be, or at the very least letting it do what it does. There is a "force immanent in life," or an "instinct" in "intelligence," much more essential than "intelligence" in "instinct," as Henri Bergson reminds us in his *Creative Evolution*.[23]

Perhaps this is also what we have forgotten even in the act of the eucharist. If "we are nourished by the Body and Blood" of Christ, according to the Eucharistic Prayer, it is not simply because a banquet or a meal has brought us together (a symbolic perspective that can be justified but that seems a bit threadbare today). The bread is consecrated bread, his body branched into ours so that we "become one body"; the wine is consecrated, his blood flowing in our veins. To be nourished with his body can and should be understood as a kind of organic transplant—a sharing of powers (the body) by which I live through his true corporal power, in the way of a community of life, even a transfusion of blood: "It is no longer I who live, but it is Christ who lives in me" (Gal. 2:20). The bodily, in the organic and Nietzschean sense of the term (*Leib*), brings us back to the spiritual. Far from fleeing it or opposing it, the body constitutes its most fundamental base, justifying that Christ should have also been incarnate to give meaning to and metamorphose it (§29). The following questions then arise: Is a return to the organic simply recourse to the biological, to a kind of organicism? Or—and putting it this time in terms of our theological project—is it enough to say (like Tertullian) that Word made flesh has "a body" like us, "muscles" like us, a "head of hair" like us, and "bone marrow" like us to demonstrate the "human reality of a body" like ours?[24] In short, is the "human substance of the body" (*humana substantia corporis*) all we need to make up the human, even when it is a question of the divine? Nothing could be less certain, for the following reasons:

(1) First, such a philosophy of the power of the body cannot be satisfied with what *is* (Aquinas), nor what *should be* (Kant), nor what *appears to be* (Husserl), but only with "what comes to be" (Nietzsche). That is the difference, as we have already seen, between Nietzsche and Spinoza, definitively marking the departure of modern philosophy from the substantialist model of the classical age. Nietzsche, in what is in effect a confrontation with Spinoza, says, "Nothing is more false than to make psychic and physical

phenomena two faces, or two manifestations, of the same substance." He tells us that "Nothing is explained in this way: the concept of 'substance' is completely useless when it is a question of explanation."[25] One could certainly regret this, even be disturbed by it, since the act of the eucharist does depend upon "transubstantiation." To affirm that "the idea of the real in itself is an ass' idea," in relying on Nietzsche, would seem to destroy the basis of what remains in transubstantiation, indeed, of the so-called "real" presence.[26] I shall come back to this later (§29). There is no "real presence" except when it is "brought to reality," and no transubstantiation except where there is the act (of being) and of being transubstantiated. It is only when Christ "becomes" his body that we "become" it also. And it is in this sharing of the body, as of its forces, that we can speak of the common becoming of humankind and God in the eucharisticized body. "Become the body of Christ" says the liturgy (of the Abbey of Sylvanés), "and eat at his immortal Passover. . . . Become the blood of Christ and drink at his immortal cup."[27]

(2) Second, it is not simply in adding spirituality to a human or animal corporality already incarnate that corporality shows its creativity. The organic can always rise to a higher level, according Nietzsche; it is not that humankind is satisfied with chemistry or a metabolism in ourselves that we cannot change. Yet simple "adjustment," or "adaptation," of the living necessitated by the biology in whose midst we evolve cannot demand of us the *power* to which we are destined. The famous "will to power" is in reality the power of the will not to "adapt itself" (which would be a misreading) nor to "dominate everything" (which would be an over-reading), but to imitate and follow the true *internal power of life* in its capacity to create forms, to seek new modalities for its existence, and to be *always becoming* so as never to remain definitively fixed:

> The democratic idiosyncrasy which opposes everything that dominates and wants to dominate . . . has acquired the *right* to force its way into the strictest, apparently most objective sciences; indeed, it seems to me to have already taken charge of all physiology and theory of life—to the detriment of life, as goes without saying, since it has robbed it of a fundamental concept, that of *activity.* . . . Life itself has been defined as a more and more efficient inner adaptation to external conditions (Herbert Spencer). Thus the essence of life, its *will to power*, is ignored; one overlooks the essential priority of the spontaneous, aggressive, expansive, form-giving forces that give new interpretations and directions.[28]

We know then, or at least we feel, according to a fundamental turn taken in the history of philosophy as well as (probably) in theology, that bodies derive from forces or powers—not forces or powers from bodies. It is not substance that exercises power, but first power, which then locates itself in substance. I have already tried to show that the Resurrection does not spring from the substance of the body of the Resurrected One, but the substance of the body of the Resurrected One from the power of the Resurrection (the force of the Holy Spirit under the impulse of the Father in the Son.)[29] This present book also aims to show this (§29). The real presence does not derive from the substance of the body reified; the substance of the body reifies the real presence. That is, we go from "the realization of force in the body," or the "act of body-making (corporization)", of Christ on Holy Thursday to the bread that is eucharisticized. *This is my body* does not make the body into a *this*, but the *this* itself can be read as the token of an "actuation" (putting into action) and transformation of a power that seeks to be incarnate and to be incorporate (the Holy Spirit in the incarnate Word, and the incarnate Word in the eucharistic bread). The power of God paradoxically seeks a body, in that He also, primarily, is defined principally as the *power of the will*—certainly to save us from straying from the straight and narrow, or from sin (in a perspective that is bestiality's role to envisage [§13]), but also to be incorporate for us, in the most simple organic matter of the eucharistic bread. The priest preparing the Holy Communion says, in a low voice, "May the receiving of your Body and Blood, Lord Jesus Christ, not bring me to judgment and condemnation, but through your loving mercy be a *protection in mind and body* and a healing remedy."[30]

It should be evident, then, even to those who might have doubted it, that the true weakness of the Christian comes not from a renunciation of power (the power of the body, in particular); that is a mistranslation of a false idea of power that is mistakenly denounced by Nietzsche. Rather, it comes from entrusting power to another (the Holy Spirit in him) so that *his* power, even *his* energy, is fulfilled in us. We read, in the incident of the woman with hemorrhages, that Jesus was "Immediately aware that power [*dunamis*] had gone forth from him" (Mark 5:30). And St. Paul, in the Letter to the Ephesians, speaks of "the immeasurable greatness of his power [*uperballon megethos tês dunameôs*] for us who believe . . . his great power [*kratous tês ischmos*]. . . . God put this power to work in Christ when he raised him from the dead" (Eph. 1:19–20).

It is apparent that the Word incarnate, transubstantiated in the eucharist and raised in the Resurrection, would find nothing to envy in Nietzsche's

Zarathustra, who comes down from the mountain to preach a new message. Dionysus and Christ are not the same (see §25). But there are points of comparison between the one and the other: in the design that reaches into Chaos; in the driven and emotional opening up of our existence. On the one side, however, the design is to be suffered tragically (the eternal return); on the other, it is to be metamorphosed joyously (the resurrection of the body). "I say to you: one must still have chaos within, in order to give birth to a dancing star. I say to you: you have this *chaos within you*."[31]

§18. Manifesto of the Flesh

With the introduction of the word "flesh," (*chair* in French), we may think we have finally arrived somewhere, quitting the raging seas of corporality (organic and creating) to reach the banks of the quiet life (auto-affective). But, as I have already pointed out (§1), and as we shall see again when the question comes up of escaping from animality in sexual intercourse (§21), the "charms of the toucher-touched" have their merits but also their limits. Because overcoming them, or no longer being contented with them, means trying to reach the depths of what a "fleshly experience" could really mean, when understood as embodiedness radically incarnate or, indeed, seen in biological terms. The "manifesto of the flesh" is not here a matter of appearance (phenomenology) but a confirmation, or at least a claim—such as one shows for the flesh, or "meters" in "the nerves." For Antonin Artaud (and his Nerve Meter [*pèse-nerfs*]), in fact, the Nietzschean physiology of the body is not something that is simply lived; it is experienced, outlined, analyzed, and dissected, so that it also comes to express itself in the most prosaic fashion possible in its true nature: "I believe only in the evidence of what stirs in my marrow, not in the evidence of what addresses itself in my reason," Artaud confides to his friend Roger Vitrac in a *Manifesto in Clear Language* that is also a manifesto of the flesh. "I have found levels in the realm of the nerve. I now feel capable of evaluating the evidence. There is for me an [obviousness] in the realm of pure flesh which has nothing to do with the [obviousness] of reason. . . . My lucid unreason is not afraid of chaos."[32]

We live in *the realm of the nerve*; this is where we recover the lucidity of Chaos (§2); or we could say we weigh up (we meter) the nerve through our pure flesh (§18). All of this is what constitutes the organic in our humanity; we hardly dare to confront it, but we are continually brought back to it: "But whatever I have been able to make of my life," Artaud protests, in a kind of passion that is almost Christ-like, "it has not stopped me gently re-penetrating into my own being, and settling myself there a bit more firmly every day."[33]

The body "spreads forth," as we have seen (§1), more than it extends or stretches out or experiences itself. To repenetrate one's own being is not simply to be incorporated into a physical or objective body (*Körper*), nor to be incarnate in a phenomenological or subjective flesh (*Leib*), but rather to "*se corporéiser*" (roughly, to be embodied). Barbara Stiegler uses what she calls "the inelegant neologism '*corporéisation* [the embodying]'" in order "to express in a single word this mutation of the *thinking subject* into the *living body*."[34] This leads us in turn to the "embodiedness" that is characteristic of the living body—embodied in an organic flesh made up of nerves, muscles, digestion, secretion, respiration, . . . things that can, like so much of *this is my body*, remain foreign to me if I am not fully able to make them my own: "What is characteristic of the *Leib* (in the organic sense) in connection with *Körper* (in the objective sense) is that it nourishes itself and that it digests: that it assimilates, that it makes identical [*ad-similare*], that it brings us back to the same."[35] The patient confined to his hospital bed knows this, as we see in hospices that are only too full, and as we easily forget: the suffering body becomes nothing more than a body spread out on a bed, concerned with enduring suffering. My body weighs on me, not in that it is first of all mine, but in that sickness makes it so difficult to see it as really mine, though I have to continue with it all the same—I have no option but to put up with it. Judging by our propensity to accidents, to ageing, to senility, the sick person sees himself eaten away as far as his organicity is concerned. Only those who have not yet endured all this can deny it: "I am human by my hands and my feet, my guts, my meat heart, my stomach whose knots fasten me to the rot of life."[36]

What Artaud says in this context is not simply an acknowledgment, not simply something poeticized, but clearly something conceptualized. "On November 28, 1947," Deleuze writes, "Artaud declares war on the organs."[37] Like Nietzsche, and like Bergson later on, Artaud will not be, or will no longer be, content with organs, or more simply with the organism. The organ, in effect, kills life because it holds or restrains it in one function; it is as though the functional, or the neuronal, could be sufficient to define us: the grasp for the hand, digestion for the stomach, respiration for the lungs, thought for the brain, and so on. To reach the radicality of a "manifesto of the flesh" and the truly "embodying" sense of *this is my body* we can turn to the famous hypothesis of a "body without organs" (Artaud, Deleuze). This hypothesis is not that of a body stripped of its organs; on the contrary, it is that of a "body that is this side of organic determination, a body that is becoming."[38] In other words—mine, this time—if the hypothesis is a return to the organic on the basis of the power of the body (Spinoza, Nietzsche; §17), and of the manifesto of the flesh (Artaud), it suggests that it is not enough for biological life to be exploited and expressed with and by the organs. Chaos or Tohu-Bohu is the opening of our existence, certainly (§2), but in wanting it to be too "cosm-etic"—that is, organized into a world (*cosmos*), as also into the beautiful (*cosmetic* products), we come all at once to conceal the world, to disguise it in makeup, even to forget it. I warned earlier—and it is appropriate to remember this now, so that we don't redo what has so far been undoing—that Chaos is where we come from, not simply what is there (§2), at least as Hesiod described it (Chaos) or as we find in the book of Genesis (Tohu-Bohu). As we saw, Chaos engenders nothing, yet it is the base on which all will be engendered (§2). Beneath organs, then, but not in opposition to them, we find the "body without organs." And in the body "dis-organized," the organic takes on its role, as it were, in a mass made up of "pressures," or "passions," and of "drives," where the power of life is expressed without being immediately integrated or technicized. The "body without organs" is neither the lived body (phenomenology) nor the extended body (positivism), but it uncovers to some degree what my description of the body "spread out" was seeking (§1). "Beyond the organism [biological positivism?], but also at the limit of the lived body [phenomenology?], there lies what Artaud discovered and named: the body without organs."[39]

The real embodiedness—a movement from thinking subject to the living body—when the organic shows itself or is confirmed, is not primarily embodiedness of a *self* capable of auto-affection (Michel Henry); it is, rather, of a *non-self*, something in relation to which one becomes, paradoxically, the powerless, even the disinterested, spectator: "I know myself because I watch myself, I watch Antonin Artaud."[40]

One could certainly talk of schizophrenia here, or of a doubling of the personality—without doubt the diagnosis that was once made of the poet (as with Nietzsche and Van Gogh, both similarly confined for medical reasons). All the same, it is in experience at the limits that we find our limits. The disconnection between self and self in illness can make us strangers to ourselves; the "nerve meter" that is unbearable for us is no less unbearable for others.

Our nearest and dearest know all this. They have difficulty in consoling us when our bodies are affected, and they can appeal to nothing but consciousness, since the Chaos of pure embodiedness is also unliveable for them. Eros itself does not escape from an invincible blockage in the "ultra-materiality" of the body of another (see §21). It is as if some other organicity were always hiding behind experiences of tenderness and the caress, and as if the materializing of the body were the basis of a true alterity. "And yet," Levinas concedes, contrary to all expectations, faced with a lived experience that is, first, spiritualized (the caress), "this extreme fragility [of the Eros] lies also at the limit of an existence 'without ceremonies,' 'without circumlocutions,' a 'non-signifying' and raw density, an exorbitant ultra-materiality. These superlatives, better than metaphors, denote a sort of paroxysm of materiality. . . . [Ultra-materiality] designates the exhibitionist nudity of an exorbitant presence coming as though from farther than the frankness of the face, already profaning and wholly profaned, as if it had forced the interdiction of a secret."[41] We thus make up "one flesh" (Gen. 2:24), as we shall see later (§23), only through the heterogeneity of our different fleshes, indeed, through the opacity of an embodiedness that none of us is in a position fully to fathom.

I should like to show this in terms of painting, and here we need only turn to England—this time toward Lucian Freud rather than Francis Bacon, toward the painter of the density or solidity of the body rather the painter of the movement of the body. Certainly, before Freud there was already something intriguing in Courbet's *Origin of the World*, with its pure density of organic flesh, shown only in its objectivity.[42] But the body in its bulk, such as Lucian Freud makes us see in works from *Naked Girl* (1966) to *Lying by the Rags* (1989)[43], says more than a simple play of forces in embodiedness. It calls up more "embodiedness," as well as animality, in a "hyper-materiality of the flesh" which has probably never been equalled: "I paint people not because of what they are," Lucian Freud says, "nor exactly despite what they are, but *how they happen to be*."[44] The art critic Sebastian Smee comments that Freud "allows us to see the human individual with no trace of sentimentality. . . . Through his work, the flesh and muscle, the weight and the substance, the age and the expression become incarnate on the surface of the canvas. . . . There where Bacon dissolves the features of his models in a convulsive chaos, his friend Lucian Freud swells out the flesh, details the muscles and immobilises his models as though to underline the weight of their existence."[45] From another point of view, the contemporary artist Lydie Arickx shows the organic body open, when the organs definitively lose their function and are only exposed because they contain what is vital, and thus also organic: "The artist lands up in the anatomy demonstration theater of the Faculty of Medicine," writes her friend, the art critic Patrick Grainville;

> Several bodies are there with an élite group of doctors and students, who comment on them, carrying out their daily work. A dissection.

After all, since Rembrandt's days, the same ritual! But what does she see? She sees what she has never seen, what she would never have believed she would see. A mighty revelation. The excess of the open bodies. The entire labyrinth within, the magnificence of what yawns open. The immensity of what rushes toward her. The theater of the thorax, raw, extreme. . . . Her vision penetrates. She sees where this goes in, where that goes out. . . . No cadavers. They are open: they flourish. The flesh swoons in the skeleton made up of bones. She sees death.[46]

Body in movement (Bacon), body in bulk (Freud), and the open body (Arickx): painting moves toward the "incarnating" that philosophy hopes to think through (and theology to recover). The contemporary metamorphosis of art is no longer that of body into flesh—as it would be in a Rembrandt or Roualt of our time—but of flesh into body. It is for us to initiate things, or at least to renew them, in the context of our approach to the eucharistic mystery that is both philosophical and theological. As in Picasso's *Demoiselles d'Avignon* (1907), "the transition from face to mask takes place in a *metamorphosis of the flesh into body.* . . . The question of the flesh, or rather the double question of the *flesh* and the its *incarnation* in painting is reversed by Picasso. In other words, there where most aesthetic attempts try to guarantee a kind of *becoming-flesh of the body*, Picasso looks for the *definitive solidity of the body starting from the flesh.* The question of incarnating is turned around, as the flesh hardens, even stiffens, to become an armour, a sculpture, a fetish."[47]

There is, then, incarnating in art as there is in theology—of the flesh into body this time, and not simply of body into flesh.[48] What the human body "can do" (Spinoza, Nietzsche; §17) becomes what the body of Christ "can or could" do (§29); further, the "manifesto" of the flesh (Artaud, Deleuze, Levinas, Bacon, Lucian Freud, Arickx, Picasso) confirms at the same time the "corporal profundity" of the Son (§30). There is in art, as in philosophy and indeed in theology, a kind of sinking into corporality, after which any other possibility of existence disappears. We should perhaps conclude, along with Ludwig Binswanger, that "*Leib* (in the organic sense of the term) becomes the innermost recess of our being, coming to the limit of an existence turned in on itself. It is an inner recess which by no means gives an impression of ease and intimacy, but which seems like the 'site' of the vital *thrust*, at present disturbing, blind and without aim, that torments, terrifies and makes us anguished."[49] This is the "there" of the "flesh" that God himself in his incarnate Word comes in reality to inhabit, and the "site" also of the Chaos of our own embodiedness that the *this is my body* of the consecrated Host tries to espouse, going so far as to be fully included in it, to be strengthened and narrowed down to it. Although this has often been forgotten, eighteenth-century baroque unceasingly celebrated this site. "It is in this narrow space of the consecrated host [*hujus hostiae strictus angustiae*] that He lives in the midst of us [*nobiscum habitat*], present so that in each one of us remains [*remaneat*] the inexhaustible memory of so much grace."[50]

The Nerve Meter then counts for us, but also for Him, since we are originally constituted of such an embodiedness (Chaos, passion, drives . . .), and our embodiedness does not derive solely from sin. There is at least a sharing between humankind and God, in which Christianity precisely, and from the start, escapes from the confusions of mysticism and Gnosticism. We are never more ourselves than when we conform to, and embrace, the organic character of our bodies that belongs to our created being. Certainly the human is not *only* body, but the human is *first* body—a body in which Christ's incarnation is different from all other forms of angelic apparition.[51]

That is precisely the pact, or the adoption of the body, that the Christian *corporandum* will definitely seal, sharing organicity to some extent with God himself, when flesh is truly inhabited by the divine in the incarnation. As we come to terms with our "spread-out body," the body made up of flesh, of passions and drives—that which becomes incarnate in our body in movement (Bacon), body in bulk (Lucian Freud), or the open body (Arickx)—Christ takes the burden of this embodiedness along with us, and for us. He meets it in the Trinity and stays with it in his filiation (§28).

There is nonetheless a turn—in this study, certainly, but also in the transition from the corporal to the carnal, or the organic to the phenomenological. If the "power of the body" (§17) and the "manifesto of the flesh" remain undoubtedly the basis on which embodiedness is shown, we might still wonder whether the *conatus* (Spinoza), the creative will (Nietzsche), the Nerve Meter (Artaud), or the body without organs (Deleuze) say all that we need to say about embodiedness. Because, if Christ in his Resurrection appeared in "flesh and bones" (*sarxa kait ostea*) in the sight of and the understanding of his disciples (Luke 24:39), such an apparition does not signify, retrospectively, that he will be there in the consecrated Host with this "flesh" or with these "bones"—as though something physical, even anatomical, or of the cadaver, were to be chewed or crunched (§27). It would seem appropriate here to follow in the footsteps of a long tradition—eucharistic as well as phenomenological—that tells us Christ remains there *in person* in the eucharistic sacrifice. He is there, phenomenologically speaking, "bodily" (Husserl: *leibhaftig*),[52] which is to say, as himself: "A ghost does not have flesh and bones as you see that I have" (Luke 24:39).

§19. In Flesh and Bones

It is necessary, then, to move from the organic aspect of the body—or rather, to return to the perception of the flesh. The living being is not simply "body," or even "flesh," in the vital sense of the term, if we understand by that the necessary drives of the body. Once we have placed, weighed, and analyzed the world of the organic, and not simply postulated it, the body appears also as "flesh" (*Leib*), in the phenomenological sense of the term this time—that is, as the lived experience of a body affected by itself. This turn is indispensable: it will not lead us to the substructure of the corporal, but it changes our orientation toward the carnal, or the experience of the corporal. Different layers of embodiedness must then be distinguished, as Husserl (privileging, however, the corporal at the expense of the carnal) would suggest to us. We can consider the following:

(1) The *physical body* (*Körper*). It is inert, ontic and objective, mineral, indeed thing-like, something with which "physical nature" and "scientific naturalization" are concerned. Being "extended" is its principal characteristic.

(2) The biological body (*Leib* or "flesh" in the ordinary sense of the term). Here insofar as it is rooted in the thing-like body, something whose profundity I have tried to show in the concept of the *body spread out* and in its extensive deployment as the unconscious of the Nietzschean body.

(3) The body of lived experience (*Leib-körper*). The site of the immanent and non-reflexive knowledge of oneself, where habits form a *habitus* and way of being in the world (our situating ourselves unconsciously in space for example).

(4) The *corporal and spiritual flesh* (*Leib* in the phenomenological sense of the term). Where the lived experience of the flesh is translated into knowledge of the body and an "auto-affection"[53] of the self by which I am constituted and individualized.[54]

I have bracketed the first of these (the objective or *extended* body) and given place of honour to the second (the biological or body *spread forth*). What remains, in the context of the eucharistic act, is to reintegrate or reconsider the last two: the body of lived experience as subjective body, immanent and non-reflective on the one hand (habitus), and the site of a possible consciousness of self on the other hand (auto-affection). Since I am not *only* "body," I am also "flesh," not simply in forgetting body or the organic living being this time, but in my perceptive faculty of understanding the world, or of receiving it and relating to it.

This other perspective opens toward a new horizon, one that is often visited these days, especially when following our previous topics of discussion: from the organic we return to the phenomenological, from Spinoza and Nietzsche (or Deleuze), we climb back to Husserl or Michel Henry. But the key question is not one of writers, or even simply of persons. The protagonists are not really significant if the discussion itself moves forward. What counts most is the necessity to integrate all this, in philosophy as in theology, and not to stay put comfortably in the organic power of the eucharistic body, so that nothing remains for the subjective experience of the believer to assimilate and to work on in the encounter with God himself. As far as theology is concerned, the eucharist cannot be understood independently from the Resurrection, any more than the "biological body" can be considered independently from the "phenomenological flesh" in philosophy. As I explained earlier, this book was inspired by my sense of something lacking, or rather something left over, after my book on the *Metamorphosis of Finitude*: the topic of the "living or biological body." This body is not simply or purely objective, but acknowledged in the act of the eucharist and probably observed when we define the Resurrection in terms of the lived experience of the flesh, or according to the manner of being of our bodies (§1). It is not only that we can see how phenomenology has its "limits," and afterwards encounter a triple blockage concerning the "flesh on the body," the "meaning of Chaos," and "passivity as opposed to activity" (§3, §4). Problems arise also in theology itself—even if the discipline does not readily acknowledge them—when, after the primacy of the flesh over the body in the act of Resurrection (*Metamorphosis of Finitude*), we encounter the primacy of the body or the flesh in manducation (the act of chewing). The retroaction of the "lived experience of the flesh" over the "organic body" thus marks a necessary return toward the *wholly incarnate*, a move that should lead us to forget nothing in either the philosophical (the double sense of *Leib*) or the theological (Resurrection and eucharist) sphere.

But we still need to connect the one with the other: the organic body with the lived experience of the flesh, and the eucharist with the Resurrection. Because, if there is something "uneasy" in the history of theology, as also perhaps in that of philosophy, it most likely stems from a "growing distance" between the eucharist ("body") and the Resurrection ("flesh"), which is also the distance between the vitalist and organic tradition of the nineteenth century (Schopenhauer, Nietzsche, Feuerbach) and the phenomenological and auto-affective tradition of the twentieth century (Husserl, Scheler, Henry, Levinas) "The scepticism that shakes the faith of Catholics today in the eucharistic Presence," Gustave Martelet maintained, in a still-relevant diagnosis, "is perhaps the symptom of unease, caused by the theological rupture between the eucharist and the Resurrection, which is itself explicable by the absence of a true anthropology of the body."[55]

Let us return to the traditional question: "Is Christ there in flesh and bones in the consecrated Host or the eucharistic bread?" We can remind ourselves that a ghost has neither flesh nor bones, but all the same, it was with flesh and with bones that Christ seems to have appeared to the Eleven: "a ghost does not have flesh and bones as you see that I have" (Luke 24:39).

The question can certainly look ridiculous, especially as it is provoked in the Bible by the apparition of the Resurrected One, rather than by the eucharistic Last Supper. Yet it is traditional to link these two mysteries (Resurrection and eucharist) even though doing so has led to some eccentric readings. Because if nobody today, or since the end of the apostolic era, sees or will see the Resurrected One, and this will be true until the end of time (Acts 1:11), certain believers nonetheless affirm that the *organic body* of Christ is given to us to eat and to touch in its presence in the eucharist. "The body of our Lord Jesus Christ is physically manipulated or touched by the hands of the priest," according to Cardinal Humbert in the Council of Rome of 1059. He maintained this against Berengarius in a kind of "dispute over meat" that we shall need to consider further (§27): "It is crushed by the teeth of the faithful, not simply as a sacrament, but also in truth."[56] Certainly, as I shall discuss later (§26), this kind of a sensory approach to the eucharist cannot be sustained without its symbolic counterpart.

The liturgical prohibition against breaking the eucharistic body by chewing has been happily and definitively lifted, as has the direction for exclusive reception by the faithful in the mouth, rather than the hollow of the hand. In the past, such recommendations came from a confusion between the *eucharistic body* of Christ resurrected and the *historical body* of Jesus of Palestine.[57] On the other hand, if we over-spiritualize the eucharistic body, if we side with Berengar (symbolism) against Lanfranc (realism), we risk losing that *Catholic* sense, which at least had the merit of maintaining the consistency of the eucharistic body, of a "real presence" (§29). If the Resurrected One is present in flesh and bones in the account of his apparition to the Eleven, and if a "ghost has neither flesh nor bones," we still need to know exactly what "flesh" and "bones" are here, in this presence of the "thing itself" that phenomenology will come to name as "in person," or "bodily" (translated in French as "in flesh and bone") (*leib-haftig*). And this is something that we can find exactly in the gospel, where no denial of the consistency of the flesh is signified: "Look at my hands and my feet; see that it is I myself" (Luke 24:39).[58]

In the act of the eucharist, as on the day of the apparition to the Eleven, Christ presents himself, in person and in his own person: "It is I myself" (*egô eimi autos*). What is at stake here, whether in philosophy or theology, is that there is "somebody" and not "nobody" who presents himself "in person"—that is, with a body (*some-body*) and not without a body (*no-body*), as the English etymology puts it. To appear and present himself "in person" is probably what counts; it is what counts in the phenomenological perception of the flesh, anchored here in the biological determination of the body. The *épokhê*, or phenomenological reduction, frees the being-ness (*étantité*) and brackets off objectivity to focus on the intentional acts: perception, imagination, understanding, remembering, anticipation, reaction, passion, and so on. But the "thing itself" (*Sache selbst*) remains—or rather, what remains is what ensures that it is "in person," and that it is precisely what concerns me and what I am dealing with here: *my* thing (*die Sache*) rather than just *that* thing (*das Ding*).

So, we are left with an essential question concerning the real presence and the eucharist: Is the real presence in consciousness enough to ensure real presence? In other words, doesn't the way that objectivity is suspended in phenomenology lead us, as far as the eucharist is concerned, to rely on the modalities of consciousness (the faithful) rather than on what was actually intended (the body of Christ per se)? The question, which is very much alive today, separates off different modes of intentionality.[59]

To reply, to accept that one sees, even touches and eats, him "in flesh and bone" ("bodily," *leibhaftig*) means that we have to try to understand what "to appear in the flesh" could mean in phenomenological and theological terms. A form of perception remains involved in the vision (offertory) and the eucharistic manducation (communion), where the change in direction of feeling leaves a mark, as does the living reality (see §32). And though in phenomenological terms the perceptive lived experience is only one form of the gift (or donation)—with, or beside, the form of memory or anticipation—the "incarnate auto-donation" of that thing there "in flesh and bone" (*leibhaftig*), precisely in the mode of perception, says more to us than simply an "auto-donation" relying on imagination or memory. Heidegger, commenting on Husserl, underlines that "what is perceived, as such, has the character of the *incarnation in flesh and bones* [or bodiliness] (*Leibhaftigkeit*), which signifies that the being which presents itself as perceived has the character of the *there in flesh*."[60] In other words, if phenomenology extends the modes of donation to all modalities of consciousness (imagination, memory, anticipation, reaction, and so on), it nonetheless accords a privileged form of donation to perception, in such a way that the thing is given there (*da*), as perceived, truly "in flesh and bone" (*leibhaftig*), or "in person."

In this context, Heidegger's example of the Weidenhausen Bridge, cited by Didier Franck, can clarify for us the meaning of perception of the eucharistic body. Like Heidegger, I can "*re-present* to myself the bridge at Weidenhausen, and I can even imagine myself, at least *in my thoughts*, in this re-presentation in front of the bridge. This bridge as *imagined* in such a fashion is *truly* the bridge at Weidenhausen," just as the bread that recalls the body of Christ is truly the body of Christ in the Protestant tradition.[61] In either case (re-presentation of the bridge, or re-call of the body)—in fact, in every case—the "thing" is given in itself (*Sacher selbst*), although only in the form of a representative donation, and not in an auto-donation "in flesh and bones." The bridge that I see here is not a simple image of the bridge, nor a fantasy of the bridge—as though we were to say, for example, that the eucharist was nothing in the Protestant tradition but an illusory double. It is truly the bridge, or truly "body," but it is not given to me "in flesh." For it to be so given, Heidegger continues in his commentary on Husserl, it is necessary that "I *go down* to stand in front of the bridge itself."[62] There is, according to the Catholic tradition this time, an immeasurable difference between the recall of the famous body (donation according to the modes of consciousness) and the presence in person, or in flesh and bones, of Christ in the Host (incarnate auto-donation according to the mode of perception).

Certainly, in phenomenology as in theology, perception doesn't tell us everything about the thing; it is always a bit hazy in its different modes of donation. Perception cannot give us the whole bridge; the vision of the body is not the whole body: we have only sketches, profiles, or "adumbrations" (*Abschattungen*). It remains the case that the bridge as such is given to us in a mode that is privileged, according to the mode of perception or the incarnate donation (in *going down to stand in front of the bridge itself*). Similarly, the body of Christ is given according to a unique mode, according to the mode of the eucharistic transubstantiation, as the viewing and manducation of the eucharistic bread (§29). Since I come to the Mass not simply with the *I can of my consciousness*, but also with the *I move by means of my body*, I participate and communicate to some degree liturgically in a conversion of the "presence as recall of the body" into a "body appearing there" (*da*), truly present, as it were in person, or in flesh and bones. Moreover, the account of the apparition to the Eleven confirms what I have so far simply outlined: "Look at my hands and feet; see that it is I myself.

Touch me and see; for a ghost does not have flesh and bones as you see that I have" (Luke 24:39). The presence in flesh and bones does not mean here that the body of the Resurrected One is primarily "made of flesh and bones," as if simply raising the dead body were enough to make an improbable return into something credible. This presence points rather to the identity, or to the act of recognition of the "thing itself," or "that person himself," who comes to show himself and to give himself in the form of an incarnate auto-donation—or in flesh and bones (*leibhaftig*)—in such a way that it speaks to us of the importance of the "there" of he who has no other aim but to manifest himself. The "it is I myself" is what directs and stimulates the presence in flesh and in bones of the Son who offers himself and also shows himself. The flesh and the bones do not simply indicate the biological body that I have so far insisted upon as the eucharistic body, but also the phenomenological flesh that now becomes the form of the incarnate presence, at least as it appears as resurrected flesh. It is opportune to recall Heidegger's view, cited by Franck, that "the incarnation in flesh and in bones [*Leibhaftigkeit*] is an *excellent form* of the auto-donation of a being,"[63] Heidegger points out that one flesh is given in a privileged fashion to another flesh when the two fleshes meet, coming across each other first in the mode of perception.

A profession of faith of this kind is far from indicating an anomalous empiricism. It is rather a question here, as it has traditionally been, of the realism of the thing itself: not what makes the thing exist only in its beingness or its objectivity, but what the *ré-alité* (spatio-temporality) of the thing indicates is really present there, "in person." It does, however, wait for me to invite me (the reserved sacrament) and is there until I can also present myself (adoration of the sacrament). The spatio-temporal reality of the real presence (see §32) is not something I want to deny here, but rather something to be reaffirmed, precisely in that what is real in the resurrected body can very well be there without me, and before me (he awaits me and directs his intention toward me). At the same time, I must also hold on there with him, to do full justice to his incarnate auto-donation (responding intuitively to the direction of his intention toward me). A "certain peasant" in front of the tabernacle used to say to the Curé of Ars, "*I look at him and he looks at me.*"[64] This signifies, as it were, that the donation of the eucharistic body takes place fully in this intersection of perspectives, though it also continues independently of such a reciprocal conjunction.

The question remains, and we no can no longer avoid it: Can the "real presence" of the eucharist (myself with him) be identified with his actual presence (the possibility of him without me)? To put it another way, do I have to be "there" (*da*) so that he is there in "flesh and bones" (in person, *leibhaftig*)? Is he never there independently of me, or without me? Here again the phenomenological perspective can help with the theological point of view. To suggest that the "presence in flesh and bones of the thing itself" ("It is I myself") depends upon "I myself who intends it" ("I am there to see you") is for me to subjugate the thing so that it all comes to depend on me. It is then no longer because of the thing itself, or because of him, that the thing appears and is given to me. We find the inevitable question that faces any philosophical or theological discussion of the eucharist (and particularly our topic here, of the Wedding Feast of the Lamb). As Jean-Luc Marion puts it, "Can the eucharistic presence of Christ as consecrated bread and wine determine itself and simply in itself the conditions of its reality, the dimensions of its temporality and the arrangements for access to it?"[65]

The "gift of presence" here must retain the "present of the gift." Or, in other words, the "real" presence (myself making the presence present) does not negate the "real" presence (the thing itself that is given independently of me). Rather, and we must follow Marion closely here, "The theology of transubstantiation alone offers the possibility of distance, since it separates my consciousness from Him who summons it."[66] The real presence still holds, then, as it is understood in Catholicism, and the reserved sacrament can only be understood on the basis of such a survival—something that may be most fully manifest in the intersecting perspectives shown in the Adoration of the sacrament. But such an act of survival, as we have already seen (§11; see also §36), says nothing about the mode of the substance, at least in the sense of how it subsists, or its thing-ness—as though God were shut up in the bread, hiding himself there definitively and not giving of himself any more. Rather, there is a kind of maintenance, an "abiding" by which God performs the act of "dwelling" (in the bread) and by which we also find another way of living this (us in him and he in us), after which, paradoxically, he invites us to be assimilated: "Those who eat my flesh and drink my blood abide in me, and I in them" (John 6:56). The distance that the "real presence" secures for the body of Christ in the consecrated bread then justifies, and is in a way the basis for, the "real" presence that we encounter when we communicate. When I am there ("real" presence), the body of Christ is *de facto* there, and even there where I am, in the same way that all auto-donation gives us the "thing itself" in the community where it is rendered present ("'Emmanuel' . . . 'God is with us'" [Matt. 1:23]). But when I am not there and he, on the other hand, is there even in his body this time (real presence), he is himself paradoxically totally present at last as he summons me there, in an incarnate auto-donation that is waiting to be fully realized. As Heidegger says,

"What is itself given need not be bodily given, while conversely anything which is bodily given is itself given."[67] The "distance" of the transubstantiation guarantees the true mode of his presence, in that the "there" (*da*) "in flesh and bones" of the eucharistic body (on the altar, but also as reserved sacrament in the act of adoration) also awaits me and requires "my own flesh," in a quasi-amorous act of inter-embodiedness. I can gather myself together there and welcome the presentness of the gift of he who never ceases to give himself there. As the encyclical *Mysterium Fidei* tells us, "This presence is called 'real' not to exclude the idea that the others are 'real' too, but rather to indicate presence par excellence, because it is substantial and through it Christ becomes present whole and entire, God and man."[68]

As in the artworks that I mentioned earlier, which can "capture these . . . forces,"[69] the consecrated Host thus captures in some way the force of the Resurrected Christ, and it holds onto it so that I can always communicate and participate. It waits for me in its Force, its Holy Spirit, at the Mass, on the altar, at the Adoration of the sacrament, or even in the reserved sacrament, even when I am not still there. As we have seen (§17) and shall examine further (§29), it is not so much the substance in the act of transubstantiation that produces the Force, or the power of the body of Christ. It is rather the power of the body of the Resurrected Christ that produces the substance and holds it in the mode of presence in the act of the eucharist.[70] The philosophical power of the body (Spinoza, Nietzsche, Deleuze, Artaud) ties up here with the phenomenological donation of the flesh (Husserl, Heidegger, Marion); thus, the "gift in person"—or the "in flesh and bones" of the "It is I myself" of the resurrected body and the eucharisticized body (phenomenology of the flesh)—responds to the corporal density of "it is truly *Him*," which is a taking on of responsibility as far as, and including, the organicity of our own embodiedness (philosophy of the body). As the Eucharistic Prayer in its form for Epiphany proclaims, "Your Only Begotten Son, eternal with you in your glory, appeared in a human body, truly sharing our flesh."[71]

§20. The Work of Art in Prose

The "Word became flesh" (John 1:14): that is the very least we can say. He "lived among us," as one lives in the "sojourn of humankind," taking on and transforming what is most powerful in our embodiedness: Chaos, passions, drives, the mass of sensations, the area of what cannot be spoken, animality, power of the organic, unconscious of the body, capture of forces, apparition in flesh and bones. But the Word is still *word*, or put another way, is "speech." And in the act of the eucharist, that is something we must not forget. The Last Supper establishes, or is established, first of all by the operation of speaking, so that it is the verbal declaration of *this is my body* that comes to transform the eucharisticized body. If the "pure—and so to speak, still mute—psychological experience" in phenomenology is such that it precedes and is the foundation of every speech act (§16), it cannot in this way be secondary to a speech act.[72] It is not a subterfuge, or at least an appendix, of the flesh as it appears, or as it is given to be eaten. God creates in speaking—"God said, 'Let there be light'; and there was light" (Gen. 1:3)—and it is by the Word also, that is to say, by his Son, that he recreates: "He took a loaf of bread, and after blessing it he broke it, gave it to them, and said, 'Take; this is my body'" (Mark 14:22). Consecration is an act of speech (see §31), not simply the depth and manifestation of embodiedness. As a result of the Word proffering the word, the bread becomes body and the wine blood. Speech contains in itself a transformative power that we need to remember in the act of the eucharist—even though it might be said that recent symbolic and hermeneutic exegeses of the eucharistic tradition have a tendency to overemphasize it at the expense of the content and the power of the eucharistic body.

To place the act of the eucharist in a linguistic tradition that fully justifies its meaning, we could certainly begin with reference to the manna in the desert given to the people of Israel (Exod. 16), which prefigures the "bread from heaven" and the bread and wine transubstantiated for Christians (John 6:31–33). Bread, whether in Jewish territory or in Christian mysteries, is not simply a matter for mouths to eat, but also for mouths to speak—or rather, it is for mouths to eat because they are also mouths that speak. As we have already seen, following Marcel Jousse, "The history— the Palestinian history—of man is the history of his *mouth*." And we should add, from Jousse, "for the world of the Palestinian reciters, we now know, to eat was to repeat. Eating was *articulating*: eating was giving *rhythm*."[73] The noun "*manna*" indicates that this bread is first of all a matter of speaking and not simply of food, as we can see both from the questions it raises among the Israelites and from the question of what it is itself and in itself: "When the Israelites saw it, they said to one another, 'What is it [*Mân hou*]?' For they did not know what it was" (Exod. 16:15). Paradoxical as it may seem, the bread of the manna, probably like the flesh given to eat in *this is my body*, is given in response not to an immediate hunger, but to a more innate appetite. The "What is it?" of the manna does not concern definition or knowledge, but is the form of "the question" itself (*Mân hou?*). This bread, even if only temporarily, escapes the determinant, or the "It is," that would delimit and define it. It is far from what

Derrida calls "the empire of the *ti esti*."[74] And neither God nor his body say exactly what they are, except insofar as they speak of an *unfinished* history that is not yet traversed ("I am what *I shall be*" [Exod. 3:14]).[75]

Giving himself in the form of the manna, God is giving himself in the form of a question (*Mân hou?* What is it?); it is also *as a question* that the offering of the eucharistic bread becomes for us a linguistic act, one that cannot immediately be reduced to objective and reified presence.[76]

But language does not simply question, it creates—and there is also a kind of invisibility contained in what it presents. Merleau-Ponty underlines that "there is all the same this difference between perception and language, that I *see* the perceived things and the significations on the contrary are invisible."[77] The distinction here is not unimportant: what is invisible in language often makes manifest what is in perception, precedes it and even sometimes transforms it. I do not simply say what I see, or what I do (assertive speech act), but I also see and do what I say, or rather, my speaking itself is an act (performative speech act). Language makes us go from nonbeing to being, certainly—it says that which did not exist before being seen (signification)—but it also allows what exists to be recognized (perception). Translating this into theological terms for what happens in the eucharist, the invisible signification of language that regards the bread as body (*this is my body*) in fact makes it body, although it does not stop being perceived visibly as bread. And the invisible signification that regards the wine as blood (*this is my blood*) makes it blood without stopping it from being perceived visibly as wine. As we shall see later, in discussing the act of "transubstantiation" (§29), the bread and the wine do not simply remain "veils" of the body and blood of Christ but are totally present in the form of "accidents" of a substance that is totally transformed. A triple function of language thus does its work in the case of the eucharist: (1) the performative or illocutionary function—the speech act of the consecration produces the thing (*this is my body*) at the same time as it is spoken; (2) language is pronounced by the celebrant, who in his vicarial role (as representative of Christ) carries out what was proposed; and (3) language does not just repeat what has already been done, but creates a world in which to speak is to do the work, in the same way that an artist produces a world that is his own and is worked on each time by himself.

(1) The performative usage of language is so well known in sacramental theology today that there is no need to insist upon it here. What is valuable in this approach comes down to the recognition that the language has an "illocutionary" role, that there is a unique possibility to "do things with words" (Austin) and thus to produce through speech a new state of

affairs that had not existed before. It is not enough simply to recognize what the body of Christ "can do" as a force (§17), the "manifesto of the flesh" (§18), and the presence "in flesh and bones," or "in person," of the body that has been eucharisticized (§19). It is still necessary to produce the transformation and examine the result—something that only the work of language will stimulate and reiterate each time in a newly constructed world: "[He] said, 'This is my body that is for you. Do this in remembrance of me'" (1 Cor. 11:24). In "saying" *this is my body*, the *this* (of the bread) becomes body (of Christ) by a kind of enchantment of speech [*magie*] that only the illocutionary act is in a position to carry out. Neither verified nor verifiable (the bread become body—assertive speech act), neither declared nor with even a possibility to declare it (to decree that this is the body), the speech act of the priest works here in such a way that what it asserts (take and eat, this is my body given for you) becomes through the power of his speech, or rather through speech of God in him, that which has been asserted: the *this* of the bread to be eaten becomes the *this* of the body given. It is a unique situation: the celebrant, as the delegate of Christ, is so far one with that which he asserts (Christ himself) that the *this is my body* of *that* which he speaks (the bread become body) is, at the same time, the *this* of the body of *the One* who speaks (Christ as the Word), who through him becomes "this, the body, which has been spoken about" (Christ as Flesh). Flesh and Word are identified at this point in the consecration of the eucharist so that not only the Word becomes flesh (incarnation) but also the Flesh becomes word (eucharist and Resurrection). The speaker (who officiates and, through him, Christ) becomes the spoken (the body and blood under the two species of bread and wine). If it is the speech that is expressed, it is a body that is transmitted. The diffusion of the body that has been transubstantiated consolidates, by its establishment, our union, at the same time as it operates our transformation and feeds our quasi-eucharistic metabolism. St. Bonaventure insists "this sacrament contains Christ's true body and immaculate flesh in such a way that it penetrates our very being [*se nobis diffundes*], unites us to one another [*et non invicem uniens*], and transforms us into him."[78]

What makes this into a speech act in the eucharist is both the moment of consecration by which a word or speech transforms the bread into body (language as illocution) and the moment of the communion in which a body (that of Christ) addresses another body (that of the believer), to be incorporate there and also to change it—the body as performance or as act of transformation (to perform), whether of the believer or of the Church. If illocution remains the principal act by which, at the moment of consecration, the bread becomes body and the wine blood, it is linked to and leads us nonetheless to an occasion of speech where the speech act cannot be limited to that moment in which it is pronounced (this is my body) if it is at the same time to accomplish what it is meant to bring about ("the body of Christ. *Amen*"). It is not that speech is on the one side (the illocutionary act of the consecration) and flesh is on the other (manducation, eating, in the process). On the contrary, speech itself is the flesh once it is incarnate in the eucharisticized body (Christ); it offers by the same token another body taking it on and sojourning within it (the disciple). The body-to-body of the believer with the consecrated Host does not place the consecration and the embodiedness of the manducation in opposition. Rather, it consecrates speech as body (in the transformation of bread into body) and makes the body into speech (in the assimilation and incorporation of the disciple to Christ himself).

Therefore, we cannot simply be satisfied by the symbolic and its theology. Or, what we need from symbolic theology is that it does not stop at the reunion of flesh and speech, as though speech in itself were not already a kind of becoming-flesh, and the flesh were not the expression in itself of speech, or speech expressed to itself (§30). We speak, above all, by our bodies—indeed, more than by language—and that is what the eucharistic Last Supper in its celebration must not forget. A silence of the flesh is what is necessary, or at least expected, so that the surplus of speech does not cover what the body, by itself, has already known how to say better or say otherwise (§32). As the theologian Hans-Urs von Balthasar so rightly points out, "The Eucharist, in particular, is the adaptation of our being to God by the descent of the Word *into our senses*, indeed, into our substance, which is something even *below the senses*. Not only does the Spirit speak to spirit, but *Flesh speaks to flesh*."[79]

(2) The illocutionary formula of the eucharist cannot simply remain independent of the situation of the linguistic act that is directed at the thing or the transformation. It is not enough, in some kind of alchemy, to take the bread and say *this is my body*, so that it becomes the body, and pour out the wine saying *this is my blood*, so that it changes into blood. As Jean Ladrière says, what is necessary is "an 'intentional aim' that takes on the semantic properties of the mechanism to bring the appropriate operation to the act. . . . It is that by which Christ has wished to make himself present through the centuries, not simply in memory but in a real way . . . under a sign that is localized, and specific to each occasion, creating around him the unity of a particular community that is defined in terms of time and space. It . . . [is not then through its leader but through] the faith of the Church that this speech has the power to make what it says real."[80] The priest is here the Vicar of Christ, especially as he "lends himself" in some

way for the uttering of "the Word," so that, repeating the words (*verba*) of the Son as they were expressed by himself in the body, a new body-to-body can in some way be constituted through which he comes each time to be given. The illocution of *this is my body* does not then suffice to bring about the eucharist (Austin), unless it is also placed in the liturgical situation by which speech is authenticated, and by which it is thus rendered capable of newly producing its effect once it is reiterated.[81]

(3) But it remains true as far as language is concerned that, although it has been dominant from the first and can be reexamined in sacramental theology, we cannot simply speak of it producing this transformation of something in an illocutionary act, in a given situation. Language conquers the flesh at the same time as it stands for it, indeed, imitates it. The words of a particular culture, as also their employment, have in fact "a life"—"a life that is also our life." Signifiers do not just operate changes; they carry in themselves a part of the "pure—and, so to speak, still dumb—psychological experience" that the work of the poet—in prose this time—as also the protagonist of the Last Supper, aims precisely to stage.[82] Merleau-Ponty underlines that "it is the error of semantic philosophies to close up language as if it spoke only of itself: language lives only from silence; everything we cast to the others has germinated in the great mute land which we never leave."[83] In terms of exegesis of the eucharist, and despite the brilliance of the enterprise and the great Carolingian theological corpus that has been so meticulously examined (Irène Rosier-Catach), I feel that we cannot be satisfied simply with the reduction of the eucharistic *this is my body* to a question of logic or semantics. Certainly what is spoken is what takes effect, and this is especially true with regard to transubstantiation, where hermeneutic debates have made real progress concerning linguistic topics (§27). But the eucharist is not only or simply a matter of "preaching," in which the spoken part of the text would always take precedence over the body (Protestant perspective). The eucharist focuses on and leads principally toward "incorporation" (§30), in that what is spoken has no other autonomy than to produce a metamorphosed body. That is its aim, and the spoken cannot take its place (Catholic perspective). We need to renounce, in philosophy as in theology, the "spectre of a pure language," or the "myth of a universal language." Logic—and, even less, logicality—cannot exist without a body to adopt and work with. In other words, the spoken does its "work" insofar as it "opens up" a world: that of God, where the prose entails that we are able to join the venture and integrate ourselves into its particular narrative. The spoken is "language" as painting is "style." The one and the other send us back to a common lived experience, rather than feeding

themselves off a hermeneutic that would have no other reference than the text and its self-deployment.

The spoken does not simply precede the body (consecration); it is the body itself that proffers the first speech that is manifest in the eucharistic act (manducation or adoration). In philosophy as in theology, the lived experience of the flesh—to use Heidegger's term, the *hermeneutic of facticity* (i.e. the hermeneutic of "thrown-ness" or the way in which we are "thrown into the world")—takes precedence over what is spoken in language, or the *hermeneutic of the text*. We could say that the hermeneutic of language is itself always a hermeneutics of the body and its li While they translate what we are in our fleshly manner, words still say what we shall be in our bodies, in that all performative speech "takes on world that up to then has been foreign, not simply starting off from spe, but in that coming-and-going, or "chiasmus," in which the body and eech remain intimately joined. What counts for phenomenology coun also for the eucharist, where the crossover of *this is my body* is spoken , as much as the body is given to eat—where there is the exhausted silen of the Passion, given full meaning in the brilliance of the Resurrecti I want to emphasize, following Merleau-Ponty (faithful disciple of Huss that "philosophy is the reconversion of silence and speech into another." Merleau-Ponty quotes Husserl's *Cartesian Meditations*: "It is experience . . . still mute which we are concerned with leading to the pu expression of its own meaning."[84] The eucharistic act develops then here work of art in prose not simply in that it works on embodiedness (transub stantiation) but also as it opens up a world through the act of speaking (consecration). Only an "aesthetic" conception of the eucharist can help release the bread from its production and authorize us here to read the "work of art" of God, who "opens" himself to his own world-ness.[85]

The *hoc est corpus meum*—first, "illocutionary" (speech that is perfor mative as act); then, "in situation" (a linguistic and ecclesiastical context for the spoken); and finally, "victorious" (chiasmus of flesh and speech)— opens up a world by the work of art of language that is also the work of art of God. There is an intention to transform before the consecration, and then the eucharisticized bread becomes the expression of this transforma tion after the consecration. In both cases (see §31), there is no doubling and no trickery between the language and the body, or between the sign (*signum*) and the thing (*res*), but only a kind of mutual cooperation that ensures that the first (the language) transforms what the second expresses (the body), while the second imprints on this (the body) what the first searches for (the language). We should recall here the second Eucharistic

Prayer: "Father most holy, through your beloved Son, Jesus Christ, your Word through whom you made all things. . . . Make holy, therefore, these gifts, we pray, by sending down your Spirit upon them like the dewfall, so that they may become for us the Body and Blood of our Lord Jesus Christ.[86]

The Son Word made flesh, as he is flesh of the Word, offers himself in the consecrated Host as flesh for the flesh of others, rejoining the disciple to allow himself to be assimilated. After having discovered in the figure of the "sacrificial lamb" (Chapter 2) and in the deployment of the "animal that therefore I am" (Chapter 4), the eucharistic heritage that it concerns God to take on, our "philosophical essay on the body and the eucharist" has attempted to draw from the "Chaos" and "Tohu-Bohu" of our existence (Chapter 1) and from the power of the body (Chapter 4) the eucharistic content that the Word himself comes to expose in order to sojourn here. It remains then now to decode *this is my body* as the expression of the "eroticized body" (Chapter 3), or the embrace and the differentiation of the spouses—a modality of the eucharist that is still to be explored. In Pope Benedict XVI's words: "the mutual consent that husband and wife exchange in Christ . . . also has a eucharistic dimension."[87]

6

Embrace and Differentiation

The body on its own, whether we consider it as organic or as manifesting itself in flesh, is still not enough to define the content of the eucharist. The eucharisticized body is, first of all, a *body given*. The oblation in the eucharist belongs analytically to love, not in what theology or liturgies proclaim it to be, nor in what the benevolence of charity demands. The *way of the body* is that it gives itself: if it does not, it perishes in the wish to take and be taken. The carnal embrace (*eros*) is part of the most spiritual gift (*agape*). The *this is my body*, as I have constantly underlined (§9), does not firstly or solely proffer the words of Christ to his disciples on the day of the eucharistic Last Supper, but these are also, in effect, the words of the spouse to his espoused in the erotic scene—a scene that only gains sense in the Christian system through the eucharistic Last Supper. Our topic, then, is *philosophical* even before it is theological. It is as "donation," and, as we shall see, "humanly desired" that the body leaves off its animality to some degree—and goes from a difference of *male-female* to one of *man-woman*. Christianity cannot, of course, set itself up as the sole arbiter of such a destiny, as though the mass of humanity had to remain on the animal threshold of eros before sharing the human embrace in the charitable form of the eucharistic communion. Such a mistake would simply lead us to a negation of the mode of creation. The difference *man-woman* (*ish-ishah*) remains constitutive of the act of creating and is nourished by the *male-female* difference (Gen. 2:23). It is in the province of what is "simply human," and not just in terms of our genitals, that we can sexually differentiate ourselves. Many couples would quite rightly claim that the offering of one to another, and the quest for fidelity, does not belong uniquely to Christianity, even if the offering in question is transcended differently in Christianity in a *confidence*, or in a *faith*, that probably only God could give. If the eucharistic act has something to teach us, it is not that it will assure us, nor that it will reassure us, but that we receive through it a conversion of the eros by the agape, in which the couple are, as it were, entwined, and held through their eros in Christ, in the form of a true model of the agape. Bodies make love (*eros*) "in" the love that makes the bodies (*agape*). And it is this true humano-divine interpenetration of bodies that feeds the embrace of those who are to partake in a Christian way in their fleshly union. In other words, it is in the integration of the only One who in a paradigmatic way knew how to speak and to achieve *this is my body*. It is not human love (*eros*) that serves as model for divine love (*agape*), but rather divine love (*agape*) that, in espousing human love (*eros*), succeeds in integrating and transforming it at the heart of the eucharistic act.

I have already underlined with regard to a *charitable* God (§10) that we cannot be satisfied with the total "equivocity" of the eros and agape (Nygren), nor accept simple "univocity" (Marion). The former risks separating divine charity from human love to such a degree that nothing remains in common between the two; the latter considers the modalities of divine love on the model of human love so comprehensively that nothing remains that is particular to God. The excesses of the one or the other do not prevent us, however, from linking them; far from it. The metamorphosis of eros by agape has as its role not simply to sustain the experience of the agape (eucharist) on the model of eros (sexuality), but also and above all to integrate the eros (sexuality at the heart of its conversion by the agape). As I pointed out earlier (§10), the erotic is not fulfilled for a couple unless God contains and transforms them in his agape. Auguste Rodin's sculpture *The Hand of God* shows us a couple in one another's arms but also, significantly, within the hand of God. This is so important that the Roman Catholic ritual joins and integrates in its liturgical practice the sacrament of marriage in the sacrament of the eucharist, the *this is my body* of and between the couple is joined to the *this is my body* of Christ to his Church: "Matrimony, unless a just cause excuses from the celebration of Mass, must be celebrated within Mass."[1]

We can say it directly: the body certainly makes love. And it does so in the ordinary way of human beings, when it is enough to know one another as sexually differentiated to love one another as different, and to desire not simply the other, but the *Desire of the desire* of the other (§23). Love makes the body, in the Christian mode this time, precisely in that a third, divine, comes so as to unify or, rather, incorporate the couple. We need to be bold here and not hesitate to affirm this. The *this is my conjugal body* owes its origin to, and finds its accomplishment in *this is my eucharistic body*, even if the former will sometimes (indeed, will often) do without the latter. The conjugal erotic does not come, or does not simply come, to elucidate or express the Sunday eucharist, but it is incorporated in it and is found here as metamorphosis. St. Bernard, speaking about the ministry of the altar, but also of the couple themselves, says importantly, "*There* in this sacrament of sacraments of the eucharist, the spouse [the wife] unites with her spouse [the husband] becoming a single flesh with him [*haec efficitur una caro sponsa cum sponso*], the pious soul, at one in spirit with the Christ."[2] We approach such an incorporation of the erotic union in *this is my eucharistic body*, not through confessionalism or by dogmatism, but because the mystery requires it and philosophy formulates it. The "body donated" in the eucharistic act is neither a simple eroticization, nor an abstraction in pure charity; it is a transformation and integration of the erotic into the charitable. It ensures that nothing escapes the work of he who came to recapitulate all (Chaos, passions, drives, animality, embodiedness . . .), in the bread that uniquely, having become the *wheat of our humanity*, is metamorphosed in him: "Allow me to become food to the wild beasts, through whose instrumentality it will be granted me to attain to God," says Ignatius of Antioch, in his eucharistic martyrdom. "I am the wheat of God, and let me be ground by the teeth of the wild beasts, that I may be found the pure bread of Christ."[3]

In human love in its erotic form it is the gift that makes the body, and not simply the body that is the gift. This is what we see in paradigmatic form in the act of the eucharist, which is the site of a transformation of eros by agape. And it is the essence of the message of the eucharistic consecration, according to its modality: the eros. But there is also more, and better, in the eucharistic offering, as there is in the erotic gift. The formula "take, eat; this is my body" (Matt. 26:26) cannot be limited to the literal sense. Luke adds to this: "This is my body, which is given for you [*uper umôn didomenon*]" (Luke 22:19). According to St. Paul, "he broke it [*uper umôn, eklasen*]" (1 Cor. 11:24). Just to take it, or to eat the body, is not enough: the embodiedness would be simply consumed without being truly eroticized, or offered in the agape. The call of the body to another body that has been shown, offered, and given, also accomplishes its vocation and its dimension, as it is a desired being. The satisfaction of needs may be an attempt at fulfillment, but it produces nothing except another and new dissatisfaction. The momentum of desire, on the other hand, "does not fulfill it, but deepens it."[4] With an other, particularly in the realization of a differentiated sexuality, the loved partner is not content simply with pleasing the desired one, but also draws toward and excites through difference, to the point where it can be seen that neither will be fully satisfied. The hollow of desire is never reabsorbed into the fullness of need, and it is precisely in this difference, as we shall discuss later (§23), that we find—still and always—the distance of animality (male-female) from humanity (man-woman). It is less that we are lost, the one in the other, in the *coincidence of bodies*, than that the other remains the other of the one, and the one remains the other of the other. Emotion is not reason, nor is it simply *pathos* or suffering; it is action and the desire to love, when it is appropriate at the same time to "differentiate oneself." One is never as close to oneself, yet never as far from oneself, as when one is simply self-satisfied, carrying the burden of the self for oneself, and solely oneself: "When I shall cleave unto You with all my being . . . my life shall be a real life, being wholly full of you," says St. Augustine, "but now . . . I am a burden to myself [*oneri mihi sum*], as not being full of You."[5]

What is true, today as yesterday, of the eroticized body, is probably also true of the agape in the eucharistic act. There is no gift of the body without a body of the gift. The excitement of *this is my body* as the *passion* of giving, in the active sense of the term, takes precedence over the passive sense of to suffer or to receive. The passion of Christ is the "Passover of desire" on the day of the Last Supper, before being simply a "way of suffering" at Gethsemane or on Golgotha (see *Le Passeur de Gethsémani* [The guide to Gethsemane]), and waiting for the "rebirth or resuscitation" at Jerusalem and beyond in all Samaria (see *Metamorphosis of Finitude*). Thus we find, precisely at the dawn of the Passover, the redoubling of desire at the exact moment of the eucharist. The erotic remains in the approach to the eucharist, as though it were necessary each time to prepare and make ready, and that is something that the gospels emphasize: "'I have eagerly desired [*epithumia epethumêsa*] to eat this Passover with you before I suffer'" (Luke 22:15).

We do not go simply to the eros of the body in the conjugal union without an eager desire for the desire of the other; otherwise, it is just a kind of consumption. But neither should we go to the conversion of the eros by the agape in the eucharist, and thus to the liturgical Last Supper, without desire—desire not simply to consume one's God, as if simply to absorb him were enough to satiate oneself, but desire to *dig into* the emotion that thirst and hunger for the divine intensify rather than calm. The "given body," when it is "given and broken" for you in the congregation (as *for you* in the carnal act of the erotic), has for its first aim to be desired rather than simply consumed. Only too often we go to the body of the other without self-discipline or ascesis, without preparation, at least without interior preparation. And the eros knows this, because it is then, on each occasion, imperfect. But neither should we go to the "body of Christ" without preparation, like those foolish virgins invited to the wedding feast among the "Ten bridesmaids [who] took their lamps and went to meet the bridegroom" (Matt. 25:1). Consummation without desire shifts rapidly into desire of consumption/consummation once the excitement is lost, and all that remains is the satisfaction of a need that actually satisfies only those who allow themselves to be still deluded. In the same way as there is sometimes a consummation "of bodies" without loving hearts in the erotic act, so there will be sometimes—or even, regrettably, often—the eating (the manducation) of "the body," without spiritual hunger in the eucharistic act. In both cases we can recognize certainly the Chaos or Tohu-Bohu that constitutes our humanity (Chapter 1); we can turn toward the sacrificial lamb (Chapter 2); we can also recognize our part of animality (Chapter 4) and even an organic body ready to show itself (Chapter 5). But what is missing is the sense of having "given" the body and thus also of it having been eroticized. The scenic conversion in the Last Supper of the eros by the agape is the condition for a scenic conversion of the eroticizing act (Chapter 6).[6] From a strict Christian perspective that anyone may or may not share, one reaches authenticity of eros or of agape only to the extent that the scene [*scène*] of the body (the conjugal couple) is integrated also into the Last Supper [the *Cène*] of the body (of Christ), and only as far as both find the most profound grounds for the act of love: "If I speak in the tongues of mortals and of angels, but do not have love [*agapên de mê ekô*], I am a noisy gong or a clanging symbol" (1 Cor. 13:1).

It should go without saying that it is not a question here of good intentions, nor of a charitable vision according to an exclusivity that would be, to say the least, out of place (a radical inauthenticity of love outside its eucharistic conversion). Rather, in this context there is consistency even of the eros, insofar as it is, first, carnal and human and, afterwards, can be offered—and at the same time integrated into—the eucharistic agape. St. Paul recommends to the Romans, with a precision concerning the eucharistic and the erotic that may seem surprising, "present your bodies as a living sacrifice [*parastêsai ta sômata umôn*], holy and acceptable to God, which is your spiritual worship" (Rom. 12:1). The erotic difference, or, in other words, the sexual difference, is there from the start—and to think this through is what is now at stake for us, so that we can make sense of the *modality* of the eucharistic act: *this is my body*. In their embrace, as we have already seen, the man and the woman differentiate themselves and discover each other as they really are, rather than melting into one another to unify themselves in a state of indifference. Probably the same applies, in the same way, to the act of "communicating"—where one will never become more human (one of humankind) than when one is nourished by God. Or, perhaps we could say that one does not become son (a son) until one receives *passionately* the Son, recognizing oneself along with him as dependent on the Father.

§21. The Difference at the Origin

There has been a gradual loss of animality in the history of philosophy (§15). It is probably also necessary to indicate another omission, indeed, a complete effacement this time of the "sexual difference"—something that it behooves us now to bring into the light: "Every epoch has one thing to think through," says Heidegger. "One thing only. Sexual difference is that thing for our time."[7] It is easy to say this, but difficult to make it work. Just stating it is not enough to put it into effect (1) philosophically and (2) theologically.

(1) In philosophy, on the one hand, we have difficulties partly because psychoanalytic theory has taken up the so-called sexual difference, fundamental from the origins of humanity. Psychoanalysis has been constantly and increasingly tempted to appropriate such difference (the transition from the genital to the sexual, according to Freud). I have already made plain—in respect to Chaos and the Tohu-Bohu (§1)—that what I am attempting here is not so much psychological as *philosophical*. But if we claim the universality of that which takes place for *all persons* too forcefully (a pervasive tendency in philosophy), we shall forget singularity, or the difference between man and woman. Levinas certainly proposes a philosophical treatment of femininity as a site of interiority, or a topos where woman's "mode of being . . . consists in slipping away from, the light." We cannot, however, seriously maintain this—at least, not without deceiving ourselves. To hold that femininity is interior, and masculinity exterior, is not adequate as a way of marking a difference that is, to say the least, constitutive and originary. It does not work in a humanity that, at least today, will not stand being divided up in such a way.[8]

(2) As for theology, one cannot affirm so easily that sexual difference is there from the origin, or indeed originary. Adam as a figure of the *Earth* (*adâmah*) certainly appears to be, if only at the start, asexual (Gen. 2:7). At least, he is as long as Eve has not been presented to him and nothing has been taken from his ribs (Gen. 2:23). The common origin of Adam

and Eve in the same humanity that has been so justly postulated[9] can, if misunderstood, push sexual difference into the background—as though the difference between the sexes were not metaphysically first (the original asexuality of the first man in Eden), nor last (the asexuality of man and woman in the Kingdom). In short, we find in this context the very apposite criticism of Jean-Paul Sartre regarding Heidegger: "his 'Dasein' appears to us as asexual."[10] And this can also be extended to the history of philosophy (the neglect of sexual difference), indeed, to misunderstandings in the history of theology (the absolute neutrality of Adam).

Among philosophers, only Kant—to do him justice, in his roundabout way, in a note in *Anthropology from a Pragmatic Point of View* that is often passed over—asks the appropriate question, without, however, being tempted to think it through, or even trying to do so: "What is the reason for the fact that all organic beings that we know reproduce their species only through the union of two sexes (which we then call male and female)[?] . . . In what darkness does human reason lose itself when it tries to fathom the origin here, or even merely undertakes to make a guess at it?"[11] I wouldn't make too much of this if it were not that the question remains: How can sexual difference be "at the origin"? How can it be there *originally* at the start—but more importantly, *originary*— in a differentiation that we still depend upon and that has not ceased to exist for us? The erotic imperative by which sexual difference cannot be considered simply to be original, but is also considered originary, part of our destiny, comes not from any author, but from the founder himself, as Christianity understands it: from Christ.

That is where the turning point takes place, and where the new start occurs, which constantly initiates a Christian reading of the Holy Writ. Of course, the Pharisees will question the master to "test" him: "'Is it lawful for a man to divorce his wife for any cause?'" (Matt. 19:3), or, "'What did Moses command you?'" (Mark 10:3). The "trap" they place here is well known: to forbid the renunciation of a wife is to go against the prescriptions of the Mosaic Law ("writes her a certificate of divorce" and "sends her out of his house" [Deut. 24:1]). And to authorize repudiation is to reject the recommendation of Genesis that a man "[leave] his father and mother" and "become one flesh" with his wife (Gen. 2:24). Christ's reply actually conserves the sense of the Mosaic prescription and justifies the interdiction, making a show of getting out of the trap: "'Because of your hardness of heart he wrote this commandment for you'" (Mark 10:5). But the last words of his solution still hold true, and as I see it, they do so in a new start by which the Christian hermeneutic places sexual difference at the origin: "*From the beginning of the world* [or of creation] [*apô de arkês ktiseôs*] 'God made them male and female'" (Mark 10:6). Or, even better, "Have you not read that the one who made them *at the beginning* [*ap' archês*] 'made them male and female'" (Matt. 19:4). If Christ had not made a conscious decision here, a mistaken interpretation of the Old Testament would exist in the gospel narrative, or at least something that would have weakened a new and distinct reading and another way of starting at the beginning. After all, what we read in the first chapter of Genesis, in the first narrative of creation, is this: "In the beginning when God created the heavens and the earth" (Gen. 1:1). And it is only on the sixth day that "God created humankind in his image, in the image of God he created them; male and female he created them" (Gen. 1:27). It is a very significant inversion, although one rarely put into the spotlight, and yet it is fundamental: the *sixth day* (the creation of man and woman) is substituted in Christ's speech for the *first day* (the creation of the heavens and the Earth).

Bereshit, en archê, "In the beginning"—God does not start, or no longer starts, with the world, according to Christ, but with man and woman, or sexual difference. This takes place as if, in the eyes of the founder of Christianity, there were no other origin but sexual differentiation, or no other beginning but humanity differentiated. The New Testament hermeneutic offers us not a misinterpretation of the Old Testament, but a reinterpretation. The man-woman difference marks for Christians the first and true beginning, "the beginning of creation" (Mark 10:6), or the beginning *of* the world, rather than the beginning *in* the world—a difference that is ontological and not, or at least, no longer, ontic. The sexual difference taken and included in the eucharistic act marks, in fact, in the Christian system the origin of the act of loving, and thus also of the creation or production of alterity. Neither the Earth nor the people constitute here the first given (Judaism); yet Eve does so for Adam, or the woman for the man, precisely in that by his woman (or wife) the man escapes from his solitude, in the image of the Trinitarian God that the community also makes his specificity (Christianity): "'This at last is bone of my bones and flesh of my flesh'" (Gen. 2:23). Creating the world, as we shall see later (§22), God rejects solitude for man and wants him to be, as a creature, in the form of his own image and never as isolated as when he had been unable to find a counterpart among the animals in whom he could confide. Here, where the animals have seemed at least contemporaneous with humankind (§14), humankind goes ahead in some way and starts to takes precedence. Without in any way negating the genealogical descent (Darwin), the human oversteps the animal metaphysically and theologically, in that it establishes and is established in a differentiated alterity that zoology can neither reach nor even imagine. The Christian sense of the creation projects the "man-woman" difference (and no longer the difference *male-female* or *God-world*) in the form of the start and principle of everything. It is the primordial stuff and the difference of everything, in which God has designed all differentiation as well as all acts of love.

The reversal in Christianity—of the *sixth* to the *first* day (the creation of man and woman in place of the heavens and the Earth)—remains crucial. The rest of the reply to the Pharisees ("Is it lawful for a man to divorce his wife for any cause?") is only what might be expected, at least in that this time the claim of unity concerns what lies behind rather than what lies ahead. Only this stand on difference at the origin can provide a release from the myth of fusion: "They are no longer two, but one flesh" (Matt. 19:6). The unity of the flesh comes from their original differentiation and not the other way around. It is not a question here, as in the Platonic myth of Aristophanes, of a unity constituted at the separation of the sexes (male species, female species, and androgynous species), but of the separation of the sexes (male-female) at the formation of a new unity (one sole flesh). God created man, or "humankind," in his image, but also, as far as man and woman are concerned, "he created them" (Gen. 1:27) so as to signify the loving plurality and *sponsale* (spousals) of his own Trinity. "'Let us make humankind in our image, according to our likeness'" (Gen. 1:26). The bringing together and the double shift between singular and plural that has often been commented upon ("Let *us* make humankind" [Gen. 1:26], and "he created *man*" [Gen. 1:27 (JB)]), does not make a simple unity of the man-woman difference, but inscribes an original in God, whose love, as we have seen, is an "act of differentiation" (see Introduction). The difference in unity that makes the Trinity is the same that is repeated in sexualized difference, starting not from a divided unity but from an act of differentiation that is constitutive of the act of loving.

Clearly Christ himself, in his reply to the Pharisees, initiates a new start at the origin: "From the *beginning* of creation, 'God made them male and female'" (Mark 10:6). To neglect this would be to deny the originality of Christianity—though in fact it has rarely been remarked upon. "In the beginning there is the difference of the sexes," says Jean-Pierre Sonnet, taking up the commentary of Bernard of Clairvaux on the Song of Songs. "The difference of the sexes is that which prevents each of us from a self-totalizing as 'man'—in the generic sense—and that which inscribes in each of us a fundamental lack, which makes us bearers of a wish to know the other, and to be known by him or by her."[12]

It is true that the displacement of the origin in the reply to the Pharisees concerning divorce—from the start of the world to the start of the difference between the sexes (Mark 10:1–12)—is already there, but in a more complex way, in the question about the resurrection at the heart of the conflict with the Sadducees (Luke 20:27–40): Supposing that a woman had seven husbands, after a repeated series of widowhoods, "In the resurrection . . . whose wife will be the woman be? For the seven had married her" (Luke 20:23). If we put aside the slightly improbable and exaggerated character of this example (a woman widowed so many times), the argument does possess at least the merit that it concerns us all—not in the possibility of our remarrying, but in defining our position *in via* (in this life) as determinant of our state *in patria* (in the life to come). There are essential questions that we all confront without daring to articulate them: (1) Will the man recognize his wife once in heaven (Matt. 22:30)? (2) Which wife will he recognize if, by chance, he has had legally and by this relation of marriage, many wives (the stringent inquiry advanced here)? Unusually, metaphysics comes together with ethics; the survival and identification of conjugality depends upon the difference man-woman and the bonds by which they are united in a communion of saints that the Catholic Church has never ceased, quite rightly, to affirm.

(1) The reply to the first question—recognition *in patria* of one's own wife or husband—remains essential, because it is only through such recognition that we can give meaning to a fidelity that will transcend the laws of mortality: "To say that I love you is to say to you that you will not die."[13] There are only too many well-known discussions of this, often misunderstood or indeed found to be incomprehensible by believers, in which the "protological" difference (i.e., the difference related to the study of origins), affirmed by Christ in relation to the origin of the man and the woman (in the reply to the Pharisees), seems annihilated in the eschatological prospect of the annulment of their identity at the end of time (in the reply to the Sadducees). The response is the more surprising because even the order of the text (Matt. 19:1–9: the origin; and Matt. 22:23–33: the end) seems to suppress, in the last part, that which has been established at the start with so much care. "You are wrong, because you know neither the scriptures nor the power of God," Christ replies to the Sadducees. "In the resurrection they neither marry nor are given in marriage, but are like angels in heaven" (Matt. 22:29–30). More clearly, and the reply this time comes from St. Paul himself in his letter to the Galatians, the complete loss of difference is something that also concerns the present, so far as it might lead us, falsely, to regret not having been born different: "As many of you as were baptized into Christ have clothed yourselves with Christ. There is no longer Jew or Greek, there is no longer slave or free, there is no longer *male and female*; for all of you are *one* in Christ Jesus" (Gal. 3:27–

28). This leads to the frequent question we find in theology—an existential demand as much as a metaphysical or theological one: Will the husband find *his* wife in the Kingdom? And the wife her husband? Or will the fusion of husband and wife in Christ be such that their conjugality can melt into a higher unity, one that is certainly made to raise them but that could certainly—and in the light of the creative fidelity already involved—nourish a certain nostalgia for what has been lost, or the dissolution of that preference for the being who was the most dear, or the most loved?

We need to say without hesitation, following Joseph Ratzinger (Pope Benedict XVI), "Male and female are thus revealed as *belonging ontologically to creation* and destined therefore *to outlast the present time,* evidently in a transfigured form. In this way, they characterize the 'love [that] never ends' (1 Cor. 13:8), although the temporal and earthly expression of sexuality is transient and ordered to a phase of life marked by procreation and death."[14] The abolition of differences in the gospel (man-woman), as also in the letters of St. Paul (Jew-Greek, slave–free man, man-woman), is not the suppression of differentiation, but rather the opposite. It is a matter of divisions rather than the construction of uniformity, of the sinful modality of the bestial rather than the renunciation of a sexualized animality that has been transformed by God (§13). What will become of the woman who recognizes her husband, we could reply to the Sadducees, if it is not precisely that such recognition will now be exempt from all desire, as it will be exempt from jealousy? And what of the abolition of differences in Christ, according to St. Paul in this Letter to the Ephesians, if it is not that racial discrimination (Jew-Greek), as well as social discrimination (master-slave), indeed even cultural, political, and familial (man-woman) discrimination cannot continue in order to be established sexually?[15]

This is central to our topic—as we shall see later in relating eros to the act of the eucharist (§33)—in the incorporation of the Word, and not in a denial of the act of differentiation. We are concerned with the taking on of the flesh in his flesh, rather than a rejection of the lived experience of the flesh and the difference of bodies: "For all of you are one in Christ Jesus" (Gal. 3:28). *Sexual*—that is how men and women are from start to finish, according to Freudian categories, though the difference here in this world, as well as the difference in the hereafter, not only is a genital difference, but will relocate *in patria* (in the life to come), or in the communion of saints and even in God, those sexual characteristics that make up masculinity and femininity. To put it another way, everything that functions in differentiation in the act of construction of sexuality will certainly be Christianly transported and incorporated in God on the day of entry into his Kingdom, even though we shall no longer use our genitality in order to be unified. Far from being cultural (as in gender theory), the difference of the sexes is given to us first of all as natural and remains something that we cannot shrug off. But our nature is not based on genital difference except insofar as it is also sexualized. Without this it just comes back, as so often, to animality; indeed, it slides into bestiality. There is no sexual difference beyond a nature onto which desire is grafted and that modifies it (§23). Without this, the genital (male-female difference) would never pass into sexuality (man-woman difference).[16]

The Pauline imperative for husbands to "love their wives as they do their own bodies" (Eph. 5:28) and for wives to "be subject to your husband as you are to the Lord" (Eph, 5:22) (see §22) has nothing to do with domination or the destruction of differentiation, but in fact the opposite. The man-woman relation is the more unified, as the terms are differentiated, the bodies cross and encounter, as swords do, more keenly as they are more resistant, and are more attached to one another to the extent that they exist in their own substance or embodiedness. A husband will then recognize a woman, *his wife*, in the Kingdom; this is the least one can say. And the man, her husband, will still be such for his wife, or we risk denying the idea of fidelity capable of going beyond anything—even death. Lived and experienced in another way, sexual difference and the preference for the loved one will then continue to be expressed, even if independently of the genital and above all in an act of differentiating that will be marred neither by jealousy nor by division.

(2) In addition to the necessity of remaining sexual (but not genital) up to the Resurrection, at least—in order to recognize one another there, in what is also the basis of our humanity—another question arises, and it is by no means a minor one: What about the permanence of the sacrament of marriage when there is a possibility of plurality? What happens to this woman who has had several husbands, seven brothers one after the other, in a perfectly legal way, through the successive deaths of each previous one (Matt. 22:23–33)? This exercise in casuistry is crucial because it sends us back to the question of preference as well as to fidelity, indeed, to the pleasure that, with eros, cannot be forgotten. Christ's reply is in fact shocking—more so than the question itself (which is slightly ridiculous): You shall be "*like* angels in heaven" (Matt. 22:30). Everything hangs here on the mode of comparison—"like" (*ôs*)—which shows us precisely what we are not and what we shall never be. Moreover, it is because we are not angels, and are not called to become so, that the comparison can be made; even more significantly, it points to an analogy where the identity of the relation makes us see the heterogeneity of the terms. As far as we are and shall be in heaven *like angels*, we shall not be such as asexual beings, but we shall be, as

the gospel makes clear, *like them* "in heaven continually in the presence of my Father in heaven" (Matt. 18:10 [JB]), or we shall be those who "cannot die anymore, . . . like angels" (Luke 20:36). The hypothetical and false hypothesis of the asexual man gives way here to the oblation of the body: offered, turned toward, and integrated into God in the act of the eucharist. If they are neither husband nor wife in the sense of a possible domination, the husband and wife remain forever as such in the sense of oblation. The call to angelism in Christianity is not—is not ever for humankind—a claim to escape from our state as creatures; on the contrary, it is a model of integration at the limit in God, in order to be transformed rather than to be left behind. The in-the-world show their *difference* with respect to the divine, the human with respect to the angelic, and woman with regard to man (and vice versa). In the gap stands the truth of the differentiated. And, rather than filling in that gap, we should strive to explore it.

There is still fidelity, even when a wife has had several husbands—a hypothesis that explores a limit rather than being concerned with the norms of reality. Concerning eros, we don't consider that fidelity is simply the staying-power of vows, as a condition of the persistence of the erotic phenomenon. The *yes* once spoken is not enough of a commitment if all it does is coerce the "automatic flesh" where this "is triggered off" and "gets under way" upon the "rack of eroticization."[17]

A faithful person (in the double and admirable sense of the term, referring to husband and wife as well as to belief and the believer) shows fidelity above all in the flesh and not uniquely in what is spoken. And it follows in Christianity that a union has not been fulfilled sacramentally if it is not consummated erotically. The ratified marriage (*matrimonium ratum*) has been definitively linked since the Middle Ages and in Canon Law to the "consummated marriage" (*matrimonium consomatum*), in such a way that the absence of a physical union of bodies (*copula carnalis*) renders the sacrament of marriage "not indissoluble," if not invalid.[18]

If there is fidelity to the (marriage) vows, it cannot be simply a matter of the role of constraint. "Creative fidelity" is faithful to the flesh, not exclusively to the spoken vows. There is a risk that sustaining spoken vows may simply be the result of constraint, and the embrace at the heart of the conjugal union may simply become a matter of fact. But, as Gabriel Marcel underlines, movingly, from his own experience (after the death of his wife, Jacqueline Boegner, in 1947), "It is because fidelity is creative that, like liberty, it infinitely transcends the limits of what can be prescribed."[19] The fidelity to each other in a couple is sacramentally fidelity through eros in action. This is particularly so because their embrace of the differentiated in the union of their bodies changes and moves in the eucharistic agape of the gift of the flesh. We cannot say that there is automatic and eroticized flesh on the one hand and the vows of fidelity in the name of the sacrament on the other; the flesh itself becomes that sacramental monstrance of the transformation of the eros into agape. Christ himself concludes, in his address to these same Sadducees, "What God has joined together, let no one separate" (Matt. 19:6). He proclaims precisely the unity of the differentiated flesh of man and woman in his own body that is summoned to be offered and transubstantiated. The woman who has had several husbands was not unfaithful to *her* flesh, but simply is inscribed—exceptionally, in a plural fashion—into the eucharistic flesh of God, transforming the ordeal of mourning (for those among the dead she had loved) into a union of hearts as well as of bodies (union with the body of God before all other fleshly unions).[20]

There is no lack of desire, or of joy (*jouissance*), here-below as well as in the hereafter—that is, not in the multiplication of flesh that is unified, but primarily in fidelity to that Christly eucharisticized flesh, in which all differentiated flesh takes on meaning through enactment of the erotic. Only the coincidence of their bodies subsides, not the *desire of great desire* that we find in "'I have eagerly desired to eat this Passover with you before I suffer'" (Luke 22:15). And that desire does not end with either the consumption of the Passover meal or the proclamation of the Resurrection; far from it. The eros is so well and so thoroughly integrated with the eucharistic agape in fleshly and faithful love, and tries to stay as such, that enjoyment of it is not reserved only for here-below, even if it is so much desired that one would wish never to leave it. It is even spread to the hereafter, by which the act of the eucharist and its manducation of the Host become also the site of the celebration of a desire that is increased tenfold. Aquinas tells us that "the loftiest pleasures which we share with the angels are expected" in the Resurrection [*ubi expectantur delectationes altissimae*]. He distinguishes these from sexual pleasure, talking instead of "the pleasures in the vision of God which will be common to us and the angels."[21] Far from abandoning our limits, we keep to them here-below as in the hereafter, even though they may be lived otherwise and newly incorporated in He who comes to glorify them. What constitutes our particularity and is the great strength of our created being until its beatification is, as I see it and as Aquinas indicates, a *limited phenomenon* rather than a *saturated phenomenon*: "The created light of glory received into any created intellect cannot be infinite [*Non posse esse infinitum*]."[22] Far from maintaining the privilege of the elect in a glory that would certainly be expected but not unanimously shared, God rejoins "man as such," or our pure and simple humanity, making our limits themselves the place where essentially—and in the self-emptying and receptivity of the will (kenosis)—he comes to sojourn for us. If there is to be a resurrection, or a *metamorphosis of finitude*, it will never be made at the price of a breaking up of frontiers, but will simply be another way of living within our limited being.[23]

The title of this chapter, "Embrace and Differentiation," suggests that embrace *is* differentiation, in that man and woman unite rather than differentiate, here (*in via*) and in the hereafter (*in patria*). Or, we could say that they exist, the one for the other, only as far as they identify each one for himself or herself—even if primarily this means the one for the other. I have my limits, certainly. But the other, and my spouse in particular, shows them to me, makes me love them as well as desire them (see §22). That is what is at stake in the wedding feast—that of the Lamb, certainly (the sacrament of the eucharist), but also that of spouses (the sacrament of marriage). The latter takes place within the former, in that it serves as an experiential model that aids understanding of the eucharist; at the same time, it finds in the eucharist its own ontological basis. The limit of the couple, the one for the other, in the differentiation of their bodies, will thus be a reflection of the limit of God for human beings that is given in the sacrament. *This is my body given* tells us here that the limited, for once, do not suffer from our limitation, but are waiting for an other who will help to love, rather than dramatically to bear, our limitation. In heaven "there is no marriage," according to Hans-Urs von Balthasar, "but the Marriage of the Lamb is celebrated"[24]—a statement that resonates exactly with the theme of this book. What God does for the Chaos of passions and drives concentrated in the power of our bodies and our part of animality (Chapters 1 and 4; Chapters 2 and 5) he does also with eros or difference sexualized, this time in the form of the act of the eucharist (Chapters 3 and 6). It is as the gift of a transformation, or a transubstantiation, by which nothing of our humanity is lost, and we wait for our filiation in the act of the eucharist (§29). If there are no limits *in* love, or *of* love, a *love of limits* is still, however, its basis. Nothing takes us further from Christianity than the false desire of man or woman to wish to leave their rank of created beings and to aim at some form of angelism. The act of the eucharist invites us to recognize our own created humanity; the role of this viaticum is both to nourish and to recall us to our humanity.

§22. Love of the Limit

Why then create? Why, if the eucharistic act will come in some way to recreate, or rather, to *recapitulate* what God himself has already done? Or perhaps we should ask this instead: Why make human beings? God could well have been satisfied with making the world, or with simply contemplating himself as God—as the God who says, "Let us make humankind in our image" (Gen. 1:26). There is only one answer to these questions: Because of *his love and respect for limits*, he the Unlimited had need of a different limited one, capable of being itself for him as a face-to-face for his own act of loving. "God does not recognize himself in his work," as Bonhoeffer says in his commentary on the sixth day of creation. "He sees his work but he does not see himself. . . . Man differs from the other creatures in that God himself is in him, in that he is God's image in which the free Creator views himself."[25] The Unlimited is on one side and the limit on the other. The solitude of God precedes in some respects the creation of the world, as the solitude of man anticipates the creation of Eve. There is a period of waiting for an image for God in the first narrative of the creation (Gen. 1:22), and there is a desire for an other taken from his own flesh for Adam in the second narrative (Gen. 2:2). The two narratives reflect one another and sanctify mutual love in the blessed state that characterizes them (the limited and the unlimited). This is the basis of a sharing that, if it is not a taking on, is at least an offering, in the form of a responsibility sometimes too heavy to shoulder.

(1) *The solitude of God.* Like Adam later in the other narrative, God must no longer be satisfied with the creation of the animals (fifth day), because he goes beyond it to the creation of man, to find at last a face-to-face and a resemblance (sixth day). In man, here his image, God sees and in some way encounters a reflection, so that the human, at this point precisely, does not remain—or remains no longer—in simple animality. Certainly the Chaos of the passions and drives belongs to the human, perhaps more obviously today than in the past. But through his image in the human, God finds himself integrated and transformed—once the act of creation has taken place. Or, rather, it is particularly in the Son that God finds this integration and transformation. Human beings alone, and Christians in particular, have the means both to deny their part of animality and to make it the site of a fleshly offering, and not solely one of corporal pathos. Thus in certain translations of the Bible we read of the couple male-female (not man-woman) who, related to the image of God in humanity, lose nothing of their animality but suggest that it has to be shouldered and transformed: "God created humankind in his image, in the image of God he created them; male and female he created them" (Gen. 1:27).[26] The "extra" of the human is not philosophical in the first place, because what really counts, in phenomenological terms, is access to our proper animality (§16). It is, rather, and more originally, theological:

"We can know about the man of the beginning only if we start from Christ."[27] In other words, Adam carries already in him, and did to some degree in advance, the image of the Word; paradoxically, the Word finds there exactly its first and principal prefiguration. As Eve will later be for Adam, so man is for God in his solitude the helper who is suitable for him. At this limit of the human, the future limit of the incarnate Word is conceived in advance, so to speak, in the double choice of limitation in a body: the decision to bring about incarnation, and the narrowing down as far as the transubstantiated bread in the act of the eucharist. Irenaeus reminds us: "Adam [was] himself termed by Paul *the figure of Him that was to come*' (Rom. 5:14), because the Word, the Maker of all things, had formed beforehand for Himself the future dispensation of the human race." And thus "the commixture of the heavenly wine" with the "water of the world" mean that "the Word of the Father and the Spirit of God . . . [have] become united [in us] with the ancient substance of Adam's formation."[28]

(2) *The solitude of man.* God himself is disturbed by this solitude and speaks out against it in the second narrative of creation: "The Lord God said, 'It is not good that the man should be alone; I will make him a helper as his partner'" (Gen. 2:18). Does Adam know that he is alone? It does not really matter. Solitude is not recognized until one leaves it; it is when one has already left it that one really suffers from it. Its other name is always confinement—a confinement whose frontiers one doesn't know precisely because there is nothing beyond the closure for whoever remains immured there. The act of naming the animals had a goal, if not for humankind, then at least for God: to give the human male the companionship he lacked, to "find a companion among these brothers, for the animals really are of the same origin as he." Moreover, "according to the Bible men and animals have the same bodies!"[29] There is, however, a failure: the man does not say this, but it is obvious in what God sees: "for the man there was *not* found a helper as his partner" (Gen. 2:20). One thing is certain, even though Adam does not yet know it: to live truly is to agree to be helped or to find help. Help does not indicate weakness before danger, but rather shows an understanding of the necessity of a face-to-face with what is both the same and different, in order to be loved. One may be disappointed, and will remain disappointed, instead of Adam, or like Adam: naming the animals was not enough to release him from his solitude, even if it was essential in order to discover the "community of animality" that the Bible continues to affirm (§14).

In the void, fullness speaks: in the lack, there lies a petition. Adam must, paradoxically, help God find him a helper, or rather, find help. From that comes (a) the "rib" taken from his side, and (b) the "deep sleep" into which he falls.

(a) First of all, the "rib." Eve is given side-by-side (literally, rib-to-rib: *côte-à-côte*) and not face-to-face: "[God] took one of his [Adam's] ribs and closed up its place with flesh" (Gen. 2:21). A face-to-face is in fact never enough, because while putting God in the front, one always and at the same time finds the other at the side (*sur le côté*), or very close (*tout à côté*). And it is also thus, symbolically, with the structure of the human body: eyes to the front to see God and the world, ears at the side to hear the neighbour at our side. Hugh of Saint-Victor points out, charmingly, in his commentary on Ecclesiastes, "In the human body the eyes are properly placed *in front*, to see and gaze upon the works of God in the world. But the ears are also properly placed: situated at *the side*, they help us understand that our intentions should only be directed toward our neighbour in the second place, and principally toward God."[30] From another perspective than that of the "asymmetry of the face-to-face" (Levinas), the other appears and remains "always on the margins" in some Christian thought, as in a certain kind of phenomenology. Merleau-Ponty explains, "The other, in my eyes, is thus always on the margin of what I see and hear, he is this side of me, he is beside or behind me, but he is not in that place which my look flattens and empties of an 'interior.'"[31]

Adam does not expect mainly, or solely, a face-to-face in speech or directed to his speech. He waits a long time before he hears Eve speak. Even then, her first speech is a reply to the serpent, not simply one in which she expresses herself.[32] God, with the help of Adam, looks for a side-by-side (*côte-à-côte*) of the flesh—or rather, he looks *to the flesh*—of a man, at once similar and different: similar in that Adam gives his flesh, or rather, his bone, so that the woman can be drawn from him; and different in that only the power of God can make the transformation: "The rib that the Lord God had taken from the man he made into a woman and brought her to the man" (Gen. 2:22).

By the flesh and in the flesh, principally but not uniquely (§20), the other is said and found to be both the same and different. The couple know this through the erotic, as parents know it through filiation, and God himself knows this as he takes on responsibility for the form of the creation. In every case, the other (in particular *my* son or *my* daughter) seems always as if drawn from my flesh, so that to suffer for this other comes back to suffering for myself, in a carnal body-to-body that can only finally be the mystic union with a spiritual body. St. Paul expresses this remarkably: "I am completing what is lacking in Christ's afflictions for the sake of his body, that is, the church" (Col. 1:24). Silence is called for when the flesh is exposed, whether it is a question of the loving couple, the suffering child, or the creative God. A kind of "divine surgery" operates here (*cheriourgia*) by which Adam—in a way the pioneer of all patients who have been anesthetized—lets God work without him but always starting from him, by this "rib," or this "rib-to-rib," that comes from him.[33]

(b) Next, the "sleep." The mystery that envelops the creation of Eve from Adam's rib—it also probably envelops eros between the couple and, indeed, the *this is my body* of the eucharist—needs a night when the human does not know, and will never know, exactly how things have proceeded, except that they took place starting from him and practically without him: "The Lord God caused a deep sleep to fall upon the man, and he slept" (Gen. 2:21). The depth of the sleep here matches his surprise when he wakes: "Then the man said, 'This at last is bone of my bones and flesh of my flesh; this one shall be called Woman, for out of Man this one was taken'" (Gen. 2:23). His words follow here the transformation of the flesh. He gives it sense, ensuring precisely that he makes sense of our possible and erotic experience of the senses. What is it that Adam saw this time that he had not seen when he was naming the animals? His wife, Eve, now has her part, like him, of organic flesh—indeed, is also animal and taken from the same dust as him (flesh and bone). But above all, what she is made of in terms of *matter* is demonstrated this time in terms of *manner*, or at least in a synchrony of lived experience. What distinguishes the flesh of Eve from that of all other animals is that it is seen by Adam as like *his* flesh, with the same texture, having the same possible habitus or sensations of movement: "bone of my bones and flesh of my flesh."

The interpenetration of flesh, or of lived experiences, now takes precedence over the simple confrontation of bodies or of organs. Eve is bone of *his* bones and flesh of *his* flesh in that their passions (or rather, *pathema*) can merge without ever losing their identity. There will be common lived experience that takes on meaning only within the divine project, in that the solitude of both seems to have been definitively broken ("'It is not good that the man should be alone'" [Gen. 2:18]). And at last the helper who will suit Adam has been found, so that he can live with her, and in God, totally incorporated ("'I will make him a helper as his partner'" [Gen. 2:18]). The solitude of God, waiting for man as "his image" (first creation narrative), and the solitude of Adam, waiting for Eve as "bone of my bones and flesh of my flesh" (second creation narrative), answer to one another here—not so much in simple complementarity as in the integration of the second (carnal unity of the man and the woman) into the first (man as the image of God). As Karl Barth says so strikingly, "Man like God is not solitary. . . . In the couple man-woman, the human being is the image and the reflection of God. It is thus in the double face-to-face of God with his likeness, that he reproduces the face-to-face that exists in God himself."[34]

A question remains, and it is not a minor one; indeed, it is central: How can Eve be a true helper for Adam, to the point that he is able to cry out about it, in the same way that the viaticum of *this is my body* in the eucharist will (see §34) be able to help us, not just to live, but to recognize ourselves through God, newly constituted and differentiated? The woman is first referred to in a narrative where Adam does not speak directly but rather seems to address himself to God, or to himself, like a patient in front of his doctor, surprised to find himself suddenly cured of so much solitude, either organic or simply psychic. "This one shall be called Woman, for out of Man this one was taken" (Gen. 2:23). The woman (*ishah*) comes, then, from the man (*ish*) etymologically and in terms of flesh. But above all, she is identified—indeed, singled out—as "his" woman and not as "the" woman. The singularity of the "this" of the woman in Genesis connects with the *haecceity* (thisness)[35] of the "this" in *this is my body* on the day of the Last Supper (Mark 14:22). Both times, love is only given and it only loves that which is singularized. No universal salvation exists in philosophy, or in theology, independently of love of the singular. We learn this from a Franciscan, Duns Scotus, based on a formula that we will find useful to recall even today: *amo, volo ut sis* (I love *you*, I want *you* to be).[36]

The special help that Eve gives has no other function for Adam than to bring with it something singular—that is, it brings into play the limit exactly by which we are constituted: "Woman becomes man's helper in the carrying of the limit imposed upon him."[37] The created being is limited, as I have emphasized, and as has been a basic theme of theology through the works of its most illustrious doctor (Thomas Aquinas). Phenomenological finitude is reread theologically as a kind of theological limit wished for and desired by God. As I have pointed out elsewhere, the limitation of *nature* to *my nature* is not a turning back to oneself in the critical subjectivism that has often been wrongly attacked; on the contrary, it is an opening to the world starting from me, from mine, that respects the state of the creature and his distance from the Creator as it was willed and desired by God himself.[38] We should not mix up *limit* and *limitation*. The former acknowledges our ontological being in the face of God; the latter wrongly regrets that we are not like him, not infinite (without limits). Eve's help, given by God to Adam, is not there solely to release him from his solitude; it will also help him to bear his limit, and thus his created being—indeed, will help him to love it. "In this limitation he had his life," Bonhoeffer tells us, "[. . .] but he could still not really love this life in its limitation. . . . Out of this mercy [the Creator] created a companion for man who must be at once the embodiment of Adam's limit and the object of his love. . . . The other person is the limit placed on me by God. I love this limit and I shall not transgress it because of my love."[39]

What goes here for Adam's rib goes also, and paradoxically, for Eve's rib. In this rib-to-rib—of Adam to Eve and of Eve to Adam—we cannot in fact privilege one "rib," or rather one "side," at the expense of the other. All the (mistaken) critiques of the inequality of man and woman in St. Paul's writings neglect how much the Apostle to the Gentiles brings about a true "foundation for universalism," of woman for man, and of man for woman. The first Letter to the Corinthians insists on this, drawing on Genesis: "Indeed, man was not made from woman, but woman from man" (1 Cor. 11:8). However, this is followed almost immediately by: "Nevertheless [*plên*], in the Lord woman is not independent of man or man independent of woman. For just as *woman came from man*, so *man comes through woman*; but *all things come from God*" (1 Cor. 11:11–12). Far from remaining in asymmetry, as Genesis and Judaism might suggest ("The rib that the Lord God had taken from the man he made into a woman" [Gen. 2:22]), St. Paul and Christianity stretch out the difference man-woman to such a degree of originality and universalism that we can no longer say from whom—the man or the woman—the one or the other was taken. God is (*the*) difference from which all differences come, since "all things come from God," including the differences themselves; we thus learn to desire rather than spurn them. Alain Badiou, speaking as a well-informed nonbeliever, says on this point, "What matters for man or woman, Jew or Greek, slave or free man, is that their *differences are what convey the universal that has come to them through grace.*"[40]

It could not be better put. A "love in common of limits" of God for the world and of Eve for Adam, and vice versa, leads to the avowal of sexual difference, indeed, to the "reciprocal incarnation" (§23) in place at the origin and from then onwards. Man is never so much masculinized as when he encounters his woman (wife) erotically, and woman never so much feminized as when she is united in terms of the flesh with her man (husband). Union in eros, once again, does not suppress difference. It reveals it and always reinforces it, in order to convey it, indeed, to love difference together. Leaving his father and mother, the man "clings to his wife" and "they become one flesh" (Gen. 2:24), not because the union of flesh destroys the difference of bodies, but because it intensifies the difference and recognizes it also as something to be lived. Adam and Eve are *one flesh* but do not give up being *two bodies*, remaining so all the more in the common discovery of a masculinity and femininity that eros teaches them both to fulfill and to put into action: "I shall not overstep the limits of the other that God has given me and that he has established for me because of my love . . . in that the two beings, who remain two, become as creatures of God *one body* (or *one flesh*), that is to say, in the love they reciprocally call their own."[41]

We don't simply take the limit of the other for granted; we do not even welcome it or accept it. We strive to desire it, as we must desire this created world and also this single spouse whom God has given us. Drawing back from the limit, humans actually draw back before what is created, before the other, or before love, after loving becomes an act of differentiating (oneself). After all, without limits there is no differentiation, only the myth of fusion or the trap of a false union. The Trinity, and even more so the eucharist, serves as a model in which the couple, in Christian terms, are unified while allowing their bodies to remain separate, in a unity of flesh that is all the more strengthened because they are braced against each other: "'I have eagerly desired to eat this Passover with you before I suffer'" (Luke 22:15). The active passion of desire takes priority here over the passive reception of suffering, in humankind as in God. It consecrates the embrace of *this is my body* as well as the vigour of differentiation in the act of loving; it is not a trap in which we just melt into the oblivion of our embodiedness. Eros differentiates, and eucharistic communion also leads us in this direction—not lifting our eyes to the heavens in the illusion of a forgotten unity but, like the disciples at Emmaus during the first eucharistic meal with the resurrected Son, leaving at "that same hour" and returning "to Jerusalem" (Luke 24:33).

§23. Desire and Differentiation

God does not wish for suffering, any more than human beings do, but desires and leads toward the Passover as a gift of his self and of the body, much as happens in the erotic of the body. Christ "eagerly desired" to eat the Passover supper (Luke 22:15). The Last Supper of the body is an "act of desire" that precedes the suffering and gives it meaning. Passion in the sense of the desirable (the eucharist: "'Take; this is my body'" [Mark 14:22]) makes sense in terms of pathos, or of what cannot be represented (the cross: "'My God, my God, why have you forsaken me?'" [Mark 15:34]). The first and most ardent "desire" of God, as also of humankind, is, paradoxically, to meet a body and to be given bodily, rather than to endure everything or to suffer for the sake of bearing it. Only desire gives meaning to suffering—not the desire to suffer, but the pull of the gift of one's body to the other, regardless of whether this includes suffering. God only suffers because he loves, as I have tried to show; it isn't that he loves to suffer or that he loves suffering. The "missed opportunity" of giving a proper place to suffering in Christianity derives usually from an unjustifiable confusion between the love of suffering (Stoicism) and suffering even in love (Christianity).[42] We can bring up here how it is through "desire" that humans progressively leave animality, without ever forgetting it entirely. And it is through desire also that Christ gives his body, making the site of eros that is incarnate between the espoused couple also the site of a communion with the resurrected God. "There is no sexual understanding that is not *theological*, at least as far as the Christian system is concerned, we should say with and in relation to Tertullian. The decisive biblical expression 'two in one flesh' that Tertullian cites four or five times in his works immediately invites a connection with the question of man and woman in the great Christological affirmation of which he remains the sympathetic inventor: Christ is 'one person in two natures,' a formula that we find in *Against Praxeas* [Chapter 27]."[43]

Christ, however, as I have suggested, does not simply desire. He desires with his characteristic desire—an ardent desire or "desire of a great desire"—to eat the Passover with his disciples. Translating literally this time—"With great desire [*epithumia*] I have desired [*epethumêsa*] to eat this Passover with you" (Luke 22:15 [AV])—this redoubling of desire seems, at first sight, simply an indication of his insistence: to desire with an eager desire as if one simply desired more. But in fact to talk of the *desire of desire* is to say more and something else entirely. The desire is not simply "great"; it is "other." Or rather, it is "great" in that it is "other." The fervour of the desire makes the desire truly Desire—"desire of desire"— and not just a need. It is certainly a hunger to eat, as well as a hunger for the erotic, or for satisfaction with what is consumed. But the desire in the act of the eucharist is not a simple need to eat one's fill, nor abandonment to the point of self-oblivion in the consecrated body. It is a recognition, even a birth, or alterity, as if he who came to give himself by his desire wished already to show us what there is of his divinity in it. Certainly, animals are not without *desires*, or rather, without *needs*. And in such needs, as Hegel shows famously in his *Phenomenology of Mind*, the animal attains at least a certain "sentiment of self." Desiring, or at least wishing, the animal reveals himself to himself as having appetites and being (at least, to a certain extent) conscious. There is an "I" who wants to eat, to copulate, and to dominate who reveals himself to himself, even in wanting these things, and thus has a certain identity. But humankind—and only humankind, Hegel tells us—wants more than desiring in the simple sense of the satisfaction of needs. Through desire, not simply through "need" that is often mimed in the act of knowing (the absorption of the known and the knower), humankind arrives at "self-consciousness" rather than the "sentiment of self." Alexandre Kojève tells us in his commentary on Hegel that "anthropogenetic Desire is different from animal Desire . . . in that it is directed, not toward a real, 'positive,' given object, but toward another Desire. Thus, in the relationship between man and woman, for example, Desire is human only if the one desires, not the body, but the Desire of the other; if he wants 'to possess' or 'to assimilate' the Desire taken as Desire . . . human history is the history of desired Desires."[44]

Animality—accepted in the Chaos of our passions and drives (§2), defining a community with those who are living (§14), and making up my embodiedness (§17)—appears this time to have been transcended, without, however, having been forgotten. To desire another and be desired by her or him, when one is or becomes human, comes down not to absorbing the other in one's own pleasure, but to taking pleasure in the pleasure of the other—which is precisely what provoked the desire. Humanity is born in alterity, which comes from the meeting of desired Desires. The movement, certainly dialectical here, also consecrates, in my view, the force of divinity and not uniquely that of humanity. For if the Desire is "human," or is a "generator of humanity" (anthropogenetic) between man and woman, insofar as it is not solely a need for the body of the other, but is *Desire of the desire of the other* (not simply to consummate or to be consummated with the other, but to stimulate the desire of the other so as to give birth to one's own desire and to recognize one another reciprocally), this intensification of desire belongs above all to the eucharistic Last Supper before figuring on the erotic scene: "With desire I have desired to eat this Passover with you" (Luke 22:15 [AV]). Anthropogenetic desire, which causes man and woman to be born in their irreducible difference at the heart of the human eros, becomes in some respects *theogenetic* in the eucharistic agape, as far as the relation of human beings to God is concerned. God is also born to himself, and above all to us, in that he wishes to share this Passover with us—and thus gives himself to us in the form of the eroticized body, but it is a body capable of taking on responsibility, as well as metamorphosis.

Ego do corpus meum—Accipio ("I give you my body—I accept it"). This exchange formed part of the marriage rite in Avignon in the fifteenth century.[45] What we find here of this couple in their marriage vows, which for once are not uniquely verbal but also and above all corporal, will be even more true for Christ, who accomplishes his Desire of desire of the Passover in the eucharistic Last Supper: "Take this. . . . This is my body, which is given for you" (Luke 22:17, 19). The analogy of the union of the couple between themselves and the union of Christ with the Church is direct here, without being vulgar. It is not the couple who eroticize the eucharist, but the eucharist that in some way "agapizes" or "makes charitable" the erotic union of the espoused. As we have seen (§9), the eros of the couple between themselves, in the (erotic) *this is my body given for you*, represents neither univocity (Marion) nor equivocity (Nygren), but is the test of their transformation and conversion to the Christian agape in the eucharistic *this is my body given for you* of Christ to his disciples. The union of the bodies emerges from this transformation not simply more eroticized but, above all, charitably incorporated in a God who is alone capable of receiving such union and spiritualizing it in his own unity. Because the Trinity defines a plurality in unity (three distinct persons, but one substance: Council of Nicaea), and the incarnation a unity that has been pluralized (two natures in one person: Council of Chalcedon), it is also given to the man-woman couple to share in the differentiated structure, in the incorporation of their bodies to his body—where being unified is not this time a fusion but accentuates a difference all the greater because it is reciprocally shared. "That they may all be one. As you, Father, are in me and I am in you, may they also be in us, so that the world may believe that you have sent me" (John 17:21).

As the woman is *desire of the desire of the man* and the man is *desire of the desire of the woman*, showing one another limits to share and to aim at, so Christ is *Desire of desire to share his Passover with us* ("'I have desired with a great desire'" [Luke 22:15]) or to be given for us to communicate, indeed, to eat ("'This is my body, which is given for you'" [Luke 22:19]). The difference from the divine is given fully to the human being, as the difference of the masculine is given to the feminine and becomes visible there. The man (husband) is all the more man in that he receives his masculinity and its difference in giving himself to his woman (wife)—like God now, who is, at least for us, all the more God because he reveals himself in his divinity in being given to our humanity. "Without confusion . . . or separation," the Word holds in himself a unity (of the human and the divine) that teaches us to unite our differences in him and like him, in strengthening them, uniting our bodies in eros in *one sole flesh* (difference of man and woman), without, however, fusing them but rather keeping up a tension and to some extent interpenetrating them (difference of man and God): "Truly God and truly man, composed of rational soul and body; consubstantial with the Father as to his divinity and consubstantial with us as to his humanity: 'like us in all things but sin.'"[46]

But the desire in the conjugal eros is not simply human; it humanizes—in the same way that the gift of the body in the eucharistic agape is not simply divine; it divinizes. The dynamic of Desire must be such in the erotic night (as it is in the eucharistic Mass) that the meeting of the bodies produces a profound transformation of the self. It does not fade away in an ephemeral fashion, as if to forget the union. The erotic scene makes conjugal life, in the best sense, *fecund*, forming and transforming even its quotidian quality, begetting—just as in the eucharistic Last Supper when the priest prays silently: "May this mingling of the Body and Blood of our Lord Jesus Christ bring eternal life to us who receive it."[47] On the one hand, there is a meeting of bodies (conjugal eros); on the other hand, there is attendance of a Mass (eucharistic agape). In both cases there is embodiedness, and thus also a conversion of the self in what is encountered, or in "this person" that is encountered and, as it were, eroticized. One becomes one's own body in uniting with the body of the other (human in difference from God, masculine or feminine in difference from each other), and so much more than if one just *were* a body united to the other, and always self-made forever.

To become body, or become one's own body, through the body of the other in embrace or desire, so that the differentiated become the act of love (Part II), means placing difference at the origin (§21) but also establishing what it will become, indeed, what will be its future. Moses Maimonides translates and emphasizes the verse of Genesis 2:24 as follows: "They *shall* become one flesh."[48] The unity of man-woman is not simply given to them; it is also something becoming and to come, according to a dialectical movement of "man and woman" (Gaston Fessard) that reverses the more famous dialectic of "master and slave" (Hegel). Marx, in a remarkable aside to a manuscript of 1844, commenting on the relationship of man to man, says: "The secret of this approach [to woman as the *spoil* and handmaid of communal lust] has its *unambiguous*, decisive, plain and undisguised expression in the relation of *man* to *woman* and in the manner in which the *direct* and *natural* species-relationship is conceived."[49] This reversal (of master-slave to man-woman) was certainly often taught, particularly during the period when it was analyzed and developed by the Jesuit thinker Gaston Fessard (in 1960), at a time when Marxist theory was dominant and greater response to it was needed. The well-known episode hardly needs to be recalled here, but there is still the matter of the *impetus of desire*, and this concerns us here even more than reversal of the dialectic.

Man and woman, at least at the start, were also involved in some form of struggle and are shown as such—whether in making love or in wooing one another. Fessard comments, interestingly, "So that this union of man and woman appears not simply as the effect of a biological attraction, but the fruit of a physical choice, it is necessary that the difference of the two desires is revealed in the course of a competition that is a true *amorous struggle*. . . . The courtship that the man and women pay to one another, even in its most evolved and refined forms never loses it character of a 'struggle.'"[50] This is basic knowledge that theology and philosophy, at least up to Hegel, has often neglected to consider or to use. All struggle is not necessarily bad (see Heraclitus rather than Parmenides) or sinful (as in naive interpretations of Genesis). In a pioneering account of unsocial sociability, Kant tells us that trees with a "beautiful, straight stature" are those that "in seeking to take the air and sunlight from others must strive upward." Those that remain "isolated" and that "put out branches at random . . . grow stunted, crooked, and twisted."[51] In reality, everything depends upon what happens in, or what becomes of, the struggle—to the death (dialectic of the master and slave) or for life (dialectic of man and woman). "Whatever it appears to be," Fessard adds, "this *amorous struggle* is at bottom the very opposite of a *struggle to the death*. Since, for both of the adversaries, it is not a question of showing one's courage in risking one's own life despite or thanks to mutual threats of death: on the contrary, it is a matter, through reciprocal assurances of life, of provoking the other to show the worth that he attributes to his partner in giving himself to the partner."[52]

After this first period of reversal of the man-woman dialectic, when a couple make love or during their courtship, their aim is no longer the subjugation of the other as object of domination, but choice and discovery as a site of desire for an other and desire of another desire. "It may also be that the onslaught of courtship comes to nothing," Fessard says, "but its true end is unfailingly to find an 'accord,' an 'understanding,' that plays its role in knowledge as much as in the will of the partners. And by that it makes them bring about a new mutual being . . . the virile initiative of one of the parties involved calls up from the other the response of a feminine reception."[53] As we have seen, the *Desire of the desire of the other* is not simply the end result of a nature that has been progressively humanized, but there at the start for sexualized persons who come to "know" one another (i.e., are born together) or are in some way "hominized" (i.e., become human). It is not simply survival of the self that is at stake in the amorous struggle, as in a struggle to the death; it is survival of the life of the other, or even more of that of a third—a child—whose birth constitutes the true labor (the final reversal): "The fecund woman, through the virile power of man enters into labor to accomplish the plan that their mutual love conceived: to give an objective being to their unity. It is a labor very different, in truth, from that of the slave. For, rather than feeling her being dissolved in the anguish of death, the woman happily sees her existence affirmed by the promise of the life that she carries inside her . . . the woman gives her substance to the man whom she carries for a long time in her womb. . . . In the child nature is not simply *humanized*, a source of joy for the master and of understanding for the slave, it is *hominized*—truly becoming man as Marx wished."[54]

This homily will no doubt seem complaisant to some readers, but it does ring true, despite its seemingly naive and benevolent character. The struggle in love, as we have already seen, is not denied here, it is transformed—just as the union of bodies in eros is not, as I have tried to make plain, one of fusion but one of tension, of opposition in the encounter of difference, and identification of the self in and through the limit of the other. The child here has the role of a "recognition of love," but it is in such a distancing that the humanization of nature (master-slave dialectic) gives way to a hominization (man-woman dialectic) that is unthinkable, as I see it, and as it is seen in Christianity, independently of true filiation (§28). The other being who is engendered opens up a future and a pathway leading to Desire—which is much more than a nature that could be tamed and humanized. In theology, if not in philosophy, humanism in itself is not an end (see §28). In philosophy we note that a human being's essence lies in his "ek-sistance" and cannot simply be defined in terms of *animalitas* (Heidegger), even if we must still take account of *animalitas* because we find there "shared community" with our own organicity (§14). In theology, hominization (Fessard, Teilhard de Chardin) cannot in itself constitute a goal, even in the eucharist, if it is not at the same time transformed and integrated into filiation. And there is no humanism without the Trinitarian conception of God in Christianity (§28). No theology is "of liberation" except that which will liberate humankind even at the heart of God—*for God* and not simply *for humankind*, allowing human beings to move and search at the heart of the incarnate Word and to participate in the Trinitarian perichoresis.[55] The man-woman dialectic, moreover, does not find its fulfillment in itself, any more than eros is sufficient to explain agape. Seen in relation to God, humankind can never be called self-constituted; the couple become themselves not simply in a "coupling" but also in a willingness and desire to eroticize even at the heart of charity.

What is true of Christian marriage is also true of other sacraments (e.g., confirmation, ordination, anointing of the sick) even if it works in another way—without leaving our humanity, or indeed our animality, to offer and transform that animality at the heart of our filiation. The *hoc est corpus meum* (*this is my body*) characterizes an experience that human beings have in common with God, in the erotic scene as also in the eucharistic Last Supper, even when the latter gives meaning to the former and comes to include it as well as to engender it in a Christian mode: "Husbands, love your wives, just as Christ loved the church and gave himself up for her" (Eph. 5:25). The appeal in the Letter to the Ephesians does not shift from "this is my conjugal body" to "this is my body in the eucharist," but rather moves from "this is my body in the eucharist" to "this is my conjugal body." God, in this analogy of eros and agape, is the paradigm, and not humankind (§10). Spouses who share their Christian faith learn from this; what has come first for them (their love for one another) will in fact become what is last; and the last (the love of God) will always be first. It is not a question of renouncing egoism, or indeed the erotic; rather, the human aspect of the erotic finds and takes all its meaning from the divine banquet at the agape by which the couple, unified sacramentally, is consti- tuted, divinely this time. Certainly, our part of animality remains always there, along with the passions and drives that must be accepted and even eroticized (Chapter 4). But in the union of the agape, God gives them a meaning that they have not themselves suspected (Chapter 6). The third Eucharistic Prayer asks that "we, who are nourished by the Body and Blood of your Son and filled with his Holy Spirit may become one body, one spirit in Christ." And the nuptial blessing of the sacrament of mar- riage prays "that (partaking of the Body and Blood of Christ) they may always be bound together by love for one another."[56]

Desire in the conjugal embrace is not enough for the couple's incorpo- ration, any more than the eucharistic sacrament is enough, unless it is consummated (§33). Because what belongs to the order of will (Hegel, Marx), indeed, of love (Fessard), is not fleshly unless it is justified by the "reciprocal incarnation" of the one in the other, and of the one by the other. Sartre tells us, "The being which desires is consciousness *making itself body*. . . . Thus desire is the desire to appropriate a body as this appro- priation reveals to me my body as flesh . . . it is my body as flesh which causes the Other's flesh to be born."[57] This philosopher—seen as an existentialist, the phenomenological aspects of his work consequently neglected—tells us a great deal here. He shows an exemplary capacity to describe the encounter between bodies that are incarnate and always dif- ferentiated. We shall go on, however, to consider the workings of the inter- embodiedness of humankind and God that Christian manducation discovers, takes responsibility for, and transforms. We shall look at (1) how the consciousness becomes embodied; (2) how I become flesh in the presence of the other; and (3) how the birth of the flesh of the other starts off from my own fleshly body.

(1) Consciousness becomes embodied through desire—just as the desire to eat the Passover with his disciples will finish by embodiment in Christ and become incarnate in the gift of *this is my body*. But desire, at least for man and woman, is always first sexualized, so that we can appropriately reproach the Heideggerian *Dasein* (along with "Tintin of Hergé" [!]) because it "appears to us as asexual," because "ek-sistant" man and woman appear with no reference ever being made to sexual difference.[58] Sartre writes, "Man, it is said, is a sexual being because he possesses genitals. And if the reverse were true [i.e., because he is a sexual being he has genitals]?" In fact, the famous and much discussed theories of gender, whether in the work of Robert Stoller (1968) or Judith Butler (1990), are not far from our concerns here—proof, if it were needed, that today's questions always derive from those of yesterday, and indeed also from their answers. But Sartre remains original in his description of the erotic phenomenon and can probably help us escape from the blind alley of gender theory. Following neither pure naturalism (biologism) nor simple culturalism (the "making of gender"), he sees in human beings a "fundamental sexuality" as well as a "fundamental ontology." A human being only "[possesses] genitals" and is "originally and fundamentally a sexual being" insofar as that human is a "being who exists in the world in relation with other [human beings]"; further, sexuality, far from being "contingent," is "indispensable to the being of the For-Others." Brought back to desire, and solely to desire, sexuality takes body, rooted certainly in the biological (substantial ontology) yet also oriented toward the psychic (relational ontology): "To have sexual organs means . . . to exist sexually for an Other who exists sexually for me."[59]

(2) It is not enough, though, for my desire to take bodily form, even when that is the gift of the *this is my body*. The Desire of the desire of the other also makes me "flesh in the presence of the other," revealing to me "my own body as flesh." The famous distinction between "body" and "flesh"—of *Körper* and *Leib*—is certainly not new; indeed, I have relied upon it, going back in this book toward the *Körper* or the *Leib* in the sense of organic life, at the expense of *Leib* in the sense of fleshly lived experience (Chapter 5). But when we come back to Sartre we find that, characteristically, he has made *desire incarnate in the flesh* and thus has shown how only an intentionality of desire transforms the structure directed toward the other of the incarnate being. As I have already underlined, there is an "extended body" (mechanical object), a "lived body" (site of psychosomatic unity), and above all, the "body spread out" (biological body between the extended body and the lived body) (see §1). The extended body, or the body spread out, is still not the lived body; a doctor would not

have the same relationship with the biological body spread out on the operating table as he would have with a lived body that awaited him in the marriage bed. Everything here is a question of the "situation" rather than just the body. There is a "liturgy of eros" in the lovers' night (sexuality) as there is a "liturgy of agape" in the place of the Adoration (eucharist). Each time, what comes into play is (the same?) "putting into its situation of the body," holding itself as at once hidden and revealed, and ready to be exposed. We apprehend the other's body through its "situation in the world," as Sartre emphasizes. Certainly "Desire is defined as *trouble*," and desire remains desire of a body: "an arm or a half-exposed breast or perhaps a foot." But we do not desire the arm or the uncovered breast except on the basis of the body as an organic totality: "My desire is not mistaken: it is addressed not to a sum of physiological elements but to a total form— better yet, to a form *in situation*."[60]

The most ordinary erotic experience is enough to demonstrate this. A leg or a breast are not simply troubling because they are hidden *and* exposed, and because they are waiting to say more to us, but because they can signify so much to us. The transition in me of "the body" to "flesh" is what brings desire into play and is its essence. It is desire itself that becomes desirable and, Sartre tells us, "The error here stems from the fact that we have learned that the sexual act suppresses the desire."[61] It is as though we have learned that, as far as desire is concerned, all that matters is need (satisfaction of the drive). Desire does point to a certain way of existing through my body, and thus in flesh. Certainly, I am body, but through desire I become flesh, because in this way I am put in the situation of desiring and being desired. Paradoxically—and it is not far-fetched to suggest this—the eucharist itself and, even further, the act of adoration are not too far from this game of hide-and-seek. The bread and the wine, or the species, hide the body and the blood of Christ, or are like the "veil" or the "clothing (*velutum*)" suggested by St. Augustine, even before thought of the sacrament turns toward the "thing" (*res*) instead of the "sign" (*signum*) (§30). There is then a putting in place, or a putting in situation, of the body in the eucharistic agape as also in the conjugal eros. We see this in the liturgy, certainly, but also in the bread and the wine that express the whole of the body and blood of Christ only insofar as it remains hidden and this secret maintains the mystery of the agape that, like the eros, is never exhausted. "[God] remained concealed under the veil of the nature that covers him till the Incarnation," Pascal writes movingly in a famous letter to Charlotte de Roanez (1656). "And when it was necessary that he should appear, he concealed himself still the more in covering himself with humanity. . . . And in fine, when he wished to fulfill the promise that he made to his apostles to remain with them until his final coming, he chose to remain in the strangest and most obscure secret of all, which are the species of the Eucharist. It is this sacrament that St. John calls in the Apocalypse *a concealed manner*; and I believe that Isaiah saw it in that state, when he said in the spirit of prophecy: *Truly thou are a God concealed*."[62]

(3) It is my body of flesh that finally "gives birth to the flesh of the other." This is both the heart and the center of the "double reciprocal incarnation." The caress serves here as a model for Sartre—as it would do later, though in a slightly different way, in the work of Emmanuel Levinas. It is "the ensemble of those rituals which *incarnate* the Other."[63] But in the emergence of the caress, it is a question not simply of ignorance or of "not knowing" (Levinas), but of the emergence of the other and of myself in what is our own flesh. "The caress causes the Other to be born as flesh for me and for herself."[64] The caress does not entail taking hold of a part of the other's body; rather, it is "placing one's body against the Other's body. Not so much to push or to touch in the active sense but to place against."[65]

Once again the erotic takes precedence over the medical, and lived bodily experience for once recovers its right over the extended or spread-out body. Far from all kinds of physiotherapy or new methods of kinesthesia, or indeed haptonomy (the "science of affectivity"), the touch of the caress marks here a contact where the totality of the other, as also of myself, is engaged, and not simply a part that has been chosen to heal or manipulate. In caressing the flesh of the other, I transmit my desire of becoming flesh, not simply a body as far the other is concerned. And, letting myself be caressed by the other, he or she is incarnate for me in his or her own body to become flesh—and I appear thus as flesh to myself. A "double reciprocal incarnation" is produced, in which a mysterious inter-lacing of flesh takes shape, without confusion or separation. It is a fleshly union such that, through the other as flesh, I arrive at my own flesh, rather than always determining my own flesh myself in the lived experience of my own body. In some of his strongest and finest lines, Sartre explains how "In desire and in the caress which expresses desire, I incarnate myself in order to realize the incarnation of the Other. The caress by *realizing* the Other's incarnation reveals to me my own incarnation; that is, I make myself flesh in order to impel the Other to realize *for-herself* and *for me* her own flesh, and my caresses cause my flesh to be born for me in so far as it is for the Other *flesh causing her to be born as flesh*. I make her enjoy my flesh through her flesh in order to compel her to feel herself flesh."[66]

One couldn't sum up better what the human eros is, but also what there is in the feast of the eucharist and the recommendation of St. Paul that "husbands should love their wives as they do their own bodies" (Eph.

5:28). Certainly, as I have tried to show, the eucharistic paradigm precedes and contains the conjugal eros rather than simply making it explicit or illustrating it: "Husbands, love your wives, just as Christ loved the church and gave himself up for her" (Eph. 5:25). But this sexualized love (of man and woman), caught up in the mystery of the body given for us (God eucharisticized), becomes itself through an other who is differentiated, rather than expressing itself through a reified alterity, or a biology that is simply a given. It is for this reason, St. Paul explains, that "husbands should love their wives as they do their own bodies. He who loves his wife loves himself" (Eph. 5:28). One looks after one's own body, certainly: according to St. Paul, "no one ever hates his own body, but he nourishes and tenderly cares for it" (Eph. 5:29). But this love of oneself, even if it is fleshly (care, nourishment, nursing, and so on) is not enough truly to love oneself, unless there is an other incarnate and desired. The husband "loves himself" in loving his wife, the epistle tells us, and not the inverse ("loves his wife" in loving himself). Love of the other precedes love of the self and gives meaning to it. The incarnation becomes here a matter of reciprocity, because there is a question of loving flesh(es) and not simply carnal love, the union of bodies. Nor is there simply a meeting of consciousnesses: one should "love" one's wife as one loves one's "own body." The love of the body (loving one's body) is what effectively constitutes the body through love (loving one's wife). But love of the other in himself or herself, including the other's body ("he who loves his wife"), becomes in part the condition of an access to the self, insofar as it is truly fleshly and not simply bodily (loving oneself). My body becomes flesh for the other at the same time as the body of the other is transformed into flesh for me.

This double transition of the body to flesh (being body and discovering that I am flesh through the flesh of the other) is, I think, what we find also in the transition—theological this time—from the eucharist to the Resurrection. Clearly, and I want to hold on to this idea firmly, the "eucharist" is still the manducation of a *body* that has been through the experience and history of an earthly pilgrimage. It is not something that derives solely from the *flesh*, and to insist simply upon the lived experience of the flesh is what tends toward Gnosticism and makes Christianity lose consistency. But the "Resurrection" (and here I am continuing with a thesis put forward in *Metamorphosis of Finitude*) is what promotes the transition of the body to flesh; it would be unreasonable today to imagine a raising of the biological body with its organs necessarily present but lacking the power or right to use them (e.g., according to Aquinas, the genitals or the stomach).[67]

The eucharist is a matter of the "body," as the Resurrection is of the "flesh." And in this crossing from the body to the flesh lies all the mystery of both the Passion and the Resurrection. God is incarnate for me in his body, which allows him to be seen in the flesh (in *flesh and in bones* or in *person*; see §19). And through his body that we eat, I am also incarnate in my own body; in turn, I can express and make this known through the monstrance of my own flesh. The incarnation, in the form of a model for sexual difference, is also reciprocal and shows that there is no eucharistic embrace without the act of desire, in a corporal and mutual search that alone can justify the gift of self of the incarnate God: "For in him the whole fullness of deity *dwells bodily*, and you have come to fullness in him, who is the head of every ruler and authority" (Col. 2:9–10).

Consider (a) the Desire of desire to take bodily form that goes as far as the eucharist; (b) the liturgy "in its place" with what is hidden and revealed under the species of consecrated bread and wine; and (c) the reciprocal incarnation of the self by the other in the laying bare "in the flesh" of the mystery of the Passion by the Resurrection—then eucharistic agape does not seem simply a miming of conjugal eros, but is what precedes it and then contains it through and through. All sacraments (especially the sacrament of Holy Orders, sacrament of marriage, and sacrament of the eucharist) draw first on the fleshly and eucharistic experience of God, so that the body eaten recapitulates and contains all of the Word incarnate as also our own proper humanity. As the eucharistic song attributed to Thomas Aquinas tells us,

> In twofold form of sacrament,
> He gave his flesh, he gave his blood,
> That man, of soul and body blent,
> Might wholly feed on mystic food.[68]

In a rereading and inclusion of the conjugal eros into the eucharistic agape, the whole of the mystery—or almost all of it—can be condensed into the mystery of the Word that was incarnate and then came to play its role in the eucharist. There remain, however, the *gaps of the flesh*, and here speech is also necessary as signifier (§24), even if the performative act has already shown its efficacy as well as its creativity (§20).

§24. The Gaps of the Flesh

First of all for the body, as we have seen, the speech act speaks the flesh and transforms the body into flesh (conjugal eros); indeed, it transforms the bread into body (eucharistic agape) according to the illocutionary act of *this is my body* in the strict sense of the performative (§20). Next for the body, in the embrace or birth of my flesh, starting from the flesh of the other, something remains—something like a residue or a part that cannot be shared of the lived experience at the heart of the union of these bodies. In the amorous locking together of the embrace, as in the Adoration or eucharistic manducation, the "body-to-body" turns out to be, in fact, a "flesh-to-flesh" that can never be fully spoken or communicated. A *blessed failure* burdens the union of flesh and necessitates that the flesh can be expressed in ways other than by sensitivity or sensuality—namely, by the spoken. "Anxiety" innervates all flesh after the fleshly couple seek to be unified: "Can I feel the other there where he (she) feels himself (herself)?"[69] The question brings forward a new dimension of bodily suffering that neither the conjugal eros nor the eucharistic agape can neglect, lest they risk a failure in the power of speech and a clinging to the myth of the pure transparence of the body as opposed to its necessary obscurity. Because not to feel the other *there* where he (she) feels himself (herself), even if in the lived experience of one's own flesh, points clearly to an obvious feebleness in the conjugal eros, though one that is also part of its power. Let us agree with Michel Henry—though only after having noted the prime necessity of proceeding by way of animality (§14)—that "Desire is not at all a natural phenomenon, with some material process—biological or chemical. Desire is only possible in anxiety."[70]

True anxiety, at the approach of the union of flesh, is not simply a question of the success of copulation, whether or not it is "automatic." It derives rather from the impossibility, and at the same time the necessity, of feeling that the other is *there* and feeling *how* the other feels—that is to say, being with the other in the flesh but never quite getting there: "In front of the magical body of the other," Henry tells us, "the anxious desire of joining the life in the other awakes an anguishing possibility of being able to do so: the two dark rivers of anxiety, as it were, unite their streams."[71] It is in this expectation (of meeting what the other feels in the flesh), and in this failure (to actually be able to feel what the other feels), that the alterity of the eros and its inescapable darkness operate. Sexual difference in fact appears to be such—at least in heterosexuality, which constitutes its modality—that one could never experience, either physiologically or affectively, exactly what is felt by the other sex. The greater the difference, the greater the strangeness, but also the more alterity that remains.

Thus we find a *blessed obscurity*, or indeed a happy failure in the union of the flesh, precisely and essentially in that we are differentiated in terms of flesh and genitals. The dancer on the balcony after a dance party or ball, in taking the "hand of his partner," cannot say what his partner experiences "in herself," or rather, "under the skin." The lover approaching his love falls into true *anxiety* at the moment of the erotic—which certainly shows his liberty (Kierkegaard); indeed, a potential bad faith (Sartre); and yet also, and above all, his flesh (Henry): "It is the anxiety of one who doesn't touch the thing anymore, the body that is like a thing, but a body of flesh that is inhabited by a real life. . . . The powerlessness of these drives to reach *the other in her* intensifies the pressure of desire until it reaches its paroxysm of satisfaction in the orgasm, so that each has their orgasm without being able to experience what the other experiences. . . . It is in the immanence of the drive that desire *fails* to reach the pleasure of the other, there where it is itself achieved. It is in the night of the lovers that for each of them, the other remains at the other side of a *wall* that separates them for always."[72] Alterity appears here as something radical, and eros corroborates it rather than denying it or trying to amalgamate the bodies without differentiating the flesh. The masculine strengthens itself in its masculinity in contact with the feminine, and the feminine in its femininity through contact with the masculine (§23). Difference produces the most radical strangeness but also gives birth to the self and its true identity. In the coincidence of the bodies (eros) they find where they truly belong (masculinity-femininity). It is in celebrating the other that I find my own self. It is not that *I* identify it, but rather that it differentiates *me*.

From the night of the lovers to the night of adoration, or the manducation of the eucharist, is no great distance. The union here is also real, no less than the necessary failure or fusion was real, or indeed the impossibility of feeling the other—in this case, Christ—to be *there*, and feeling *how* he felt. St. Paul was not mistaken when he tried to achieve a common pathos with the Word made flesh and knew at the same time that it was impossible. At least he tried—and tried to bring us to participate: "It is no longer I who live, but it is Christ who lives in me" (Gal. 2:20). This loving empathy is of the essence of Christianity. And it is the great virtue of St. Bernard of Clairvaux, as of William of Saint-Thierry after him, to have shown it. "There will certainly come a day when the work conforms [*conformet*] and is in accord [*concordet*] with its Author. It has to be then, that one day or another we shall enter into his feelings [*in eundem nos affectum transire*]."[73] The "concord of hearts" accompanies and precedes the "union of the bodies" up to and including the eucharistic act, as a double way of "sympathizing" and "incorporating." More precisely, the act of eucharistic manducation, like the eros, seeks (1) to experience what the other experiences (concordance of hearts); and (2) to feel what the other feels (union of bodies).

(1) In the concord of hearts, first of all, the attempt is to be as open as possible, indeed, to have complete empathy: "Let the same mind be in you

that was in Christ Jesus" (Phil. 2:5). I am not Christ, nor is Christ entirely me; through the mystery of the Resurrection, however, or by the "intimacy of the life of God in me," a kind of inter-affectivity or a form of empathy is woven between humans and God, of the sort that only Christ (or, only Christ in an exemplary fashion) can feel and then, through it, be affected by what I sense and feel. And thus he lives through these feelings with me.

(2) As far as the union of bodies—and, indeed, its continuation in shared flesh—is concerned, certain obvious traces of this can be found in the aim of the eucharist (incorporation), but also, and in an even clearer way, in the *compassion of flesh* by which nothing that I go through in my fleshly lived experience is immaterial to God. Nor is what Christ goes through in his own body (the Church) strange to us: "I am completing what is lacking in Christ's affliction for the sake of his body, that is, the church" (Col. 1:24). The Church is not a body, as we shall see, unless it is also and first of all a *community of flesh* (Conclusion). And the eucharist is surely a step in the direction of that act, by which the fleshly lived experience of the human being becomes also the fleshly lived experience of God, in a total assumption of embodiedness that does not ignore his Chaos, his share of animality, his passions, or his drives but *recapitulates* them in himself, to metamorphose them completely and give them meaning at the heart of his filiation. As in the episode of the "hand of his partner" (on the balcony after the ball), a kind of standing back or "anguish of the flesh" comes into being at the moment of eucharistic manducation, a moment when the believer is invited in exemplary fashion to feel what the other (Christ) feels—in his affect as well as in his embodiedness. The mystics, and in particular the French school, were concerned with this possibility—one that we might also hope to recover—in specific pathos at the time of communion: "Our Lord is not simply the sacrament in the Blessed Sacrament," according to Jean-Jacques Olier, taking up the position of St. John Eudes. "But he is also communion, insofar as he comes *to communicate to us the religious and respectful feelings* that he holds in relation to his Father. . . . As our Lord made his Church through the Holy Spirit and the Holy Ghost, our Lord now wishes to remake his Church *in taking on those qualities and provisions of the spirit that are found in the Blessed Sacrament on the altar.*"[74]

If there are "gaps of the flesh" in the conjugal eros, they are also certainly there in the eucharistic agape. But the second sacrament, as we have seen (the Christly agape or the eucharistic transformation), realizes and contains the first (the conjugal eros or the sacrament of marriage). Where lovers cannot fully encounter one another through the flesh—meeting the "wall" so convincingly described by Henry in the night of the lovers—married spouses can perhaps do so, and hypothetically do so through marriage, at least as far as their fleshly union is integrated into the heart of the incarnate Word through the sacrament. The union of flesh is not "better" in sacramental marriage; it is "other," or rather, differently oriented. While lovers may simply be content to be part of humanity—which alone is very significant in their relationship—and they may believe also in the fidelity of the flesh, married spouses search for God, to be incorporate with him and to live their lovemaking in another way. The gaps of the flesh certainly remain and must stay thus: I shall never be able to experience what the other feels (affectively), any more than I can feel what the other feels in the flesh. The situation of a differentiated alterity remains in place. But because God was made flesh and, moreover, lived our flesh, he and only he can, through his resurrected flesh, experience the pathos of our flesh: "Through him, and with him, and in him," as we say in the famous Eucharistic Prayer, the mystery of our eroticized flesh is communicated otherwise, in that it becomes part of the pathos of the eucharisticized Word.[75]

The *me* implied in *this is my body*, for one spouse, will meet even more strongly the *you* of *this is my body* for the other spouse, integrated as they are in the *we* of *this is my body* addressed by Christ to his Church and to humanity in general. It is not that a mystical vision would be difficult to share, and would hold conviction only on the basis of a faith that was not binding for anyone. Rather, it is necessary here that we should not be blocked into a duality and, further, should always be ready for a third, for the ultimate figure of alterity. What responds to the *we* of the *Trinity* of God in the act of creation ("'*Let us make* humankind in *our* image, according to *our* likeness'" [Gen. 1:26]) is the *conjugal we* of the man and woman incorporated in God ("Therefore a man *leaves* his father and his mother and clings to his wife, and they become *one flesh*" [Gen. 2:24]).

But the lived experience of the flesh, even if it is in the Word incarnate and resurrected in the form of a helper and vessel, will never conquer the blessed obscurity—indeed, the felicity of failure—that is also and definitively inherent in the union of bodies. For, despite the Holy Trinity, the incommunicability of fleshly lived experiences and affect remains the guarantee of their perfect alterity. One can certainly accompany the other in his or her suffering, but one can never truly suffer *with* the person, or in his or her place, with the probable exception, to a certain degree, of the figure of the Resurrected Christ.[76] We have to accept, not simply regret, what is at the heart of these "gaps of the flesh." If, in our encounters with one another, flesh has such difficulty, it is precisely because both sides in the encounter hold firmly to their personal singularity. So, speech that is expressed comes to signify and address what the flesh cannot or can no longer say. It is true that the words of eros speak often "to say nothing" and in a way to take us out of the situation, or touch on what can be "squalid," if they are "obscene" or "childish," or indeed "mystical."[77] So many of these words undoubtedly say "nothing" except "to allow the flesh to become excited in speaking"—an incontestable aspect of love, and one that can be phenomenologically described.[78] But it is also the *words* that "express" love, as much as they "excite"; or, perhaps we should say that they excite more and better in that they express the play of the flesh and its gaps. And this is all the more true because they eternally mime their success in exempting themselves from precise meaning. The *fidelity of the flesh* is also written in "words [*mots*]," so that (all punning aside) one "can avoid problems [*maux*] through fidelity." Clearly, then, there is a language that excites, but there is also speech that expresses something, and only the latter (expression) gives sense to the former (excitation), at the risk of becoming enclosed in the play of the carnal and in attempts at success in what speech comes to say when just trying to fill a gap. As Merleau-Ponty says, "The other who listens and understands joins with me in what is most singular in me. It is as though the universality of feeling . . . has finally ceased to be a universality for me and in the end redoubled itself through a recognized universality. . . . It is not enough for speech to convey a meaning already given to either side, speech must bring meaning. Speech is the gesture which suppresses itself as such and goes beyond itself to a meaning."[79]

It is apparent then that if, before embodiedness, language speaks its performatives to the extent of consecrating its expression through action (§20), along with embodiedness goes expressivity and its capacity to address what the flesh tries to live through without actually speaking it. After communion the priest says quietly, in a heart-to-heart prayer, "What has passed our lips as food, O Lord, may we possess in purity of heart, that what has been given to us in time may be our healing for eternity."[80] Far from spiritualizing everything, the body is here, in the eucharistic act, fully acknowledged and metamorphosed. The incarnate Word takes, in its offer of the sacrificial lamb, our part of animality fully distinguished from bestiality (Chapters 2 and 4). It handles the Chaos of our embodiedness that cannot be reduced to the lived experience of an ethereal flesh (Chapter 1). Finally, it makes the eros the true concern of an action to convert and transform the flesh and speech in the agape (Chapters 3 and 6). The eucharist thus finds its legacy, as I have tried to show, in the elements of animality ("'Look, here is the Lamb of God'" [John 1:36]); it finds its content in the body ("'Take; this is my body'" [Mark 14:22]); and it finds its form in the eros ("'I have eagerly desired to eat this Passover with you'" [Luke 22:15]). The wedding feast is completed—or, we could almost say, perfected—not by thinking of agape in the form of eros, but in integrating the erotic into the eucharistic (Chapters 3 and 6), by speaking of the body regarding its conversion into the flesh (Chapters 1 and 6), and in not trying to flee the Chaos of our passions and drives that have their part in us of animality, but waiting for humanization as well as filiation: "Let us rejoice and exult and give him the glory, for the marriage of the Lamb has come," the book of Revelations tells us. "And his bride has made herself ready; to her it has been granted to be clothed with fine linen, bright and pure. . . . Blessed are those who are invited to the marriage supper of the Lamb" (Rev. 19:7–9).

What remains now is to change, or better, to "metamorphose"—philosophically first—that which was given. Because if, with humankind, God "descends into the abyss" (Part I), and if, as well, it was proper then for him to "sojourn in man" (Part II), only the incorporation of God could demand its "Passover" from this animality, "transubstantiation" from this bread, and "conversion" from this desire (Part III). Without denying anything of what has been *philosophically* studied so far (animality, embodiedness, desire), it is appropriate now to shift our attention to the theological (Passover, transubstantiation, the wedding feast). The eucharisticized body said something, and says it still today, that nobody, apart from God, had ever formulated, and that humankind had not been prepared for. The poet Paul Claudel put it for us in a cry that needs to be repeated still, in the famous Hymn to the Blessed Sacrament, and in a way that philosophical prose needs to state clearly, at least to ensure that we do not take it for granted: "It is You, yourself who tells me I can eat your flesh. It is written. It is not I who have invented it! How could I doubt for a moment, when your words are so clear? Only you, O my God—because as for me it is not of my business—are responsible for this enormity."[81]

PART III

God Incorporate

Nothing involves (in reality) a man so much as the eucharist.
—François Mauriac, 1931[1]

Like birth or resurrection, the eucharist denotes first of all a passage. It is a passage of body to body in a transubstantiation (of bread to body and of wine to blood), an assimilation (of God in man through manducation), and an incorporation (of man in God through the mystery of the Church, of spouses). It brings about a Passover (*pèsah*) on the day of the Passover, or rather, it speaks the Passover. After that time when everything centred solely on the assumption of the body of Christ in the consecrated Host, we have now come to a time for the expansion of the Last Supper—expanded to the incorporation of humanity into all divinity. The incorporation *of* God, or God incorporate, is not simply that of God to the human through the consecrated bread, but also that of the human to the divine by the Host that is eaten. Everything was certainly in humankind and in humankind first of all, even when God abided here—from the descent into the abyss (Part I) to the "sojourn of man" (Part II). Nothing, however, even after the fact, was to remain strange to his nature, apart from sin, once the Son as man had come to be incarnate and to "incorporate us to him" by the manducation of the eucharisticized body (Part III). Perhaps it is only Montaigne who opens a pathway for us here—a pathway entailing a possibility for human beings, not without God or against God but *starting off from* our need for depth and autonomy at the level of our existence, or our humanity: "Let us then, for once, consider a man alone, without foreign assistance, armed only with his own proper arms, and unfurnished of the divine grace and wisdom, which is all his honour, strength, and the foundation of his being. Let us see how he stands in this fine equipage."[2] The petition of "man alone" contains, as I see it, his own consistency, at least in laying bare the depths of his conscience, as well as in his dialogue with contemporary humankind, which is imbued with a sense of finitude.

But, as I have tried to show elsewhere,[3] the closed horizon of our existence as part of humankind is not satisfying (at least in Christian terms) for this man alone, even if he is "armed only with his own proper arms."

Because "divine grace and wisdom" remain the "honour, strength, and the foundation of his being" as a human being, as Montaigne makes clear; moreover, no humanism can be founded without recognizing a certain transcendence that also belongs to the spirit of humanity, if only to be recognized after the event (in the vision and the prospect of the Resurrection). But—and we confront here a certain tendency in theology that sets itself up, wrongly, as a form of liberation (Christian as well as political)— neither humanization nor hominization can constitute in themselves the purpose of the act of the eucharist, since they risk neglecting the act of filiation as also that of re-creation. Certainly, without God, man is still a being worthy of existence, and is even, up to a point, capable of taking responsibility for himself. And it is part of the desire of God that we should be able to take responsibility for our humanity and offer a true vis-à-vis for his divinity. In attributing too much to man, however, we forget God, especially if the filiation in the Trinity does not come to integrate and transform the weight of our humanity. But through the figure of the Completely-Other— in fact, only through this figure—we see the other, or our neighbour, who is always derived from such a figure. A certain form of transcendence, seen in phenomenology as openness (Husserl) and in theology as an elevation (St. Augustine), is always and ineluctably found in immanence.[4]

Anxiety, suffering, and death are not self-sufficient in this sense, and they wait in some way for the Son to consecrate his offering so that they do not remain definitively confined (see *Le Passeur de Gethsémani*). The burden of finitude—of the world, or time, as also of man—can hope for some kind of transformation, if not an alleviation, in the act of transition to the Father in the Resurrection of his Son under the power of the Holy Spirit: a new birth and the transfiguration of the flesh of man (see *Metamorphosis of Finitude*). What remains to us is the "body" as such, in which drives and animality are rooted, and in which we see organic composition and erotic tensions. It also desires wholly its own act of transubstantiation, something that only God can carry out and where only God is the model in the moment of consecration. "The eucharist is not simply an application of the *vinculum substantiale* [substantial bond] of Leibniz," Blondel maintains in his Latin dissertation on Leibniz, "but . . . the perfect example, the *total and perfect realization*. . . . By this first vital taking into possession [of the Word made flesh by the supreme incorporation of all that there is in the incarnate Word] the *vinculum proprium Christi* [what is the characteristic property of Christ] prepares, as far as the domain of the subconscious, the spiritual configuration that, without confusion and without consubstantiation, is realized in a *transforming union*. . . . The 'universal binding' is not a transnaturalizing embrace for spiritual beings, but an embrace that binds them while respecting their nature."[5] Transubstantiation, once again, does not deny or go beyond the body, but takes on the body in transforming it, making our interior Chaos the property of the divine, and not, or at least no longer, solely a site for the human's debate with himself.

I should like to emphasize that animality (the eucharistic legacy), embodiedness (the content of the eucharist), and eros (the modality of the eucharist) wait for and hope for their *translation* in the act of transubstantiation, so that the response to the appeal of a transformed humanity (the simple proclamation of humanism) will be echoed in a filiation that has been acknowledged (difficult but necessary in Christianity). The incorporation of God, or the God incorporate (Part III), after the "descent into the abyss" (Part I [Chaos and Tohu-Bohu, sacrificial lamb, eros eucharisticized]) and the "sojourn of man" (Part II [the organic body, animality, and differentiation in the embrace])—all this does not simply incorporate God to man and man to the bread in the particularizing movement of kenosis (a subjective genitive), but also, and even more, integrates man with Christ and Christ with the Church in the universalizing project of eschatology (an objective genitive). The ultimate meaning of transubstantiation is not solely corporal; it is also related to the Trinity—or rather, it is corporal in that it is of the Trinity, once the Son goes so far as to offer his body to the Father ("Not what I want, but what you want" [Mark 14:36]) and it is inspired by the Holy Spirit ("through the eternal Spirit, offered himself without blemish to God" [Heb. 9:14]). "The eucharist is not *simply the concern of the Son*, otherwise he would bind himself alone with mankind," as Adrienne von Speyr so aptly suggested. "It is equally the *concern of the Father*, and that is why the Son communicates with his Father, and remains united with him in the making of the eucharist."[6] In centering everything on the Son, we leave things with Christ, and we confuse the celebration of the blessed Last Supper with a simple "shared bread" (*cum panis*) or a companionship (with bread) in which his incorporation in God himself is completely forgotten. But what is known as the Bread of Life Discourse (John 6: 25–29) insists on this. Neither what made up the meal nor the well-being of the community on the day of the Last Supper could express the basis of the act of the eucharist (one drift of certain symbolic theology). Only a return to the Trinity (in that it also must be integrated into the dynamic of the eucharist) justifies the rationale of he who comes to be given (Trinitarian monadology). "I am the bread of life. . . . I have come down from heaven, not to do my own will, but the will of him who sent me" (John 6: 35, 38). We need to understand this because the faithful, to say the least, too often forget it; they stick too closely to Christ alone at the time of communion. The epiclesis (invocation of the

Holy Spirit) and the preface (communion with the Father) belong wholly to the eucharistic liturgy, and it is thus not simply as Christ but as a person of the Trinity that the Son comes to give himself in the eucharist.

In the Last Supper, then, and in the ultimate Trinitarian and Christly motion that it is up to us now to perform, our animal passions in their driven force, our bodies in their organic dimension, must also be completely accepted and transubstantiated—not only in order to constitute a new humanity, but principally to bring us into a kind of Trinitarian perichoresis (relationship among the persons in the Trinity) where blessedness as *pleasure* also contributes a true happiness: "The happy life is joy based on the truth," according to St. Augustine in his *Confessions* (10.23.33). "It is therefore pleasure that is something like the weight of the soul," he adds in *De Musica* (6.11). "There where your pleasure is, *there* is your treasure; *there where* your heart is, *there* is beatitude and misery."[7]

The Passover of Animality

The first movement of incorporation of God corresponds to humankind's initial stage of animality. I am referring to the introduction and transformation of *our* animal part—made up of interior Chaos, or passions and drives (Chapters 1 and 4)—into the Word himself, who takes responsibility for all our humanity as far as and including the preserve, or district, of "that which can no longer be said" (Chapters 2 and 7). Our animality, present and offered in the bread of the eucharist, also awaits its Passover; indeed, it awaits its metamorphosis into a humanity that will recognize its divine filiation. Christ himself is not identified with any particular animality (Council in Trullo; §5), and does not fall into the sinful errors of bestiality (animality and bestiality; §13). As Christ incarnate, he makes what we have of animality in us the site of an offering, specifically in the bread of the eucharist. Since he is the Word incarnate, nothing in our constitution escapes him, and all that we are as sons of the Son comes from the Father, under the power of the Holy Spirit, "in him" incorporating and transformed in the crucible of the Trinity: "Our Lord Jesus Christ, who did, through His transcendent love become what we are [*factus est quod sumus nos*], that He might bring us to be even what He is Himself [*uti nos perficeret esse quod est ipse*]."[1]

From the question posed by Nicodemus when he opens the topic of Resurrection (*Metamorphosis of Finitude*)—"Can one enter a second time into the mother's womb and be born?" (John 3:4)—we move now to the question, raised by the Jews of Capernaum, that brings us to the eucharist:

ι this man give us his flesh to eat?" (John 6:52). In both cases ιe same outrage, stemming in fact from the same misunderstand- of fetal regression in the obscurity of the Resurrection (Nicode- ιd that of cannibalism in the misinterpretation of the eucharist ιaites). We can dispose of these problems easily, at least on the suʋⱼᵤₓ of the eucharist, but at the risk of over-spiritualizing; there is also a risk of overlooking the radical strangeness of what is given to us to eat. The great mystics realized this, and St. Augustine in particular showed how this act of communion should initially repulse us: "It seemed that it was madness [*furor*] and extravagance [*insania*] to give men his flesh to eat and his blood to drink," Augustine says in his commentary on the Psalms. "Doesn't it seem that it was a piece of extravagance to say: eat the flesh and drink my blood? And in saying: 'Whoever does not eat my flesh and drink my blood you have no life in you' (John 6:54) doesn't it seem that Jesus was raving [*quasi insanire videtur*]?"[2]

§25. Return to the Scandal

In philosophical terms, "the strangest thing"[3] is that we have lost the sense of what is revolting in the part of Christianity that is the mystery of the eucharist. Nobody, in fact, except young children, dares to question out loud what everybody questions silently: What are we to make of this act and its meaning, indeed of its "autophagy," where humans have problems devouring each other—or *eating the flesh of the other*? Accusations of can- nibalism with regard to the eucharist have been abundant, from the start of Christianity (the Montanist crisis) up to the present day (ethnology, psychoanalysis, anthropology . . .), even though Christian theology has chosen to believe that such accusations have been definitively overcome. John Chrysostom, in his hyperrealism (like that of his contemporary, St. Augustine), provides some dazzling testimony; he anticipates that the tongue is reddened by the colour of the blood in the eucharistic potion, and he sees the mouth full of flesh as the place for a Host that must not be chewed in case the body of the Resurrected One is crushed. "In order that we may become this not by love only, but in very deed [*non solum per dilectionem sed reipse etiam*], let us be blended into that flesh," he says forcefully. "He has given to those who desire Him not only to see Him [*vivendum modo*], but even to touch [*tangendum*], and eat Him [*comeden- dum*], and fix their teeth [*dentibus terendum*] into His flesh, and to embrace Him, and satisfy their love."[4] Chrysostom continues, "What then ought not he to exceed in purity that hath the benefit of this sacrifice [*manum illam quae hanc carnem secat*], than what sunbeam should not that hand be more pure which is to sever this flesh, the mouth that is filled with spiritual fire [*os quod spirituali replectur igne*], the tongue that is reddened by that most awful blood [*linguam tremendo sanguine tinctam*]?"[5] It would be nice to think that this problem is finished with, or that it was simply a passing—indeed, an isolated—error. However, the spectre of anthropophagy has continually been reactivated during the history of the theology of the sacraments and of the practice of ritual (not chewing the Host); "Eat, this is my body" has, unsurprisingly, had difficulty escaping from it. In wishing to fight against accusations of cannibalism, Christianity has quite often only reinforced them, substituting a realism that is necessary in order not to spiritualize everything. And it has often lost the sense of what is the basis, for us now as well as throughout the Catholic tradition, of the eucharistic assumption: the taking on and transformation of the whole of the human being, up to and including his organicity, his passion and his drives—indeed, his part of animality.[6]

Aquinas himself is not exempt from such fears, or from the obsession with autophagy. His famous argument on the permanence and change of species, at the heart of his doctrine of transubstantiation, is there precisely to curb understandable feelings of repulsion at the taste of blood to be drunk, or the smell of flesh to be chewed, at the time of communion. It would be useful, then—*theologically* apart from anything else—to ensure that the bread remain bread and the wine remain wine, though the one and the other *really* become the body and the blood of Christ, as far as substance is concerned. The discussion of the eucharist in the *Summa Theologica* underlines how "It is evident to sense that all the accidents of the bread and wine remain after the consecration."[7] In other words, the persistence (*remanence*) of the bread and the wine justifies believers in continuing to eat bread when they eat the body and to drink wine when they drink the blood; however, this is a matter of *accidents*, rather than of substance or essence. The bread remains bread but connected to the body, and the wine remains wine but brought back to the blood. When I communicate and receive the body and blood of the Lord, I *truly* eat his body and *truly* drink his blood, but I do this under the species of bread and wine that are not suppressed, but only converted. The substance of the bread has become, through the consecration, an accident connected to his body, which constitutes its true substance, and the substance of the wine is an accident connected to his blood, which is its true reality.

Nonetheless, the question remains, and it is significant: Why is there such a persistence, or *remanence*, of the species? In other words, doesn't the doctrine of transubstantiation stem from some barely acceptable, or ulterior, motives that lie underneath or at the heart of the *Summa Theologica* itself? According to Aquinas, there are two further reasons for the persistence of accidents, given in the form of answers to objections in the treatise: "First of all, because it is not customary, but horrible, for men to eat human flesh, and to drink blood. And therefore Christ's flesh and blood are set before us to be partaken of under the species of those things which are the most commonly used by men, namely, bread and wine. Secondly, lest this sacrament might be derided by unbelievers [*infedelibus irrideretur*] if we were to eat our Lord under his own species."[8] Apart from the metaphysical reasons for the persistence of the accidents of bread and wine in the eucharistic sacrament (e.g., the solidity of the matter, the earthly and celestial nourishment, the fruit of the vine and the work of men, the shared meal), two motifs, one subjective and one inter-subjective, justify its retention. There is the necessity *for us* (in our heart of hearts) not to sink into a feeling of horror at the prospect of eating true flesh and drinking true blood. It has to reflect what we habitually eat and drink (bread and wine). There is also the importance *for others* (nonbelievers) of not exposing ourselves to mockery as cannibals, when we know very well that we do eat the "true body" of Christ and drink his "true blood" when we participate in his own sacrifice. It is fairly clear that the accidents of bread and wine persist also (though not primarily) as a way of camouflaging the scandal of anthropophagic flesh, which remains in some way behind these things, indirectly, even if the accidents come to be suppressed in their conversion through the act of transubstantiation.

St. Bonaventure—in the same period (thirteenth century), and this time strictly following the lead of Peter Lombard's *Book of Sentences*, in which the sacrament is theorized as a "vie" (*velum*), and no longer as "thing" or "sign of a thing" (*res signata*)—started and justified arguments for a prohibition on crushing the body of Christ "with the teeth." Prohibition was based on, first, a holy horror of the "meat" or "raw flesh" that the consecrated bread would nonetheless contain and, second, the necessity of not destroying Christ, who is there and always living. "It is also unseemly," Bonaventure says in his *Breviloquium*, "that the flesh of Christ be actually torn by our teeth [*carnem dentibus attrectare*], because of the loathsomeness of such crudity [*proptem horrorem cruditas*] and the immortality of his body. It was therefore necessary that the body and blood of Christ be imparted under the veil [*velatum*] of the most sacred symbols and by means of congruous and expressive likeness [*similitudinibus*]."[9] As with the doctrine of transubstantiation that is so impressive in the work of Aquinas, the thesis of eucharistic conversion in Bonaventure's work certainly has its own integrity—in particular, as we shall see (§30), insofar as it concerns the assimilation of the believer to Christ himself through this act of transformation: "Whoever receives them worthily, eating not merely sacramentally [*sacramentaliter*], but also spiritually [*spiritualiter*] through faith and love, is more fully incorporated [*magis incorporatur*] into the mystical Body of Christ."[10] These deliberations on the "integrity of the body that has been chewed" and the "prohibition on crunching it" are found throughout the Middle Ages, and there are traces even in certain liturgical hymns: "The one and the other of these species are only pure *signs* [*signum*] and not things [*non rebus*], they veil the real divine," according to the Hymn of the Blessed Sacrament of Corpus Christi, composed by Aquinas for the festival instituted by Urban IV (1264). A translation from 1922 reads as follows:

> Though His Flesh as food abideth,
> And his blood as drink—he bideth
> > Undivided under each.
> Whoso eateth It can never
> Break the body, rend or sever;
> > Christ entire our hearts doth fill:
> Thousands eat the Bread of heaven,
> Yet as much to one is given:
> > Christ though eaten, bideth still . . .
> The Saviour still abideth
> > Undiminished as before.[11]

Such formulae would certainly seem slightly ridiculous today if we tried to follow them to the letter. The debate over realism in the eucharist is no longer concerned with the breaking or division of the body once it is chewed, its disappearance once it is swallowed, or its reduction in becoming contained in the Host in the eucharist. However, something engrossing, and eminently fair-minded, remains in these suggestions, making it inappropriate to mock them or simply ignore their concerns. Everything has a certain basis in fact and is thought through, at least in the Catholic tradition, so as not to lose the consistency of this body that is given to us to eat. Eucharistic realism consecrates the body of Christ "in the confined space of the consecrated host" (*hujus hostiae strictus angustiae*), as the site of a true *reality* and transformation: in a sense, the *something* of a *something to eat* that is not, or is no longer, our daily bread; or, the *something* of a *something to drink* that is not just wine drunk for pleasure. This does not depend simply on *we who eat* (*ex parte manducantis*); that would be an error of symbolism and an overdependence on the subject that would not help us understand all about the fleshly donation (see §12). Realism about eucharistic conversion comes also from *that which is eaten* (*ex parte manducati*) and has a consistency, perhaps a phenomenological consistency, such that it cannot be satisfied solely with the illusions of subjectivity.[12]

From Chrysostom (the tongue reddened by blood) to Augustine (the folly and madness of a flesh given to eat), and from Aquinas (hiding under the species a repulsion at what we eat and warning us of the mockery of nonbelievers) to Bonaventure (not touching the consecrated Host with the teeth because of the horror we feel at raw flesh), the *eucharistic scandal* is in fact less hidden than embellished, although everything has been done to avoid showing it or bringing it into view. A deeper reading of the history of sacramental theology of the Fathers in the Middle Ages, or indeed of the period of the Counter-Reformation (reinforcement of eucharistic realism in a certain form of thing-ness), would bring out the full spectrum of a thought experiment in which the unimaginable becomes somehow imagined, even if only to be pushed aside—as in the piercing question from the Jews of Capernaum: "How can this man give us his flesh to eat?" (John 6:52). The horror at cannibalism remains the inescapable, and quite simply the philosophical, horizon of the transformation of bread into body and wine into blood, even though numerous theological attempts have been made to minimize it. Thomas Hobbes castigates priests in his *Leviathan*, insisting that when, by the words *this is my body*,

> the nature or qualities of the thing it selfe is pretended to be changed, it is not Consecration, but either an extraordinary worke of God, or a vaine and impious Conjuration. But seeing (for the frequency of pretending the change of nature in their Consecration,) it cannot be esteemed a work extraordinary, it is no other than a *Conjuration* or *Incantation*, whereby they would have men to beleeve an alteration of Nature that is not, contrary to the testimony of mans Sight, and of all the rest of his Senses. . . . [Priests] require men to worship it, as if it were our Saviour himself present God and Man, and thereby to commit most grosse Idolatry.[13]

Recent research in the human sciences has not put an end to such questions or suspicions, but rather the contrary. Yet it may help the believer wake up from "dogmatic slumber" (Kant)—or perhaps it should be called "liturgical" slumber—and avoid taking for granted his or her procession through the eucharist. As far as cannibalism in psychoanalysis is concerned (André Green), cannibalism with the economic order (Jacques Attali), or the distinction between the raw and the cooked in ethnology (Claude Lévi-Strauss), Christianity with its doctrine of the *body given to be eaten* cannot be ignored—far from it. As Green, writing from his psychoanalytic point of view, says, "*Cannibalism in Christianity* allows us along with other things (cannibalism in art, in mythology or in psychiatry) a theoretical approach to cannibalism that introduces us to psychoanalytic theses."[14]

As we have seen, the transformation of the sense and of the threshold of cannibalism by Christianity is not enough to exempt the eucharistic mystery completely from the suspicion that weighs on it: that one is eating the man (anthropophagy) and, indeed, eating God (theophagy). This mutation of cannibalism does not suppress it, but gives it another significance. Surely the mystery of incorporation has its source in a symbolic assimilation with ancestors; the manducation of the body allows us to see the solid element in this transmission, while the wine sends us back to the blood that runs through our veins and thus also to the life of the tribe. Speech has here a performative effect, certainly, as it does in the act of recognition of two people who have been separated and then reunited. But in all of these examples, something cannibal and something of cannibalism still remains today, which the believer would be mistaken not to mull over—whether to reject it or simply to call it into question. René Girard stated in his *Dialogues on the Origin of Culture* (making reference to his seminal work, *Violence and the Sacred*), "To those who say that the Eucharist is rooted in archaic cannibalism, instead of saying 'no', we have to say 'yes!' The real history of humankind is religious history, which goes back to primitive cannibalism. Primitive cannibalism is religion, and the Eucharist recapitulates this history from alpha to omega."[15] Whether or not one escapes from the charge of anthropophagy (and it is probably important to find both a way out and a reply to the charge), the issue remains problematic in a consideration of the start of the eucharistic Last Supper, when it is no longer ethnological and anthropological (Girard) but becomes, in my view, a metaphysical and theological question.

§26. Getting around the Scandal

There are two ways of getting around, or at least reducing, the scandal in the eucharist of flesh given to humans to eat, or even to chew (*trogôn*) (John 6:56–57): (1) through exegesis, and (2) in philosophical terms.[16] These are both technical moves, but they also serve as an excuse for the believer not to be, or no longer to be, satisfied simply with what Péguy calls the "habituated" soul.

(1) *The exegetical objection to the notion of a scandal.* It is frequently said—and has been repeated constantly in sociological rereadings in historico-critical mode of the eucharistic Last Supper—that the body destined to be eaten (*this is my body*) or the flesh before being chewed (*eat my flesh and drink*

my blood) cannot show, at least as far as the Jewish sacrificial world is concerned, either the organic and material that the Greek *soma* would lead us to or the blood and its hemoglobin that the Hellenic *aïma* would point to and show us through the veins. Marcel Jousse, in his anthropology of gesture, says, "It is obvious that if you take these formulae 'crudely' (this is my body, eat/ this is my blood, drink) you will say: 'But these are cannibal processes or worse!' But we need to see what is said and done *in context*, to ask what were the reactions of those around and what reverberation there were."[17] We thus come back, so as not to confuse things with a major anachronism, to what is fundamentally justifiable and the basic principle of Jousse's enterprise: "When we study Iéshoua of Nazareth, if we don't bring into play Palestinian anthropology and ethics, we straightway risk misinterpretation."[18] In the Palestinian history "of man" as a "history of the mouth," as we have already seen in the context of the image of the sacrificial lamb (§5), the meaning of the sacrificial formulae "take, this is my body" and "drink, this is my blood" need to be resituated and thought through.[19] To employ the terms used by Jousse, in the "mime of the Bread and the Wine" it is the flesh and the blood, or "the entire being," that is designated.[20]

All this, along with what has become commonplace in the exegetical reading of the sacrifice, needs to be said and is solidly based in rationality. In the tradition of Jesus, that of Israel, flesh and blood point to "the man insofar as he is of the earth and mortal and not just two components of the organism." The body is not then entirely material, but "a way of pointing to the presence of the man who shows it in its entirety." And the blood is not primarily the fluid blood, but the "principle of life, that belongs to God and to him alone"—thus we find the prohibition, in Israel, of consuming the sacrificial blood. "To eat the *flesh*, that is to be *incorporated into the person*. And to drink the *blood*, that is to take communion with this life that is of God; it is to claim that life."[21] In eating his body, we are incorporated into the body of God and thus also the Church (to be "one body" [1 Cor. 12:12]), and in drinking his blood we receive his life, dedicated in such a way that it comes and flows in our own veins ("and it is no longer I who live, but it is Christ who lives in me" [Gal. 2:20]). The analogy here is perfect and it is indeed what is performed in the eucharist. The assumption behind it is that one cannot understand *this is my body* except by the yardstick of the figure of the Galilean and the context that produced him.

Yet such a contextualization cannot, in my opinion, be truly satisfying for us today, because it risks imposing on us a reading of the Bible that is simply not of our time. Neither demythologization (Bultmann) nor de-Hellenization (Küng) nor Palestinianization can be applied any longer.

There is no such thing as chemically pure Christianity, and wishing to reach it will only bring us back to, on the one hand, abandoning the effort of translation through the tradition and, on the other hand, abandoning the attempt to bring it up to date for the purposes of transmission. The difficulty for readers and interpreters of the biblical narrative, and the difficulty of the transcription of the message of *hoc est corpus meum* in the greco-latin tradition (Tertullian, St. Augustine, Thomas Aquinas), is not that God is incorporate in a human being and that we receive his life—as so much of the discourse that surrounds the eucharistic sacrifice has told us. Rather, the true *lectio difficilior* is in recognizing that the body given to us to eat is also—for us and in our culture (see §27)—a true body (*corpus verus*), or rather, "tru(ly) body" (*corpus vere*), and that the blood given us to drink is a true blood (*sanguis verus*), or more precisely, "tru(ly) blood" (*sanguis vere*).

In our Western tradition, and not just in the Palestinian outlook of the Hebrew Jesus, the body is (materially) body, and the blood is (materially) blood. The exegetic way around the scandal of cannibalism is certainly right in underlining the incongruity of such a scandal, but our point of departure remains the need to overcome the scandal *for ourselves*—that is, to take into account the mystery as it exists in our culture, and reckoning from our culture. Believers reply to the formula *Corpus Christi* ("the body of Christ") with an *Amen* that makes us see, or at least believe, that they are in accordance. But what are they saying yes to at the moment of communication, or rather, of eating? The way around the scandal through arguments from exegesis brings us back to where we started, even though its basis in history (the historico-critical method), justified in many respects, has tried at all costs to avoid this.

(2) *Philosophical objections to the notion of a scandal in the eucharistic sacrifice.* These may rely so heavily on the symbolism of sacrifice that they drain it of all consistency, or at least of all realism. Such a tendency is widespread today and is a result of basing all forms of sacramental theology simply on the distinction between sign and symbol. "Thus the sign is the union of a signifier and a signified," says Edmond Ortigues, following the lead of Ferdinand de Saussure. "The symbol is the operator of a relation between a signifier and other signifiers."[22] The ancient Greek sense of *sumbolon* as a "sign of recognition" (as in the case of shards or fragments of pottery) is cited in arguments for a eucharistic theology founded on a relationship between the bread eaten and the body of Christ identified with it—concerning which it is sufficient to say that it is registered by the believer. In the "good meal," action of grace (*eu-charis*), or the house of bread (*bethléem*), the symbolic aspect of the eucharistic bread becomes

more important than the reality of what we swallow. We even forget sometimes that the believer is incorporated, and that it is not just the believer
who decides upon the symbol.[23]

In reality, the symbol signifies something quite different, at least in the
context of medieval theology. Symbolic theology (*theologia symbolica*)
should teach us the correct use of "sensible things" (*recte ultamur sensibili-
bus*), as St. Bonaventure insists in his *Journey of the Soul into God*.[24] The
symbol is not the recognition of a meaning, but an acknowledgment of
consistency—precisely that of a body, or of matter, that the sacrament
must not give up easily. Maurice Blanchot echoes this in *The Book to
Come*: "Symbol does not mean anything, expresses nothing. It only makes
present—by making us present to it—a reality that escapes all other capture and seems to rise up, there, prodigiously close and prodigiously far
away, like a foreign presence. . . . If symbol is a wall, then it is like a wall
that, far from opening wide, not only becomes more opaque, but with a
density, a thickness, and a reality so powerful and so exorbitant that it
transforms us."[25]

Symbolic theology does not call into question the real presence—far
from it—but it can also neglect what is strange, or indeed impossible to
assimilate, in the reality of the eucharisticized body, precisely because it
relates it to the overly familiar notion of a shared meal. The Last Supper,
as we have seen, is not simply a meal, even if it is the transformation and
conversion of the Jewish rite of the Passover. It is above all a gift of the
body (*this is my body*), something that patristic and medieval theology
constantly emphasized, though it also, in part, aimed to diminish the
strangeness. We need then, once again, to dare to go beyond the figural to
the literal. The *hoc est corpus meum* of Catholic tradition is not simply there
to gather the faithful around the eucharistic bread. It gives us "some
thing" or rather "some one" to eat. All our theological good intentions
cannot disguise what lies at the base of the mystery: the body given to eat
is truly body, if not a true body (§27). Under these conditions (and only
under these conditions), *eating the flesh* finally loses its ethereal meaning
and we are brought back to all that there is in us of animality, of passions
and drives, with a presence that is so rightly called *real*, becoming transformed (§29).

A reading of this kind, of the Bread of Life Discourse (John 6), that is
primarily literal—or at least philosophical—does entail the emergence of
the scandal rather than an ordinary recognition of an easily digestible
food. But perhaps it is enough to mention, and to read closely, the exact
words of Christ: "Those who eat my flesh [*trogôn mon ten sarxa*] and drink
my blood [*pinôn mon aïma*] abide in me, and I in them . . . whoever eats

me [*ô trôgen me*] will live because of me" (John 6:56–57). Whether it is a matter here of the exegetical reading (the flesh as the entire human being and blood as the life of God), or of using a symbolic reading to avoid the scandal (primary recognition of the community), or indeed of a theological justification (the permanence of accidents fixed to the substance), the same question remains—that posed by the Jews in the synagogue at Capernaum: "The Jews then disputed among themselves, saying, 'How can this man give us his flesh to eat [*tên sarxa auto phagein*]?'" (John 6:52). Further, "'Is not this Jesus, the son of Joseph, whose father and mother we know? How can he now say, "I have come down from heaven?"'" (John 6:42). I would emphasize, once and for all, what can be (and what ought still to be) a cause of amazement to believers in the eucharistic sacrifice: that a man could thus *give himself to be eaten.*

The impossibility of getting around this scandal is what confronts us when we read *strictu sensu*, or start by reading the Greek, of the Bread of Life Discourse in St. John's gospel. A man—or worse, a God—claims or claimed to give himself to be eaten, indeed to be chewed and digested: "He who *chews* me [*trôgon*][26] will live because of me" (John 6:57); "For my flesh [*sarx*] is true food [*brôsis*] and my blood [*aïma*] is true drink [*pôsis*]" (John 6:55). This is not far from the Greek Eleusinian Mysteries or the placing of blood from sacrificed animals on the altar of the Great Temple in ancient Jewish tradition. There is also an obvious proximity between eucharistic sacrifice and ancient Dionysian rites (see §35). The conception of the eucharistic sacrifice in St. John's gospel does nothing to disguise its radical strangeness, something that some kinds of exegesis (contextualization) as well as some theology (symbolic) often try to obscure. The gospel writer himself emphasizes the unpleasant aspect of the affair instead, basing his whole argument on the objection of the Capernaites. Certainly, the bread "which comes down from heaven" does not resemble the "manna" that "our ancestors" ate (John 6:31–35). The former comes to satisfy hunger, while in the case of the latter, our hunger is insatiable. The difference lies not, or does not lie solely, in the way it was eaten (i.e., whether the eaters were insatiable or not); rather, it is in the reality of that which is eaten (bread or body): "*I am* [*egô eimi*] the living bread that came down from heaven. Whoever eats of this bread will live forever; and the bread that I will give for the life of the world is *my flesh* [*ê sarx mou*]" (John 6:51).

It must be understood, then, that because they have become used to it, the "righteous"—those who are "habituated souls," so that "their moral skin, constantly intact, becomes their shell and armour of faultlessness," and they "do not offer to open themselves for grace" (Péguy)[27]—do not understand the indignation that their procession toward the altar of sacrifice must provoke. Mauriac says in *Le Jeudi-Saint*, "Do not believe that communion is an easy gesture, a meaningless routine, or even a mere consolation, an emotion, a certain manner of closing one's eyes, or resting one's head in one's hands." It is rather the summit, or the ultimate stop, where "the Christian tastes, at that moment, the passionate life that Nietzsche values so highly, that 'purple life,' and infinitely better than what was ever relished by the Borgias and all those feeble enslaved brutes whose derisory example was given to us by Zarathustra. . . . Nothing involves (in reality) a man so much as the eucharist."[28] We can insist on this because simply reading the gospel has the effect of breaking up our habitual assumptions. From the Capernaites to the Fathers of the Church, and from the Fathers of the Church to Hobbes or to the human sciences, a single nagging question hangs over the eucharist—one that the philosopher must ask the theologian, either to get rid of it or to make it real without taking away its substance: What is it that believers eat when they are said to take communion with this body ("the body of Christ. *Amen*"), even if it seems as though they are just chewing bread? And a second question: What does a believer drink when he or she is said to drink blood ("the blood of Christ. *Amen*") but seems simply to be drinking wine? These questions may seem trivial, but they come up with an appropriately infantile naïvety to which we ought to listen. The force of the transformation in the mystery will be all the greater if we acknowledge it, in human terms, and if we also take stock of its impossibility.

§27. The Dispute over Meat

We are brought, then, in this historic debate concerning the eucharist, if not to a solution (to the difficulty that still exists over cannibalism) then at least to some attempts at finding a solution. If *this is my body*, as I have emphasized throughout (Parts I and II), tells us all about embodiedness, including its organic aspect (the eucharistic tradition), its element of animality (the eucharistic content), and the shared eros (the eucharistic modality), all of this must be borne in mind, and reconsidered, in terms of a theological dispute where *meat* keeps turning up like a bad penny.

I recall here Deleuze's words in relation to Francis Bacon, mentioned earlier: "Bacon is a religious painter only in butchers' shops."[29] In philosophy, in aesthetics, and indeed in theology, truth can't be measured simply against the yardstick of carnal realism, or indeed of its obvious cruelty. There is evidently something that revolts us and at the same time draws us toward *this is my body* that we can come back now to question, even at the risk of somehow watering things down with an answer. If it is necessary to underline the thesis of eucharistic realism, one can first take the *body of Christ* literally. One can see it as *body* truly given to be eaten in the consecrated Host, whatever historical analyses we need to put forward to clarify the statement. Despite a theology of carnage (accidents on the doctrinal route and meat cut up in the eucharisticized body), which remains a threat today as it was yesterday, there is still something right, indeed, something existential, that can be read in the depth of the questions posed in the past. If it has become (quite rightly) unseemly to dare to think or even write that "the tongue appears reddened with blood" (Chrysostom), or that "the teeth risk breaking the flesh in chewing the bread" (Bonaventure), a middle way needs to be found between pure "sensism" (i.e., the view that there is nothing in the mind that has not been in the senses)[30] and strict symbolism. The consecrated Host is truly a body given to eat (the sensationalist path), but it is one that cannot be reduced simply to an organic body or to the physical body of the historical Jesus (the appropriate reaction from the point of view of symbolism). A rapid historical detour becomes necessary in this respect, since precision in relation to these questions helps largely to overcome the ensemble of approximations that follow on from them (transignification, transfinalization, and so forth) and that fail to express truly the reality of that which is given to us to eat.[31]

At the start of the ninth century, when the Carolingian Reform was in full swing, the emperor Charles the Bald kicked off the debate. It would take four centuries more for it to be fully opened (on the doctrine of transubstantiation): "Is what the mouths of the believers receive in the Church," Charles asked theologians in his palace, "*in mysterio* or *in veritate*? And is this the body that was born of Mary, suffered, died and was buried, and that after resurrection and ascension is seated at the right hand of the Father?"[32] It is difficult to imagine today how novel and original these questions seemed at the time (in 838). Deliberations over the eucharist among the Fathers of the Church were such during this Carolingian period, and according to major initiatives that we do not need to rehearse here,[33] that direct focus simply on the body given to eat (*caro spiritualis*) would progressively eclipse its connection with the flesh of the Resurrected One (*caro mystica*) as well as its connection with the mystic body of the Church in which the believer becomes incorporated (*corpus mysticum*). The consecrated bread (on the altar) would incidentally, as it were, take over the place and the trace of the Resurrected Son (at the right hand of the Father) and of the integration of the community (the ecclesiastical body) through the eucharist.

Despite all this, the questions remain open, demanding a wider examination of the "this" that we eat: Is it a body in the figurative sense and a mystery? Or a body in reality and in truth? And if the body is given here in reality and in truth, is it the historical body of Jesus incarnate that is eaten here, and/or the spiritual body of he who today is resurrected and sits at the right hand of the Father? Such questions may seem surprising, but they possess at least the merit of getting to the *thing itself.* They ask us, as in all good meals, what *it is* that we have actually been given to eat. The history of the concept (moving toward a so-called real presence in the eucharist) thus helps to clarify the *disuptatio*, or debate.

The problems expressed by Charles the Bald concerning the status of the body that is eaten stem in fact from the "triform body" described by Amalarius of Metz, Bishop of Trèves and successor of Alcuin, who talked of the "three bodies," or "three types of the body of Christ," distinguishing them according to the way in which the consecrated bread was considered in each case:

> The body of Christ is of three kinds, those that have tasted death and those that will die: first, the *holy body without stain* that is born of the Virgin Mary; second, the *body that wanders the earth*; third, the *body that lies in the sepulchre.* The portion of the host that is placed in the chalice represents the body of Christ now resurrected from the dead [*quod jam resurrexit a mortuis*]; the portion that the priest and the people eat is that which still wanders the earth [*ambulans adhuc super terram*]; and the portion that is kept on the altar represents that which lies in the sepulchre [*jacens in sepulcris*].[34]

We would then have three bodies—the immaculate body, the wandering body, the body that dies and is resurrected—and three states of the eucharistic mode corresponding to these three bodies: the immaculate body that joins the blood (the Host in the chalice); the wandering body that is eaten (the bread of the faithful); and the resurrected body that is conserved (the reserved sacrament and later the tabernacle). Apart from the complexity of the debate, which helps us grasp at least how the manducation of the eucharistic body remains obscure to us even today, one comes to understand from this how, at the very least, these things don't just go without saying. Because, if we eat the "immaculate body" it is not the historical Christ that is assimilated; if we stick to the "wandering body" we cannot avoid the danger of having to break and chew it; and if we conserve only the "Resurrected Christ," we shall forget the historical dimension of his humanity. The "full Christ" (*Christum totum*) will not be found except at the price of a radical separation of the flesh in the eucharist and the body that remains intact in heaven: how that could be done," Lanfranc says to Berengarius in a k render, "I shall reply briefly for the moment: it is a *mystery of fa rium est fidei*]; it is profitable to *believe* it [*credi*], it is not useful the matter [*vestigari*]."[35]

We need to escape from these ruts of "fideism"; it is not my aim in this book to explore them fully and I shall not pretend to retrace their paths completely. Nonetheless, two essential questions lead us toward the *content* of what is eaten. They concern the *status* of an organicity made up of passions and drives that the eucharistic body comes to take responsibility for, and to transform: (1) Is it in truth or simply figuratively that we eat the eucharistic body? (2) What type of body are we talking about when we speak of eating it—the historical body or the resurrected body? A brief reply to these questions should allow us to escape from the *aporia* of cannibalism (§26), after we have nonetheless given some appropriate attention to the matter (§25), so that we can use all this as a springboard for a line of argument that, after all, started off with an untenable strangeness.

(1) Is it the body in truth or figuratively? The arguments put forward by Paschasius Radbertus, then Lanfranc (advocates of realism), and then Ratramnus and Berengarius of Tours (advocates of symbolism) would appear to be all the more decisive insofar as the sacramentality of the body eaten here is undermined, or is at the very least called into question. The one side (the realists), already giving a reply to Charles the Bald's question, see in the consecrated bread a body *in veritate* and not *in mysterio*. That is, they see a true body to eat and not simply something that represents a body in our thoughts or our understanding. Relying upon the definition of the sacrament as a "sacred sign" (*sacrum signum*), Lanfranc maintains, "It is truly the invisible flesh and blood of the Lord [*invisibili Domini Jesu Christi carne et sanguine*] that remains under the visible appearance of these elements [*visibile elementorum specie*]."[36] We can see here a form of (philosophical) sensism, or at least an obvious realism. The two species simply "veil" (as *velum*) the reality of the body and blood of Christ, and in removing the vestment or the superficial appearance of the species, the true reality of a flesh to be eaten or a blood to be swallowed will be uncovered anew. On the other side of a debate so severe that it will lead to the double and definitive condemnation of Berengarius (Councils in Rome, 1059 and 1079), the symbolists insist that the presence of the body of Christ in the consecrated bread must be understood solely *in mysterium* and not *in veritate*—figuratively and not in reality.

The symbolist argument is based on an Augustinian definition of the sacrament as sign or symbol (*signum aut figura*); the presence of Christ is considered as spiritual rather than fleshly or material. Berengarius insists in opposition to Lanfranc that "The bread and the wine are transformed into the body and blood of Christ according to the intelligence [*intellectualiter*] but not according to the senses [*sensualiter*]." In other words—and without increasing the complexity of the *disputatio*—we can say that the transformation of bread into body and wine into blood is produced less in the bread and wine themselves than in "the one" who receives communion through the body and blood of Christ. The beliefs of the person communicating count more than what is eaten.[37]

In short, either the initial definition of the sacrament rests on the thing signified (*res sacramenti*, Isidore of Seville) and it is the bread itself that is transformed into body and the wine into blood, or it refers to the sign or symbol (*signum aut figura*, Augustine) and it is the believer who is transformed rather than the matter itself. As we know, Berengarius lost the debate in the Middle Ages against Lanfranc, and thus symbolism lost to realism. There was a return to the reality of what is eaten—a debate that we would be wrong to forget today—when symbols (e.g., the meal, the wheat, the work of humankind, the community) go so far sometimes as to obscure what is to be signified (the transubstantiation of the bread into body and wine into blood). Berengarius avows—unwillingly, one suspects—in the profession of faith that he was required to make at the Second Roman Synod of 1079,

> I, Berengarius, believe interiorly and profess publicly that the bread and wine, which are placed on the altar, through the mystery of the sacred prayer and the words of our Redeemer are substantially changed into the true, proper and life-giving flesh and blood of our Lord Jesus Christ. After the consecration, it is the true body of Christ, which was born of the Virgin, and which hung on the cross as an offering for the salvation of the world, and which sits at the right hand of the Father. And it is the true blood of Christ which was poured forth from his side. And Christ is present not merely by virtue of the sign and the power of the sacrament but in his proper nature and true substance as is set down in this summary and as I read it and you understand it.[38]

(2) What type of body is given to be eaten? The resolution of the conflict (*in veritate* vs. *in figura*) depends on how one *envisages* the body, once one has been invited to communion. The formula of "The body of Christ.

Amen" (*Corpus Christi. Amen*) frees us definitively from the aporia of cannibalism only under the condition that what is chewed is not cannibal flesh, in terms of either theophagy or anthropophagy. As I have already made plain, the consecrated Host is considered to be the flesh of the Resurrected Christ and not simply that of the historically incarnate Jesus. Charles the Bald's initial question amounted to asking not simply if what "is received in the mouths of the believers" is there in symbolic terms or in truth, but also if the body is the historical body born of Mary and/or the resurrected body that sits at the right hand of the Father. The emperor's question is a good one because it does not fix on one option; that is, he leaves it open for theologians to decide. And the limitation of Berengarius, as well as of, to a slighter degree, Lanfranc, is that they wished to decide too quickly. Either it was to be the resurrected body and not the historical body (in such a way that continuity from one to the other could not be assumed in the eucharistic consecration: Berengarius), or it was to be the historical body and not the resurrected body (so that a physicalism, or indeed cannibalism, remained always possible: Lanfranc). Is it really necessary to choose between the body in heaven and its presence on Earth? Don't we find in the New Testament both the recognition by the disciples at Emmaus of the presence of Christ in his eucharist, beginning with his appearance as the Resurrected One (Luke 24: 13–35), *and* the celebration of the Last Supper in the historic body of Christ on the eve of his Passion (Mark 14: 22–25)? It is when we put one directly in opposition to the other that there is either nothing to eat (where Berengarius takes us) or too much to eat (where Lanfranc takes us).

Nonetheless, the distinction (between the historical Christ and the Resurrected Christ) made in the course of this heated debate did lead in the eleventh century toward a certain resolution of the problem. The distinction was retained and recovered in the context of the doctrine of transubstantiation. "The true body [*verum corpus*] and the true blood [*verum sanguinem*] of Christ," Berengarius writes to Adelman of Liège, "cannot be identified with his *real body* [*corpus verus*] nor with his *real blood* [*sanguis verus*]." In other words, if "after consecration the bread and wine themselves become, in terms of faith and our intelligence, the true body and the true blood of Christ [*verum Christi corpus et sanguinem*]," this formula does not suggest that the body eaten is exclusively the historical body; it is also, and above all, Christ's resurrected body. *Truly body* (*corpus vere*) does not inevitably indicate his true body in the somatic meaning of the term (*corpus verus*), nor does *truly blood* (*sanguis vere*) strictly invoke the hemoglobin (*sanguis vere*).[39] Returning to the power of the body and its material organic aspect (§17) does not contradict the phenomenological modes of apparition in flesh and bones (§19). It is simply that in thinking of the one (the flesh, *Leib*) too independently of the other (the body, *Körper*), phenomenology runs the risk of limiting its field too narrowly: to the significance only of lived experience (§3). And theology risks foundering in a form of Gnosis that to some extent turns away from the Incarnate One understood in his organicity (Introduction). Flesh and body hold together in the act of the eucharist. The matter is not more important than the manner (as for Lanfranc), nor the manner more important than the matter (as for Berengarius). We need to think of a kind of continuity, from the body to the flesh, or from the historic Jesus to the Resurrected Christ.

As I understand it, only Lanfranc can really help us, in this case with his *De corpore et sanguine Domine* (his treatise on the body and blood of the Lord). However, this treatise has drawn recent criticism for its over-realist tendency and because it has been found insufficiently symbolic. "The body of the (resurrected) Lord retains [*retinet*] some of its [historical] qualities," Lanfranc very rightly maintains. "[In] the sacrament of the body of Christ it is his flesh [*caro ejus*] that we receive, covered by the form of bread."[40] There is, then, according to the treatise, a kind of resemblance (*similitudo*) and a continuity or retention (*retinere*) between the body of the Resurrected Christ and the body that was the historic body, ensuring that in taking communion through the body of Christ on the altar, one communicates first of all with the resurrected body (which is why we can eat it and drink it without risk of breaking it or making it disappear). But at the same time, it inherits the qualities or forms that we can identify with the suffering (the *pathiques*) of the historic body (which is why it is truly [*vere*] the body of Christ that we eat and the blood of Christ that we drink). What is important here is no longer the *dispute over meat*—something from which we have extricated ourselves definitively with the distinction between the real body (*corpus verus*) and "truly body" (*corpus vere*)—but the fleshly continuity of the biological body with the resurrected body that ensures the presence of Christ in the eucharist. The eucharistic procession comes back to *eating* him when we assimilate him, and to *recognizing* him as we draw near. A kind of amorous empathy brings us in our own bodies to the body of Christ, in such a way that the organic leaves its trace in the phenomenological. At the same time, we communicate precisely with *his* life, made up of flesh and blood, given to us first of all in temporality and shed for us at Golgotha: "Put your finger here and see my hands. Reach out your hand and put it in my side. Do not doubt but believe" (John 20:27). The "body [physique] of the eucharist" (Claudel) does not reduce Christ to *his* physique, but rather consecrates what makes up and was in him, of *his* body as the basis of *a* body, or of a nourishment, that we today can assimilate and be incorporated in. Claudel writes, "Give us this day our super-substantial bread. I have had enough of that manna that changes into shadow and image. We have had enough of that taste of the flesh and the blood, of milk, of fruit and honey. Tree of life, give us the *real bread*. You yourself are my nourishment."[41]

We learn both from Paschasius Radbertus and Lanfranc of Pavia, on the one hand, and Ratramnus and Berengarius, on the other. From the former we learn not to give up on the reality of he who is to be eaten (realism, but still tinged with a certain sensism), and the latter assure continuity between the historical Jesus and the Resurrected Christ (symbolism, but with the added danger of spiritualization). Certainly, transubstantiation will provide a solution (see §29), but according to a definition of substance where, as I shall show, one cannot accept simply its "subsistence" (Aristotle) if we do not also include its "force" (Leibniz) as well as its "act of being" (Aquinas). We close here the dispute over meat, if such a debate could ever really come to an end, while noting that it has at least the merit of showing us in theological terms the place of the body in the resurrected being (Chapter 5). But it remains for us to think through the way in which our part of animality, of passions and drives, is still to be metamorphosed, to become in the eucharist completely hominized and filialized: "[The Son] shared our human nature in all things but sin," as the fourth Eucharistic Prayer reminds us. "To the poor he proclaimed the good news of salvation, to prisoners, freedom, and to the sorrowful of heart, joy."[42]

§28. Hominization and Filiation[43]

We saw in Chapter 2 how the wedding feast of the lamb classically came to celebrate the Passover of God with his people (Judaism) or of Christ with the Church and with humanity (Christianity). But it is my view that *this is my body* was originally to celebrate a Passover, or *passage from animality to humanity*, recognized in its filiation (in other words, from Chaos to cosmos) (§5). Nothing is optional, then, in the act of the eucharist, even if it is only considered as drawing humankind from their animality. Certainly—and happily—we do not remain animal (Chapter 7), even when we don't join the communion. But the reason for this—our humanity that cannot be reduced to a simple animality—is not, or is no longer, philosophical; it is theological. The aim of the eucharist is not achieved through the act of hominization if it is independent of the recognition of filiation. In the transubstantiation of our interior Chaos, of our passions and our drives, through the body given for us, the eucharistic sacrifice does not take us back simply to humankind or to a transfigured cosmos (Teilhard de Chardin). Nor does it take us to a more advanced state of science (Martelet). It takes us to the Son who, in his relation to the Father, and under the power of the Holy Ghost, comes with their unanimous consent to incorporate us.

It is important to recognize the immense merit of Pierre Teilhard de Chardin's having opened up the liturgical Last Supper to the stage of the world. In a remote part of Asia, on August 6, 1923, when he was confronted by the cosmic proportions of the Ordos desert, the altar for the Mass became for him the whole Earth, and the offertory (the first principal part of the Mass) "the labour and suffering of the world." Enlarging, so to speak, the flesh of Christ to "the world of Matter," Teilhard de Chardin found that the universe changes into an "immense Host" and "is made Flesh." God consecrates the world as "his descent into the *universal species*," and a "new Humanity" is now born every day, in such a way that the Word, by the act of the eucharist, "prolongs the unending act of his own birth" through its "immersion in the World's womb."[44]

This perspective is tempting, not to say fascinating. I would point out that it recalls the *corpus mysticum* of the Fathers of the Church that was so convincingly explored and developed later by Henri de Lubac. But major questions remain. Is it really satisfactory to suggest that the act of the eucharist hominizes, or leads us to what Teilhard de Chardin calls a "new Humanity"? Can the cosmic and Christ-centred perspective on the Host really abandon in this way its Trinitarian formulation and identity? If there really is, as I have suggested, an organization of Chaos, or an assumption and transformation of our interior Tohu-Bohu through eucharistic manducation (§2), this process of humanization aims principally at the recognition of our filiation. It is "when we cry 'Abba! Father!' " that, addressing the Father through the power of the Holy Spirit, we see ourselves as "[adoptive] children of God" (Rom. 8:15). And it is then that our humanity shows itself through our filial dependence as created beings. Our humanity is not simply a question of the deployment of our capabilities. No humanism is envisaged by Christianity, even in the act of the eucharist, unless it is integrated into the heart of the first and fully recognized mystery of the Trinity. As Hans-Urs von Balthasar says, developing the thought of Adrienne von Speyr (who so inspired him), "In the eucharistic surrender of Jesus' humanity the point is reached where, through this flesh, the triune God has been put at man's disposal in this final readiness on God's part to be taken into and incorporated into men."[45] There is no hominization—even in the cosmic vision of the eucharistic celebration, independent of a filiation that it comes, newly, to bring to being in us.

As for Martelet, it has to be said that rarely has there been an account of the eucharist so bold and comprehensive (see his *Résurrection, eucharistie, et genèse de l'homme*). We can find everything, or almost everything, there, from Martelet's account of the eucharist as a meal to the medieval debate over the status of the body of Christ—and this last part is directed at Teilhard de Chardin. Still, as I see it, there is an important question that cannot easily be dismissed: Is all of this done at the price of the integration of everything in the act of the eucharist? The analysis of natural symbols (the bread and the wine) and, even more, of the cultural components (e.g., the Big Bang, the emergence of humankind starting from the animal) cannot in fact justify or clarify on its own the eucharistic enterprise. Neither an attempt at harmonization nor concerns of modernity can be used to cover up the mystery, or can aid us in grasping its full weight. Our questions remain metaphysical above all (and thus we have posed questions about animality rather than just about the animal), and indeed theological (the Trinitarian dimension), but not epistemological or scientific (the origin of the world, conformity with Darwinism, the history of humans in the universe standing upright, and the organization of the human body). I do not want to suggest that one learns nothing from science; however, one does not learn from science what science cannot teach: where we come from and where we are going according to the eschatological purposes of God rather than the scientific discoveries of human beings. The two (eschatological purpose and scientific discovery) are certainly not always in contradiction. But their non-contradiction does not imply or impose upon us their coincidence, and even less their concordance. We lose our grasp of the eucharist if we try to conceptualize it in epistemological terms, and we lose our grasp of science if we try to theologise it.[46]

Neither humanization (theologies of liberation) nor hominization, nor metabolism (Martelet), can give us the final word on transubstantiation. I would agree, without hesitation, with the Jesuit theologian François Varillon, who says, "It is when man becomes truly the *Body of Christ* that he becomes *fully man*."[47] Rather than a profession of faith in humanism, this is the recognition above all, and quite simply, of the weight of humanity that comes—in the eucharist, in Trinitarian terms, and in terms of human filiation—to offer itself and transform itself, going so far as the complete realization of our created nature. By the act of communion, our viscera address themselves to his viscera; or rather, that which makes *my life* becomes also and above all *his*—and this is what constitutes first and foremost the great strength of the act of transubstantiation. As the priest pronounces in the Ablutions of the old form of Mass: "May Thy Body, O Lord, which I have received and Thy Blood which I have drunk, *cleave to my inmost parts [adhaereat visceribus meis].*"[48]

8

"This Is My Body"

I am not going to attempt here a history of the doctrine of transubstantiation. This is neither the place nor the time to attempt something that has been done perfectly well and fully discussed by others.[1] The thread of my argument here leads me instead to try to think through the transformation of our embodiedness in the act of the eucharist (eucharistic *content*), having rooted it in an animality that is converted into humanity through recognition of its filiation (eucharistic *heritage*), and before performing the donation in an agape that loses nothing of its erotic genesis even in relinquishing its own body to the body of the other (eucharistic *modality*). *This is my body* (Chapter 8) takes over from the Passover of animality (Chapter 7), waiting for the "lost body" while the viaticum nourishes us on our voyage, as it keeps us in God (Chapter 9). As we have seen, there is a cultural problem. The formula *hoc est corpus meum* constitutes for Western thought our *Om mani padne* (Sanskrit mantra recited in Buddhism), our *Allah ill'allah* (Islamic creed: There is no god but God), and our *Schema Israel* (section of the Torah recited in Jewish prayer: Hear O Israel), and so it needs to be analyzed as such. Above all, it is a statement made when the *this* has become *my body* and will purportedly be reified at the same time as it is spoken by the priest.[2]

If such an analysis (§8) remains philosophically correct, at least in part, it is worthwhile now, however, to place it against the theological motif. While the body in its formulation here can certainly appear as reified (*this is my body*), neither Christ in the Palestinian tradition, nor theology in its

199

substantial argument on the topic, ever intended such a reification. The *this is the bread* becomes the "body of Christ" not as a result of some misunderstood Western invective, but through the will of Christ, who gives himself according to the strongest objectivity. A *thing-ness* paradoxically underlies the substantialism, or rather the operation of the transubstantiation. Rejecting philosophically the modality of the thing, we no longer see how God himself is made theologically *thing* or *matter* (bread and wine), so that the matter itself can be transubstantiated (body and blood), and our bodies assimilating it come also to express this. Marcel Jousse, in Palestine, says, "You have no right, anthropologically, to deny the real Presence and Transubstantiation. And this solution I inflict upon you as an anthropologist. . . . The word 'symbol' which in the modern mentality has taken on the soft meaning of allegory, takes on here its primitive meaning, its real sense . . . 'I am come not to destroy, but to make into a thing [*chosaliser*].'"[3]

§29. Transubstantiation

Let us come back to the most basic question, which has been put forth clearly by Joseph Ratzinger: "What happens in transubstantiation, since nothing *chemical or physical* happens?"[4] If we don't take up the challenge of answering this, the dogma remains so enigmatic that the problem of cannibalism keeps cropping up and the "truly body" of the Resurrected One (*corpus vere*) becomes confused with the "true body" of the historic Jesus (*corpus verus*) (§27). We do not look for the molecular flesh in the bread, even if it had been veiled so as not to frighten us, or for the blood in the form of hemoglobin in the wine, even if it were sweetened so as not to disgust us. On the contrary, we recognize that "a conversion is made of the whole substance of the bread into the substance of the body of Christ," and that "the whole substance of the wine [is converted] into the substance of His blood," while "the species of bread and wine" remain. This is the "conversion [*conversio*]" truly and correctly called "transubstantiation" by the Holy Catholic Church, which the Council of Trent (1551), following the lead of the Fourth Council of the Lateran (1215), definitively established as such.[5]

In fact, what counts as far as substance is concerned—or rather, what counts in the doctrine of transubstantiation—is first of all the theological deployment of this mystery, which tries here to define a "form of presence"—in contrast, as we have seen, to all the false accusations of presentification, or acts of making present (§11). But such a "being-there of God" in his body and blood, under the species of bread and wine, is not simply an encounter or incorporation; at least, the Middle Ages did not see it only as such. It was also considered a localization, indeed, an assumption and transformation of matter, there where the Christ is least bound within the matter that he transubstantiated in order to be corporally incorporated in it. "Christ's body is not in this sacrament in the same way [*eo modo*] as a body is in a place, which by its dimensions is commensurate with the place," Aquinas tells us in his *Summa Theologica*, "but in a special manner [*quodam speciali modo*] which is proper to the sacrament." And this special manner, proper to the body of Christ in the consecrated Host, Aquinas continues, in what was to become almost the canonical article, "does not begin to be there by a local motion, nor is it contained therein as in a place," but "by conversion of the substance [*per conversionem substantiae*] of bread into itself."[6] However complex the doctrine of transubstantiation may be, we cannot disregard one important aim here: that is, giving an account of the so-called real presence of the body and blood of the Lord in the bread and wine after consecration, without confusing the historic Jesus and the Resurrected Christ or totally suppressing the species of bread and wine—if not as substance, at least in the form of accidents referring back to substance and preserved here by God alone: "It is evident to sense that all the accidents of the bread and wine remain after the consecration. And this is reasonably done by Divine providence [*virtute divina*]."[7] Some people will certainly prefer to assert that the bread and the wine are not transformed chemically, and that in any event their continued existence is solely in terms of an analogy with *eaten nourishment* (symbolism), that the business of substance and accident is obsolete, and can usefully be forgotten (modernism). But as I see it, such attempts, or such errors, risk destroying the wholeness of the eucharistic conversion, or of the transubstantiated body. *This is my body* points above all to a body made of flesh and blood that is the body of the Word incarnate, one that is in another mode (not localized but transubstantiated) and has another presence (of the Resurrected Christ and not simply of the historic Jesus). To take communion is to participate in the life of the Resurrected One, not to share fragments of a flesh that it would be forbidden to chew: "It is no longer I who live, but it is Christ who lives in me" (Gal. 2:20).

Certainly, I *have* a body. But also I *am* my body—which the eucharistic sacrifice takes one step further: *This is my body*. The passage from the "body that I have," to the "body that I am," which has become classic in the context of philosophy and theology, is the first step in the process by which God himself is given in a *this* that is his body. After the disappointment of theoretical mechanism and positivism, which attempt to reduce the living person to a simple "statue or earthen machine"[8] that can be repaired and has been repaired (from Descartes to Auguste Comte), many modern philosophers have quite rightly attacked such avatars of an exaggerated rationalism (from Nietzsche to Gabriel Marcel, and including Michel Henry). "*Body am I* through and through, and nothing besides; and soul is merely a word for something about the body."[9] What Nietzsche says about the Overhuman in a heroic proclamation is in some sense worthy of Christ in his prophetic "exinanition" (exhaustion, humiliation). Speech is gradually buried in the flesh on the day of the Passion; it is his flesh that speaks out in his cry ("Then Jesus gave a loud cry and breathed his last" [Mark 15:37]), rather than his speech, which keeps silent in his *logos*. *Body am I through and through*: this could also be the expression of the Word suffering in Gethsemane and in agony on Golgotha.[10]

The *this is my body* of the eucharist—which is neither the simple "I have a body" of good health nor the "I am my body" of Gethsemane or Golgotha—takes a step further, then, speaking here the true sense of transubstantiation. Because becoming the body here is becoming *bread* and not simply becoming flesh, even though flesh would then entirely constitute the *topos* of the bread. To put it another way, the body becomes a thing so that the thing becomes body; or, the subject becomes object so that the object can be seen as subject. The eucharistic imperative of the liturgy (*this is my body*) sparks off the Kantian dissociation of hypothetical imperative and categorical imperative. While the hypothetical imperative denounces the thing and swallows it up in the subservient role of a means to another end ("if . . . then"), the categorical imperative frees the person as an unqualified end and forbids reduction to the simple rank of a means ("it must because it must"). What I call here the eucharistic imperative holds the hypothetical and the categorical imperatives together, as I see it, and in a way that is, to say the least, paradoxical: "At the time he was betrayed and entered willingly into his Passion [*categorical imperative*], he took bread and, giving thanks, broke it, and gave it to his disciples, saying: *Take this* all of you and *eat* of it [*hypothetical imperative*]: For *this is my body* which will be given up for you [*eucharistic imperative*]" (Eucharistic Prayer II).[11] In making his body a *this*, the Christ given for us borrows in his humility, or as his *humus* (ground), the road of the thing, while the bread is given to us as nourishment to fortify us. But in consenting freely to this, he raises up and makes seen his person as subject—or as an end that is irreducible to any particular means—after the *this* of the thing, or of the means, becomes something deliberately chosen rather than simply necessary: "He has achieved here the equivalence, the identity of the most opposed extremes: he who presided and who spoke has come to *identify himself as the thing shared* between us all: 'This is my body' (Luke 22:19)."[12] The objectivizing of the self into the thing, which contains in its terms the transubstantiation itself (*this* is my body), is not always to be rejected outright, once it is understood as an act of giving, going as far as, and being included in, the assumption and transformation of his *own body* (flesh) into *objective body* (bread) and then *transubstantiated* (body of flesh).

We have to take a path, then, that in some sense leads us backward—from the Resurrection to the Passion this time. While we go from the body to the flesh on the route to the Resurrection (*Metamorphosis of Finitude*), we now return from the flesh to the body through the viaticum of the eucharist. The route is the same, but the direction has been reversed. In his pilgrimage on Earth, God showed himself in a body (physical), and learned about his own flesh (lived experience), up to the glory of his new birth (Resurrection). But through the eucharist (after the fact, as it were, even though the mystery was there chronologically beforehand), he remained body, at least for us, under the species of bread and wine transubstantiated into body and blood. This is although the *eucharis*, or the shared meal, would speak fully of the action of his flesh (lived experience) as resurrected. The route of the incarnation (*Verleiblichung*) is that of the Resurrection, and the route of embodiment—perhaps even more difficult—is that of the eucharist. What corresponds to the *becoming-flesh of the body* (Resurrection) is the *becoming body of the flesh* (eucharist). Not only are the two mysteries placed against each other, but also they are linked theologically, and indeed phenomenologically.

As we have seen (§7), in discussing Cézanne's letter to his son, the priest, like an artist, and God through him, lends in some way "his body to the words," rather as though there were a transubstantiation of the body in painting.[13] A "wonderful exchange" takes place here from the thing to the work of art, or from the reification to its manifestation (on the canvas or in the bread). Because if the body, at least initially, becomes thing or reifies (*this* is my body), reification alone is not enough; it works at the same time through the power of donation and of expression. In fact, nothing compels us (in Aquinas, or even less so in Leibniz) to think of the substance as a form of subsistence (food), whether it is a question here of its reification or its supposed autonomy or independence. Implied in the context of "trans-substantiation" (which necessarily implies "substance") is (1) an act of being (Aquinas), or even (2) active force (Leibniz).

(1) *An act of being*, where substance escapes definitively from any accusations of reification. Aquinas says in the *Summa Theologica*, talking of the simplicity of God, "'To be' can mean either of two things. It may mean the act of essence [*actum essendi*], or it may mean the composition of a proposition [*compositionem propositionis*] effected by the mind in joining a

predicate to a subject."[14] Clearly, when "being" is not logical (*a copula*) but ontological (existing), it is the *act* of accomplishment rather than the *thing* defined: "This conversion does not come about by the passive potentiality of the creature, but solely by the active power [*per potentiam activam*] of the Creator."[15] So, we can conclude, God is actually present in the eucharist, "but with an eschatological presence that time cannot 'reify.'"[16]

(2) *Active force.* Substance is "a being that is capable of action," Leibniz says in his "Principles of Nature and Grace." An active force, or a substantial chain (or bond) (*vinculum substantiale*), unites us creatures with the Creator. As Maurice Blondel later explains, the "bond that is Christ himself [*vinculum ipsius Christii*] in the Transubstantiation" does not join the bodies of humans among themselves and the *body* of Christ to them simply as a bond but as a "coagulant." By transubstantiation, which can be understood as an active force, God allows us to participate in his Work (of Art) as in his Being itself, in such a way that the eucharist is not simply the "implementation [*application*]" but the perfect example of the Leibnizian *vinculum.*[17]

When the bread and wine are transubstantiated they are converted along these lines into body and blood as a result of a power (Holy Spirit)— by which God is offered and sustained in his "act of existing" (Aquinas), at the same time as he "connects" those beings, or those "monads," in the Word—that has no other wish than to gather them together (Leibniz, Blondel). If we can suggest that all force is looking for a body, and that the resurrection does not come from the substance of the body of the Resurrected One, but the *substance of the body of the Resurrected One comes from the force of the resurrection* (§ 17), then it comes back to the Spirit of God, or to the Holy Ghost, to bring about, through its "force," the transubstantiation of the bread and wine—precisely the thing that the epiclesis (calling on the Holy Spirit) invokes and celebrates at the heart of the eucharistic liturgy: "Be pleased, O God, we pray, to *bless*, acknowledge, and approve this offering in every respect; make it spiritual and acceptable, so that it *may become for us* the *Body* and *Blood* of your most beloved Son, our Lord Jesus Christ."[18]

Transubstantiation, which is neither metaphysical in the way it is rendered to the consciousness (Heidegger) nor a response to some unacknowledged weakness (Nietzsche), is not one of those terms that can sensibly be dispensed with today. The *now* of the body, understood here as the eucharistic gift, is a challenge to our concept of presence (the act of being) as well as to our concept of what links us together (bond or *vinculum*), and it is sustained all the more through a *being-there* to which it surrenders itself, in its reification as well as in its communion. Emptied—in a way, literally—of his substance, in the bread and the wine, God paradoxically gives us something of his substance as we eat the bread and drink the wine, or, more exactly, of his force and power for those who then "abide in me, and I in them" (John 6:56). Hans-Urs von Balthasar remarks (only in passing, unfortunately) that "When [Jesus] exercises this power by giving to this surrender 'for his friends' (John 15:13) the form of a meal, of eating and drinking his Flesh and Blood (John 6:55) . . . he fills his friends with his own substance—body and soul, divinity and humanity. Granted the mystery of Jesus' inseparably divine and human reality, this act of love that 'loves to the end' (John 13:1) exhibits a compelling and transparent logic."[19]

§30. Incorporation

In this movement, then—and through this power that reaches right to the substance—assimilation (the descent of God into the world and also into ourselves) precedes incorporation (the mounting of ourselves to be integrated in God in forming his body). We should emphasize that the *eucharis* is what points to the action of grace and the "meal" through which we assimilate God in eating him. But the communion, even if it is first, is not satisfying only because of the presence of a small Jesus at its heart; rather, it incorporates human beings to the heart of Jesus—that is, as a "living sacrifice [or offering of oneself], holy and acceptable to God" (Rom. 12:1). Nobody simply eats God, but we are always in some respect eaten by him. From our being anthropophagous (eating the body of Christ) what becomes clear is a kind of theophagy (to be eaten or incorporated into the body of Christ). Certainly the aim is different. In this inverse movement of eating we find, figuratively of course, the double sense of digest: (1) the *assimilation of the body*, and (2) the *incorporation in his body*.

(1) The model of assimilation stipulates first that God makes himself ours and that we are able in some way to swallow or digest him. The alimentary and nutritional aspects of the eucharistic sacrifice—updated according to current tastes, sometimes to the point of forgetting the substance of the body in the eucharistic conversion—are in fact thoroughly ancient. Through "the Eucharist of the body and blood of Christ . . . the substance of our flesh is increased and supported," Irenaeus tells us, insisting that Paul, in the Epistle to the Ephesians, refers to "an actual man, consisting of flesh, and nerves, and bones—that [flesh] which is nourished by the cup which is His blood, and receives increase from the bread which is His body."[20] Such considerations are important once the eucharistic sacrifice is taken to be, far from any Gnosticism, above all a gift of the organic to the organic (§4). The route of the nourishment that spreads

from our vascular system into the whole body emphasizes how, through the assimilation of the life of God in us, our corruptible bodies become in some way incorruptible, simply by the act of communion: "As the bread, which is produced from the earth, when it receives the invocation of God, is no longer common bread, but the Eucharist . . . so also our bodies, when they receive the Eucharist, are no longer corruptible, having the hope of resurrection to eternity."[21]

In short, the metaphor of assimilation along with nourishment allows us to take into account the movements of the body—or its *power*, organic and bodily (Spinoza, Nietzsche; §17)—and to recognize the carrying over of a life of God. It is a life of God that weaves its way like the ineffable and discreet movement of blood in our vascular system, or like the more or less conscious burden of our nerves (Artaud; §18). God is made a human being through a penetration-incorporation, so that the sacrament of the eucharist completes the movement of incarnation of the Word and of its kenosis. It is a kind of incorporation, or a "becoming body," starting from the flesh (*Verkörperung*), through which annihilation in "de-creation" reaches its furthest point in a process of total identification: "In so far as I become nothing, God loves himself through me," says Simone Weil, talking of "Catholic communion" with a kind of eucharistic hunger for the body of Christ. In her case the hunger was never satisfied, because she only ever felt ready to approach communion, never taking part.[22]

(2) As far as *incorporation* is concerned, the movement is different, or even opposite. That which is assimilated by us, in the unique case of the body of Christ, is what assimilates us; or rather, paradoxically, it incorporates us even into Christ-there whom we eat. The eucharistic sacrifice is a form of "anti-digestion" rather than something that simply contains or ingurgitates. "The priest is a man eaten," according to Abbé Chevrier.[23] He shows by his work and even by his death that a human being becomes progressively "food for God," so as to be transformed and reintegrated into the life of the Trinity. At stake here is the act of incorporation in theology, as with intentionality in phenomenology—that is to say, a movement of inversion of all assimilation, which means that "to know" is, above all, to go out toward rather than to interiorize everything. In fact, an extraordinary misunderstanding has existed throughout the history of philosophy, and probably also throughout theology: Jean-Paul Sartre, commenting on Husserl's view of intentionality (in phrases like "He devoured her with his eyes [*Il la mangeait des yeux*]") says, "This expression and many other signs point to the illusion common to both realism and idealism: to know is to eat." In other words, it has been necessary since the matching of ideas and things (Plato), or the identification of the knower

and the known (Aristotle), to believe in the "spidery mind" that "trapped things in its web, covered them with a white spit and slowly swallowed them, reducing them to its own substance. . . . Nutrition, assimilation! Assimilation, Lalande said, of things to ideas, of ideas by ideas, of minds by minds."[24] The criticism is certainly severe—to say the very least—and reflects on the whole history of philosophy, as indeed on theology, including theology today.

If anything is new or fresh in phenomenology as far as intentionality is concerned, perhaps it could clarify for us the topic of incorporation in sacramental theology, not simply as "becoming body" (*Verkörperung*) but as a going out toward and into an other who is not me and will never be reducible to me. Husserl's famous formula—"all consciousness is consciousness *of* something"—says more than a simple reference to the noetic-noematic of the consciousness. It is not a matter of connecting the consciousness that is me to an object that is not my consciousness, but of recognizing "oneself as another" (Ricœur). In regarding something, one certainly sees it starting from one's own position, but one then discovers in it meanings that belong to it and that cannot be exclusively reduced to oneself. "You see this tree, to be sure," Sartre says, and it is certainly a tree, or even better, *this* tree that I see. It isn't important (to me) whether it is exterior to me (realism) or interior (idealism). All that counts is the fact that I cannot dissolve the meaning of the tree in myself so that it becomes simply the projection of my own fantasies onto what I would call a tree. The "return to things themselves" (*zurück zu den Sache selbst*) is a return to *things* as they are part of the lived experience of the consciousness, or as far as they concern me. They do not exist as objects in themselves (*Ding*), but rather because I am preoccupied by their "kind of thing" and by their signification (*Sache*). "All consciousness is consciousness of something," Sartre says, recalling Husserl's phrase. And then, "No more is necessary to dispose of the effete philosophy of immanence, where everything happens by compromise, by protoplasmic transformations, by a tepid cellular chemistry. The philosophy of transcendence [understood here as openness] throws us onto the highway, in the midst of dangers, under a dazzling light. Our own being, says Heidegger, is being-in-the-world. One must understand this 'being-in' as movement. To be is to fly out into the world. . . . This necessity for consciousness to exist as consciousness of something other than itself is what Husserl calls intentionality."[25]

Without any further commentary, and bearing in mind Sartre's impressive review of intentionality in Husserl, we can say that what goes for phenomenological intentionality applies also to eucharistic incorporation, in terms of the rupture they both represent from previous models of assimilation or of digestion. In eating the body of Christ, as we have seen, the believer is in some way eaten by him or incorporated in him: "Now you are the body of Christ [*sôma Christou*] and individually members of it" (1 Cor. 12:27). What is ordinarily interpreted in terms of pure functionalism, or in terms simply of the organism, should rather be understood as empathetic incorporation. Making our communion through the flesh of Christ—in being unified with the true body of the Resurrected One (including and going beyond the true body and the history of Jesus of Nazareth)—we take part in the life of the Resurrected One in its otherness; we make our communion with his Life rather than focusing on ourselves or confining ourselves solely within our egoisms. In presenting myself for communion, and this time in the mode of incorporation and not simply of assimilation, I do not simply bring forward my own concerns and the sufferings of my flesh; he brings forward his divine mode of being in his body, through which he embraces and takes responsibility for all the sufferings of our flesh.

The major switch from assimilation to incorporation—so essential for the integration of the spiritual flesh of the eucharist (*caro spiritualis*), the mystic flesh of the believer (*caro mystica*), and the mystic body of the Church (*corpus mysticum* [Henri de Lubac])—determines what is specific to the eucharistic dynamic and our total integration in God. If we ourselves are also "completely body" (Feuerbach, Nietzsche, G. Marcel; Chapter 5), as well as being the inheritors of a certain form of animality in our selves (Spinoza, Deleuze, Bacon; Chapter 4), and are caught in an interior Chaos or Tohu-Bohu that the significance of the phenomenon is not able to express (Husserl and Heidegger on limits; Chapter 1), then it is appropriate now that all of that—perhaps we should talk of a cluster of things, of our passions, our drives, and "the region of what can no longer be said" (Heidegger on Husserl; Chapter 1)—should be integrated and transformed in God. It is with our inmost parts (*viscera*) or with all that makes up our being, up to and including that part of ourselves that we do not dare contemplate, that we go toward the table to communicate. And all of this is already—in advance, so to speak—taken on and transformed in the body of Christ. God has no need of an angel, or indeed a ghost, who would come spiritually to the Wedding Feast of the Lamb without being hungry: "It is not, as some would wish, simply the soul that is fed by this eucharistic mystery," Paschasius Radbertus tells us, impressively, arguing against the excess of symbolism in Ratramnus. "Because it is not simply the soul that is redeemed and saved by the death of Christ; *our flesh*, also, is brought to immortality and incorruptibility by this mystery. *Introduced spiritually to our inmost parts*, the flesh of Christ becomes *transformative*, so that the substance of Christ *finds itself in our flesh*, just as it is obvious that he took on our substance in his divinity."[26]

There is, then, a double sense of God incorporate (Part III), or a double movement of the incorporation *of* God (§30): that by which the Word is incorporated or assimilated into the bread in its kenosis (subjective genitive), and that by which we are ourselves caught in this act of integration and transformation (objective genitive). Forming in this way "the fount and apex of the whole Christian life,"[27] the eucharistic sacrifice ensures that we are ourselves offered, rather than that we consume it. We are ourselves cast into it; we do not just assimilate or digest it. "This sacrament contains Christ's true body and immaculate flesh in such a way that it penetrates our very being, unites us to one another, and transforms us into him."[28]

We are nonetheless left with a significant problem: Is what was true in the past for transubstantiation (§29) and incorporation (§30) still valid today? If we "celebrate the memorial of our redemption" (liturgy of the eucharist), isn't that memorial duty simply dedicated to the *memory* of that which is past? Or does it incorporate us newly in every instant in the movement of assimilation and transformation that ensures that nothing of ourselves, of the most individual and personal kind, is left out or forgotten in a transubstantiation of bread into body—of which I am, for my part, the most fitting wheat? The eucharist is not simply something from the past (in memory of the Last Supper), nor merely an opening to the future (expectation of the Second Coming). It is given to us as a *present*—as in being a gift and for the present time, when and where it is exactly a question of abiding (John 6:56). The remembrance of the body of Christ speaks also, and now, to our own bodies and to our own memories, or perhaps we should say to our memory of our bodies. Because this has been too often forgotten, the mystery has sometimes been, at least historically, interrupted (e.g., the Great Schism of Michael Cerularius, the Reformation). Catholicism would try, and still tries today, to work in an opposite direction, to be incorporate in a communal and silent embodiedness. St. Thérèse of Lisieux reminds us, "In the heart of the Church, my mother, I will be love."[29]

§31. Consecration

Transubstantiation (§29), incorporation (§30), and consecration constitute three stages of a *this is my body* that is capable of taking on and transforming our humanity, and indeed also our animality, in the expectation of an adoration that can bring us back to our nature as created humans and that integrates us in a definitive and radical filiation (§32). Pronounced liturgically, and each time reiterated, the words of consecration have their source in a formula that derives from scripture: "On the same night that he was betrayed, the Lord Jesus took some bread, and thanked God for it and broke it, and he said, 'This is my body, which is for you; do this as a memorial of me'" (1 Cor. 11:24 [JB]).

The commemoration, or *anamnesis*, referred to here is not simply the celebration of a memory. If the eucharistic Last Supper needs to be read as anticipation of the Resurrection, the commemoration does not consecrate an event in the past. It reactualizes each time in the present what happened and what continues still to come to us. Celebration of the eucharist is not a rehearsal or repetition but a performance, or actualization, of a mystery that is freshly given each time. In the words of the Catechism of the Catholic Church: "Christian liturgy not only recalls the event that saved us but actualizes them, makes them present. The Paschal mystery of Christ is *celebrated*, not *repeated*. It is the celebrations that are repeated, and in each celebration there is an outpouring of the Holy Spirit that makes the unique mystery present."[30]

A question, however, remains here, and the duty of remembrance demands that we address it—precisely because we are concerned not only with a matter of memory or duty, but with one of life, of body and blood, newly given and shared. Our question is this: How can we philosophically think through this mode of memory, if we are most often just celebrating events of the past? In the anamnesis—and in the actualization today of this event in the past ("Today we celebrate Jesus-Christ come *in our flesh*" [Orthodox liturgy of the Mass])—all our body must be involved, as Christ also is given here in the flesh. Because we participate in the Mass consciously, or rather, through our consciousness, we are inclined to forget the silent experience of the body-to-body of human and God that should guide us here. Two philosophical stumbling blocks—leftovers of so-called classic philosophy—make the translation into theological terms difficult: (1) the reduction of memory to a simple phenomenon of consciousness, and (2) memory seen as a container, in which a mass of recollections is piled up.

(1) The claim to the memory of Christ's self must first be envisaged as a memory of the body: *in mei memoriam facietis* ("do this in memory of me"). This reiteration of the past (in memory of me) is deliberately inscribed in the heart of a future (do this), rather than invoking the memory of a gesture or a moment whose repetition would ensure that neither his person nor his gift are forgotten. There is a willingness to be open toward a gift of the present and the presence of a now that has never been interrupted—and, moreover, that is actualized each time. Memory here cannot be identified simply with recollection, in that it does not just

celebrate an instant in time; rather, it draws upon what is imm
an act from the past that has never been superseded. *This is my b*
to something from our origins—from one spouse to the other, ⟨
("the man [Adam] *knew* his wife Eve" [Gen. 4:1]), but also from C
the Church ("for in him the whole fullness of deity dwells bodily'
2:9]). What we find here is not simply a beginning or restarting of ,
but a founding act by which the world becomes in some way newly created
and, in the figure of the Lamb, precisely and definitively ratified: "And all
the inhabitants of the earth will worship it, everyone whose name has not
been written from the foundation of the world [*apo katabolês kosmou*] in
the book of life of the Lamb" (Rev. 13:8).[31]

We do not just celebrate the past—something that the simple continuity of the liturgy could not guarantee on its own; if it pleased God to come
among humankind, the will of believers alone would not be enough to
make him stay (§12). What was necessary (what we needed here) was the
body, so that something could be developed in a way that was ante-
predicative, like the eros and beyond all speech, in our fleshly memory:
something to ensure that my entire being participates in this sacrifice
made for me. We might have thought only consciousness and the knowledge of what was going on were to be celebrated; actually, the whole body
must participate—not just as a complement that brings things into balance, but in the form of a kind of compendium, or a backwash, of that
which in our deepest selves remains hidden (Chaos, Tohu-Bohu, passions,
drives . . .). There is no particular organ of memory, Nietzsche says in his
notes published as *The Will to Power*. "All the nerves, for example of the
leg, recall their previous experiences. Every word, every number is the
result of a physical phenomenon and is fixed somewhere in the nerves. All
that the nerves have assimilated continues to live in them. The waves of
emotions have summits where this life comes into consciousness, where
we recall."[32]

What was metaphysical for Spinoza and Nietzsche (§17, §4) and has
been verified by recent biology or psychoanalysis (the memory of the
body) is given, as I see it, in a liturgical form in the eucharistic sacrifice. A
simple act of consciousness is not enough for the memory celebrated in
this is my body, nor indeed is the act of will concerning whether or not we
attend a Sunday Mass. The memory is inscribed, or should be inscribed,
in our own bodies—just as the memory of food leads us always, almost
biologically, to look for it. Henri Bergson reminds us how we need to find
a kind of *instinct*, or a *second nature*, something much more than the intelligence, to lead us to the Mass, to give us the desire for an ardent desire to
communicate, and allow our bodies to be spiritually entwined with He

who gave everything.[33] There is certainly a fatigue in the liturgy, as we shall see later when we look at the viaticum (§34); at least, it signifies that we have not yet reached the end of time. But the nerves, our nerves, carry also the trace of our existentiality, as in Artaud's Nerve Meter, which expresses the purity and solidity of embodiedness (§18). The eucharistic memory cannot then remain indifferent to the body, to its weight and its wounds that are endlessly reactualized; otherwise, it risks being held and kept simply by the consciousness, as the memory of a past that has been superseded. Everything is inscribed in our bodies, and nothing has been forgotten of the body of the Resurrected One in the total of the eucharisticized bodies. By eating his body and drinking his blood, we don't simply celebrate the memory of an event, even if that event was foundational for all humanity. We drink the blood of *his* life that flows as far as our veins, and we eat the flesh of *his* body that feeds us even in our inmost organs. Celebration of the Last Supper is not a conscious and intellectual remembrance of Christ, who was given (to the world), but a sharing of the embodiedness that ensures nothing of my body—even what is most intimate to me—remains foreign to Christ, who espoused it in order to transform it. Drawing a parallel between the Lord's Prayer and the bread of the eucharist, Tertullian says, "In petitioning for 'daily bread,' we ask for *perpetuity in Christ, and indivisibility from His body.*"[34]

(2) The memory of the Last Supper is, then, a memory of the body, and not simply an epiphenomenon of the consciousness piled upon the brain in the form of a Pandora's box that Sunday celebration forces us to open. Nothing is more destructive for the meaning of the liturgy (see §34) than the mode of bracketing it off, or abstracting it from time—making it belong to no time and certainly not to the continuous present of our ordinary daily lives. The eucharistic imperative of the anamnesis ("do this in memory of me") is undoubtedly rooted in a kind of immemorial past that removes it from all memories. But the immemorial Word outside time breaks in, in full embodiedness and in time, on the day of Holy Thursday. Giving his body, he offers what is there for all eternity, but this time in a way that is fully manifest. The memory becomes rooted in history and is then a criticism of forgetting, especially as this memory constitutes an immemorial resource in which all the events of the world are in a sense implanted and reactualized.[35]

The eucharistic consecration cannot just celebrate a yesterday—even if it is to reactualize it in our today. To "do this in memory of me"—and thus, for us, "of him"—belongs also and integrally to *our* own memory, because nothing that humanity has been through, or goes through now, and will go through in the future, remains (or will remain) foreign to him.

There is not, speaking of the eucharist, something like the before and after Exodus, or before and after Exile, or before and after the Holocaust. The immemoriality of human history is inscribed entirely in the memory of the body—of human beings, certainly, but also and above all the body of God. His body celebrates the *this is my body* along with our bodies. In the eucharist the priest speaks quietly as he performs the gesture of mixing wine and water in preparation for the celebration: "By the mystery of this water and wine may we come to share [Chaos, passions, drives] in the divinity of Christ, who humbled himself to share in our humanity."[36]

In the eucharist, what was yesterday, what is the past of memory ("do this in memory of me"), turns today into the present of the gift and the gift of the present. And it opens the way to a total assumption and transformation of humankind for tomorrow. At present, however, we still have to apply ourselves to see this, to see him, because all has been effectively taken on and transubstantiated in the eucharisticized body. It is not enough to *eat* him to participate in his mode of incorruptibility. We can still, and we should still, lead ourselves to *see* him and to love him as the power of transformation. The basis of the act of adoration makes for us, in this sense, today, a kind of paradoxical asceticism (spiritual-discipline) of Chaos. In the eucharistic Adoration, none of our senses, up to and including that of sight, will be forgotten as we try to come to an understanding of the One who, by the act of manducation, will be tasted. Of course, this form of worship can seem outdated to some people, and all the more because it was established by the Council of Trent to counteract the eucharistic disputes of the Reformation. However, it still holds a form of empathy and a sharing of affect (§24) that Christ's embodiedness in his modes of being—or in his "mind"—comes to communicate to us. Pierre de Bérulle, founder of the Congregation of the French Oratory (1611) and initiator of the French School of Spirituality, tells us, "In the Eucharist, the life of God is given to mankind in the fullness *of his mind* and of *all his mysteries*. And it is given as *life* and as eternal nourishment."[37]

§32. Adoration

Certainly the desire to see the Host was not there from the start. It was only gradually that sight became implicated in the dynamic of the eucharist. The history of the Church shows this, along with well-known excesses: People in the Middle Ages went from Mass to Mass to see the elevation of the Host, to the extent that, with the establishment of the Feast of Corpus Christi (1264) and then the promulgation of the Council of Trent (1563), the practice of the Adoration was to become a veritable institution, separated from the eucharistic Last Supper.[38] The tradition of the Adoration of the Blessed Sacrament does involve an exercise in contemplation—of God, but also of the self, in that the whole of my interior being, itself made up from Chaos, passions and drives, is projected and transformed in God. I do not simply see God, who sees me and who contains me in him. The Adoration is a matter not simply of detachment but also of attachment, not uniquely the will to "unpack" myself but also the desire to remake myself, or to be remade by him. The asceticism of Christ becomes a kind of exercise, in the sense of the Jesuit spiritual exercises, in which the totality of my being—up to and including its part of animality (the human inheritance), indeed, of bestiality (sin)—is transformed in the crucible of contemplation of the divine. We learn gradually to turn our senses to contemplation of the eucharistic bread. Then, our whole being, including our sensibility (as opposed to sensuality), is exerted gradually to become reoriented, turned toward the other of God rather than toward the me of humankind, and to become a place of letting go and not simply one of attempting control. Bonaventure says that when a person possesses the spiritual sense [*sensus spiritualis*] "then the sublime beauty of Christ the Bridegroom is *seen*, insofar as he is Splendor; the highest harmony is *heard*, insofar as he is Word; the greatest sweetness is *tasted*, insofar as he is the Wisdom which contains both Word and Splendor . . . the most sublime fragrance is *smelled*, insofar as he is the Word breathed into the heart; the greatest delight is *embraced*, insofar as he is the Incarnate Word."[39] To see the splendor of Christ (contemplation), to hear his Word (speech), to taste his wisdom (manducation), to feel his inspiration (the whole of Christ in me), and to touch his incarnation (embrace in prayer) are also acts or modalities in the apprehension of a God who belongs to ordinary Christian life, insofar as this exercise, or form of asceticism (here the Adoration), calls for and authorizes the transformation of ourselves, reaching to what is most powerful in our being. Not being able to formulate any better our inner being and that region of what can no longer be said (Chaos or Tohu-Bohu, passions, drives, life of the body . . .), we try at least to offer it up, in the crucible of our vision of the consecrated bread, to allow ourselves to be transformed.[40]

Our "pure—and, so to speak, still dumb—psychological experience" (Husserl), achieves then, in some way, its highest point in the exercise and experience of the Adoration. Because even if silence seems to be common practice in this kind of devotion, it is because one does not speak, or says so little, that the flesh becomes apparent—and so fully apparent that words to speak the experience would seem enough to destroy it. The Adoration is a pre-affirmation of incorporation as well as its point of completion.[41] This applies to the Last Supper, as I have tried to demonstrate, as well as to the erotic scene. Speech is second, not first, and falls within the imperfections of the flesh (§23). The unity here is never one of fusion but rather one of differentiation (§21), and the "love of limits" is not something one can charge with limitation (§22). It is precisely in the eucharistic Adoration that we find what is perhaps both the greatest difference and the greatest resemblance. Nothing is further away than this body that is given to us to contemplate: bread transubstantiated such that only recognition of the mystery ensures that our adoration (*latria*) does not turn into idolatry. But also, nothing is closer—nothing is more my neighbor—than this body offered and always given in advance, already there, not to be consumed, but awaited and respected in an alterity that is not to be suppressed.

"I look at him and he looks at me," to repeat the famous formula of the Curé of Ars. Not simply a matter of piety, this statement brings into play a metaphysical structure that the eucharistic Adoration transforms and completes rather than contradicts. Because, in all this—and we come back here to Levinas, who showed it so convincingly—the face of the other "disorients the intentionality that sights it."[42] In other words, when I see the world I include it in my intentionality, even if that means the presence of the other in me and undermines any kind of digestive philosophy (§30). But when I see the other, I see that he sees me; it is in seeing myself seen that I uncover myself along with he who sees me (the face [*le visage*]; Levinas), or because he is a voyeur with regard to me (shame [*la honte*]; Sartre). The other does not simply give me access to the world (Husserl, and even Heidegger), but makes me give up or remove that egoism that wants too much heroic domination of human beings or wants to dominate any breakthrough of alterity (Merleau-Ponty, Levinas, Ricœur, Marion, Jean-Louis Chrétien, Michel Henry). Inverse intentionality[43]—something that has been celebrated in the context of contemporary French phenomenology—in this sense also speaks the truth of the eucharistic Adoration.

After all, when I see him, in his body and under the stable form of the species of bread, I think—no, I believe—that he sees me: me, in my body that lives and shares with him that mute experience of a body-to-body, where my sense and my interior Chaos will emerge so that I take responsibility for them and they are changed. I see him seeing me, and seeing him thus I kneel before the mystery of the Blessed Sacrament. Liturgical practice here rejoins theology, and theology is buttressed by the truth of philosophy. The *this is my body* of transubstantiation (§29), of incorporation (§30), of consecration or of the memory (§31), and of the Adoration

(§32) form and transform the power of embodiedness (§17), not just as it is produced by me, but where it is offered and driven by an other in me. The epiclesis (invocation of the Holy Spirit) affirms, and the Holy Spirit brings this about—starting with the bread and the wine, but also with our "bodies as a living sacrifice, holy and acceptable to God" (Rom. 12:1): "May this same Holy Spirit graciously sanctify these offerings that they may become the Body and Blood of our Lord Jesus Christ. . . . May he make of us an eternal offering to you, so that we may obtain an inheritance with your elect."[44] The eucharistic bread is of course a form of nourishment, but also, and above all, it is an active force and a transubstantiation at the heart of reality (§29), so that he who says, "I am the resurrection and the life" (John 11: 25) incorporates us and confers upon us his own power of transformation. "The eucharist is a *source of strength* for those who *receive* it," according to St. Cyprian of Carthage, speaking to his people threatened with martyrdom (start of the third century). "That is why we arm those whom we wish to be strong against the adversary, by providing them with the repast of the Lord."[45]

Appearing in flesh and in bones, the Son, as we have seen, is not given in the bread and the wine *with* the flesh or *with* the bones. It is, rather, a question of his "person," or the "thing itself" (*Sache selbst*), and not simply a compound of organs. Such a compound would be insufficient on its own to define him, even if he bears this body and assumes total responsibility for it, to transubstantiate it and to live in it along with us (§19). "Touch me not [*Noli me tangere*]" (John 20:17 [AV]): The words of the Resurrected One to Mary Magdalene apply perfectly to the eucharistic self-discipline of the Adoration, as well as to the experience of the conversion of the senses in which my own interior Chaos is put together in another way—indeed, becomes better regulated—once offered and transformed in the act of eucharisticizing. In fact, one does not touch the body that one sees when one adores it (in the Adoration); one assimilates it and is incorporated in it when one eats it or consumes it (manducation). The procession we join in the Adoration and the procession we join for manducation complement one another, in two distinct liturgical stages, nourished together by the same act of transubstantiation. Neither the Adoration nor the manducation, however, are enough to justify in themselves that God should be given to us. Because if one contemplates the consecrated Host, or if one eats his body in consuming the bread, it is above all to fortify and make up *our* own bodies (including what we are as organisms) and *his* own body (the Church). The *for the self* of the Passover of animality (Chapter 7) and of *this is my body* (Chapter 8) becomes and is transformed here into a *for the other*—a kind of headlong, unreserved plunge, or an act of renunciation (Chapter 9). Both the reunion and the transformation of the eros (Chapters 3 and 6) open up here in the agape (Chapter 9) and now demand of the body given that it is not held back, at risk of being neither spread out nor widespread: "Touch me not; for I am not yet ascended to my Father: but go to my brethren, and say unto them, I ascend unto my Father, and your Father; and to my God, and your God" (John 20:17 [AV]).

9

Plunging Bodily

There is a paradox here: The body finds itself all the more when it is lost, or when it plunges unreservedly into something. Or at least, we can say that the body is most present when it surrenders itself. This is common knowledge. Nothing blocks a gift more than the knowledge that it is a gift; Christ's words to the Samaritan woman—"If you knew the gift of God" (John 4:10)—are less a sign of nostalgia for ancestral knowledge than thoughtfulness concerning a desire that, in essence, could destroy the gift. As Jean-Luc Marion has pointed out, "The words 'If you knew the gift of God' (John 4:10) can serve here as a paradigm [not a theological paradigm] for all the phenomenology of the gift. The recipient does not know and will not get to know what gift comes to him, precisely because a gift can and must surpass all consciousness [that it is a gift]."[1] The embrace and differentiation of desire in the eros (Chapter 6) wait now to pass into the crucible of the eucharistic agape (Chapter 9). The modality of the eucharistic body (the eros) finds its inheritance here (animality), and its content (the body), giving us the sense of incorporation where nothing that is either human or of God will be forgotten. On the day of the first celebration of the Last Supper by the Resurrected One, in the inn at Emmaus, the enraptured disciples were not satisfied simply by attending the first Mass that divinity had invented. When "he took bread, blessed and broke it," they recognized him (Luke 24:30). But at once "they got up and returned to Jerusalem" (Luke 24:33), to "'go to my brothers'" (John 20:17). Following the Resurrected One is not just a pastoral recommendation addressed to Mary Magdalene; it is the logical imperative of the eucharistic mystery. Eating his body in the mode of assimilation, and being eaten by him in the form of incorporation, we constitute *ad intra* and phenomenologically his embodiedness, which allows him *ad extra* to appear and be manifest. The eucharistic body is given from the start, and today, as mystical body, even if in later history (as well as in some earlier history) this is forgotten or obscured. "From the start of Christianity, the Eucharist was considered in its relation to the Church," Henri de Lubac rightly reminds us.

> This reciprocal bond, seen for a long time as essential, takes account of the meaning of the *corpus mysticum* applied to the Church. . . . However later theologians, who could base their ideas on one or two passages from Thomas Aquinas, thought that *mysticum* was opposed here rather to *naturale*. According to them "mystic body" was in contrast to "physical body." . . . The result of this was a temptation, in the case of the Church as well as the Holy Writ: the temptation to see hardly anything in this metaphor but the metaphor itself, and to consider "mystic" as a reduction or attenuation of "real" and of "true."[2]

I should like to make it clear once and for all that the mystic body of the Church should not be opposed to the true body of the eucharistic sacrament; it is its manifestation as well as its perfect expression. The unreserved bodily plunge offered on the day of the Last Supper ("Take; this is my body" [Mark 14:22]), and later shared by the disciples at Emmaus after the Son has disappeared into invisibility ("Then their eyes were opened, and they recognized him; and he vanished from their sight" [Luke 24:31]), is present all the more in that it is a letting go (an 'aban-donation') and very far from the kind of consciousness that it is a gift, which might destroy its donation ("If you knew the gift of God" [John 4:10]). He plunges in bodily [literally, in French, "the body lost"] (Chapter 9), just as one forgets oneself and lives as an other when there is a task ahead or the body is to be constructed. We find this exemplified in the narrative of the washing of the disciples' feet, which is placed there to establish the community through the eucharist, or in Charles Péguy's words, to "assume the flesh." It comes in the episode of the Last Supper, duly placed so as to suggest its meaning in another way: "Now before the festival of the Passover, Jesus knew that his hour had come to depart from this world and go to the Father. . . . [Jesus] got up from the table, took off his outer robe, and tied a towel around himself. Then he poured water into a basin and began to wash the disciples' feet and to wipe them with the towel that was tied around him" (John 13:1, 4–5).

§33. The Assumption of the Flesh ["*encharnement*"][3]

There is an analogy to be made between the way in which the flesh of humankind has been assumed by Christ in the washing of the feet and the way he is incorporated in the bread on the day of the Last Supper (at the same meal and on the same day): "He had always loved those who were his in the world, but now he showed how perfect his love was" (John 13:2 [JB]) "'This is my body, which is given for you. Do this in remembrance of me'" (Luke 22:19). The gift of the body is the same: it is given, or given up, to something, even if it is oriented differently—toward a form of incorporation in matter according to the narrative of the Last Supper, and toward a way of establishing the community according to the episode of the washing of the feet. An ethos of the eucharist is born in this way in St. John's gospel, where the gift of the body is not, or is no longer, limited to the transubstantiated bread but spreads out to a *habitus* through which all believers become themselves the shared bread: "Now you are the body of Christ and individually members of it" (1 Cor. 12:27). This is recalled famously by St. Augustine: "It is your own mystery that is paced on the Lord's table! It is your own mystery that you are receiving! . . . Be what you see; receive what you are."[4]

With the towel he used to wash his disciples' feet wrapped around his waist, Jesus stands, as it were, body-to-body with them, just as in transubstantiation he stands body-to-the-bread. The scene (of the washing of the feet) replicates the scene (*la Cène*) of the Last Supper, or rather, they are nothing but obverse and reverse of the same scene/*Cène*. In Péguy's terms this is "history that has arrived on the earth and history that has arrived in the flesh."[5] What happens here to the bread of the eucharist happens in the same way to the bodies of the disciples and then to the Church, even if in another mode (symbolic gesture rather than consecration) and with another aim (establishment of the community rather than transformation of *this* given to eat). We are ourselves the wheat of the transubstantiated bread, and that is the great lesson in the assumption of the flesh in the washing of the feet. A form of *toucher-touched* invigorates the episode of the foot-washing and incorporates that which the (earlier episode of the) woman with the issue of blood only symbolically signified: "If I but touch his clothes, I will be made well" (Mark 5:28).[6]

We can see clearly that, having delivered man and woman from the master-slave dialectic (§23), God is now freed from all domination as also from servitude, and himself sets up a model of service: "You call me Teacher and Lord—and you are right, for that is what I am. So if I, your Lord and Teacher, have washed your feet, you also ought to wash one another's feet. ... Very truly, I tell you, *servants* are not greater than their master, nor are messengers greater than the one who sent them. If you know these things, you arc blessed if you do them" (John 13:13–17). To talk of *assumption of the flesh by the feet* is to put it in a way that might seem provocative but is nonetheless phenomenologically appropriate. What this assumption of the flesh opens up, in the place of the eucharistic Last Supper, is the gift of the body that goes so far as its "loss," because nothing of the self is really given unless it is surrendered in gestural terms. It is as a "viaticum"—provisions for the journey—that this body is offered to us every day in order for us to continue. And yet it is also by a gesture that, in a contradictory fashion, Judas came to deliver Christ up. Gesture against gesture: body against body. St. John's gospel places the body-to-body of the washing of the feet (John 13:1–20) directly against the body-against-body of the betrayal by Judas (John 13:21–30). The eucharistic viaticum achieves for us what would otherwise never be dared. Inscribing the gift at the heart of what should be, or placing obedience at the strongest moment of vengeance, ensures that the relationship between bodies is capable of taking on anything, and the blood of the Lamb becomes definitively able to redeem us: "Here is the Lamb of God who takes away the sin of the world" (John 1:29).

§34. The Viaticum

In light of both our salvation and our errors, we see that animality can reach as far as bestiality (§13), and thus there is a eucharistic heritage (the Lamb of God) as well as eucharistic forgiveness (that "takes away the sin of the world"). With Judas's betrayal, the bread of our humanity and the wine of our vitality are not enough, at least on their own, to be transubstantiated; equal are the bread that "our enemies have also eaten" and the blood poured out "for many for the forgiveness of sins" (Eucharistic Prayers). There is "sin at the door like a crouching beast hungering for you" (Gen. 4:7 [JB]) or the "scarlet beast that was full of blasphemous names, and it had seven heads and ten horns" (Rev.17:3) (see §13). These also wait for salvation. Not content with baptism—which certainly, once and for all, has struck it down—the monster of sin needs (still, and every day) the power of *this is my body* that alone is definitively capable of pushing it away from our quotidian.

At this Last Supper, in fact, he who is offered unreservedly (plunging in bodily; "this is my body *given* for you") becomes simultaneously given up and taken bodily: "'Very truly, I tell you, one of you will betray me' [Fr. *livrer*: give me up]" (John 13:21). Bread for bread: mouthful for mouthful. Thus, against the *this is my body* of Christ's eucharistic offering on the day of the Last Supper (Mark 14:22) is opposed the "this is *his* body" of the eucharistic betrayal by Judas after the washing of the feet. "'One of you will betray me. . . . It is the one to whom I give this piece of bread [Fr. *bouchée*: mouthful] when I have dipped it in the dish'" (John 13:21, 26). As we have seen in Marcel Jousse's analysis, "The history—Palestinian— of man is the history of his mouth" (§5).[7] A *mouth-to-mouth*, or better, a *mouthful* against *mouthful*, can also be read into the form of the eucharist, and it makes the meal that is given to us meaningful. As it is a kiss that sanctifies the affection of Mary Magdalene (Luke 7:45) as well as the betrayal of Judas (Luke 22:47), so on the day of the Last Supper the apostate is condemned by that with which Christ has chosen to save others: the sharing of a mouthful of bread. Those who go wrongly to the banquet of the Wedding Feast of the Lamb without "first be[ing] reconciled to your brother or sister" (Matt. 5:24) and those "who eat and drink without discerning the body, eat and drink judgment [Fr. *condamnation*] against themselves" (1 Cor. 11:29). The eucharistic viaticum will thus give us two meanings, as different as they are naturally complementary: (1) that which frees us and saves us at the hour of our passing (death), and (2) that which nourishes us in the state in which we remain (life here on Earth).

(1) Ordinarily, and according to a tradition that goes back to the Middle Ages, "viaticum" describes the mode by which the eucharist was given in the form of the "last sacrament of the Christian," and "in addition to the Anointing of the Sick," at the time of passing from death to life, or from this world to the Father.[8] That is to say, the eucharistic sacrament was important because, without being the first sacrament (baptism at least preceding it or going together with it), it remained the last (along with extreme unction). The viaticum would then first work as the liberation from sin, to the point that one would wait (or did wait in the past) for the last breath to make one's communion and to be immediately saved. Life, as understood in Christian fashion, reaches its climax in this communion. The last mouthful is joined to the last breath. The body-to-body of the Living One to the dead comes into play, also *for us*, in this last meal. At the moment of the corruption of our organic body, at the day of our death, the Son gives himself, in the flesh, in the eucharist, in order to promise us incorruptibility and lead us to remake ourselves, or at the very least, to *rise up*: "Those who eat my flesh and drink my blood have eternal life, and I will raise them up on the last day" (John 6:54). Death in communion (the theology of the viaticum) joins here with communion in death (theology

of empathy). The passage presupposes suffering, though the illusion of a simple leap into divinity might make us (erroneously) forget the spasms of our humanity. We need to cry out, like Teilhard de Chardin, "*It is not enough that I should die while communicating. Teach me* to treat my death as an act of communion."[9]

(2) All the same, the excesses of spirituality of the *Transitus*,[10] or of *humans as pilgrims*, have been abundant from the Middle Ages up to our own day, and there is no shortage of false justifications for leaving this Earth on which we are set. There has been an excess of angelism, justification of suffering by recompense in a future life, denigration of earthly life in the name of heavenly life, and so on. The eucharistic viaticum holds us to Earth, this time in its second sense: no longer as a passage from death to life at the last breath, but as daily bread for those who are committed to their sojourn and who do not seek readily to escape. Although on Earth we may be "visitors [*paroikous*] and pilgrims [*parepidêmous*]" (1 Pet. 2:11 [JB]), according to the First Epistle of Peter, our earthly pilgrimage does not indicate, in biblical terms, that it is necessary to leave anything, and still less that we have already arrived at that point. The "creation [that] waits with eager longing for the revealing of the Children of God" (Rom. 8:19) remains always as it were *in labour* in the Son, at the impetus of the Father who also works and remains at his task. "'My father is still working, and I also am working'" (John 5:17). The rest on the seventh day (Gen. 2:2), or the Sunday celebration of the eucharist, extends thus to all the days (the six days of creation of the *Hexameron*) and makes sense of the whole of our daily lives as of our humanity. As Benedict XVI points out in his *Sacramentum Caritatis*, St. Ignatius of Antioch—with his phrase "living in accordance with the Lord's Day"—emphasized that this "is defined by something more than the simple suspension of one's ordinary activities, a sort of parenthesis in one's usual daily rhythm. . . . Sunday is thus the day when Christians rediscover the eucharistic form which their lives are meant to have."[11]

Rather than sending us "on the way," the eucharistic viaticum holds us and keeps us "on the right road." The route certainly winds uphill and is also our destiny, but it reminds us above all of our state "of being(s) here below." The itinerary (*Itinerarium*) of humankind toward God is justified only if we dwell also *on* and *in* the state of earthly pilgrimage (*status viae*) that constitutes our pure and simple humanity (Aquinas). Rather than transgressing our limits, the eucharistic viaticum—in the sense this time of our daily bread—teaches us to love them, indeed, to long for them (§22). Even though life *in patria* (the life to come) teaches us to relativize our world here-below, God accepts, teaches us, and desires that we are to

)onsibility for our being-here *in via* (in this life), if only in order have something to offer, and in a sense to transform, from all our y. Edith Stein, commenting on Aquinas, and faithful here at least rizontality of the lifeworld in phenomenology, says, "At our goal, at we know *in via* [on our earthly journey] and what we take on faith *in via*, we know in another way. The possible extent of our knowledge during our pilgrimage on earth is fixed; we cannot shift its boundaries."[12] "Finitude" in phenomenology (Husserl) joins here with "limits" in theology (Aquinas), and the rapture of the wedding feast comes back to pay its tribute, indeed, to let God transform these limits, so that the act of the eucharist will not be consecrated as a simple passage or transition into another place of existence.[13]

§35. The Rapture of the Wedding Feast

There is, and there should be, a dionysiac element in the eucharistic banquet. Such a formula may seem surprising, especially because it can lead to a kind of "New Gnosticism"—something that actually has been widely propagated and developed (from Novalis to Manfred Franck). We can, however, agree that the choice offered by Nietzsche in his note of 1888— "The two types: *Dionysos* and the *Crucified One*."—indicates the most radical of exclusions, something to be respected and then transgressed. There appears to be no possible common ground between the drink drawn from the Earth (Dionysos) and the blood shed from heaven (the Crucified One). There is a "tragic" sense of suffering on one side (Dionysos isolated as the promise of life, eternal recurrence, and lust for destruction) and the "Christian sense of the suffering of the other" ("'The God on the cross' is a curse on life, a hint to deliver oneself from it").[14] Many interpreters have pointed out—Rudolf Bultmann, in particular—a certain concomitance between the Christian miracle of the wine at Cana (John 2:1–11), and the wine ritual of Dionysian legend. We find on the one hand the "fantastic exuberance of life" conferred on the Greek god of the Earth ("of her own accord the earth proffers her gifts . . . [and] the earth yields milk and honey"[15]), and on the other, the enthusiasm fostered by the miracle at Cana (the miraculous transformation of water into wine in jars filled to the brim [John 2:1–12]), or in the parable of the Good Shepherd ("I came that they may have life [*zôên echôsin*], and have it abundantly [*perisson echôsin*]" [John 10:10]). We need then to return to the posthumous fragment of Nietzsche, too often neglected today: "The *Gospel according to St. John* born out of Greek atmosphere, out of the soil of the Dionysian."[16]

The question, or rather the comparison, of Dionysos and the Crucified One certainly needs to be cross-examined carefully, especially according to those who have reservations about syncretism, or about all forms of vitalism. One cannot in fact give too much credit to speculations on the comparison, because current studies in exegesis seem, quite correctly, not to follow philosophers on this particular route.[17] But all the same—and precisely as a way of thinking about the eucharistic act in the light of the banquet and of *our own embodiedness*—we are led to ask, Is the blood spilt simply the *curse of life* leading to the passage to another life? Or is it the *blessing of our own life* that waits to be incorporated in He who is "the life" (John 14:6).

German Romanticism, despite its excesses and a theosophical Gnosticism that has quite appropriately been censured, has something to teach us here. The parallel between the Eleusinian Mysteries and the eucharistic blood poured into the chalice is not new. Hölderlin writes, "Bread is the fruit of the earth, yet it's blessed also by light. The pleasure of wine comes from the thundering god." And in his "Spiritual Songs" Novalis writes, "Of the Last Supper/ The divine meaning/ Is to the earthly sense a riddle;/ But whoever has breath'd/ From warm, beloved lips,/ Drew breath of life; . . ./ Will eat of his body/ And drink of his blood,/ Everlastingly."[18]

Certainly such declarations are enough to cause practitioners of rational theology to cringe, or at least to blush: they would quite rightly not let themselves by carried away in such a fashion. The problem is not solved, however, nor the question answered as long as it is not posed precisely: Is there in the eucharistic banquet something that we can see in the cases of Dionysos *and* the Crucified One, of the kind that, sending us back in liturgical terms to the Mass, is not just a matter of complaining about this life or wishing for another and better refuge? We can put it another way: By pushing aside the rapture or intoxication of the banquet (something, as we have seen, that St. Paul appropriately accomplished when denouncing the Philippians whose "god is their belly" [Phil. 3:19], or again Tertullian, who says in *On Fasting*, "Your belly is god, and your lungs a temple, and your paunch a sacrificial altar, and your cook the priest, and your fragrant smell the Holy Spirit"[19]), have we not forgotten, indeed, deliberately left out, all that there could also have been of *joy*, or of *pleasure* and *interior* rapture in the eucharistic sacrifice as such? "Blessed are those who are invited to the marriage supper of the Lamb," according to the beatitude of St. John in his Book of Revelation (Rev. 19:9), and this was shown with precision and force by the Van Eyck brothers in their altarpiece of the Mystic Lamb (see Preface).

In fact, suffering hangs on to that eucharistic joy, or rather, "the meaning to be given to suffering." No joy, as we know, is realized without passion, just as transubstantiation (§29) shows certainly the transformation of bread into body but also the passage (*trans*) by Christ himself from our corporal substance (*substantia*): "when he had given thanks, he broke it and gave it to them, saying, 'This is my body, which is given for you'" (Luke 22:19). It is not then the suffering that counts in the end, nor even the efforts we make to overcome it (Stoicism) or to deny it and rid ourselves of it (nihilism). What matters is the manner in which we experience the suffering, and the meaning we attribute to it—Christian meaning (the Crucified One) or tragic meaning (Dionysos): "The opposition between Dionysos and the Crucified isn't what is at stake between the atheist's way of life and the way of life of the Christian or believer, between what marks immanence and what marks transcendence, between what is this side and what is beyond: it points to two religious relationships with life."[20]

The dionysiac rite is concerned with the divine, as is the Christian rite; however, its nature is not the same, and neither is its meaning. There is also rapture in the eucharistic sacrifice, but belief in the Resurrection distances it from the idea of the eternal return, as does the attempt at a total auto-assumption, or an over-resurrection in this life itself: "Dionysos cut to pieces is a *promise* to life: it will eternally be reborn and come home out of destruction." Nietzsche assures us, as the prophet of the overcoming of nihilism, that "'the God on the cross' is a curse on life, a hint to deliver oneself from it."[21] The truth is that the act of the eucharist on its Sunday celebration does not consecrate humankind's ambition to return (eternal recurrence), or even to escape (a false interpretation of resurrection, or resurrection falsely included in the "false life," as Nietzsche expresses it).[22] 22 The burden of the flesh offered and the flux of blood spilled is not an exaltation in the eucharistic sacrifice of the ideal of their return. Instead, the sacrifice celebrates their impossible "starting again of the same," and "in the same way," even if they are tragic. That which was given—the body in the sacrifice of the Last Supper—was given *once only* and *once for always* in Christianity. There would be nothing to be started again, or even to await, if it were a question of other gods for more celebration. "In these sacrifices there is a reminder of sin year after year. For it is impossible for the blood of bulls and goats to take away sins," the writer of the Letter to the Hebrews says. He is speaking of Judaism, but this could equally apply, in the same period, to Dionysian sacrifices. He mentions "the offering of the body of Jesus Christ once for all," and says that "when Christ had offered for all time a single sacrifice for sins, 'he sat down at the right hand of God'" (Heb. 10:3–4, 10:10–12). We can place in opposition, then, the uniqueness of the eucharistic sacrifice, which definitely saves us from sin and death, and the plurality of the Dionysian sacrifices, fed on the fantasy of being able to reboot everything, as if the burden of life could still encumber itself with the ambition to start again or could be worn in a new way. As Paul Valadier reminds us, "The horizon of death (in Christianity) is what gives meaning to life, what gives it its fullness. And this is appropriate because one does not die an infinite number of times, but it was necessary to have said yes to life a multitude of times in order to say (perhaps) in the form of the Crucified One resurrected, *once*, yes to death."[23] In Christian existence, life is not "torn apart," as though nourished only through fragmentation, or by the constant possibility of coming back into a form of life about which it is nostalgic—even when it is tragic and a heavy burden. For the Christian, life is "crucified": that is, not denied, but at risk in another way.

§36. Abiding ["*manence*"]

To do everything to dwell, or to "abide," not just in the world such as it is, or ought to be, but insofar as we are incorporated through the eucharist in God (§30)—this is the primary concern of communion in the Church and the consecrated bread: "Those who eat my flesh and drink my blood abide [*meinein*] in me, and I in them" (John 6:56). The passage from "birth" (*Metamorphosis of Finitude*) to dwelling or abiding (§11) crosses a ford that is the finitude of the body, or goes from transformation in the resurrection to transubstantiation in the eucharist. What is at stake is not a parting (the tendency of Platonism), or a wishing to end (the perspective of nihilism), but living in a fashion of "continuing to exist," where subsisting or remaining is defined as "an effort to dwell in the presence."[24] Far from distorted accusations of substance as "permanence," or a form of "presentification" (i.e. giving the intentional object as real) (Heidegger to Derrida), there is in fact in the act of taking communion a *per-manence*, or a kind of *manence* (Latin *manere*: to remain, stay, endure, abide). By this *per-manence* I abide "in him" and he "in me" (John 15:4), as also he in "the Father," so that "they also [are] in us" (John 17:21).

The Bread of Life Discourse in the Gospel of St. John—"Those who eat my flesh and drink my blood abide in me, and I in them" (6:56)—reflects onto the parable of the true vine and its branches ("Abide in me as I abide in you" [John 15:4]), as well as onto the final prayer of Jesus, through which the couple man-woman in particular (but not only them) find themselves integrated and incorporated into the Trinity: "That they may all be one. As you, Father, are in me and I am in you, may they also be in us" (John 17:21). Apart from the union of bodies in his body that I have emphasized at length (§30), there is a logic of permanence, or of abiding in, the eucharistic act. Inhabiting that permanence is what makes our community, as does a certain acceptance of being exiled from it, since we are never truly as "at home" as when we are "in him" and "with him."[25]

One could then regret that we don't always stick to this and even that we don't remain with God as paraclete (or comforter); Christ himself, however, is always with us: "Truly I tell you, I will never again drink of the fruit of the vine *until that day* when I drink it new in the kingdom of God" (Mark 14:25). What is this saying? Is it that the body given for us (Mark 14:22) has not been truly given up, and the wine "poured out for many" (Mark 14:24) not universally circulated? The expectation of the "new wine" (despite the interdiction in Leviticus 10:9 of drinking wine) needs fulfillment, even though it may always be postponed because we have strayed from the right path, or because of our sins. We do not abide always in God, in that we leave that sphere of the Trinity where the Father has corporeally integrated us, through his Son in the act of the eucharist. The Holy Spirit needs to come and search for us, and in some way bring us back. Origen comments, magnificently, "It is sufficient that *one Christian* [*christianos*] is put on trial for *the Christ* [*o Christos*] to be put on trial." In short, the saints and the Son will then "cry when we cry" and "rejoice when we rejoice."[26]

What this means is that there are not two worlds in Christianity—the world of human beings and the world of God. There is just the unity of one world (that of God) in which we can stay and abide (through the grace of the eucharistic viaticum); or, we can pull out of it, and let ourselves be expelled (through the power and temptation of sin).[27] The *body that was given* to us in the eucharistic act was truly offered and given up; the blood poured was wholly poured forth, to give us life. It is we and only we who can refuse it, and we can decide not to go there, to the Mass as the eucharistic sacrifice. The body and blood are offered to us to abide in our daily lives, so as not to break the vine branch on which we are grafted and to "bear much fruit" (John 15:5). In the creative fidelity of sexual difference, as also in the unique sacrifice of the eucharistic gift, the abiding—or the imperative that tells us to stay—becomes the condition of our permanence[28] and is the principal requisite of all true fruitfulness.

A kind of *disquiet of the created* at the heart of the *mystery of iniquity* (which I hope to portray or recount in a projected future book) is something that spreads through the nerves to us, and indirectly to the whole of creation—along with the possibility of committing sin. As far as humankind is concerned, there is the possibility of falling away from the Trinity (never mind that we "may all be one. As you Father are in me and I am in you" [John 17:21]. And as far as God is concerned, there is the anguish of seeing humanity fleeing from that which was given in advance ("'[Adam,] where are you?'" [Gen. 3:9]).

We cannot be surprised if there is now an eschatological fatigue concerning the liturgy, and particularly concerning the celebration of the mystery of the eucharist: "The experience of tiredness is the daily bread of prayer."[29] The celebration of the Last Supper is in fact and in essence fatiguing, not simply or mistakenly from the tedium of its repetition, but from the burden of the bodies that it has to carry (the body of Christ and also our bodies); the heaviness of our sins that must always go with it; and our impatience at the time that has not yet come. The weight of our created embodiedness and the difficulty of remaining incorporate participate together in the Parousia, or Second Coming—the expectation of which constitutes its own liturgical temporality as well as eucharistic anamnesis (memorial sacrifice): "We proclaim your Death, O Lord, and profess your Resurrection until you come again" (Mystery of Faith: Eucharistic Prayers). In his encounter with the woman of Samaria, Jesus is "tired out by his journey, . . . sitting by the well" (John 4:6). The Word is also in some respects tired out or fatigued beside us, waiting for us to accept that we abide in him completely and are totally integrated and incorporated. Since he assumed "a body that tires," his body was *made body* along with our bodies that tire when we take communion, and this was done precisely in order to restore us.[30] It is not a question here of care, or of the burden of the years; all that counts is the modality of waiting, or the being *in* unquiet, by which the "intermediate coming" of the liturgy, or the *medius adventus*, is given to us today, in order for us to be able to live through it as eucharist. "'A little while, and you will no longer see me, and again a little while, and you will see me'" (John 16:16). But, as Bernard de Clairvaux laments in his sermon on the Song of Songs, "I do not want to throw accusations at the words of my Lord, but the time seems long to me [*longum est*], extremely long [*et multum valde nimis*]."[31]

Conclusion

The Flesh in Common

Ite, missa est. Go forth, the Mass is ended.[1] Or, rather, our bodies have been thrown and taken into the "enlarged body" of the Son and the Church, where the "supplement of soul" will not now fail us.[2] I have written the three books in this triptych; thus, there are three conclusions containing "the flesh," one in each part. First, I discussed "the silent flesh," or the figure of the *in-fans* (speechless one) in the form of a paroxysm of suffering and death waiting to be transformed (*Passeur de Gethsémani* [The guide to Gethsemane]). I looked then at "the waiting flesh," which signified the final resurrection as a community of all the resurrected (*Metamorphosis of Finitude*). Finally, we arrive now at "the flesh in common," as embodiedness shared and, at last, achieved in part. With the eucharistic viaticum there is a community of embodiedness for us today, *in via*, and not just the satisfaction of our individualities in the hereafter, *in patria*. Eucharistic communion—in a rapture that is Christian, not Dionysian—should in fact, everywhere and always, give rise to enthusiasm (*en-thou-siasme*). That is, it is the act by which human beings find themselves projected in God (*en-theos*), not just taking in the divine and assimilating it or, as it were, digesting it. The true joy is not simply to possess God in himself (assimilation), but to give oneself up to him (incorporation), without ever losing that difference that always and forever forms the site of self-identity as well as the site of pleasure (desire and differentiation). Since the eucharist is the "sacrament of sacraments [*Sacramentum sacramentorum*]," we should recall, along with Henri de Lubac, that its mystery reaches its completion

231

in a "sacrament of unity." There is unity of humankind and God, certainly, but also of man and woman as far as they are empowered and incorporated in the coincidence of their bodies. St. John Chrysostom exclaims, "Let us learn the wonders of this sacrament. . . . We become one body, says the Scripture, members of his flesh, bones of his bones [1 Cor. 12:12]. That is what the food that he gives us effects: he joins himself to us that we may become one whole, like a body joined to its head."[3]

What has been said here in theological terms also translates to philosophy. As we have seen, the gift of the body depends upon a human existence that only the eucharist has the power to take responsibility for and transform. We have, first, the organic body—irreducible simply to the lived experience of the flesh—that the *this is my body* comes also to signify (the eucharistic content). Next, there is our part of animality, made up of drives and passions, in an interior Chaos that, moreover, we cannot forget (the eucharistic inheritance). Finally, there is the eros, or the body given and given up, converted here by the agape (the eucharistic mode). Embodiedness, animality, and love: Let us call them the three characteristics of the Wedding Feast of the Lamb. So that they are never diminished (see the Council in Trullo [§5] and the necessary distinctions between animality and bestiality preserved [§13]), they will take upon themselves all that makes up *our* nature, to convert it into the supernatural. Far from simply being a question of adaptation to our experience of humanity, to embodiedness (*this is my body*), to animality (the Lamb), and to love (eros), the mystery of the eucharistic incorporation comes in fact to overturn even that for which it has already taken responsibility.

We don't simply make claims for the organic body itself (Chapter 5), but we do for its incorporation, when it is taken as such in the act of transubstantiation (Chapter 7). It is not the animal in us, duly distinguished from the Beast, or sin (§13), that demands God not deny it (Chapter 4); it is the figure of the sacrificed lamb, which anticipates not simply humanization but also filiation in the act of the eucharist (Chapter 7). What serves in the last instance as a model for the "gift of the body of Christ to the Church" (*agape*) (Chapter 6) is not the "gift of the body of the spouses" (*eros*). On the contrary, it is "the gift of Christ to the Church" (*agape*) that holds and maintains in him "the gift of the body of the spouses between themselves" (*eros*) (Chapter 9).

What I have called the *staging* of the Last Supper—playing on the French words *scène* and *Cène* [Last Supper]—has not forced us to leave the human scene. Far from it: Through Holy Thursday, God helps us philosophically reintegrate our own embodiedness in the filial transubstantiation of the eucharistic bread. We have believed that the body could belong to us (I *have* a body), or that we could use the body to define ourselves (I *am* my body). He teaches us, at least through his example, that to truly give oneself is also to accept objectivizing oneself, and becoming in some way reified (*This* is *my* body; §29). There is nothing in the radicality of all this that escapes him, up to and including our organic embodiedness that is waiting to be transformed in the eucharist.

The limits I have acknowledged from the start of this book, both in philosophy and indeed also in phenomenology, might seem surprising. But our inquiry must try to reach out to that great interior Tohu-Bohu, or that "region of what can no longer be said," that only a divine otherness can take on and in a sense transform (Chapter 1). All the same, the discourse on such frontiers is nothing, or almost nothing, in comparison with the "silent experience of the flesh" that is told, or rather, that is lived, when the eros is transformed into agape (Chapter 3) in the act of the manducation of Christ eucharisticized (§26) and in contemplation of his body in the Adoration (§32). My ending (agape, filiation, adoration) takes us back at once to the start—or to that with which it will now be appropriate to start everything. I chose to start off this book with humankind (Part I: Descent into the Abyss; Part II: The Sojourn of Humankind), and I realize now as I close how God himself has taken all this on, up to and including our humanity (Part III: God Incorporated). There are no "loaded dice" here. There is simply a logic of the incarnation that is also a logic of incorporation, from the Word made flesh to the flesh transubstantiated. Irenaeus speaks of "The Word of God who dwelt in man, and became the Son of man, that He might accustom man to receive God, and God to dwell in man, according to the good pleasure of the Father."[4] We are left with a question that we can no longer avoid and that lies beneath the whole of the analysis attempted here. If there is a "disquiet of the created" and a straying of humankind (to the extent that they have found themselves expelled, or "sent forth" [Gen. 3:23]), how can "salvation" now allow us to dwell at the heart of Christ eucharisticized? Or, we can put it another way: Must I not wait for the Son himself before I can reach the difficult "abiding," or *manence* (blocked by sin)? Must I not wait before I can accede to my own embodiedness? Humankind's transgression is not simply a matter of failing to follow a rule; rather, it is the chasm in which we probably would be plunged (would plunge) by dint of not knowing *where* or *how* to reach ourselves or the Trinity. Incorporation, then, goes along with its dis-incorporation; the construction of Christianity with its de-construction; and the raising up with the Fall. The point is abstruse— not in the eucharistic mystery and its redemption, as we have seen at length (§13), but rather in the possibility for human beings to shut themselves up within a barrier that is certainly philosophical (death) but not, theologically, the destiny of God (Resurrection).[5]

Therefore, the Wedding Feast of the Lamb, or the liturgical practice of the eucharist, can provide for us—or, perhaps better, can be said to reassure us—because we can be nourished by it and incorporated into Christ, who is waiting there to sojourn with us. He who, in a redoubling of the desired and the desirable, has "eagerly desired to eat this Passover with you before I suffer" (Luke 22:15; see §23), invites us now to a Last Supper of desire. The future of Christianity (if it makes sense to think that God himself would not in every way give it the means to endure) will not depend simply upon "religious fervor," or "a joyful way of being together," or "friendly proximity," or "passionless egalitarianism" (which could simply be a new form of tribalism). It will come in reality solely from that quality that is "interior to man and that will give the necessary vitality."[6] The *fidelity to the body* that God himself gives witness to, in the movement from Incarnation to the eucharist and from the eucharist to Resurrection, awaits in response a *fidelity to the flesh* in the believer himself—as much in his existentiality as in the erotic gift to the one from whom he is differentiated in a face-to-face, and in the eucharistic offering from the depths of his unspoken interior Chaos. We shall not find in such a trust of the humano-divine body-to-body either the heroism of the subject or a point-blank indictment of the practices of modernity, but rather the simple certitude of the possibility of endurance for all human beings of an eros of fleshly fidelity (Chapter 3). And this implies also that the believer may remain in a Christly incorporation that is still always proposed (Chapter 8). Gabriel Marcel says, in his commentary in *Creative Fidelity*, "There is no valid reason to think that *fidelity to oneself* should be more intelligible than *fidelity to another* and should clearly come first. It seems much rather that the opposite that is true. I am undoubtedly less immediately present to myself than is the person to whom I have given my word [or in whom I have faith]."[7]

Notes

Translator's Note

1. For an account of the first generation involved in this movement, see Part I of *Phenomenology and the "Theological Turn": The French Debate*, ed. Dominique Janicaud. With essays by Jean-François Courtine, Jean-Louis Chrétien, Michel Henry, Jean-Luc Marion, Paul Ricœur, trans. Bernard G. Prusak (New York: Fordham University Press, 2000).

2. A conference on Falque's work was held in July 2014 at the École Franciscaine de Paris, under the title "Une analytique du passage: Rencontres et confrontations avec Emmanuel Falque." A volume containing the conference papers along with Falque's responses is under preparation. Falque also recently published a volume of his discussions of contemporary phenomenology and theology: *Le Combat amoureux: Disputes phénoménologiques et théologiques* (Paris: Hermann, 2014).

3. "Pope John's Opening Speech to the Council," October 11, 1962, *Vatican II–Voice of the Church*, last modified October 31, 2015, http://www.vatican-2voice.org/91docs/opening_speech.htm.

4. Falque, *Le Combat amoureux*, 12.

5. *Le Passeur de Gethsémani* (Paris: Éditions du Cerf, 1999). English translation forthcoming.

6. *The Metamorphosis of Finitude: An Essay on Birth and Resurrection* (New York: Fordham University Press, 2012).

7. *The Wedding Feast of the Lamb*, chap. 6, §23.

8. Paul Ricœur, "Experience and Language in Religious Discourse," in Janicaud et al., *Phenomenology and the "Theological Turn,"* 130.

9. See Charles Taylor's note on the term "expressivism," in *Hegel* (Cambridge: Cambridge University Press, 1975), 13.

10. Karl Jaspers, *Way to Wisdom: An Introduction to Philosophy*, trans. Ralph Manheim (New Haven: Yale University Press, 1964), 76.

11. See Falque's own analysis of his methods, in *Passer le Rubicon: Philosophie et théologie: Essai sur les frontières* (Brussels: Éditions Lessius, 2013).

Opening

1. "Pope John XXIII's Address to Open the Council," October 11, 1962, "The Second Vatican Ecumenical Council," *Papal Encyclicals Online*, http://www.papalencyclicals.net/vatican2.htm.

2. [The title of this book in French is *Les noces de l'agneau*, which can also be translated as "The Nuptials of the Lamb," "The Wedding Supper of the Lamb," or even "The Marriage of the Lamb." The translation "Wedding Feast" has been chosen here, as it seems appropriate in order to refer to the description in the Book of Revelation as well as the image on the altarpiece at Ghent (see Preface). It should be noted, however, that the author's key reference in choosing the title was the passage in Revelation 19:7, which has been translated as "wedding feast" but also as the "marriage" or the "marriage supper" of the Lamb. In French the word *noces* refers both to the festivities at a marriage and to the alliance of the wedded couple. —Trans.]

3. Thomas Aquinas, *Commentary on the Gospel of St. John* 14.2, trans. Fabian R. Larcher (1870; Albany, NY: Magi Books, 1998), http://dhspriory.org/thomas/John14.htm.

Preface: The Ghent Altarpiece, or, The Adoration of the Mystic Lamb

1. See Peter Schmidt, *Le Retable de l'Agneau mystique* (Paris: Éditions du Cerf, 1995). The Ghent altarpiece can be seen in detail on the website *Closer to Van Eyck: Rediscovering the Ghent Altarpiece*, accessed November 3, 2015, http://closertovaneyck.kikirpa.be/#home/sub=altarpiece.

2. Forthcoming in English translation.

3. [Translations of biblical passages are from the New Revised Standard Version of the Bible (NRSV), except where the Jerusalem Bible (JB) or the Authorized (King James) Version (AV) comes closer to the French translation used by the author. In those cases, the source is indicated. —Trans.]

4. [The pronunciation in French suggests a play on words, between the "scène" and the "Cène," or Last Supper. —Trans.]

5. This part of the altarpiece was damaged in a fire in 1822 and has since been partially restored.

6. "Pope Gregory XI: The Condemnation of Wycliffe 1382," *Medieval Sourcebook*, Fordham University, accessed 1998, http://www.fordham.edu/halsall/source/1382wycliffe.asp.

7. See, for example, Jaume Huguet, *The Last Supper*, c.1470, painting on wood, Museu Nacional d'Art de Catalunya, Barcelona.

8. The Council in Trullo, or the Quinisext Council, was held in Constantinople in 692 AD, in the same domed hall as the Sixth General Council (the name refers to an Italian building style of huts with conical roofs, or *trulli*). Canon 82 in *Acta Conciliorum*, the Canons of the Council in Trullo, reads, "We decree that the figure in human form of the Lamb who takes away the sin of the world, Christ our God, be henceforth exhibited in images, instead of the ancient lamb [*Christi Dei nostri humana forma characterem etiam in imagines deinceps pro veteri agno erigi ac depingi jubemus*]." "Council in Trullo," in *Nicene and Post-Nicene Fathers*, Second Series, vol. 14, trans. Henry Percival, rev. and ed. Kevin Knight (1900: New Advent, 2009): http://www.newadvent.org/fathers/3814.htm. This is a rejection of figuration in animal form that is not motivated by the avoidance of animality. On the contrary, it is a question of indicting a symbolism in which the anticipatory figure (the lamb) had been given preference over the achieved model (Christ incarnate). "It is likely then that this text provides a way for Christian art to *distinguish itself from Jewish art* and from the reproach of idolatry that Jews in that period were directing against the Church. The practice of using indirect symbols (for example, the lamb) was no more than a vestige from the past. According to these theologians 'it is a question of a deviant practice that detracts from *the reality of the Incarnation and the visibility of Christ in human flesh*.' Several later popes would revive this canon officially (in particular during the Second Council of Nicea in 787 during the arguments over iconoclasm); but Christian art took little notice of the canon, as is witnessed by the rich Carolingian iconography of the adoration of the Lamb." François Bœspflug, *Dieu et ses images, Une histoire de l'Éternel dans l'art* (Paris: Bayard, 2008), 113–15.

9. Blaise Pascal, *Pensées*, trans. A. J. Krailsheimer (Harmondsworth: Penguin, 1966), 678 (358).

10. Fabrice Hadjadj, *L'Agneau mystique: Le retable des frères Van Eyck* (Paris: Éditions de l'Œuvre, 2008), 50.

11. John Chrysostom, "The Decollation of S. John Baptist," in *The Golden Legend*, vol. 5, comp. Jacobus de Voragine, Archbishop of Genoa (1275), *Medieval Sourcebook*, Fordham University, accessed December 10, 2015, http://legacy.fordham.edu/halsall/basis/goldenlegend/.

12. Aristotle, *On the Generation of Animals* 1.2, trans. Arthur Platt (1912; Adelaide, Australia: University of Adelaide/eBooks//ebooks.adelaide.edu.au/a/aristotle/generation/complete.html.

13. Hadjadj, *L'Agneau mystique*, 50.

14. "Apologia of St. John Damascene against Those Who Decry Holy Images" (1898), 1.16, *Medieval Sourcebook*, Fordham University, accessed December 10, 2015, https://legacy.fordham.edu/halsall/basis/johndamascus-images.asp.

Introduction. The Swerve of the Flesh

1. See Falque, "Y a-t-il une chair sans corps? (Michel Henry)," in *Le Combat amoureux: Disputes phénoménologiques et théologiques* (Paris: Hermann, 2014), 197–238. First printed with Michel Henry's response, in *Phénoménologie*

et christianisme chez Michel Henry, ed. Philippe Capelle (Paris: Éditions du Cerf, 2004), 95–133, 168–82.

2. Friedrich Nietzsche, *Thus Spoke Zarathustra*, trans. Graham Parkes (Oxford: Oxford University Press, 2005), Book I, Part 4, 30–31.

3. Martin Heidegger, *Nietzsche*, vols. 1 and 2, trans. David Farrell Krell (New York: HarperCollins, 1991), 99–100. Translating *leiben* as "embodied" rather than "incarnate" is justified here because *Leib* in Nietzsche (as we shall see later), far from signifying the lived flesh of phenomenology, brings us back to the organic body of biology. There is an inversion of Nietzsche in phenomenology. He uses *leiben* in the "organic" sense of the term, and in the context of phenomenology the concept is reserved for "the lived experience of the body" (see also §4).

4. See in particular the appropriate comments of Medard Kehl, quoted by Jean-Baptiste Lecuit (in connection with our joint research on this topic) in *L'Anthropologie théologique à la lumière de la psychanalyse* (Paris: Éditions du Cerf, 2007): "*Leib* is an essential and indispensable moment of the life accomplished in the resurrection. In contrast, the corporal 'purely in itself,' can be completely given over to the earth and its laws of biological corruption and reversal. Undoubtedly a certain *spiritualization* characterises such an interpretation of the resurrected body, being a question of a purely corporal [*körperlichen*] moment of our bodies [*Leibes*]." What sparks this just comment on *The Metamorphosis of Finitude* can be found in Emmanuel Tourpe, "Dieu et l'être: Échange autour d'un livre recent," *Revue philosophique de Louvain* (May 2006): 387–91. "In trying as hard as he can to bring us to understand the baptismal 'birth' as spiritual generation, the author, E. Falque gives the impression of proceeding to a transcendental reduction of the body, which brings us back to a *subjective manner* of behaviour. The constant opposition between the lived flesh [*Leib*] and the living body [*Körper*], which allows the author to assume that the Resurrection is a 'metamorphosis,' cannot escape the strong charge of 'modalism' [seeing manifestations of the Trinity as facets of God's nature, as opposed to distinct parts of God's nature. —Trans]. The 'modalism' that attempts to rebuild an anthropology around the topics of *manner, translation*, and metamorphosis, is not simply a lifeless replacement or rejection of substance, but one cannot escape from the impression that it is a sophisticated form of such an objection—'in the footsteps of a belated Kant [*sic*].'" See also the reply by Falque, in *Revue philosophique de Louvain* (May 2006): 392–403.

5. See Falque, *Le Passeur de Gethsémani* (Paris: Éditions du Cerf, 1999), and *The Metamorphosis of Finitude: An Essay on Birth and Resurrection*, trans. George Hughes (New York: Fordham University Press, 2012).

Part I. Descent into the Abyss

1. In *Nicene and Post-Nicene Fathers*, First Series, vol. 1, trans. J. G. Pilkington, rev. and ed. Kevin Knight (1887: New Advent, 2009), http://www.newadvent.org/fathers/110104.htm.

2. Michel Tournier, *Friday, or, The Other Island*, trans. Norman Denny (1967; London: King Penguin, 1984).

3. ["Tohu-Bohu" is a Hebrew term found in Genesis 1:2, usually translated as "formless and void" (or empty), or "without form and void." In modern English, or French, it can also be used informally to mean a state of chaos or utter confusion. —Trans.]

4. Xavier Léon-Dufour, "Shéol," in *Dictionnaire du Nouveau Testament* (Paris: Éditions du Seuil, 1975), 62.

5. See Jackson Pollock, *The Deep*, 1953, oil on canvas, Centre Georges-Pompidou, Paris. An image of the painting and further commentary can be found at "The deep," *ArtySplash* (blog), January 21, 2010, http://www.artysplash.com/the-deep.

6. In this respect, one might view this Part I, "Descent into the Abyss," as a sequel to the "Précis of Finitude" (Part I, *Metamorphosis of Finitude*).

7. *Dictionnaire encyclopédique Quillet*, vol. 1 (Paris: Librairie Aristide Quillet, 1934), s.v. "abysse."

8. Ibid., s.v. "abîme."

9. See Edgar Allan Poe, "A Descent into the Maelstrom" (1841), in *Edgar Allan Poe: Poetry and Tales*, ed. Patrick F. Quinn (New York: Library of America, 1984). "When it is in flood, the stream runs up the country between Lofoden and Moskoe with a boisterous rapidity . . . if a ship comes within its attraction, it is inevitably absorbed and carried down to the bottom, and there beat to pieces against the rock; and when the water relaxes, the fragments thereof are thrown up again" (p. 435).

10. Jean-Pierre Vernant, "L'origine de l'univers: Au tréfonds de la Terre: la Béance," in *L'Univers, les Dieux et les Hommes: Récits grecs des origins* (Paris: Éditions du Seuil, 1999), 15–16. This is a book that I welcomed warmly and that spoke to me in a very personal way. I should also like here to underline how much I owe to, and how strongly I sympathize with, the research, undertaken from the point of view of a "psychology of depths," by Sabine Fos-Falque, psychoanalyst and author of *La chair des émotions* (Paris: Éditions du Cerf, 2014). I offer my profound thanks, in words that are certainly inadequate, to her (see this book's dedication).

11. Provisional title: *Le Mystère de l'iniquité: Essai philosophique sur le mal et le péché*.

12. "Second reading at Office of Readings on Holy Saturday," in *Patrologia Graeca*, vol. 43, ed. J. P. Migne (Paris, 1857–1886), sec. 439–45, 462–63.

13. Édouard Ade, *Le Temps de l'Église: Esquisse d'une théologie de l'histoire selon Hans-Urs von Balthasar* (Rome: Pontifica Universitatis Gregoriana, 2002), 193; my emphases.

14. For the position I have taken on the relationship between theology and philosophy, see Falque, *Passer le Rubicon* (Paris: Éditions Lessius, 2013).

15. Albert Camus, *The Myth of Sisyphus: And Other Essays*, trans. Justin O'Brien (1955; New York: Vintage International, 1991), 52: "Is one, on the

contrary, going to take up the heart-rending and marvelous wager of the absurd? Let's make a final effort in this regard and draw all our conclusions. The body, affection, creation, action, human nobility will then resume their places in this mad world. At last man will again find there the wine of the absurd and the bread of indifference on which he feeds his greatness." For comments on this passage, see the excellent essay by Arnaud Corbic in *Camus et l'homme sans Dieu* (Paris: Éditions du Cerf, 2007), 71.

1. Philosophy to Its Limit

1. Two major contributions by two French phenomenologists are immediately relevant here, because they have been concerned with and worked with the limits of phenomenology. First, Didier Franck, *Dramatique des phénomènes* (Paris: PUF, 2001), 105–23, on how to "trace back intentionality to our drives" without always thinking of drives in the context of intention (unlike Husserl); on recovering how "feeling and phenomenality spring in reality from force" (a return to Nietzsche); on how to make the "driven body" the condition for all that constitutes subjectivity and show that the project of a phenomenological constitution of subjectivity "retains nonetheless a sense," as long as we trace it back to sensation and to drives that it does not fulfil directly, and not in a framework derived from intentionality. Second, Claude Romano, *Il y a* (Paris: PUF, 2003), 177–224, on the "idealism of the sensible" and the "theoretism of the flesh" in phenomenology from Husserl to Merleau-Ponty.

2. Paul Ricœur, *Hermeneutics and the Human Sciences*, trans. John B. Thompson, (Cambridge: Cambridge University Press, 1981), 32.

3. "Who touched my clothes?" (Mark 5:30). See Falque, *Le Passeur de Gethsémani* (Paris: Éditions du Cerf, 1999), 147–52.

4. I would like to express my thanks here to friends in the medical profession, surgeons and anesthetists who have helped in this approach and suggested a new dimension to corporality. There are topics here that have been overlooked in philosophy, but that philosophers need to take up and formalize, including anesthesia on animals (e.g., pigs, gorillas), surgery with full anesthetic (e.g., hip replacement), surgery with local anesthetic (e.g., for abdominal hernia), plastic surgery (e.g., reconstruction), and intestinal examination (e.g., colonoscopy).

5. Friedrich Nietzsche, *La Volonté de puissance* (1935; Paris: Gallimard, 1942), §227, and *The Gay Science*, trans. Josefine Nauckhoff (1882; Cambridge: Cambridge University Press, 2001): "By far the greatest part of our mind's activity proceeds unconscious and unfelt" (p. 192).

6. Natalie Depraz, "*Leib*" in *Vocabulaire européen des philosophies*, ed. Barbara Cassin (Paris: Éditions du Seuil, 2004), 707–9. See Edmund Husserl, *Cartesian Meditations: An Introduction to Phenomenology* (1929), trans. Dorion Cairns (Dordrecht: Kluwer Academic Publications, 1950), Fifth Meditation: "Among the bodies belonging to this 'Nature' and included in my peculiar ownness, I then find my animate organism [*Leib*] as uniquely singled out—namely as

the only one of them that is not just a body [*Körper*] but precisely an animate organism [*Leib*]" (p. 97).

7. Depraz, "*Leib*," 706.

8. Ibid., 707. One notes, however, that in German—the language from which these terms derive—there used to be a term that signified an "intermediate flesh," duly biological, that was neither purely subjective nor exclusively objective. To examine this term is precisely to go back to the source of the organic here. In German, *Leib* certainly covers an intimate lived experience, but originates unconsciously from the stomach, or gynecologically from the breast, rather than signifying the enclosure in a purely self-formed and disembodied ego. One uses the term in German-speaking countries to describe both an empty stomach (*Nichts im Leibe haben*) and pregnancy (*gesegneten Leibe sein*); further, it is by the *Leib* that one is constipated or that one "trembles all over" (*harten Leib haben*), suffering feelings that one cannot control (*am ganzen Leibe zittern*). These linguistic refinements will no doubt seem too complicated to some, but they at least help us to see a "middle way" in current language (*Leib* or *Fleisch*, it doesn't matter which one here)—a middle way between the pure subjectivity of phenomenological *Leib* and the scientific objectivity of *Körper*. See Ibid., 706, for all of these expressions.

9. Gilles Deleuze, *Francis Bacon: The Logic of Sensation*, trans. Daniel W. Smith (1981; London: Continuum, 2005), 32; my emphasis. See also, in the context of phenomenology itself and from a less critical point of view, Claude Romano, "Le miroir de Narcisse: Sur la phénoménologie de l'intentionalité," in *Il y a*, 188–91: "the concept of flesh is not a break with idealism, nor with its Cartesian sources" (p. 189). A "docetism of the flesh" would be a possible reading of my previous book on the Resurrection as a recovery of the mode of being or our bodies (see Falque, *Metamorphosis of Finitude*, trans. George Hughes [New York: Fordham University Press, 2012]) if it were not balanced here by a kind of "biology of the body" in the context of a reflection starting from the eucharistic *this is my body*. I should like to thank in particular Professor A. Moulonguet, medical doctor, student, and friend, for having pointed out the possible drift of my earlier work, which I now wish to take into account, counterbalancing one mystery (resurrection) with another (eucharist), but without at all denying our options in one (flesh) as in the other (body): "there is a contemporary sabellianism [view that the Godhead was differentiated only into a succession of modes, and that the Father suffered as much as the Son] of the body, in the spiritualization of the flesh in the resurrection" (A. Moulonguet, letter to author, Nov. 8, 2004).

10. For Zeno, see "Tatian's Address to the Greeks," trans. J. E. Ryland, *Early Christian Writings*, 2015, chap. 3, http://www.earlychristianwritings.com/text/tatian-address.html. See the commentary on Zeno's view in Dominique Weber, *Hobbes et le corps de Dieu* (Paris: Vrin, 2009), 62; and Michel Spanneut, *Le Stoïcisme des Pères de l'Église, de Clément de Rome à Clément d'Alexandrie* (Paris:

Éditions du Seuil, 1957), 85–90. For the modification of this view by Tertullian, see Jérôme Alexandre, *Une chair pour la gloire: L'anthropologie réaliste et mystique de Tertullien* (Paris: Beauchesne, 2001), 241–56.

11. Martin Heidegger, *Nietzsche*, vols. 3 and 4, trans. David Farrell Krell (San Francisco: HarperCollins, 1991), 71.

12. Hesiod, *Theogony* 2.115, trans. Richard S. Caldwell (Newburyport, MA: Focus Classical Library, 1987).

13. Heidegger, *Nietzsche*, 3:91; Hesiod, *Theogony* 2.123.

14. A point particularly well made by Reynal Sorel, *Chaos et éternité* (Paris: Les Belles Lettres, 2006), 15: "From chaos, not given any epithet, Erebos the dark and Nix the black are born. The myth says nothing else. Above all it does not say that Chaos engenders Gaia, but that Gaia comes after." See also the critique in Pierre Pellegrin, "Physique," in *Le Savoir grec*, ed. Jacques Brunschvicg and Geoffrey Lloyd (Paris: Flammarion, 1996), 462. For a general commentary on Hesiod's *Theogony* and the concept of Chaos, see Clémence Ramnoux, *La Nuit et les Enfants de la Nuit* (Paris: Champs-Flammarion, 1986), 63–101. See also the relevant comments of Maurice Blanchot in "Terre: Chaos," in *L'Amitié* (Paris: Gallimard, 1971), 208: "If the Greek gods teach us that incest is not forbidden, they seem to have the mission to fix a separation elsewhere, between Earth and chaos. It is a separation that one cannot infringe without producing monsters. . . . To unite with chaos is to take foothold in the abyss, to go back, while turning away from the abyss."

15. I take the double etymology of Chaos (from *chaíno* and *cheïn*) from Sorel, *Chaos et éternité*, 16–17. A necessary resort to Chaos in its original sense (the open, the abyss) is very largely and justly conscripted by Henri Maldiney in "Chaos, harmonie, existence" (interview with Chris Yourés), in *Avènement de l'œuvre* (Paris: Éditions Théétète, 1997), 72–109. "Chaos is a yawning gap not simply bottomless but also directionless. There is in it neither top nor bottom, neither ahead nor behind, nor any possible system of co-ordinates. It is beyond dimension. But this word is rarely taken in its original sense" (p. 78).

16. *The Apology of Tertullian for the Christians*, trans. T. Herbert Bindley (London: Parker, 1890). The literal impossibility of reading the account in Genesis as an account of creation *ex nihilo* does not preclude such an interpretation; rather, the contrary. The Christian rereading is justified in that another beginning ("In the beginning was the Word" [John 1:1]) is, as it were, substituted for the first beginning ("In the beginning when God created the heavens and the earth" [Gen. 1:1]).

17. Medard Kehl, *Et Dieu vit que cela était bon: Une théologie de la création* (Paris: Éditions du Cerf, 2008), 150–6. This is one of the rare works of theology that tries to deal fully with the question of Chaos and Tohu-Bohu; see also the well-known work of Erich Zenger and Karl Löning, *Als Anfang schuf Gott: Biblische Schöpfungstheologien* (Düsseldorf: Patmos, 1997); and Franz Gruber, *Im Haus Lebens: Eine Theologie der Schöpfung* (Regensburg: Pustet Verlag, 2001). We await, however, a comparative study of Greek Chaos (Hesiod) and Semitic Tohu-

Bohu (Genesis), not to mention the Christian *ex nihilo/de nihilo* (Tertullian, St. Augustine). What is needed is a work that will clarify and at the same time force a recognition of that irreducible opacity that lies at the base of all transparent acts, whether we are speaking of the organization of the world (Hesiod, Plato) or simply the creation (Genesis).

18. Augustine, *Confessions* 7.7.

19. Jean-Luc Marion, *Au lieu de soi: L'approche de saint Augustin* (Paris: PUF, 2008), 334.

20. Dietrich Bonhoeffer, *Creation and Fall: Two Biblical Studies*, trans. John C. Fletcher (New York: Simon & Schuster, 1997), 18–20; my emphases. "Darkness was upon the face of the deep; and the Spirit of God was moving over the face of the waters" (Gen. 1:2) (p. 19). Bonhoeffer's is probably the greatest philosophical commentary on these first chapters of Genesis that has been written.

21. See François Castel, *Commencements: Les onze premiers chapitres de la Genèse* (Paris: Le Centurion, 1985), 18–19. For creation myths, see the following: (1) Sumerian: "When skies above were not yet named/ Nor earth below pronounced by name,/Apsu, the first one, their begetter/ And maker Tiamat, who bore them all,/ Had mixed their waters together." "Sumerian Legend of Creation," *International World History Project*, accessed November 3, 2015, http:// history-world.org/sumerian_legend_of_creation.htm; (2) Chinese: "When Heaven and Earth were yet unformed, All was ascending and flying, diving and delving. Thus it was called the Great Inception." John S. Major, *Heaven and Earth in Early Han Thought* (Albany: State University of New York Press, 1993), 62; (3) Egyptian: See the creation myth of Atum and Nu in James P. Allen, *The Ancient Egyptian Pyramid Texts (*Atlanta: Society of Biblical Literature, 2005).

22. Plato, *Republic* 9.571–72, trans. Allan Bloom (New York: HarperCollins, 1968). A foreshadowing of Freud that will be important for psychoanalysts: the tyrannic desires are those "that wake us in sleep when the rest of the soul—all that belongs to the calculating, tame, and ruling part of it—slumbers, while the beastly and wild part, gorged with food or drink, is skittish and, pushing sleep away seeks to go to satisfy its dispositions. . . . And surely this becomes plain in dreams" (571c–572b). To which we could add the dialogue *Gorgias*, in which the "intemperate" or "incontinent" is, in its Chaos, contrasted explicitly to the cosmos as "orderly" rather than "insatiate." I warmly thank my colleague and friend Jérôme de Gramont, who pointed out to me the double reference in Plato.

23. A prayer pronounced by a deacon (if one is present) as representing the "human dimension" that, along with the priest but in a different manner, he brings to the eucharistic table.

24. [See Marion's concept of the saturated phenomenon: "there are phenomena of such overwhelming givenness of overflowing fulfilment that the intentional acts aimed at these phenomena are overrun, flooded—or saturated." John D. Caputo, review of *The Erotic Phenomenon*, by Jean-Luc Marion, *Ethics* 118, no. 1 (2007): 164. —Trans.]

25. Martin Heidegger, *Nietzsche*, 3:78.

26. Franck, *Dramatique des phénomènes*, 122–23.

27. Ibid., 122–23: "Beyond and not within phenomenology because the project of establishing or constituting can still have a meaning here (if it is rooted in the drive to the roots of intentionality, and not the opposite)." In the context of phenomenology we must however perhaps recognize that Merleau-Ponty touched on this abyss. See Maurice Merleau-Ponty, "The Philosopher and His Shadow," in *Signs*, trans. Richard C. McCleary (Evanston, IL: Northwestern University Press, 1964), 178: "What resists phenomenology within us—natural being, the 'barbarous' source Schelling spoke of—cannot remain outside phenomenology and should have its place within it. The philosopher must bear his shadow, which is not simply the factual absence of future light."

28. Heidegger, *Nietzsche*, 3:77.

29. Ibid., 3:78.

30. Ibid.

31. Ibid., 3:79.

32. There is a critique of "perception" in contemporary phenomenology (which is, as always, post-Cartesian) that points out how it is always taken in the context of "apperception" and can thus be rightly said to privilege the infinite over the finite (see Falque, *Metamorphosis*, §5). Nietzsche's writings contain many references to Chaos, but these are largely spread through the posthumously published fragment, and thus I have found it necessary to stick to the simple interpretation given by Heidegger. Nonetheless, the essential references (1883–1887) can be found in Didier Franck, *Nietzsche and the Shadow of God*, trans. Bettina Bergo and Philippe Farah (Evanston, IL: Northwestern University Press, 2012), 183–84: "*chaos sive natura* . . . My task: the dehumanization of nature and thereafter the naturalization of man" (197–211, fragment from 1881). On the "mass of sensations" as Chaos, see Immanuel Kant, *The Critique of Pure Reason*, trans. Paul Guyer and Allen W. Wood (Cambridge: Cambridge University Press, 1998), A111; this concept was taken up by Nietzsche (1883–1884)—see Franck, *Nietzsche and the Shadow of God*, 253. [Falque uses the phrase "mêlée des sensations" throughout. The phrase is taken from the French translation of Heidegger's *Nietzsche*, vols. 3 and 4; the English translation of Heidegger uses "mass of sensations," while *The Cambridge Edition of the Works of Immanuel Kant* (1999–2015) uses "swarm of appearances." See also note 51 below—Trans.]

33. "In the phenomenalism of the 'inner world' we invert the chronological order of cause and effect. The fundamental fact of 'inner experience' is that the cause is imagined after the effect has taken place . . . e.g., 'I feel unwell'—such a judgment presupposes a great and late neutrality of the observer—; the simple man always says: this or that makes me feel unwell—he makes up his mind about his feeling unwell only when he has seen a reason for feeling unwell. I call that a lack of philology." Friedrich Nietzsche, *The Will to Power*, trans. Walter Kaufmann and R. J. Hollingdale (1888; New York: Vintage Books, 1968), 3:479.

34. Emmanuel Levinas, *Time and the Other*, trans. Richard A. Cohen (1947; Pittsburgh: Duquesne University Press, 1987), 46, 49.

35. Ibid, 46.

36. Ibid, 46–49. "How are we going to approach this existing without existents? Let us imagine all things, beings and persons, returning to nothingness. What remains after this imaginary destruction of everything is not something, but the fact that there is [il y a]. . . . There is, after this destruction of things and beings, the impersonal 'field of forces' of existing. There is something that is neither subject nor substantive. The fact of existing imposes itself when there is no longer anything. And it is anonymous: there is neither anyone nor anything that takes this existence upon itself. It is impersonal like 'it is raining' or 'it is hot.' . . . Insomnia is constituted by the consciousness that it will never finish—that is, that there is no longer any way of withdrawing from the vigilance to which one is held . . . this existing is not an *in-itself* [*en-soi*], which is already peace; it is precisely the absence of all self, a *without-self* [*sans-soi*]." See also the excellent commentary on Levinas, and numerous other references to Levinas, in Didier Franck, *L'Un pour l'autre: Lévinas et la signification* (Paris: PUF, 2008), 247–60. As for the expression "limited phenomenon"—differentiated here from "saturated phenomenon"—I explore this, albeit from another perspective, in "Limite théologique et finitude phénoménologique chez Thomas d'Aquin," *Revue des Sciences philosophiques et théologiques* 93, no. 3 (2008): 527–56. "What is distinctive about us, or what our condition is as created beings [Thomas Aquinas], is that we are *positively limited*. It is not so much that we feel regret about the limitations of our condition (or a desire for the uncreated [Dionysius the Areopagite]. The human creature does not expect from the Creator that he will suppress or pass beyond our proper limits, it is rather that he will come to live in those limits, to transform them from the inside, but without ever attempting to burst through them."

37. Franck, *Nietzsche and the Shadow of God*, 284–85.

38. Ibid, 285: "And if phenomenology is itself an error, then phenomenology has no right to the title of rigorous science. 'Phenomeno-Mania,' notes Nietzsche drily." The term "phenomenology" is used here with reference to Hegel, but we can extend it to the reductive phenomenology of Husserl and his followers. See also Barbara Steigler, *Nitezsche et la critique de la chair* (Paris: PUF, 2005), 48: "The fundamental thought develops in anticipation critical tools against certain tendencies in phenomenology—for a first example, that which, in the work of Michel Henry, systematically pits the immanence of life against representation and more generally against ecstatic dimensions of experience."

39. See Martin Heidegger, *Being and Time*, trans. John Macquarrie and Edward Robinson (New York: HarperCollins, 2008), §53, and its critique in Levinas, *Time and the Other*; and Jean-Luc Marion, *Étant donné* (Paris: PUF, 1997), 325. See also Falque, *Gethsémani*, 127–28.

40. Friedrich Nietzsche, from the Notebooks of 1883, quoted in Franck, *Nietzsche and the Shadow of God*, 305.

41. Didier Franck, *Chair et corps: Sur la phénoménologie de Husserl* (Paris: Éditions de Minuit, 1981), 98n25. See also Franck, *Dramatique des phénomènes*,

120: "Husserl never explained how instinct can give rise to intentionality. Or, in other words, how meaning and phenomenality derive from power." This is a question that the author has continued to pose in relation to Husserl and Levinas by way of Heidegger and Nietzsche.

42. Friedrich Nietzsche, *The Anti-Christ* (1895), trans. R. J. Hollingdale (London: Penguin, 1990), 47.

43. It is surprising how often Levinas has been taken up in the context of Christianity and used in interpretations that are to say the least doubtful (e.g., reduction of the subject in Levinas to a simple figure of passivity; confusion of the human face as "trace" with the human figure as "icon"; blissful vision of the other as against the "tragic," which is found in the figure of the self just as much as the other). On the distance of Levinas from Christianity, see Falque, *Gethsémani*, 167–69.

44. Falque, *Metamorphosis*, 79; emphases in original.

45. It seems worth recalling here that there was what Jean Greisch refers to as a "failure of the flesh in *Being and Time*." See Greisch, "Le phénomène de la chair: un ratage de *Sein und Zeit*," in *Dimensions de l'exister*, ed. Ghislaine Florival (Louvain-la-Neuve: Ètudes d'anthropologie philosophique, 1994), 157–74. This "failure" was less marked than is often thought, and it is only necessary to read the published proceedings of the Zollikon Seminars to see this. During the seminars, given to a group of scientists and medical doctors who, according to Heidegger, were concerned solely with the objective body (in line with a positivist conception of medicine that seems too narrow)—flesh was seen in subjective terms and defined from the starting point of the existentiality of man, even though flesh expresses itself in terms of the rapture of the body and not as a self-generated disposition. This topic was opened up in Heidegger's reading of Nietzsche ("the corporal starting from Chaos") and was not, as far as I can see, reconsidered later. See also Jocelyn Benoist, *Autour de Husserl: L'Ego et la raison* (Paris: Vrin, 1994), 110: "The flesh is flesh in the light of existence and not as *soma* driven by the spirit. Flesh does not express a spirit which lies behind it: above all it possesses an existential sense."

46. On the first point—the unsatisfactory understanding of flesh as an ensemble of "the lived" in the phenomenological project—see Barbara Stiegler, *Nietzsche et la critique de la chair* (Paris: PUF, 2005), 42: "The Nietzschean critique of *Erlebnis*-insight follows to the letter the reading of *The Critique of Pure Reason*. . . . The Kantian intuition is the impossible grasping of the self—and in this sense the impossibility of insight—because it is the putting to the test of a self seen as originally dispersed (critique of *Erlebnis*, lived experience), in the name of *Erfahrung* (experience as 'living through' [*fahren*] and danger [*Gerfahr*])." As for the second point—the impossibility of sticking to the notion of the "extension of the body"—this can easily be confirmed in phenomenology itself. It is still the case that taking the signification of "body" as "objective body" (see §1) ignores our normal usage of "flesh" as changeable and tactile matter through which we apprehend our own body (and with which a medical doctor deals in the

case of anesthesia, for example). As to the third point—definition of the body by its expansiveness (the "spreading out" of the body) rather than by its extension (the extendedness of the body)—one finds little about this in philosophy, except (as we shall see later on) in the commentary on the painting of Francis Bacon by Gilles Deleuze; see Deleuze, *Francis Bacon*, 22: "In meat, the flesh seems to *descend* from the bones, while the bones rise up from the flesh" (emphasis in original). See also several comments on Lucian Freud's work, more fleshly and opaque even than Francis Bacon's, in Jean Clair, "Lucian Freud: La question du nu en peinture," in *Éloge du visible* Paris: Gallimard, 1996), 171–88: "It took Freud a long time to come to this renewed conquest of the human in man, this re-presentation of the figure" (p. 176). It is probably through reexamining the most contemporary art that philosophy and theology can renew themselves. The artist is most often part of the avant-garde (open to the idea of the unexpected and a new perspective), the philosopher is in the rearguard (painting gray on gray as Hegel does), and the theologian is at the farthest distance from contemporary culture (going no further than Rembrandt or Roualt as far as any reference to art is concerned.)

47. Friedrich Nietzsche, *Beyond Good and Evil*, trans. Helen Zimmern (1886; Project Gutenberg, 2009), §36, chap. 2, http://www.gutenberg.org/files/4363/4363-h/4363-h.htm; my emphasis.

48. Franck, *Nietzsche and the Shadow of God*, 344. Franck takes the phrase *der Leib philosophiert* (the body philosophizes) from Nietzsche's Notebooks of 1882–1883 (German edition): *Sämtliche Werke: Kritische Studienausgabe*, ed. G. Colli and M. Montinari (Berlin: Walter de Gruyter, 1967), 226. See also Franck, *Chair et corps*, 98n25.

49. See Friedrich Nietzsche, "Expeditions of an Untimely Man," in *Twilight of the Idols*, trans. R. J. Hollingdale (1889; London: Penguin, 1990), 8: "The essence of intoxication is the feeling of plenitude and increased energy." Heidegger commented on this (the concept of "rapture") in *Nietzsche*, vols. 1 and 2, trans. David Farrell Krell (San Francisco: HarperCollins, 1991).

50. See, for example, Antonio Damasio, *Spinoza avait raison* (Paris: Odile Jacob, 2003). I do not disagree with the biological conclusions, but refuse to draw from them a metaphysics (a theory of the emotions reduced to psycho-chemistry).

51. Kant, *Critique of Pure Reason*, A111. I prefer the translation "mass of sensations" to others such as "crowd of phenomena" or "mass of phenomena," because nothing can guarantee that what totally escapes from synthesis and thus from the possibility of experience in the Kantian sense of the term (through categories of understanding and the schema of the imagination) can still be called phenomena.

52. Husserl, *Cartesian Meditations*, 38–39.

53. See Jakob von Uexküll, *Mondes animaux et mondes humains* (Paris: Gonthier, 1965), 19–27; see especially the illustrations of the same room as seen by a man, a dog, and an insect. See also Martin Heidegger, *The Fundamental Concepts of Metaphysics*, trans. William McNeill and Nicholas Walker (Bloomington: Indiana University Press, 1995), §46–48.

54. Heidegger, *Nietzsche*, 3:80. For a convincing critique of Heidegger's presuppositions about humanity in his discussion of animality, once he has moved on from direct commentary on Nietzsche, see Alain Seguy-Duclot, "Humanisme et animalité," in *Heidegger et la question de l'humanisme*, ed. Bruno Pinchard (Paris: PUF, 2005), 329–46: "I should like to consider that abyss located by Heidegger in humanity and animality, not starting off from the human point of view . . . but from the animal" (p. 332). The essay also includes excellent comments on "anthropocentric prejudices and their theological roots" (p. 344). See also Claude Romano, "Le monde animal, Heidegger et von Uexküll," in *Heidegger en dialogue, 1912–1930*, ed. Servanne Jollivet and Claude Romano (Paris: Vrin, 2009), 255–98: "this praise by Heidegger of von Uexküll comes along with a definite distancing on his part. In fact it is a rerun and a critical re-appropriation of von Uexküll that will lead toward an argument that does not come from him, and indeed is in complete contrast to his analysis: that of the *unfathomable difference between man and animal*" (p. 267; my emphasis).

55. Heidegger, *Nietzsche*, 3:80.

56. Ibid.

57. Friedrich Nietzsche, *La volonté de puissance* (Paris: Gallimard, 1942), §258.

58. See Barbara Cassin, *"Pulsion," in* Vocabulaire européen des philosophies, ed. Barbara Cassin (Paris: Éditions du Seuil, 2004), 1050–55; Natalie Depraz, "Pulsion, instinct, désir: Que signifie *Trieb* chez Husserl?" *Alter*, no. 9 (2001): 113–25. See also *Alter*, no. 3 (1995); and Anne de Montavont, *De la passivité dans la phénoménologie de Husserl* (Paris: PUF, 1999), 245–59.

59. Sigmund Freud, *Métapsychologie* (1915; Paris: Gallimard, 1995), 17: "The concept of drive (*Trieb*) is thus one of those lying on the frontier between the mental and the physical."

60. Gilles Deleuze, "Entretien avec Michel Cressole" (1973), in *Pourparlers* (Paris: Éditions de Minuit, 1990), 23; my emphases.

61. Heidegger, *Nietzsche*, 3:78.

62. Tertullian, *On Fasting*, quoted in Jean Steinmann, *Tertullien* (Paris: Éditions du Chalet, 1967), 274–75. See also the commentary in Alexandre, *Une chair pour la gloire*, 454–65.

63. Franck, *Dramatique des phénomènes*, 122; my emphases.

64. See "Pope John's Opening Speech to the Council," October 11, 1962, *Vatican II–Voice of the Church*, last modified October 31, 2015, http://www.vatican2voice.org/91docs/opening_speech.htm.

65. Heidegger, *Nietzsche*, 3:80.

66. For the refusal to identify Christ wholly with a simple figure of animality, see the appropriate condemnation at the Council in Trullo (see Preface).

2. The Staging of the Last Supper

1. Johannes Scotus Eriugena, *De la division de la nature: Periphyseon* 5.913b–d (Paris: PUF, 2009); my emphasis. This thesis is also put forward by, for

example, Hans-Urs von Balthasar, *Theo-Drama: Theological Dramatic Theory*, vol. 4, *The Action* (San Francisco: Ignatius, 1994). I discuss this theophanic (i.e., manifesting God) and integrative perspective in *God, the Flesh, and the Other*, trans. W. C. Hackett (Evanston, IL: Northwestern University Press, 2015).

2. These are literally recommended in what remains probably the best dictionary of Judaism in the "Old" or "First" Testament: Moses Maimonides, *The Guide for the Perplexed*, 2nd ed., trans. M. Friedländer (New York: E. P. Dutton, 1910), part 3, chap. 46 (on sacrifice and the Passover lamb).

3. See the characteristics of the image of the lamb in the two testaments discussed in Xavier Leon-Dufour, *Vocabulaire de théologie biblique* (Paris: Éditions du Cerf, 1977), 27.

4. Marcel Jousse, *La Manducation de la parole* (Paris: Gallimard, 1975), 33, 34, 197; my emphases.

5. See Preface I of the Most Holy Eucharist in *The Order of Mass: A Roman Missal Study Edition and Workbook* (Chicago: Archdiocese of Chicago, Liturgy Training, 2011), 78.

6. Benedict XVI, *Homily of His Holiness Benedict XVI*, Chrism Mass, Holy Thursday, April 13, 2006, accessed 2006, http://w2.vatican.va/content/benedict-xvi/en/homilies/2006/documents/hf_ben-xvi_hom_20060413_messa-crismale.html.

7. The parallel between the manger and the altar of the eucharist was widely discussed by the Fathers of the Church and rediscovered by Marcel Jousse, in his ethnography and ethnology of the Palestinian people. "Despite the silence of the texts, the presence of a manger in which a young infant, recently born, is laid, recalls quite naturally the actual 'users' of the manger. We can't be surprised that from these prophetic texts we find the ass and the ox emerging, and coming to feature in the story. This is not an intrusion but a taking possession. . . . A 'manger' can no longer ignore those that eat [*manger*] from it, any more than a shepherd can ignore his sheep." Jousse, *La Manducation de la parole*, 167–68n20.

8. See *Dictionnaire de spiritualité ascétique et mystique* [1880–1952] (Paris: Beauchesne, 1990), s.v. "eucharistie": "It is the essence of the sacrifice of Jesus that it inaugurates the sacrament of the universal gathering together of the new Israel. . . . The privilege of Israel passes to a new people. Nothing is more significant than that the *image of the Lamb* is mentioned *29 times* (in the book of the Apocalypse), without ever being explained, because universally known" (my emphasis).

9. Jousse, *La Manducation de la parole*, 34.

10. Maimonides, *Guide for the Perplexed*, part 3, chap. 32.

11. Hugues Cousin, *Le monde où vivait Jésus* (Paris: Éditions du Cerf, 1998), 346.

12. See the exact temporal coincidence between "the Last Supper of Christ and the disciples" and the "burnt-offering of the lamb during the Jewish Passover at Jerusalem" established in Leon-Dufour, "Agneau [Lamb]," in *Vocabulaire de théologie biblique*, 27. On the importance and presence of the animal in Jewish

sacrificial rites, see Cousin, *Le monde où vivait Jésus*, 342–48, citing the *Pesahim*: "An Israelite slaughtered it and the priest received it [the blood] passing it along to his fellow"; and "there were iron hooks fixed into the walls and pillars on which they suspended [the offerings] and flayed them." (Quoted passages can be found online: "Moed 1: Pesahim," chap. 5, *eMishnah.com*, accessed December 10, 2015, http://www.emishnah.com/pesahim.html.) According to Cousin, "after 70 and until today, a bone with a little roasted meat is used to recall the Passover lamb" (*Le monde*, 346).

13. *Acta Conciliorum* of the Council in Trullo (see Preface).

14. Heidegger, *Nietzsche*, 3:79.

15. Ibid., 3:81. The Vatican position in favor of evolutionary theory was clearly reaffirmed in Rome at the celebration of the 150th anniversary of the publication of *The Origin of Species* (by Charles Darwin). In particular, Cardinal William Levada, president of the Congregation for the Doctrine of the Faith, supported by Pope Benedict XVI, stated, "The Vatican sees no incompatibility between belief in God and scientific theories of the evolution of species ('The Vatican does not stand in the way of scientific realities'). But it would be 'absurd' to assume from this that evolutionary theories prove that God does not exist" (statement of March 3, 2009, reprinted in "Le Vatican juge 'absurde' d'opposer foi en Dieu et evolutionnisme," *Scientuss's Blog*, April 25, 2009, accessed October 29, 2015, https://scientuss.wordpress.com/2009/04/25/le-vatican-juge-absurde-d%E2%80%99opposer-foi-en-dieu-et-evolutionnisme). See "Science de la nature et foi chrétienne," *La Documentation catholique*, no. 2420 (March 11, 2009): 287–300. See also the first note in Chapter 4.

16. Gregory of Nazianzus, Epistle 101 (Letter to Clédonium), in "Critique of Apollinarius and Apollinarianism," *Early Church Texts*, accessed 3 November 2015. http://www.earlychurchtexts.com/public/gregoryofnaz_critique_of_apolliniarianism.htm.

17. I examine this topic in *God, the Flesh, and the Other*, in sections on Irenaeus and Tertullian.

18. See Nicolas Greschny, *L'Icône de la Trinité d'André Roublev* (Alba: Éditions du Lion de Juda, 1986), 81–83. See also Fabrice Hadjadj, *L'Agneau mystique: Le retable des frères Van Eyck* (Paris: Éditions de l'Œuvre, 2008), 50.

19. Apart from those in private collections, versions of this painting (c. 1635–1640, oil on canvas) are in the collections of the Bilbao Fine Arts Museum; *Museo Nacional del Prado*, Madrid; the San Diego Museum of Art; and the Walters Art Museum, Baltimore.

20. Paul Guinard and Tiziana Frati, *Zurbarán* (Paris: Flammarion, 1975), illustration 27 and dust cover. I warmly thank my colleague and friend Pierre Lequois, who drew my attention to this unforgettable image of *The Lamb*.

21. *Musée du Louvre, Paris. Posted commentary on Rembrandt's* Flayed Ox, in exhibit.

22. See Chaim Soutine, *Flayed Beef*, c.1924, oil on canvas, Kunstmuseum, Bern.

23. Francis Bacon, *Study after Velázquez's Portrait of Pope Innocent X* (1953), oil on canvas, Des Moines Art Center, Iowa; *Crucifixion* (1944), oil with sand on canvas, Guggenheim Museum, New York; *Painting* (1946), oil and pastel on linen, Museum of Modern Art, New York.

24. David Sylvester, *The Brutality of Fact: Interviews with Francis Bacon* (New York: Thames and Hudson, 1987), 45, 44.

25. Ibid., 23, 46.

26. Gilles Deleuze, *Francis Bacon: The Logic of Sensation*, trans. Daniel W. Smith (1981; London: Continuum, 2003), 24.

27. Ibid., 23, 22. One can thus interpret Caravaggio's astonishing painting in which doubting Thomas sticks his finger in the open wound in the almost biologically rendered flesh of the resurrected Christ. Caravaggio, *The Incredulity of Saint Thomas*, c.1601–1602, painting, Sanssouci Palace, Potsdam. See Duncan Bull, *Rembrandt, Le Caravage* (Paris: Hazan, 2006), plate 36. Other examples, some more contemporary (and sometimes more "shocking"), also show the carnality, or the animality, of Christ in the eucharist: *Crucified Horse* (1999), by Joel-Peter Witkin, is a photograph that radicalizes to the extreme the thesis of crucified animality (see Nissan N. Perez, *Corpus Christi: Les représentations du Christ en photographie 1855–2002* [Paris: Éditions Marval, 2002], 149); and *Novecento* (1997), by Maurizio Cattelan, is a taxidermied horse suspended from a baroque ceiling (perhaps of a church?) (see Catherine Grenier, *L'art contemporain est-il chrétien?* [Nîmes: Jacqueline Chambon, 2003], 44–45).

28. Deleuze, *Francis Bacon*, 23.

29. Ibid., 58.

30. Maurice Merleau-Ponty, "Eye and Mind," trans. Carleton Dallery, in *The Primacy of Perception: And Other Essays on Phenomenal Psychology*, ed. James Edie (Evanston, IL: Northwestern University Press, 1964), 162: "The painter 'takes his body with him,' says Valéry. Indeed we cannot imagine how a 'mind' could paint. It is by lending his body to the world that the artist changes the world into painting. To understand these transubstantiations we must go back to the working, actual body—not the body as a chunk of space or a bundle of the functions by that body which is an intertwining of vision and movement." See also Paul Cézanne, letter to Émile Bernard, October 23, 1905, in *Conversations with Cézanne*, ed. Michael Doran (London: University of California Press, 2001), 254: "I owe you the truth in painting and I shall give it to you."

31. See, in this context, Falque, "Métaphysique et théologie: De la bienveillance à la performance," *Transversalités* 110, no. 2 (2009), 125–29.

32. Paul Cézanne, *Letters*, 4th rev. ed., ed. John Rewald, trans. Marguerite Kay (New York: Hacker Art Books, 1976), 327.

33. See Denis Coutagne, *Cézanne en vérités* (Arles: Actes Sud, 2006), 17. I would like to thank this author, who has shown me—through his writings, exhibitions, and friendship—the depths to be found in the work of Cézanne.

34. In this sense, I follow Deleuze: "the extraordinary work of abstract painting was necessary in order to tear modern art away from figuration. But is

there not another path, more direct and more sensible?" (*Francis Bacon*, 11). Further, "If the painter keeps to the Figure, if he or she opts for the second path, it will be to oppose the 'figural' to the figurative" (Ibid., 2). The second path (the figural) is the one that I have tried to follow in the philosophical context of a "visibility of the flesh," in Irenaeus; see Falque, *God, the Flesh, and the Other*.

35. Benedict XVI, *Deus Caritas Est* [God is love], first encyclical letter, December 25, 2005, sec. 5, *The Holy See*, http://w2.vatican.va/content/benedict -xvi/en/encyclicals/documents/hf_ben-xvi_enc_20051225_deus-caritas-est.html.

36. Jean-Luc Nancy, *Corpus*, trans. Richard A. Rand (New York: Fordham University Press, 2008), 3.

37. Ibid., 5. See the debate opened by Nancy's celebrated chapter "The Deconstruction of Christianity" in his *Dis-Enclosure: The Deconstruction of Christianity*, trans., Bettina Bergo, Gabriel Malenfant, and Michael B. Smith (New York: Fordham University Press, 2008). In the first chapter of this book Nancy writes, "Christianity designates nothing other, essentially (that is to say simply, infinitely simply: through an inaccessible simplicity), than the demand to open in this world an alterity or an unconditional alienation. However, 'unconditional' means not undeconstructible. It must also denote the range, by right infinite, of the very movement of deconstruction and disenclosure" (p.10).

38. We can't be satisfied with the simple spoken pledge (the "yes" in marriage) as a kind of bastion against an "automatic flesh" (the uncontrolled eros), but we can propose the hypothesis of a fidelity to the flesh, itself formed in the progress from animality to humanity under the influence of the eucharistic eros. On this question, see Jean-Luc Marion, *The Erotic Phenomenon*, trans. Stephen E. Lewis (Chicago: University of Chicago Press, 2006): "Thus, the oath's endurance or, in a word, faithfulness, becomes the condition for the persistence of the erotic phenomenon" (p. 184).

39. Timothy Radcliffe, "Affectivité et eucharistie," *La Documentation catholique*, no. 2327 (January 2, 2005): 38–46. I have changed the term "sexuality" to "eros," in that the topic here is metaphysical rather than ethical, and in that "sexuality" has pejorative connotations, at least in French, that are best avoided. (The text is taken from a speech originally delivered in Spanish.)

3. Eros Eucharisticized

1. [The French word used here, *consommation*, means either "consumption" (of food, consumer goods) or "consummation" (of marriage, a sexual relationship).—Trans.] See the link between "marriage ratified" in the Church (*matrimonium ratum*) and "marriage consummated" (*matrimonium consummatum*) in the nuptial bed explicitly formulated in Canon Law (1055–1165): *Code of Canon Law* (Washington, DC: Canon Law Society of America, 1983), accessed November 1, 2015, http://www.vatican.va/archive/ENG1104/_INDEX.HTM. Canon 1141 specifies that a marriage ratified and consummated cannot be "dissolved." See also §21.

2. Bernard of Clairvaux, *Commentary on the Song of Songs* 2.3, accessed December 10, 2015, https://archive.org/details/StBernardsCommentaryOnThe SongOfSongs.

3. See Roland Barthes, *A Lover's Discourse: Fragments*, trans. Richard Howard (New York: Hill & Wang, 1978).

4. Benedict XVI, *Sacramentum Caritatis* [The sacrament of charity], post-synodal apostolic exhortation, May 1, 2007, sec. 27, *The Holy See*, http://w2.vatican .va/content/benedict-xvi/en/apost_exhortations/documents/hf_ben-xvi_exh _20070222_sacramentum-caritatis.html. This perspective would have been difficult to predict, given the general neglect of the mystical theology of the Middle Ages. We have only to recall the way in which the Song of Solomon was bowdlerized at the end of the nineteenth century, or the allegorical interpretations that definitively obliterated erotic meanings. See Jean-Pierre Sonnet, "Érotique et mystique dans le Cantique des cantiques," in *Sermons sur le Cantique de Bernard de Clairvaux*, vol. 3, ed. Jean Leclercq, Charles Hugh Talbot, and Henri Rochais (Paris: Éditions du Cerf, 2000), 365–86. "Doesn't the allegorization of the Song of Solomon present us with a textual distortion, with a form of censorship that transforms an erotic poem into a *theologically* correct text?" (p. 336). As for what is obviously erotic in the Song of Solomon, a single verse suffices to show it, even if there is also necessarily a symbolic aspect: "My beloved thrust his hand into the opening,/ and my inmost being yearned for him/ I arose to open to my beloved,/ and my hands dripped with myrrh, my fingers with liquid myrrh/ upon the handles of the bolt" (Song of Sol. 5:4–5).

5. Anders Nygren, *Agape and Eros: A Study of the Christian Idea of Love*, trans. P. S. Watson (New York: Harper and Row, 1969), Part I, 52.

6. Jean-Luc Marion, *The Erotic Phenomenon*, trans. Stephen E. Lewis (Chicago: University of Chicago Press, 2007), 211.

7. See Benedict XVI, *Deus Caritas Est*, first encyclical letter, December 25, 2005, part 1, *The Holy See*, http://w2.vatican.va/content/benedict-xvi/en/encyclicals/ documents/hf_ben-xvi_enc_20051225_deus-caritas-est.html. There is a debate here with Jean-Luc Marion's thesis in *The Erotic Phenomenon* of univocal eros and agape, though that thesis is nuanced and counterbalanced in Marion's more recent book *In the Self's Place: The Approach of St. Augustine*, trans. Jeffrey L. Kosky (Stanford, CA: Stanford University Press, 2012); here, the theological dimension and the transforming dimension of the agape are affirmed more strongly. See also Falque, "Dieu charité," *Communio* (September–December 2005): 75–87.

8. [See medieval theories of analogy from Aristotle: Analogy of proportionality is when two things are related in terms of comparison of proportions or relations. Analogy of attribution is when one term is primary and the other secondary (e.g., when "healthy" is used to describe dog food—the dog would be healthy in the primary sense, while the food is healthy only as it contributes to the health of the dog). —Trans.] See Bernard Montagnes, *La Doctrine de l'analogie de l'être d'après saint Thomas d'Aquin* (Louvain: Publications Universitaires, 1963) 24–41; and

Falque, "De l'impossible analogie de l'être chez Aristote et de sa réalisation chez Thomas d'Aquin" (master's thesis, Université Paris-X, Nanterre, 1986).

9. See the comment by Jean Guitton, *Le Christ dans ma vie: Dialogue avec J. Doré* (Paris: Desclée, 1987), 41. It is not easy to explain either the nuptial character of the eucharist or the eucharistic character of marriage. Perhaps they will be better understood in the twenty-first century. See also Joseph Doré, "Le Christ dans la vie de Jean Guitton," *Transversalités* (July–September 2008): 141–61.

10. August Rodin, *La Main de Dieu* (*The Hand of God*), 1896, marble, Musée Rodin, Paris.

11. Benedict XVI, *Sacramentum Caritatis*, sec. 11. See also Pascal Ide, *Le Christ donne tout: Benoît XVI, Une théologie de l'amour* (Paris: Éditions de l'Emmanuel, 2007), 119–30.

12. On the subject of my "triptych" of books on the fleshly forms (past, birth-resurrection; future, death-Gethsemane; present, body-eucharist), see Falque, *The Metamorphosis of Finitude*, trans. George Hughes (New York: Fordham University Press, 2012), §1. Regarding the three dimensions of the eucharist analyzed here, traces can be found in the form of "seeds of the word," animality, eros, and eucharist (*hoc est corpus meum*). For the conclusive formula on this subject, in a commanding text, see Charles Péguy, "Victor-Marie, Comte Hugo," in *Œuvres en prose complètes* (Paris: Gallimard, 1992), 235: "They needed on their side (the people of this calling) from their point of view, to consider the *incarnation* . . . that story like a story that came to earth of God as a child. . . . The incarnation as an extraordinary success of fleshly fecundity, as a culmination, as a fructification at its apogee, as a forcing-house—but natural, as a fleshly crowning moment, as a narrative (culmination, supreme, a limit), coming to flesh and to the earth." I examine this point in my article "Ch. Péguy: Incarnation philosophique et incarnation théologique: une histoire arrivée à la chair et à la terre," *L'Amitié Charles Péguy* 102 (April–June 2003): 164–78.

13. [Various biblical translations give "remain," "tarry," "stay," "dwell," "continue," and "abide." —Trans.]

14. See Jacques Derrida, *Of Grammatology* (1967), trans. Gayatri Spivak (Baltimore: Johns Hopkins University Press, 1997). The expression "metaphysics of being" derives from Heidegger; see Martin Heidegger, "Metaphysics as History of Being," in *The End of Philosophy*, trans. Joan Stambaugh (Chicago: University of Chicago Press, 2003), 6–8: "As this presence, *ousia* is called: *to eschaton*, the presence in which presencing contains its utmost and ultimate. This highest manner of presence also grants the first and nearest presence of everything which in such case lingers as this and that in unconcealment. . . . That something is and what is are revealed as modes of presencing whose fundamental characteristic is *energeia*." See also Jean-Luc Nancy, *Corpus*, trans. Richard A. Rand (New York: Fordham University Press, 2008), 5: "And all thoughts of the 'body proper,' laborious efforts at reappropriating what we used to consider, impatiently, as 'objectified' or 'reified,' all such thoughts about the body proper are comparably contorted; in the end they only expel the thing we desired."

15. Stanislas Breton, *Le Vivant Miroir de l'univers* (Paris: Éditions du Cerf, 2006), 19. On this warning, and following this perspective, see Falque, "De la préposition à la proposition: mystique et philosophie chez Stanislas Breton," *Transversalités* (July–September 2006): 17–36.

16. One welcomes in this context the "retraction" of Jean-Luc Marion, in "Saint Thomas d'Aquin et l'onto-théologie," *Revue thomiste* 95, no. 1 (1995): 279–332. It was taken up again in Marion, *God without Being*, trans. Thomas A. Carlson, (Chicago: University of Chicago Press, 1995). This "retraction" follows Étienne Gilson's charges against Heidegger; see Gilson, *L'Être et l'Essence* (1948), (Paris: Vrin, 1981), 365–77. "If one wanted briefly to describe the metaphysics of Aquinas, emphasizing precisely what was peculiar to it, one could take the opposite course to that proposed by Heidegger: insofar as Aquinas never objectifies being as being, his metaphysic always considers being itself" (p. 372).

17. Edmund Husserl, fragment written May 7–9, 1934, quoted in Maurice Merleau-Ponty, *Husserl at the Limits of Phenomenology: Including Texts by Edmund Husserl*, ed. Leonard Lawlor and Bettina Bergo (Evanston, IL: Northwestern University Press, 2002), xli.

18. Martin Heidegger, *Poetry, Language, Thought,* trans. Albert Hofstadter (New York: Harper Perennial, 2001), 203–4.

19. Ibid., 145.

20. Friedrich Nietzsche, *Ecce Homo: How One Becomes What One Is*, trans. R. J. Hollingdale (London: Penguin, 1979).

21. See the connection drawn between the "certitude of faith" (as "safe-keeping") and the *cogito* of Descartes by Didier Franck, *Nietzsche and the Shadow of God*, trans. Bettina Bergo and Philippe Farah (Evanston, IL: Northwestern University Press, 2012), 242, 243, 246. See also Falque, "Éternel retour ou résurrection des corps?" *Transversalités* (July–September 2002): 119–37.

22. See Breton, *Le Vivant Miroir*, 42; see also Breton, *Philosophie et mystique* (Grenoble: Jérôme Millon, 1996), 45.

23. Charles de Bovelles [Carolus Bovillus], *Liber de Sapiente* [The book on the sage], ed. Pierre Magnard (1509; Paris: Vrin, 2010), 55. Bovelles's remarks are intended to guard us against the temptations of lower beings (the beasts), but also apply to higher beings (the angels). Bovelles is a major author, whose work has been unjustly neglected. He contributed importantly, along with Nicolas de Cues and Jean Gerson, to the "Christian humanism" of the Renaissance.

24. This is an interpretation of Matthew 22:30 that I return to later when I consider eros, or the sexual difference, as a modality of the eucharist (*this is my body*); "in the resurrection they neither marry nor are given in marriage, but are like angels in heaven." We can accept, for the moment, the note in the French ecumenical translation of the Bible (*Traduction œcuménique de la Bible* [Paris: Éditions du Cerf, 1975–1976] [hereafter cited as *TOB*]): "The expression 'like the angels' does not aim in any way to depreciate the institution of marriage, but signifies here having no other preoccupation than that of serving and praising God" (p. 104).

25. Breton, *Philosophie et mystique*, 33 (a "Johanine" reinterpretation of the act of being in Aquinas).

26. Thomas Aquinas, *Summa Theologica* 3.80.3, ad. 3, trans. Fathers of the English Dominican Province (1920; New Advent, 2008), http://www.newadvent.org/summa/5080.htm.

27. Aquinas, *Summa Theologica* 3.83.3, ad. 2.

28. See note in *TOB* on 1 Cor. 11:29 (p. 509).

29. Augustine, "Sermon 21 on the New Testament" 71.17, in *Nicene and Post-Nicene Fathers*, First Series, vol. 6, trans. R. G. MacMullen, rev. and ed. Kevin Knight (1888; New Advent, 2009), http://www.newadvent.org/fathers/160321.htm.

30. See Jacques Attali, *L'ordre cannibale* (Paris: Éditions Grasset et Fasquelle, 1979).

31. Aquinas, *Summa Theologica* 3.75.5, arg. 4, http://www.newadvent.org/summa/4075.htm.

32. Bede, quoted in Thomas Aquinas, "Catena Aurea John 6," 54, *Catechetics Online*, accessed November 7, 2015, http://www.catecheticsonline.com/CatenaAurea-John6.php. Bede's is a perspective that we find again in the debate between Berengarius and Lanfranc (see §27).

33. See Dionysius the Areopagite (who distinguishes between mystery, which needs to be examined in the unknown, and secret, which is of the order of the unknowable): "Direct our path to the ultimate summit of Thy mystical Love, most incomprehensible, most luminous and most exalted, where the pure, absolute and immutable mysteries of theology are veiled in the dazzling obscurity of the secret Silence." Dionysius the Areopagite, *Mystica Theologia* 1 (1923; Shrine of Wisdom, 2004), http://thefintrytrust.org.uk/shrineofwisdom.org.uk/mystical_theology_and_the_celestial_hierarchies.htm.

34. Quoted in Charles M. Radding and Francis Newton, *Theology, Rhetoric, and Politics in the Eucharistic Controversy, 1078–1079* (New York: Columbia University Press, 2003), 13.

35. I am putting together here "the effort to abide" (Stanislas Breton) with the "act of being" (Thomas Aquinas), in particular to speak of the act of the eucharist: "those who eat my flesh and drink my blood abide in me, and I in them" (John 6:56).

36. Marion, *God without Being*, 178.

37. Irenaeus, *Against Heresies* 4.18.5, in *Ante-Nicene Fathers*, vol. 1, trans. Alexander Roberts and James Donaldson, rev. and ed. Kevin Knight (1885: New Advent, 2009), http://www.newadvent.org/fathers/0103.htm.

Part II. The Sojourn of Humankind

1. "Man is neither angel nor beast, and it is unfortunately the case that anyone trying to act the angel acts the beast." Blaise Pascal, *Pensées*, trans. A. J. Krailsheimer (London: Penguin, 1966), 242.

2. See the warning against "anthropological reduction" made by Hans-Urs von Balthasar to Karl Rahner in *Love Alone Is Credible*, trans. D. C. Schindler (San Francisco: Ignatius, 2004), chap. 2. Balthasar's is a severe judgment on Rahner, especially because Rahner, in his transcendental theology, aimed to recognize that God himself "made himself the measure of man" in his kenosis, rather than to reduce God to man. See Karl Rahner, *Foundations of Christian Faith*, trans. William V. Dych (New York: Crossroad, 1985). See also Vincent Holzer, *Le Dieu Trinité dans l'histoire: Le différened théologique Balthasar-Rahner* (Paris: Èditions du Cerf, 1995), 333: "If Rahner *expresses a measure of God for man*, he does not think of it as a *measure taken and understood* by man, but as a *measure of himself by God offered* to man."

3. Thomas Aquinas, *The 29 Questions on Truth* 6.4, trans. R. W. Mulligan (Documenta Catholica Omnia, 1952); my emphasis. This axiom is analyzed in Jean-Pierre Torrell, *Saint Thomas d'Aquin, maître spirituel* (Paris-Fribourg: Éditions du Cerf, 1996), 335. I discuss this matter in relation to the "limited phenomenon" (Aquinas) and "saturated phenomenon" (Dionysius) in "Limite théologique et finitude phénoménologique chez Thomas d'Aquin," *Revue des Sciences philosophiques et théologiques* 92, no. 3 (2008): 527–56.

4. See Falque, *The Metamorphosis of Finitude*, trans. George Hughes (New York: Fordham University Press, 2012), §23.

5. G. W. F. Hegel, *Lectures on the Philosophy of Religion*, vol. 3, trans. R. F. Brown, P. C. Hodgson, and J. M. Stewart (Berkeley: University of California Press, 1998), 276. The passage is quoted and commented on in Philippe Soual, "Amour et croix chez Hegel," *Revue Philosophique*, no. 1 (1998): 71–96. Hegel talks of the accomplishment of this act of love as "differentiation" in the anthropomorphosis of God, or the "absolute" union of contraries in the figure of God made Man. See also Jean-Louis Vieillard-Baron, *Hegel: Systèmes et structure théologiques* (Paris: Éditions du Cerf, 2006), 298: "The important point about the anthropomorphosis of God is that it is speculatively necessary. . . . Divine incarnations in the other religions are arbitrary and problematic. The incarnation of the Christian God is free and necessary: it is the necessary fulfilling of the divine nature manifesting its unity with human nature."

6. Jacques Derrida, *Margins of Philosophy*, trans. Alan Bass (Chicago: University of Chicago Press, 1984), 9.

7. Irenaeus, *Against Heresies* 1.22.1, in *Ante-Nicene Fathers*, vol. 1, trans. Alexander Roberts and William Rambaut, rev. and ed. Kevin Knight (1885; New Advent, 2009), http://www.newadvent.org/fathers/0103.htm.

4. The Animal That Therefore I Am

1. Martin Heidegger, *Nietzsche*, trans. David Farrell Krell (New York: HarperCollins, 1991), 3:81.

2. See, on this point, Pascal Ide, "L'homme et l'animal: Une alterité corporelle significative," in *L'Humain et la Personne* (Paris: Èditions du Cerf, 2009) 281–99.

3. Benedict XVI, *Homily of His Holiness Benedict XVI: Easter Vigil*, Vatican Basilica, Holy Saturday, April 15, 2006, accessed November 3, 2015, http://w2.vatican.va/content/benedict-xvi/en/homilies.index.html. As for the statement put forward by the double pontificate of John Paul II and Benedict XVI on the theory of evolution, see Vincent Aucante, "Création et évolution: La pensée de Benoît XVI," *La Documentation catholique*, no. 2417 (February 2009): 138–42: "After many years of condemnation, encouraged no doubt by the progress in exegesis of hermeneutic biblical studies, the Holy See took account under John Paul II and Benedict XVI of the scientific dimension of evolution." See also proceedings of the 2006 seminar of Castel Gandolfo, in *Creation and Evolution: A Conference with Pope Benedict XVI in Castel Gandolfo*, ed. Christoph Cardinal Schönborn (San Francisco: Ignatius, 2008). A conference was also held at the Gregorian University, Rome, to mark the 150th anniversary of the publication of Charles Darwin's *The Origin of Species*, entitled "Biological Evolution: Facts and Theories" (2009). The so-called critique at the heart of the Catholic Church of the theory of evolution was concerned less with evolution or mutation as such than with the theory of open-ended chance that went with it (Monod, Dawkins, Conway Morris). See Fiorenzo Facchini, *Les Défis de l'évolution: Harmonie entre science et foi* (Paris: Parole et silence, 2009), 110–11: "According to a neo-Darwinism, the world has no purpose, and man is also a chance event, accidental, like other species that are formed by natural selection. . . . According to many of its partisans, it is a world without any aim that seems to emerge from Darwin's ideas, according to which god becomes superfluous. . . . However, Darwin's theory of evolution does not necessarily imply a materialist origin of the universe. This would be an unreasonable extrapolation, even if the number of researchers who hold it is not negligible (in particular since the first biographer and disciple of Darwin, Thomas Huxley)."

4. Translations such as the *TOB* give "male and female he created them," and not "man and woman he created them" as we read in earlier editions of the Jerusalem Bible. The translation indicates, at least as far as the Jewish world is concerned, how things are linked together, though it will then be for the Yahwist Creation narrative (Gen. 2) rather than the first priestly narrative (Gen. 1) to sort out the complications, which it does by the recognition by Adam of Eve as his "Woman" (*ishisha*) (Gen. 2:23).

5. See the much-discussed work of John Paul II, "Man Becomes the Image of God by Communion of Persons," general audience, November 14, 1979 (reprinted from *L'Osservatore Romano*), accessed November 3, 2015, https://www.ewtn.com/library/PAPALDOC/jp2tb9.htm: "The meaning of man's original unity, through masculinity and femininity" (sec. 2). For similar analysis of the passage in Genesis, see François de Muizon, *Homme et femme: L'altérité fondatrice* (Paris: Éditions du Cerf, 2008), chap. 5.

6. See Henri de Lubac, *Corpus Mysticum: The Eucharist and the Church in the Middle Ages,* trans. Gemma Simmonds, Richard Price, and Christopher Stephens (Notre Dame, IN: University of Notre Dame Press, 2007), §30.

7. "Pope John XXIII's Address to Open the Council," October 11, 1962, "The Second Vatican Ecumenical Council," *Papal Encyclicals Online*, accessed December 10, 2015, http:www.papalencyclicals.net/vatican2.htm.

8. Jacques Derrida, *The Animal That Therefore I Am* (address to the 1997 Cérisy Conference), trans. David Wills (New York: Fordham University Press, 2008).

9. Benedict de Spinoza, *The Ethics*, trans. R. H. M. Elwes (1677; Project Gutenberg, 2009), Part IV, Prop. 67, http://www.gutenberg.org/files/3800/3800 -h/3800-h.htm. This proposition of Spinoza's derives not exclusively from reason, as has been wrongly suggested, but rather from the reintegration of humankind in the "empire of nature," which Spinoza understood, accepted, and even desired—without being able to transform this empire. Spinoza's position on the immediacy of life (developed in the present book) does not contradict a Heideggerian position of consciousness of death (taken up in *Le Passeur de Gethsémani* and transformed in *The Metamorphosis of Finitude*). It is simply closer to our origins, in that it reconnects with the human on this side of consciousness and thus also with our anguish over death, going back to the darkness of Chaos, the passions and drives that we experience, without being able to speak about them, or even name them (see §3—the "region of what can no longer be said").

10. Michel Henry quoted in Rolf Kühn, "Vie et animalité," in *Études phénoménologiques* 12, nos. 23/24 (1996): 239. Concerning the auto-affection of human beings in God, which paradoxically leads us back to the original pathos of life itself, see Michel Henry, *I Am the Truth: Toward a Philosophy of Christianity*, trans. Susan Emanuel (Stanford, CA: Stanford University Press, 2003), 106: "According to the strong concept [of self-affection], life asserts itself in a double sense—first, in that it in itself defines the content of its own affection. The 'content' of a joy, for example, is this joy itself. Second, life itself produces the content of its affection, this content that is itself. It does not produce this content as it might an exterior creation. . . . Life engenders it. . . . [It] is life's generation of itself to which the strong concept of self-affection refers. . . . The strong concept of self-affecting pertains to absolute phenomenological life and is suitable only for it—that is to say, to God."

11. Jean-Louis Chrétien, *The Ark of Speech*, trans. Andrew Brown (London: Routledge, 2004), 2: "Much more essential, and worthy of consideration, is the fact that God makes human speech into the *first ark*. The animals have been gathered for human speech and brought together in this speech, which names them."

12. This is an important topic that I return to later (§27). A preliminary discussion can be found in Falque, "Manger la chair: la querelle eucharistique comme querelle sacrificielle," in *Archivio di Filosofia (Il sacrificio)* 26, no. 1 (2008): 154–68.

13. Derrida, *The Animal That Therefore I Am*, 3–4.

14. Ibid., 4.

15. Ibid., 5–6.

16. Thomas Aquinas, *Summa Theologia*, 1, 56,1; René Descartes, *Meditations on First Philosophy*, Meditation II, in *The Philosophical Works of Descartes,* trans. Elizabeth S. Haldane (1911), accessed 3 November 2015, http://selfpace.uconn .edu/class/percep/DescartesMeditations.pdf.

17. On this point, see Falque, *God, the Flesh, and the Other*, trans. W. C. Hackett (Evanston, IL: Northwestern University Press, 2015).

18. Jacob von Uexküll, *A Foray into the Worlds of Animals and Humans: With a Theory of Meaning*, trans. Joseph D. O'Neil (1930; Minneapolis: University of Minnesota Press, 2010), 41–42. Von Uexküll is notable particularly for having brought together phenomenology and the conception of the "lifeworld" (*Lebenswelt*) with the world of the environment (*Umwelt*). He was frequently cited by Husserl and Heidegger, then brought into prominence in Merleau-Ponty's "Le concept de la nature: L'animalité, le corps humain, le passage à la culture," in *Notes de cours: La nature,* (Paris: Éditions du Seuil, 1995) 220–34. See the celebrated example of the tick, which I discuss below (§16).

19. Gabriel Marcel, "L'Être incarné repère central de la réflexion mètaphy-sique," in *Essai de philosophie concrète (Du refus à l'invocation)* (Paris: Gallimard, 1967), 3–31.

20. Blaise Pascal, *Pensées*, trans. A. J. Krailsheimer (London: Penguin, 1966), 242, 61, 60.

21. Tertullian, *On the Flesh of Christ*, chap. 6, in *Ante-Nicene Fathers*, vol. 3, trans. Peter Holmes, rev. and ed. Kevin Knight (1885; New Advent, 2009), http://www.newadvent.org/fathers/0315.htm.

22. Ibid., chap. 9. See, in connection with this point, my analysis of "On the Flesh of Christ" in Falque, *God, the Flesh, and the Other*, chap. 5.

23. R. B. Onians, *The Origins of European Thought: About the Body, the Mind, the Soul, the World, and Fate* (1951; Cambridge: Cambridge University Press, 2000) 168–69, 171. The distinction between animus and anima is confirmed and commented upon at the same time by Heidegger, in *Qu'appelle-t-on penser?* [What is called thinking?] (Paris: PUF, 1983), 150–51: "*Anima* signifies the fundamental determination of all living beings, including that of man. . . . The Latin word animus can also be translated by our German word *Seele* (soul). Soul does not signify the life-principle, but the presence of the spirit, the spirit of the spirit, the spark of the soul according to Master Eckhart."

24. Marcel Jousse, *La Manducation de la parole* (Paris: Gallimard, 1975), 154–55.

25. See note in *TOB* on Gen. 2:19 (p. 47).

26. Irenaeus, *Against Heresies* 5.8.2, in *Ante-Nicene Fathers*, vol. 1, trans. Alexander Roberts and William Rambaut, rev. and ed. Kevin Knight (1885; New Advent, 2009), http://www.newadvent.org/fathers/0103.htm.

27. Falque, *God, the Flesh, and the Other*.

28. Apart from the numerous films that have recently shown this, and made it directly accessible (in particular, the remarkable 2003 documentary by Jacques Malaterre and Yves Coppens, *L'Odyssée de l'Espèce*), we find an excellent graphic

illustration of the original parentage of human and animal in Jean-Christophe Camus, Michel Duffranne, and Damir Zitko, *La Bible: L'Ancien Testament, La Genèse 1re partie* (Tournai: Delacourt, 2008). See the image of Adam "crouching in the steppe," like an animal, at the time of his face-to-face confrontation with animality (here, the lion) and then with humanity (Eve) (p. 7).

29. Aristotle, *On the Parts of Animals* 1.5, trans. William Ogle (London: Kegan Paul, Trench & Co., 1882).

30. Ibid. "Latrines" is probably more appropriate than "kitchens" for the story as reported by Aristotle. "Posterity has in fact often attributed to Heraclitus the affirmation that the gods are not simply in super-celestial places, or in consecrated places on earth, but that they gratify the entire world with their presence, as far as, and including, the most ordinary kitchens, by the side of the fire. If the meaning of the anecdote is really that divine perfection is everywhere, tradition has tended to shift the Heraclitus of the toilet, where Aristotle puts him, into the kitchen, where it was without doubt more elegant to hear him speak of the divine." Jean-François Pradeau, *Héraclite, Fragments* (Paris: Garnier-Flammarion, 2004), 324n148.

31. Martin Heidegger, "Letter on 'Humanism,'" trans. Frank A. Capuzzi, in *Pathmarks*, ed. William McNeil (London: Cambridge University Press, 1998), 270–71.

32. Ibid., 252.

33. Aristotle, *On the Parts of Animals* 1.5.

34. Aristotle, *On the Parts of Animals* 1.5.

35. Irenaeus, *Against Heresies* 5.33.4.

36. See, in particular, *Dictionnaire d'éthique chrétienne* (Paris: Éditions du Cerf, forthcoming), s.v. "animalité-humanité." As for anthologies, see the very instructive work of Hélène Bastaire and Jean Bastaire, *Le Chant des créatures: Les chrétiens et l'univers d'Irénée à Claudel* (Paris: Éditions du Cerf, 1996); and Henri de Lubac, *Catholicism: Christ and the Common Destiny of Man*, trans. L. Sheppard and E. Englund (San Francisco: Ignatius, 1988), esp. chap. 4 ("Eternal Life"), in which the Irenaean perspective of "recapitulation" serves as a spearhead against "communion with the mystical body."

37. Johannes Scotus Eriugena, *De la division de la nature: Periphyseon* 5.913b–d (Paris: PUF, 2009).

38. Élisabeth de Fontenay, *Le Silence des bêtes: La philosophie à l'épreuve de l'animalité* (Paris: Fayard, 1998), 250; my emphases. This is an instructive work, despite the fact that it attacks Christianity, which is only too easy a target to accuse of all·evils (see pp. 241–50).

39. Ibid., 247–48.

40. Bastaire and Bastaire, *Le Chant des créatures*, 10.

41. Friedrich Nietzsche, *La Naissance de la tragédie; suivi de Fragments posthumes (Automne 1869–Printemps 1872)* (Paris: Gallimard, 1981), 213.

42. Diogenes Laërtius, "The Lives and Opinions of Eminent Philosophers," 6.6, trans. C. D. Yonge (1895), *Ancient History Sourcebook*, Fordham University,

2000, https://legacy.fordham.edu/halsall/ancient/diogeneslaertius-book6-cynics .asp#Diogenes.

43. Diogenes Laërtius, "Pythagoras," in *Lives of the Eminent Philosophers*, trans. Robert Drew Hicks (Adelaide, Australia: University of Adelaide/eBooks// ebooks.adelaide.edu.au/d/diogenes_laertius/lives_of_the_eminent_philosophers/ complete.html.

44. Plato, *Republic* 10, trans. Benjamin Jowett (1894), *Internet Classics Archive*, accessed December 10, 2015, http://classics.mit.edu/Plato/republic.html.

45. Aristotle, *Politics* 1.2, trans. Benjamin Jowett (1885), *Internet Classics Archive*, accessed December 10, 2015, http://classics.mit.edu/Aristotle/politics .html.

46. Aristotle, *Politics* 1.2; my emphasis.

47. Aristotle, *Politics* 1.2.

48. Aristotle, *Politics* 1.2.

49. Aristotle, *Politics* 1.2.

50. Aristotle, *Eudemian Ethics* 7.12.

51. Terence, *Heauton Timorumenos* [The self-tormentor] 1.1.25.

52. Jacques Derrida, *Voice and Phenomenon: Introduction to the Problem of the Sign in Husserl's Phenomenology*, trans. Leonard Lawlor (Evanston, IL: Northwestern University Press, 2011), 66. This analysis by Derrida awaits an echo, in the context of his "description of the voice," in exegesis and theology.

53. Aristotle, *On the Soul* 2.8, trans. J. A. Smith (Adelaide, Australia: University of Adelaide/Books//ebooks.adelaide.edu.au/a/aristotle/a8so.

54. Aristotle, *Politics* 1.2.

55. Aristotle, *On the Soul* 3.12.

56. Bonaventure, *Breviloquium*, vol. 9 of *Works of St. Bonaventure*, trans. and ed. Dominic V. Monti (New York: Franciscan Institute, 2005), 194.

57. Cicero, *On the Nature of the Gods*, trans. Francis Brooks (London: Methuen, 1896), 63.

58. St. Augustine, *On Genesis*, trans. with notes by Edmund Hill, ed. John E. Rotelle (New York: New City Press, 2002), 57, 56.

59. René Descartes, *Discourse on Method*, trans. E. S. Haldane and G. R. T. Ross (Mineola, NY: Dover, 2003), part 5, 39.

60. Nicolas Malebranche, *De la recherche de la vérité*, in *Œuvres de Malebranche*, vol. 1 (Paris: Gallimard, 1979), Book IV, chap. 9, 467.

61. Nicolas Malebranche, *Entretiens sur la mort*, vol. 2 (Paris: Vrin, 1948), 214.

62. Arthur Schopenhauer, *The World as Will and Idea*, vol. 2, trans. R. B. Haldane and J. Kemp (1909; Project Gutenberg, 2012), supplement to Book I, chap. xvii, 359, http://www.gutenberg.org/files/40097/40097-pdf.pdf; emphasis in original.

63. Ibid., 360, 372; emphasis in original.

64. Ibid., 373.

65. Arthur Schopenhauer, *The World as Will and Idea*, vol. 1, trans. R. B. Haldane and J. Kemp (1909; Project Gutenberg, 2011), 402, http://www.guten berg.org/files/38427/38427-h/38427-h.html.

66. Michel Henry, in Kühn, "Vie et animalité," 239–43.

67. Jean-Jacques Rousseau, *Reveries of the Solitary Walker*, trans. Russell Goulbourne (Oxford: Oxford University Press, 2011), 54. For a commentary that accords with my perspective, see Jean-Luc Guichet, *Rousseau, l'animal et l'homme: L'animalité dans l'horizon anthropologique des Lumières* (Paris: Éditions du Cerf, 2006), 113–246. "What man calls animal takes on then immediately a sense in *relation to himself.* . . . The animal, a problem for thought and the human subject, questions *in return* both thought and subject, and does that even more so because the *exterior form of the animal* brings up again for human interiority the question as to whether *animality* is or is not inscribed in man" (p. 14; my emphasis).

68. Heidegger, "Letter on 'Humanism,'" 246–47, 266.

69. Didier Franck, "L'être et le vivant," in *Dramatique des phénomènes* (Paris: PUF, 2001), 55; my emphases. I shall not develop here what has led to a major debate in the history of philosophy; I would simply point out that the problematic of "the Heideggerian neglect of animality as such" (even though it was often addressed by him, but always starting solely from the *Dasein* of humanity), as well as the topic of the "anthropomorphization of the animal as counterpoint to the animalization of man," has been opened up and discussed at length by Françoise Dastur in "Pour une zoologie privative ou comment ne pas parler de l'animal?" *Alter*, no. 3 (1995): 281–317.

70. Von Uexküll, *Worlds of Animals and Humans*, 44–45.

71. There is a certain fascination in such films (whether they be Walt Disney productions, *Microcosmos*, or *March of the Penguins*) that at the very least makes us aware that nothing can be foreign to the act of philosophizing. Above all, they may remind us that even philosophers share a childhood with the rest of humanity—and for them to forget it would be a mistake.

72. Franz Kafka, *The Metamorphosis and Other Stories*, trans. Stanley Corngold (New York: Bantam Dell, 2004), 3–5. See also the famous commentary in Gilles Deleuze and Félix Guattari, *Kafka: Pour une littérature mineure* (Paris: Éditions de Minuit, 1975).

73. Edmund Husserl, "Le monde et nous: Le monde environnant des hommes et des bêtes" (unpublished sketch, 1934), *Alter*, no. 3 (1995), 189–203; my emphases.

74. Rainer Maria Rilke, *Duino Elegies*, trans. Stephen Cohn (Evanston, IL: Northwestern University Press, 1989). If the "open" refers here to the eyes or the vision of the animal, Heidegger in his lectures on Parmenides will deny in a radical way the possibility of such an openness for the animal, accusing Rilke, along with Nietzsche, of neglecting the Being which is at the root of the biologism of the nineteenth century and of psychoanalysis (Heidegger, *Nietzsche*, vol. 2). It remains true that the basis of the human metaphysic here is such; for my

part, I am claiming that we learn nothing here of the animal or of animality itself—as Rilke and Nietzsche tried to do. The "Letter on 'Humanism'" cannot really pass over the biological and the animal as easily as it does, in a denial that is above all the denial of the most classical metaphysic. See, on this point, the transformation in Heidegger of the concept of the "open" (starting from his rejection of Rilke's Eighth Elegy) in Giorgio Agamben, *L'Ouvert: De l'homme et de l'animal* (Paris: Bibliothèque Rivages, 2002), 86–95; and, on the "Letter on 'Humanism'" as neglect and denial not simply of "the animal" but also "of the living in general," Alain Seguy-Duclot, "Humanisme et animalité," in *Heidegger et la question de l'humanisme*, ed. Bruno Pinchard (Paris: PUF, 2005), 329–46.

75. *Seneca*, Selected Philosophical Letters, trans. Brad Inwood (Oxford: Oxford University Press, 2007), Letter 121. A rehabilitation of Rilke or Scheler as opposed to Heidegger has been suggested by Jean Greisch, in *Qui sommes-nous? Chemins phénoménologiques vers l'homme* (Louvain: Peeters, 2009), 66: "The animal impoverished in its world, in a way envies humans their openness to the world. But could we not also envisage the *opposite hypothesis*, closer to the anthropology of Scheler, asking whether man does not feel a certain *jealousy toward animals*, who lead a life less troublesome and anxious than him?" (my emphases).

76. The origin of this concept (of *oikeiôsis* and *homologia*) can be found in the Stoic, Chrysippus of Soli, and carried on by the Epicurean, Lucretius, and the Jewish Neo-Platonic, Philo of Alexandria. See Jean Daniélou, *Philon d'Alexandrie* (Paris: Arthème Fayard, 1958), 74 (where one can also find many anecdotes and further discussion of the characteristic intelligence of animals).

77. Heidegger, "Letter on 'Humanism,'" 155–56.

78. Schopenhauer, *The World as Will and Idea*, vol. 2, 361.

79. Heidegger, "Letter on 'Humanism,'" 257.

80. Rousseau, *Reveries*, 54. See Edmund Husserl, *The Crisis of the European Sciences and Transcendental Phenomenology*, trans. David Carr (1954; Evanston IL: Northwestern University Press, 1970), §72.

81. See Edmund Husserl, *Recherches phénoménologiques pour la constitution (Livre second)* (Paris: PUF, 1982), 137–241 ("La constitution de la nature animale"; and Bruce Bégout, "Pulsion et intention: Husserl et l'intentionalité pulsionnelle," in *La pulsion*, ed. Jean-Christophe Goddard (Paris: Vrin, 2006), 138–82. See also the analysis of the intentionality of the drive in Husserl's *De la synthèse passive* (Grenoble: Jérôme Millon, 1998), 225s.

82. See preface to "L'Animal," *Alter*, no. 3 (1995), 25: "If the animal allows us to deepen our notion of phenomenological life through an investigation centered on the transcendental drive, it would seem that the way to the world of *life* is most appropriate for us to grasp the phenomenological concreteness of the *animal* (*Tier*). The meaning of *animal* (*Tier*) would then be related genetically to *drive* (*Trieb*)."

83. Edith Stein, "Le mystère de Noël" (lecture, January 1931), in *La Crèche et la Croix* (Geneva: Ad Solem, 2007), 21–23; my emphases.

5. Return to the Organic

1. See Martin Heidegger, *Nietzsche*, vol. 1, trans. David Farrell Krell (San Francisco: HarperCollins, 1991).

2. Barbara Stiegler, *Nietzsche et la critique de la chair* (Paris: PUF, 2005), 31–32. See also Barbara Stiegler, *Nietzsche et la biologie* (Paris: PUF, 2001). For a complete analysis of *Leib*, see Natalie Depraz, "*Leib*," in *Le Vocabulaire européen des philosophies*, ed. Barbara Cassin (Paris: Éditions du Seuil, 2004), 705–10. See also Natalie Depraz, *Transcendance et incarnation: Le statut de l'intersubjectivité comme altérité à soi chez Husserl* (Paris: Vrin, 1995) 344–45.

3. See, for example, Isaiah 40:6–8: "All people are grass, their constancy is like the flower of the field. The grass withers, the flower fades, when the breath of the Lord blows upon it; surely the people are grass. The grass withers, the flower fades; but the word of our God will stand for ever."

4. Martin Heidegger, *Being and Time*, trans. John Macquarrie and Edward Robinson (New York: HarperCollins, 2008), §50, 294.

5. Paul-Louis Landsberg, *Essai sur l'expérience de la mort* (1942) (Paris: Éditions du Seuil, 1951) 49. A lively critique of the "authentic" Heideggerian *Dasein*, and of "death as an immanent phenomenon in life." The book was written and published at the height of the Second World War, when the tragic element in life would find its sense not as the horizon of a possible metaphysical nothingness, but in the necessity of a personal ethic.

6. Françoise Laurent, "L'homme est-il supérieur à la bête? Le doute de Qohéleth (Qo 3, 16–21)," *Recherches de sciences religieuses* 92, no. 1 (2003): 11–43.

7. Marie-Dominique Chenu, *Théologie de la matière* (Paris: Éditions du Cerf, 1967), 13.

8. See Olivia Gazalé, "Le corps était presque parfait," *Philosophie*, no. 3 (August–September 2006): 22–27: "The contemporary cult of the body is accompanied by a *phobia in relation to the corporal*, by a *hatred of the organic body*. . . . In its essence, the life of the body is *imperfect*, odorous, sweaty, fleshy, diverse, transitory. It seethes and caws as though at a market. It is a *rebel against norms*, restive under norms" (my emphasis).

9. Benedict de Spinoza, *The Ethics*, trans. R. H. M. Elwes (1677; Project Gutenberg, 2009), Part III, Prop. VI, http://www.gutenberg.org/files/3800/3800-h/3800-h.htm.

10. Ibid., Part III, definition III; my emphasis.

11. Ibid., Part III, Prop. II: Note.

12. Ibid., Part III, Prop. LVIII; my emphasis. On this theory, and this change in relation to the emotions, see Gilles Deleuze, "Affections, Affects," in *Spinoza: Practical Philosophy*, trans. Robert Hurley (San Francisco: City Lights, 1988), 48–51. See also the very instructive analysis in Alain (Émile Chartier), *Spinoza* (1946; Paris: Gallimard, 1986), 62–76.

13. This tying together of the two philosophers is definitively theorized by Pierre Zaoui (corroborating Deleuze) in "La 'grande identité' Nietzsche-Spinoza, quelle identité?" *Philosophie*, no. 47 (September 1995), 64–84. The anticipation

of Nietzsche's ideas by Spinoza was suggested by Deleuze: "Spinoza saw, before Nietzsche, that a force is inseparable from a capacity for being affected and that this capacity expresses its power." Gilles Deleuze, *Nietzsche and Philosophy*, trans. Hugh Tomlinson (1962; London: Continuum, 1986), 206.

14. Benedict XVI, *Sacramentum Caritatis* [The sacrament of charity], post-synodal apostolic exhortation, February 22, 2007, sec. 11, *The Holy See*, http://w2.vatican.va/content/benedict-xvi/en/apost_exhortations/documents/hf_ben-xvi_exh_20070222_sacramentum-caritatis.html. We need to recover this perspective on the "Mass on the world" (Teilhard de Chardin), with the merit of its hyperextension to a universalized world, but also the limit of its dissolution in neutrality (§28).

15. Spinoza, *The Ethics*, Part III, Prop. II: Note; my emphases.

16. Ibid.

17. Friedrich Nietzsche, *La Volonté de puissance*, vol. 1 (Paris: Gallimard, 1942), §226.

18. Ibid., §227, §254.

19. Martin Heidegger, *Nietzsche*, vols. 3 and 4, trans. David Farrell Krell (San Francisco: HarperCollins, 1991), 424.

20. "That Nietzsche posits the body in the place of the soul and conscious-ness alters nothing in the fundamental metaphysical position that is determined by Descartes." Heidegger, *Nietzsche*, 3:133. See also the critique by Barbara Stiegler, in whose eyes "the power of the organic" has no other purpose in Nietzsche than to get rid of the couple of mind-body: "Putting the body in the place of the mind; what does that change?" Barbara Stiegler, "Mettre le corps à la place de l'âme, qu'est-ce que cela change? Nietzsche entre Descartes, Kant et la biologie," *Philosophie*, no. 92 (June 2004): 77–94.

21. On the possible divergences between the Freudian psychic unconscious and the Nietzschean organic unconscious, see Paul-Laurent Assoun, *Freud et Nietzsche* (Paris: PUF, 1980), 203–20. "The reality of the economy of the uncon-scious simply expresses the original principal of the Freudian economy. It is above all its most *privative* characteristic (the total absence of obstacles and planning) that serves to characterise the unconscious. We are at the opposite pole to the *Nietzschean valorization* of the unconscious as the direct language of the *instincts*. . . . For Nietzsche the unconscious is not properly speaking a psychological con-cept, because representation is what characterises the conscious and indicates in such a way its limits. The Nietzschean organic unconscious is rather so rich that it *transcends any possibility of representation*: it is none other than the shade of the thing in itself, *instinct* and the *will to power*. For Freud on the contrary, the unconscious masks a *certain organized representation* (primary process). Drives can perfectly well be the names of the thing in itself: the unconscious, which is language, marks out a *representative sphere*, accessible to *psychological and clinical investigation*" (p. 216; my emphases).

22. Nietzsche, *La Volonté de puissance*, §230, §239.

23. Henri Bergson, *Creative Evolution*, trans. Arthur Mitchell (1911; Project Gutenberg, 2008), 142, http://www.gutenberg.org/ebooks/26163. "Intelligence and instinct, which diverge more and more as they develop. But which never entirely separate from each other. . . . Intelligence has even more need of instinct than instinct has of intelligence."

24. Tertullian, *On the Flesh of Christ*, chap. 9, in *Ante-Nicene Fathers*, vol. 3, trans. Peter Holmes, rev. and ed. Kevin Knight (1885; New Advent, 2009), http://www.newadvent.org/fathers/0315.htm.

25. Nietzsche, *La Volonté de puissance*, §252.

26. Deleuze, *Nietzsche and Philosophy*, 181. Deleuze's comment is the basis for a strong critique of Christianity seen as "negation of force" and of becoming.

27. See the *Liturgie de Pâques et du Temps Pascal*, vol. 1, text by Jean-Philippe Revel and Daniel Bourgeois, music by André Gouzes (Paris: Éditions musicales Studio SM, 2013).

28. Friedrich Nietzsche, *On the Genealogy of Morals*, trans. Walter Kaufmann (New York: Vintage, 1969), essay 2, sec. 12, 78–79; emphases in original. A necessary passage from the organic to the will to power that takes root and overflows it through and through is shown in Barbara Stiegler, *Nietzsche et la biologie*, 44–85.

29. See Falque, *The Metamorphosis of Finitude* (New York: Fordham University Press, 2012), §18.

30. Priest's second preparatory prayer before Holy Communion, in Michael S. Driscoll and J. Michael Joncas, *The Order of Mass: A Roman Missal Study Edition and Workbook* (Chicago: Liturgy Training), 160; my emphasis.

31. Friedrich Nietzsche, *Thus Spoke Zarathustra*, trans. Graham Parkes (Oxford: Oxford University Press, 2005), Prologue, §5; my emphasis. On the necessary difference between the "Zarathustra of Nietzsche" and the "power of the believer in the act of communion," see in particular François Mauriac, *Le Jeudi-Saint* (Paris: Flammarion, 1931): "Nietzsche's basic mistake is not to have seen that supreme love needs supreme audacity to get to work, and that this man who comes toward the small consecrated wafer, his hands joined, throws his all into it, sustains, sometimes heroically, the vision of his entire life as if in agony, surmounts this horror, looks to the future, throws himself into an infinite adventure. That passionate life that Nietzsche places so much value upon, the 'purple life,' is something that the faithful Christian tastes, at such a time, infinitely better than all the Borgias or all the weak enslaved brutes that Zarathustra offers us in his derisory examples" (p. 97).

32. Antonin Artaud, "Manifesto in Clear Language" (1925), in *Selected Writings*, ed. Susan Sontag (Berkeley: University of California Press, 1976), 108.

33. See Antonin Artaud, *Œuvres* (Paris: Gallimard, 2004), 168–69. In Susan Sontag's translation of the *Selected Writings* we find the famous "Nerve Meter": "I have already told you: no work, no language, no words, no mind, nothing. Nothing but a fine Nerve Meter. A kind of incomprehensible stopping place in the mind, right in the middle of everything" (p. 86).

34. Barbara Stiegler, *Nietzsche et la biologie*. Specifically, Stiegler uses the neologism "corporéisation" precisely to distinguish incarnation (*Verleiblichung*) from incorporation (*Verkörperung*): "In order to express in a single word this mutation of the *thinking subject* and the *living body* (a *Leib* in Nietzsche that he takes from biology [Rudolf Virchow]), we have recourse, in what follows in the text, to the inelegant neologism 'corporéisation'" (p. 21n4; my emphases).

35. Barbara Stiegler, "Mettre le corps à la place de l'âme," 78.

36. Antonin Artaud, *Artaud Anthology*, trans. and ed. Jack Hirschman (San Francisco: City Lights, 1965), 44.

37. Gilles Deleuze, *A Thousand Plateaus*, trans. Brian Massumi (London: Athlone, 1988), 150.

38. Ibid., 149–66.

39. Gilles Deleuze, *Francis Bacon: The Logic of Sensation*, trans. Daniel W. Smith (1981; London: Continuum, 2005), 44. For a precise and careful commentary, see Anne Sauvagnargues, "Corps sans organes," in, *Dictionnaire du corps*, ed. Maria Michela Marzano (Paris: PUF, 2007) 254–57.

40. Artaud, "The Nerve Meter," in *Selected Writings*, 84.

41. Emmanuel Levinas, *Totality and Infinity: An Essay on Exteriority*, trans. Alphonso Lingis (The Hague: Martin Nijhoff, 1979), 256.

42. Gustave Courbet, *Origin of the World*, 1866, oil on canvas, Musée d'Orsay, Paris.

43. Lucian Freud, *Naked Girl*, 1966, oil on canvas, private collection; and *Lying by the Rags*, 1989, oil on canvas, Astrup Fearnley Collection, Oslo, Norway.

44. Lucian Freud quoted in Sebastian Smee, *Lucian Freud: L'observation de l'animal* (Paris: Album Taschen, 2008), 7. Freud's painting *Naked Girl* appears on p. 39.

45. Smee, *Lucian Freud*, 7. With Smee's text and illustrations, I cannot recommend this book too highly. "'What interests me truly with people is their animal side,' Freud adds. 'It is in part because of that I like to work starting from their nudity. . . . The animal is not 'closed or impenetrable' to us, as Georges Bataille says in his *Théorie de la religion*. The animal opens in front of me a depth that draws me in and that is familiar to me. In a certain way I know this depth: it is mine. It is also what is farthest from me, what merits the name of depths, that which precisely signifies what is *unfathomable for me*'" (pp. 61–68). See also William Feaver, *Lucian Freud* (London: Tate, 2002); Freud's painting *Lying by the Rags* appears as plate no. 115. As for the distance between Freud and Bacon, see Anne de Marnhac, "La vérité en portrait," *Le Figaro*, November 3, 2005, p. 6; reprinted in Smee, *Lucian Freud*. For a deeper study of Lucian Freud, see Jean Clair, *Éloge du visible* (Paris: Gallimard, 1996), 171–88. "Freud's later paintings can seem a provocation: a woman lying on the wooden floor, a mountain of flesh, of skin, of muscles, of limbs, of breasts and sex organ. She is terrifying and fascinating. Nothing here is redeemed, hidden, disguised. . . . But exactly, words cannot describe what it is that the painting gives to us to look at without com-

mentary, this disconcerting profundity of the skin, the inexhaustible sense of the envelope of which Valéry spoke at one time" (p. 188).

46. Patrick Grainville, "Vous les entendez: peindre ça! Leur stupeur . . . ," in Lydie Arickx, *Les Racines du chaos* (Paris: Servedit, 1998), 68–72. The whole of this photo collection shows magnificently the "open body," as Lucian Freud's work shows the "body in bulk."

47. Alain Bonfand, *Histoire de l'art et phénoménologie* (Paris: Vrin, 2009), 392–93; my emphases. The transition of flesh into body is found also in Cézanne: "The truth of painting as an expression of beauty is shown in the painting of the 'bathers': a truth in relation to the body! Also the truth of the painting itself becomes 'body,' not simply flesh, but organization, sense, rapport with others: painting becomes a material reality implying at the heart of its materiality, a human feeling. . . . Cézanne's paintings have no pretensions to replace reality. But they remind us that the work is a body-to-body." Denis Coutagne, *Cézanne en vérités* (Arles: Actes Sud, 2006), 364–65.

48. This is the sense of Jérôme Alexandre's *L'Art contemporain: Un vis-à-vis essentiel pour la foi,* (Paris: Parole et Silence, 2010), with whose view I am wholly in agreement. Alexandre writes, "Art is the domain of what is felt. . . . What is felt is also the domain of Faith. . . . To be Christian is to profess that *God gave himself up to the domain of feeling* in that he joined so completely the humanity of the human, and in revealing himself as being himself the Life" (p. 97).

49. Ludwig Binswanger, "De la psychothérapie,' in *Introduction à l'analyse existentiale* (Paris: Éditions de Minuit, 1971), 135. The perspective of a "sinking into corporality" in Binswanger or Medard Boss as opposed to Heidegger, is shown convincingly by Caroline Gros-Azorin in "Le phénomène du corps (*Leib*): Une entente participative," *Études philosophiques*, no. 4 (1998): 465–77.

50. Marc-Antoine Charpentier, "O Amor, O Bonitas," first movement of "O Amor," motet for six voices and continuo, H.253, performed by Olivier Vernet Ensemble (In Ore Mel), on *Pour une elevation*, recorded February 18, 2005, Ligia Digital, 202150, compact disc.

51. "No angel ever came down with the intention of being crucified, of obtaining experience of death, of being raised again from death. If there never was this kind of reason for angels *becoming embodied* [*corporandum*], you have the very reason why they took to them flesh without being born [*non nascendo acceperint carnem*]." Tertullian, *De Carne Christi* 6, trans. Ernest Evans (Society for Promoting Christian Knowledge [SPCK], 1956). See also the discussion in Falque, *God, the Flesh, and the Other*, trans. W. C. Hackett (Evanston, IL: Northwestern University Press, 2015).

52. [The usual French translation of Husserl's *leibhaftig* is "in flesh and bone" (rather than "bones"). —Trans.]

53. ["Auto-affection": "The presence of the subject to itself in its own acts of consciousness or feeling." A term used by Derrida to mean "giving oneself a presence or a pleasure," "hearing oneself speak" in the closed circuit of mouth

and ear. Jacques Derrida, *Speech and Phenomena and Other Essays on Husserl's Theory of Signs*, trans. D. B. Allison (Evanston, IL: Northwestern University Press, 1973), 78. —Trans.]

54. See Natalie Depraz, *Lucidité du corps: De l'empirisme transcendantal en phénoménologie* (Dordrecht: Kluwer Academic Publishers, 2001), 2–9.

55. Gustave Martelet, *Résurrection, eucharistie et genèse de l'homme* (Paris: Desclée de Brouwer, 1972), 130. See Chapter 2 for the history of this rupture. The extraordinary courage of Martelet's book is still striking, despite certain slightly dated features, such as the preeminence it accords the culture of the meal or food, and the Teilhard-style overemphasis on universalization and "hominization" rather than identification and filiation in the eucharistic act.

56. Cardinal Humbert quoted in Christian Brouwer, "Les condamnations de Bérenger de Tours (XIe siècle)," in *Le Penseur, la violence, la religion*, ed. Alain Dierkins (Brussels: Éditions de l'Université Libre de Bruxelles, 1996), 10. The text in Latin can be found in Henry Chadwick, "Ego Berengarius: Reply to Lanfranc by Berengarius of Tours," *Journal of Theological Studies* 40 (1989): 410. For a close commentary on the letter by Berengarius that caused this reaction from Cardinal Humbert at the Council of Rome, see Jean de Montclos, *Lanfranc et Bérenger: La controverse eucharistique du XIe siècle* (Leuven: Université Catholique de Louvain, 1971), 163–79.

57. General authorization of "crunching the consecrated host"—indeed, of "chewing" it and not simply swallowing it directly (with or without moistening it)—is after all comparatively recent. The Constitution on the Sacred Liturgy, given by Pope Paul VI in 1963, does not explicitly deal with chewing and crunching, though it does insist that "the rites are to be simplified . . . ; elements which, with the passage of time, came to be duplicated, or were added with but little advantage, are now to be discarded" *Sacrosanctum Concilium*, December 4, 1963, sec. 50, *The Holy See*, accessed November 5, 2015, http://www.vatican.va/archive/hist _councils/ii_vatican_council/documents/vat-ii_const_19631204_sacrosanctum -concilium_en.html.

58. On this question of the "manducation of the consecrated host," of which a certain trace remains in Christian practice, we can refer to older catechisms that now seem dated, to say the least, but whose prose is nonetheless eloquent. See, for example, *Catéchisme de Rome ou Abrégé de la doctrine chrétienne prescrit par Sa Sainteté le pape Pie X* (Paris: Lethielleux, 1906), 211–12 ("On how to communicate"): "*When should I swallow the consecrated Host?* —We should make every effort to swallow the sacred Host as soon as possible, and avoid chewing it lengthily. *If the Host becomes stuck on my palate, what should I do?* If the Host becomes stuck on the palate you should use your tongue to detach it, and never use your finger." See also the earlier theological justification in Abbé Ambroise Guillois, *Explication historique, dogmatique, morale, liturgique et canonique du Catéchisme*, vol. 3, 7th ed. (Le Mans: Julien Lanier, 1853), 173: "If one tries to swallow the consecrated Host as soon as the priest has placed it on the tongue,

before allowing it to moisten a little, it can become attached to the palate and could cause a problem for the communicant. It could even happen that it becomes difficult to digest in the stomach. One must also avoid chewing the Host; this is a question of appropriate respect for the body of our Saviour: the faithful should moreover show that they know how to distinguish this heavenly food that they receive from the altar from ordinary common fare." These formulae may make us smile today, but they do recall how the question of "that" which is to be eaten can no longer be avoided, even among the faithful.

59. See on this point Catherine Pickstock, *Thomas d'Aquin et la quête eucharistique* (Geneva: Ad Solem, 1999). This contains a close and careful reading of the treatise on the eucharist in the *Summa Theologica* (3.73–83), but with an unusual opening condemnation of postmodern thinking: "But first of all, since the eucharist implies sign and language, it will be necessary to take into account the critique that postmodern philosophers have developed in opposition to the possibility of a true theological discourse. We can't do this without using the *subtle jargon forged by the nihilists of postmodernity.* But this will only serve to underline how such *new sophistry* is a dead letter when faced with the simplicity of the words that actually institute the eucharist" (p. 26; my emphases).

60. Heidegger quoted in Didier Franck, *Flesh and Body: On the Phenomenology of Husserl*, trans. Joseph Rivera and Scott Davidson (London: Bloomsbury, 2014), 20.

61. Franck, *Flesh and Body*, 20.

62. Ibid.

63. Ibid., 20–21; my emphasis.

64. Jean-Marie Vianney, the Curé of Ars ("Je L'avise et Il m'avise"), reproduced in the *Catechism of the Catholic Church* (Vatican City: Libreria Editrice Vaticana, 2003), 2715, http://www.vatican.va/archive/ENG0015/_INDEX.HTM; my emphasis. We also find, in a more directly phenomenological perspective, a bringing together of the "real presence" and the "donation in flesh and bone" (*Leibhaftigkeit*) in Natalie Depraz, *Le Corps glorieux: Phénoménologie pratique de la philocalie des pères du désert et des pères de l'Église* (Leuven: Peeters, 2008), 176: "Christ himself presents his body, gives himself in flesh and blood, or offers himself *in person* (*Leibhaftig*). There is an identity that is not a dual identity in the eucharistic food of the Church with the body and blood of Christ. And such an identity is fundamentally less substantial than truly experiential: it must in fact be experienced in an equal fashion by each one."

65. Jean-Luc Marion, *Dieu sans l'être* (Paris: PUF, 1982), 241.

66. Ibid., 250.

67. Martin Heidegger, *History of the Concept of Time: Prolegomena*, trans. Theodor Kisiel (Bloomington: Indiana University Press, 1985), 41.

68. Paul VI, *Mysterium Fidei*, encyclical on the Holy Eucharist, September 3, 1965, §39, *The Holy See*, http://w2.vatican.va/content/paul-vi/en/encyclicals/documents/hf_p-vi_enc_03091965_mysterium.html.

69. Deleuze, *Francis Bacon*, 57.

70. On this identification, essential as it seems to me, of the "Holy Spirit" with the "Force of God," see Falque, *Metamorphosis*, §18.

71. "Eucharistic Prayer I," accessed October 31, 2015, http://www.liturgy office.org.uk/Missal/Text/EP1-A4.pdf.

72. See Edmund Husserl, *Cartesian Meditations: An Introduction to Phenomenology*, trans. Dorian Cairns (Dordrecht: Kluwer Academic Publishers, 1950), 38.

73. Marcel Jousse, *La Manducation de la parole* (Paris: Gallimard, 1975), 53, 33n1; my emphases.

74. Derrida, *Speech and Phenomena*, 25.

75. See, on this point, Falque, *St. Bonaventure et l'entrée de Dieu en théologie* (Paris: Vrin, 2000), §4, 55–63: "l'empire du *ti esti*." This [English] translation of Exodus as "I am what I shall be" is from the French translation in the *Traduction œcuménique de la Bible* (henceforth, *TOB*), where it is justified because of the unaccomplished (imperfect) verb form found in the Hebrew: *ehye asher ehye* (*hâwâh*: archaic form of the verb "to become"), which indicates here what is unaccomplished or is to be accomplished in the future. "Thus the phrase 'I am what I shall be' affirms 'I am there, with you, in the way that you shall see.'" *TOB*, note to Exod. 3:14 (pp. 138–39). The unaccomplished verb form is not translated as such in the *Septuagint* (*egô eimi o ôn*), nor in the *Vulgate* (*ego sum qui sum*). See Alain de Libera and Émilie zum Brunn, *Celui qui est, interprétations juives et chrétiennes d'Exode 3, 14* (Paris: Éditions du Cerf, 1986).

76. See Louis-Marie Chauvet, "Sacrements," in *Catholicisme: Hier, aujourd'hui, demain*, vol. 13 (Paris: Letouzey et Ané, 1992), 326–61. "The name of the manna is a kind of question (*Mân hou*; What is it?). Its consistency as object has all the inconsistence of an anti-object (it is delicate like frost and melts in the sun). Its dimensions defy measurement, which signifies that it is not possible to transform it into capital, and that it exists on another register from that of computation or value. . . . Manna is thus to be understood in terms of the register of speech" (p. 350).

77. Maurice Merleau-Ponty, *The Visible and the Invisible*, trans. Alphonso Lingis (Evanston, IL: Northwestern University Press, 1968), 214; my emphasis.

78. Bonaventure, *Breviloquium*, vol. 9 of *Works of St. Bonaventure*, trans. and ed. Dominic V. Monti (New York: Franciscan Institute, 2005), 241.

79. Hans-Urs von Balthasar, *The Glory of the Lord: A Theological Aesthetics*, vol. 1, trans. Erasmo Leiva-Merikakis (San Francisco: Ignatius, 1982), 392; my emphases. Despite the many and very sound advances that it has made, symbolic theology drawing on language reaches here a limit that it would be appropriate today to question. See the pioneering work on this subject: Robert Scholtus, "Sacrement, symbole, événement," *Études*, no. 377 (1992): 389–96. See also Falque, *God, the Flesh, and the Other*, §39. As for the sense of linguistic utterances so well taken up and developed in sacramental theology, see J. L. Austin, *How to Do Things with Words* (Cambridge : Harvard University Press, 1962); and

Louis-Marie Chauvet, *Symbole et sacrement: Une relecture sacramentelle de l'existence chrétienne* (Paris: Éditions du Cerf, 1987), 137–42.

80. Jean Ladrière, *L'Articulation du sens: Discours scientifiques et parole de foi* (Paris: Éditions du Cerf, 1984), 98.

81. See Ibid., on how "expressive" language (Evans) takes over from "performative" (St. Augustine): "The language of revelation is not simply enunciative; . . . it is an *auto-implicative* language. God addresses man in an event or an act which he undertakes vis-à-vis man . . . and man (when he speaks to God) undertakes something vis-à-vis God and *expresses his attitude* toward God" (p. 98; my emphases).

82. Husserl, *Cartesian Meditations*, 38.

83. Merleau-Ponty, *The Visible and the Invisible*, 126. There is an implicit reference here to Husserl's *Cartesian Meditations*: "Its beginning is the pure— and, so to speak, still dumb—psychological experience, which now must be made to utter its own sense with no adulteration" (pp. 38–39). A return to dumb experience remains today the true starting point of phenomenology. See Jérôme de Gramont, "Le monde muet et la patrie de la phénoménologie," *Transversalités*, no. 110 (April 2009): 177–95: "The first gesture of phenomenology inherited from Husserl would consist in going back, *before speech and judgement*, to the silent experience which, in the glance and in affect, but for Husserl before any glance (or perception), gives us the most simple presence of the things themselves. To be there, given to the glance, *the things do not have to be spoken*. But there will be nothing tragic as it happens for our speech if we fail to respond to their offer. It doesn't matter if, at the dawn of presence, our words are not there, as long as *presence* is entire." I wish to note here my agreement—and friendship—with this author.

84. Merleau-Ponty, *The Visible and the Invisible*, 129.

85. See Balthasar, *The Glory of the Lord*: In the context of the theological aesthetic, "The sacraments are an essential part of ecclesial aesthetics. Not only does God's invisible grace become visible and graspable in the Christ-form as such, but here, in the sacraments, the Christ-form itself in turn appears before us and impresses its shape upon us in a valid form which is free of all subjective ambiguities" (p. 566). See also Joseph O'Leary, "The eucharist as a work of art," in *Il sacrificio: Actes du colloque Enrico Castelli (Rome, 2008)* ed. Marco M. Olivetti (Rome: Archivio di filosofia, 2009), 154–68: "I propose that if we think of the eucharist *as a work of art*, we can find liberating new perspectives" (p. 169; my emphasis).

86. "Eucharistic Prayer II," accessed November 1, 2015, http://www.liturgy office.org.uk/Missal/Text/EP2-A4.pdf.

87. Benedict XVI, *Sacramentum Caritas*, sec. 27. See also §9 above.

6. Embrace and Differentiation

1. Philip T. Weller, trans. and ed., *The Roman Ritual, Complete Edition* (Chicago: Bruce Publishing, 1964). Further, "This human communion is confirmed,

purified, and completed by communion in Jesus Christ, given through the sacrament of Matrimony. It is deepened by lives of the common faith and by the Eucharist received together." *Catechism of the Catholic Church* (Vatican City: Libreria Editrice Vaticana, 1993), 1644, accessed November 1, 2015, http://www.vatican.va/archive/ENG0015/_INDEX.HTM.

2. Bernard of Clairvaux, "Sermon sur l'excellence du Très-Saint-Sacrement et sur la dignité des prêtres," in *Œuvres complètes*, vol. 6 (Paris: Vivès, 1877), 517.

3. Ignatius, "The Epistle of Ignatius to the Romans" 4, in *Ante-Nicene Fathers*, vol. 1, trans. Alexander Roberts and James Donaldson, rev. and ed. Kevin Knight (1885; New Advent, 2009), http://www.newadvent.org/fathers/0107.htm.

4. Emmanuel Levinas, *Totality and Infinity: An Essay on Exteriority*, trans. Alphonso Lingis (The Hague: Martin Nijhoff, 1979), 34.

5. Augustine, *Confessions* 10.28.39, in *Nicene and Post-Nicene Fathers*, First Series, vol. 1, trans. J. G. Pilkington, rev. and ed. Kevin Knight (1887; New Advent, 2009), http://www.newadvent.org/fathers/110104.htm. See also Jean-Luc Marion, *Au lieu de soi, L'approche de saint Augustine* (Paris: PUF, 2008), 216, 363; and Falque, "Le Haut Lieu de soi: Une disputation théologique et phénoménologique," *Revue de métaphysique et de morale*, no. 3 (July 2009): 363–90, esp. the discussion of *oneri mihi sum* and its relation to Heideggerian "facticity" (pp. 375–79).

6. [The French text here, as shown in the sentence that follows, involves a play on words in the two conversions: the *Cène* (the Last Supper) and the erotic *scène* (scene). —Trans.]

7. I borrow this quotation from Luce Irigaray, *Éthique de la différence sexuelle* (Paris: Éditions de Minuit, 1984), 13. The "omission" has been brought to light particularly by François de Muizon, *Homme et femme: L'altérité fondatrice* (Paris: Éditions de Cerf, 2008), 22–24. This is a pioneering work, important for the wealth of material it covers, and I am happy to rejoin its theme here, particularly in view of the warm and long-lasting friendship I have shared with the author.

8. Emmanuel Levinas, *Time and the Other*, trans. Richard A. Cohen (1947; Pittsburgh: Duquesne University Press, 1987), 87: "Hiding is the way of existing of the feminine, and this fact of hiding is precisely modesty." The thesis was developed earlier, in a fuller way, in Levinas, *Totality and Infinity*.

9. John Paul II, "Original Unity of Man and Woman," general audience, November 7, 1979 (reprinted from *L'Osservatore Romano*), accessed November 1, 2015, https://www.ewtn.com/library/PAPALDOC/jp2tb8.htm: "The Hebrew term *'adam* expresses the collective concept of the human species, that is, man who represents humanity. . . . The contraposition *'is-'issah* underlines the sexual difference" (Note 1).

10. Jean-Paul Sartre, *Being and Nothingness*, trans. Hazel E. Barnes (1943; Abingdon, UK: Routledge, 2003), 405.

11. Immanuel Kant, *Anthropology from a Pragmatic Point of View*, ed. Robert B. Louden (Cambridge: Cambridge University Press, 2006), 70–71.

12. Jean-Pierre Sonnet, "Érotique et mystique dans le Cantiques de cantiques" in *Sermons sur le Cantique de Bernard de Clairvaux*, vol. 3, Sources Chrétiennes no. 452, ed. Henri Rochais, Paul Verdeyen, Jean Leclercq, and Raffaele Fassetta (Paris: Éditions du Cerf, 2000), 381–84.

13. Gabriel Marcel, "La mort et l'espérance," in *Le Mystère de l'être* (1951) (Paris: Association Présence de Gabriel Marcel, 1997), 147–66. "It is not I think from a noumenal point of view that the '*indestructibility* of the loved being' can be affirmed; it is much more that of a *bond* that is not 'that of an object' [text slightly adapted]. The prophetic assurance of which I have spoken above could be formulated more or less exactly as follows: whatever the changes undergone in what I have before my eyes, *you and I—we shall stay together*. Things that happen, and which are by way of accident, cannot make void the promise of eternity included in our love" (p. 155; my emphases). See, by way of commentary, Jean-Pierre Bagot, *Connaissance et amour: Essai sur la philosophie de Gabriel Marcel* (Paris: Beauchesne, 1958), 200–11.

14. Benedict XVI, "Letter to the Bishops of the Catholic Church on the Collaboration of Men and Women in the Church and in the World," July 31, 2004, quoted in De Muizon, *Homme et femme*, 271–75: "What will happen to the man-woman difference and to conjugal love in eternity?"

15. For an analysis of these texts of St. Paul that avoids any hasty misreading, see Anne-Marie Pelletier, *Le Signe de la femme* (Paris: Éditions de Cerf, 2006), 85–98, 169–71.

16. Freud clearly states the difference between the "genital" and "sexuality" to explain the idea of "infantile sexuality." See Sigmund Freud, "Pour introduce le narcissisme" (1914), in *La Vie sexuelle* (Paris: PUF, 1969), 81–105. "Detaching *sexuality* from the *genital organs* has the advantage of allowing us to subsume the sexual activity of children and perverts within the same point of view as that of normal adults." See also Freud, *Three Essays on the Theory of Sexuality*, trans. James Strachey (1905; New York: Basic Books, 2000). The distinction between "sexuality" and "the genital" remains in the program of psychoanalysis, but obviously has a possible fecundity for theology—at least in order to establish a "sexual" difference that is not "genital" in the Kingdom. Perhaps it is in this sense that we should consider the formula of Aquinas: "Now among other organs that belong to the *integrity of the human body* are those which *minister to generation* as well in male as in female. These organs therefore will rise again in both. Nor is this conclusion impaired by the fact that there will be no longer any use of these organs. . . . We conclude that all such organs will be there, even organs of which the function has ceased: these will not be there without a purpose, since they will serve to make up the restored integrity of the natural body." Thomas Aquinas, *Summa Contra Gentiles* 4.88, on Jacques Maritain Center website, accessed November 1, 2015, http://www3.nd.edu/Departments/Maritain/etext/gc4_88 .htm; my emphases.

17. Jean-Luc Marion, *Le Phénomène érotique* (Paris: Grasset, 2003), 286, 219–20.

18. *Code of Canon Law* (Washington, DC: Canon Law Society of America, 1983), accessed November 1, 2015, http://www.vatican.va/archive/ENG1104/_INDEX.HTM. "For a just cause, the Roman Pontiff can dissolve a non-consummated marriage between baptized persons or between a baptized party and a non-baptized party at the request of both parties or of one of them, even if the other party is unwilling" (c. 1142). There is a distinction between the "validity" of the sacrament of marriage depending on "consent" (c. 1157) and indissolubility that depends on consummation: "A marriage that is ratum et consummatum can be dissolved by no human power and by no cause, except death" (c. 1141). The question of the indissolubility of the sacrament of marriage done by *copula carnalis* (physical union) was a matter of debate among the Fathers of the Church as far back as the Middle Ages. For examples of opposing views, see Yves of Chartres or Hugh of St.-Victor, "against" such a connection (the marriage of Mary and Joseph assumed to be without *copula carnalis*), and Gratian or Anselm of Laon, in favor of such a linkage (danger of the marriage of convenience, in particular among aristocratic families). We have to wait for Peter Lombard, the decision of Pope Alexander III (1159–1181), and Canon Law (c. 1142) for a decision firmly in favor of the link between the "ratified marriage" (*matrimonium ratum*) and the "consummated marriage" (*matrimonium consummatum*). This is a canonical formula taken up and translated pastorally by Pope John Paul II, in his General Audience of January 5, 1983: "The coming into being of marriage is distinguished from its consummation, to the extent that without this consummation the marriage is not yet constituted in its full reality. The fact that a marriage is juridically contracted but not consummated (*ratum—non consummatum*) corresponds to the fact that it has not been fully constituted as a marriage." For all this debate (which is, to say the least, instructive as far as the sense of the body and of speech that I discuss in Chapter 6), see the article—a little dated, but extremely well documented—in *Dictionnaire de théologie catholique*, vol. 9 (Paris: Letouzy et Ané, 1927), s.v. "mariage." For a more contemporary perspective, see John Baptist Sequeira, *Tout mariage entre baptisés est-il nécessairement sacramental?* (Paris: Éditions du Cerf, 1985); and Jean Gaudemet, *Le Mariage en Occident* (Paris: Éditions du Cerf, 1987).

19. Gabriel Marcel, *Homo Viator: Introduction to a Metaphysic of Hope*, trans. Emma Craufurd (Chicago: Henry Regnery, 1951), 133. See also Marcel, "La fidélité créatrice," in *Essai de philosophie concrète (Du refus à l'invocation)* (Paris: Gallimard, 1967), 220–59, esp. the distinction between constancy and fidelity (pp. 235–53).

20. Independently of any religious expression, and from the point of view of simple humanity, there is a confirmation of this simple unwillingness to confound the "word based upon vows" with the "liberty of making erotic" as a "form of automatism" in Claude Romano, "Love in Its Concept: Jean-Luc Marion's *The Erotic Phenomenon*," in *Counter-Experiences: Reading Jean-Luc Marion*, ed. Kevin Hart (Notre Dame, IN: Notre Dame University Press, 2007), 319–35. "The

notion of *automatism* in particular *may appear excessive*: the spontaneity of desire is not its automaticity; we do not react to the flesh of one another *like one of Pavlov's dogs* reacting to a conditioned reflex; we allow ourselves to be bewitched, we give in to a tropism which is different" (332; my emphases).

21. Aquinas, *Contra Gentiles* 4.88.13. See also Denis Moreau, *Les Voies du salu, Un essai philosophique* (Paris: Bayard, 2010): "Thomas does not affirm that the blessed will not know joy [sexual pleasure], but that they will enjoy it more and better than us. One could thus set out a history *of salvation* emphasizing the different types of pleasure of the human being in his different states" (48). Such a "history of salvation," in part, and in a very personal fashion, can also be found in this work of Moreau's. Our research has much in common (if certainly from a different perspective), and I acknowledge both the courage Denis Moreau shows in his work and our friendship.

22. Thomas Aquinas, *Summa Theologica* 1.12, co.7, trans. Fathers of the English Dominican Province (1920; New Advent, 2008), accessed November 1, 2015, http://www.newadvent.org/summa/1012.htm.

23. See Falque, "Limite théologique et finitude phénoménologique chez Thomas d'Aquin," in *Revue des Sciences philosophiques et théologiques* 92, no. 3 (2008): 527–56, esp. the "tentation de l'ange" (pp. 551–53) and the *limited phenomenon* as the counterpart here for Marion's *saturated phenomenon* (pp. 553–54). On the "breakup of frontiers," see Falque, *The Metamorphosis of Finitude*, trans. George Hughes (New York: Fordham University Press, 2012), §24.

24. Hans-Urs von Balthasar, *Theo-Drama: Theological Dramatic Theory*, vol. 2, trans. Graham Harrison (San Francisco: Ignatius, 1990), 82.

25. Dietrich Bonhoeffer, *Creation and Fall: Two Biblical Studies*, trans. John C. Fletcher (New York: Simon and Schuster, 1997), 38, 40–41.

26. The Hebrew bible language does not use "male" and "female" (Gen. 1:27, Gen. 5:2) to reduce man and woman to dimensions of animality, or to make the animal into the image of God—on the contrary. We can cite here, in the hermeneutic unity of the same narrative, Genesis 1:27 ("male and female he created them") and Genesis 2:23 ("'this one shall be called Woman, for out of Man this one was taken'"); also, the "femininity" characteristic of mankind develops as Adam and Eve experience their double face-to-face with God and with the animals over their "male-ity" and "female-ity" (neologisms I need to employ here). See Shmuel Trigano, "La différence sexuelle dans la Bible: Une lecture juive subversive," *Ètudes*, no. 391 (July–August 1989): 63–74. "Adam does not find his wife, because he only looks in her for his 'female.' He cannot find her because he has not definitively left behind his animality. Incomplete, alone, he lacks words, cannot call on the *feminine*, which is other than *female-ity*. The female for him is not a partner in dialogue. In fact the woman is in an asymmetric relation with him, a being at *the furthest limit of the power of language*, of nomination-appropriation—*outside reference to the same*" (pp. 69–70).

27. Bonhoeffer, *Creation and Fall*, 39.

28. Irenaeus, *Against Heresies* 3.22.3; 5.1.3, in *Ante-Nicene Fathers*, vol. 1, trans. Alexander Roberts and William Rambaut, rev. and ed. Kevin Knight (1885; New Advent, 2009), http://www.newadvent.org/fathers/0103.htm.

29. Bonhoeffer, *Creation and Fall*, 64.

30. See Hugh of Saint-Victor, *In Ecclesiasten Homeliae* 141d–143a, in *Hugues de Saint-Victor et son école*, trans. and ed. Patrice Sicard (Turnhout, Belgium: Brepols, 1991), 241–43 [translation slightly adapted]. On this point, see Falque, "Le geste et la parole chez Hugues de Saint-Victor," *Actes du colloque de la Société internationale de philosophie médiévale* (Paris: Centre Sèvres, forthcoming).

31. Maurice Merleau-Ponty, *The Prose of the World*, trans. John O'Neill (Evanston, IL: Northwestern University Press, 1981), 134.

32. "The woman said to the serpent, 'We may eat of the fruit of the trees in the garden; but God said, "You shall not eat of the fruit of the tree that is in the middle of the garden, nor shall you touch it, or you shall die"'" (Gen. 3:2–3).

33. For the meaning of this "divine surgery" or "loving *plasmatio*," see Falque, *God, the Flesh, and the Other*, trans. W. C. Hackett (Evanston, IL: Northwestern University Press, 2015).

34. Karl Barth, *Dogmatique* 3.1 (Geneva: Labor et Fides, 1960), §40, 198. See also the comments on Barth in François de Muizon, *Homme et femme: L'altérité fondatrice* (Paris: Éditions du Cerf, 2008), 196–201.

35. [*Haeeceity*: a term from Duns Scotus, indicating the qualities, properties, or characteristics of a thing that make it a particular thing. —Trans.]

36. See Falque, *God, the Flesh, and the Other*, chap. 9.

37. Bonhoeffer, *Creation and Fall*, 66.

38. See Falque, "Limite théologique et finitude phénoménologique."

39. Bonhoeffer, *Creation and Fall*, 66.

40. Alain Badiou, *Saint Paul: La fondation de l'universalisme* (Paris: PUF, 1997), 113; emphasis in original. Badiou describes a "Christian universalism" that starts from Jewish particularism and the man-woman difference. This universalism is clearly seen and exploited by the philosopher, who declares himself explicitly to be "atheist."

41. Ibid., 113.

42. See Falque, *Le Passeur de Gethsémani* (Paris: Éditions du Cerf, 1999), chap. 10.

43. Jérôme Alexandre, "Tertullien et la différence sexuelle," in *Les Péres de l'Église et les femmes: Actes du colloque de La Rochelle (September 6–7, 2003)*, ed. Pascal Delage (La Rochelle: Association Histoire et culture, 2003), 79–99. Alexandre, from a theological view, makes sense of sexual difference based on an accurate reading of the Fathers of the Church. I should like to express my gratitude, and very warm friendship, with the author.

44. Alexandre Kojève, *Introduction to the Reading of Hegel*, trans. James H. Nichols Jr. (Ithaca, NY: Cornell University Press, 1980), 6. Kojève comments on passages from Hegel; for the passages in question, see G. W. F. Hegel, *The Phenomenology of Mind*, trans. J. B. Baillie (New York: Dover, 2003): "Self-consciousness

exists in itself and for itself, in that, and by the fact that it exists for another self-consciousness; that is to say, it *is* only by being acknowledged or 'recognized.' . . . The middle term is self-consciousness which breaks itself up into the extremes, and each extreme is this interchange of its own determinateness, and complete transition into the opposite. . . . They recognize themselves as mutually recognizing one another" (pp. 104, 106).

45. Quoted in Xavier Lacroix, "Connaître au sens biblique," in "Amour et sexualité," special issue, *Christus*, no. 213 (January 1997): 13. Also, an interview in the same issue of *Christus* presents in embryonic form the argument of this present book and some practical consequences of the perspectives envisaged here: "Le couple dans la durée: Épreuves et communion. Dialogue avec un philosophe [Falque], une psychanalyste [Michèle Montrelay], et un évêque [Jacques Perrier]" (pp. 40–52).

46. Fourth Ecumenical Council at Chalcedon, 451 (Ds 301: cf. Heb 4:15). Cited in *Catechism of the Catholic Church*, 467.

47. See, for example, the Order for the Liturgical Celebrations of the Supreme Pontiff: "The priest then allows the particle which he had in his hand, to fall into the chalice, thus mingling the Body and Blood of the Lord, and saying at the same time: *Haec commixtio et consecratio Corporis et Sanguinis Domini nostri Iesu Christi fiat accipientibus nobis in vitam aeternam* [May this mingling of the Body and Blood of our Lord Jesus Christ bring eternal life to us who receive it]. *Amen.*" Order for the Liturgical Celebrations of the Supreme Pontiff, "The Priest in the Communion Rites," *The Holy See*, accessed November 2, 2015, http://www.vatican.va/news_services/liturgy/details/ns_lit_doc_20100316_sac-riti-comunione_en.html.

48. I owe this quotation to Shmuel Trigano, "La différence sexuelle," 73–74: "That is why man shall leave his father and mother, and shall *cleave* unto (*will cling to*) his wife, and they *shall be* one flesh" (Gen. 2:24, Jewish translation; my emphases).

49. Karl Marx, *Economic and Philosophic Manuscripts of 1844*, trans. Martin Milligan (1959; Marxists.org, 2000), 43, https://www.marxists.org/archive/marx/works/download/pdf/Economic-Philosophic-Manuscripts-1844.pdf; emphases in original.

50. Gaston Fessard, *De l'actualité historique*, vol. 1 (Paris: Desclée de Brouwer, 1960), 164. A full account of this celebrated "dialectique homme-femme" is on pp. 163–75. For a closer analysis, see also Edouard Pousset, "Homme," in *Dictionnaire de spiritualité, VII/I*, ed. A Rayez, (Paris: Beauchesne, 1969); and De Muizon, *Homme et femme*, 92–100. For a full account of the thought of Fessard, which contextualizes this dialectic and the subsequent debate, see Frédéric Louzeau, *L'Anthropologie sociale du Père Gaston Fessard*, Part II (Paris: PUF, 2009), 175–341.

51. Immanuel Kant, *Idea for a Universal History from a Cosmopolitan Point of View*, trans. Lewis White Beck (1784; Indiana: Bobbs-Merrill, 1963), fifth thesis.

52. Fessard, *De l'actualité historique*, 164; my emphases.

53. Ibid., 164–65.

54. Ibid., 166; my emphases.

55. [*Perichoresis*: relationship among the persons of the Trinity. —Trans.]

56. See "Basic Texts for the Roman Catholic Eucharist: Eucharistic Prayers I–IV," from the *Roman Missal*, English Translation, 3rd ed. (2011), accessed November 1, 2015, http://catholic-resources.org/ChurchDocs/RM3-EP1–4.htm; and Blessing B of the Sacrament of Marriage.

57. Sartre, *Being and Nothingness*, 411, 412; emphasis in original.

58. "Existential philosophies have not believed it necessary to concern themselves with sexuality. Heidegger, in particular, does not make the slightest allusion to it in his existential analytic with the result that his 'Dasein' appears to us as asexual. . . . Of course one may say that the problem of sexual differentiation has nothing to do with that of *Existence* (*Existenz*) since man and woman equally exist." Sartre, *Being and Nothingness*, 405. As for the reference to Tintin as an image of *Dasein*—an asexual one, unlike Captain Haddock or Brian Castafiore—see Jean-Luc Marion and Alain Bonfand, *Hergé: Tintin le Terrible ou l'Alphabet des richesses* (Paris: Hachette, 1996), 7–28. "Tintin is he for whom everything always goes above all according to his being—he who is in the mode of existence. . . . One understands then the very strange character of Tintin: he has no character; and also his strangest characteristic: he has none" (Preface [Marion]).

59. Sartre, *Being and Nothingness*, 405–6. On gender, see in particular Robert Stoller, *Sex and Gender: On the Development of Masculinity and Femininity* (New York: Science House, 1968); Judith Butler, *Gender Trouble: Feminism and the Subversion of Identity* (New York: Routledge, 1990); and Judith Butler, "Gender," in *Vocabulaire européen des philosophies*, ed. Barbara Cassin (Paris: Éditions du Seuil, 2004).

60. Sartre, *Being and Nothingness*, 409, 407, 408; emphases in original.

61. Ibid., 407.

62. Blaise Pascal, *Letters*, vol. 48, Part II, trans. Mary L. Booth (1909–14; Bartleby.com, 2001), accessed November 2, 2015: http://www.bartleby.com/48/2/11.html. See also Xavier Tilliette, "Pascal: le Dieu le plus caché," in *Philosophies eucharistiques de Descartes à Blondel* (Paris: Éditions du Cerf, 2006), 27–32.

63. Sartre, *Being and Nothingness*, 412 (in a deviation from Levinas, for whom the caress tends toward the "not knowing" of the body of the other, rather than toward "reciprocal incarnation"). See Levinas, *Time and the Other*: "The caress is a mode of the subject's being, where the subject who is in contact with another goes beyond this contact . . . the caress does not know what it seeks. The "'not knowing,'" this fundamental disorder, is the essential" (p. 89).

64. Sartre, *Being and Nothingness*, 412.

65. Ibid.

66. Ibid., 412–13.

67. See Aquinas, *Contra Gentiles* 4.88.2: "Neither is this opposed by the fact that there will be no use for those members, as was shown above. For, if for this reason such members are not to be in the risen, for an equal reason there would be no members which serve nutrition in the risen, because neither will there be use of food after the resurrection. Thus, then, a large portion of the members would be wanting in the body of the risen. They will, therefore, *have all* the members of this sort, even though there be no use for them, to re-establish the integrity of the natural body" (my emphases).

68. Thomas Aquinas, "*Verbum supernum prodiens*," eucharistic hymn for Lauds at Corpus Christi, trans. John Mason Neal and Edward Caswell, in *The New English Hymnal* (Norwich: Canterbury, 1989), 293.

69. Michel Henry, *Incarnation: Une philosophie de la chair* (Paris: Éditions du Seuil, 2000), §29–41, 284–305.

70. Ibid., 290.

71. Ibid., 291.

72. Ibid., 288, 302; my emphases. For a fuller development of the meaning of this "night of the lovers" by Henry, but at the risk of making it a "flesh without body," see Falque, "Y a-t-il une chair sans corps?" in *Phénoménologie et christianisme chez Michel Henry*, ed. Philippe Capelle (Paris: Éditions du Cerf, 2004), 95–133, and Henry's response (pp. 168–82). See also Eric Rhode, "La promesse de la nuit," in *Dossier H: Michel Henry*, ed. Jean-Marie Brohm and Jean Leclercq, (Paris: L'Âge d'homme, 2009), 233–43.

73. Bernard of Clairvaux, *Traité de l'amour de Dieu* [*De Diligendo Deo*] SC.393 (Paris: Éditions du Cerf, 1991), 131. Taken up and developed in William of Saint-Thierry, *La Contemplation de Dieu* [*De contemplando Deo*], Sources Chrétiennes no. 61.1 (Paris: Éditions du Cerf, 1999), 59. "Consideration, intentions, wishes, thoughts, affections, and all my interior life, come, climb the mountain, *to the place where* the Lord sees and is seen." For St. Bernard in particular, see Falque, "Expérience et empathie chez Bernard de Clairvaux," *Revue des Sciences philosophiques et théologiques*, no. 89 (October–December 2005): 655–96, esp. pp. 678–95.

74. Jean-Jacques Olier, "Mémoires," (1642–1652), in *Le Traité des Saints Ordres*, vol. 4, (Paris: Saint-Sulpice, 1676), 123. This discussion of the dimension of empathy in the eucharistic mystery contains an echo of St. Bernard and also, above all, the figure of the founder of the Order, St. John Eudes. See Eudes, *La Vie et le Royaume de Jésus dans les âmes chrétiennes*, in *Œuvres complètes*, vol. 1 (Paris: P. Lethielleux, 1905), 468: "Unite me then with you, oh divine Jesus, because it pleases you that I offer with you now this very blessed sacrifice. May it be that I offer it also with the blessed disposition with which you offer it."

75. "Through him, and with him, and in him, O God, almighty Father, in the unity of the Holy Spirit, all honor and glory is yours, for ever and ever." See "Basic Texts for the Roman Catholic Eucharist."

76. See Falque, *Gethsémani*, part 3.

77. See Marion, *Le Phénomène érotique*, §28, 224–34, esp. pp. 231–34.

78. Ibid., 231: "These transgressions privilege a marginal, eccentric, even crazy lexicon that says nothing and describes nothing and thus allows the flesh to become excited in speaking."

79. Merleau-Ponty, *The Prose of the World*, 141.

80. "Missal: Ordinary: The Order of the Mass," *iBreviary*, accessed November 3, 2015, http://www.ibreviary.com/m/messale.php?s=ordinario&id=22.

81. Paul Claudel, "Hymne du Saint-Sacrement" from *Corona Benignitatis Anni Dei* (1915), included in *Œuvres poétiques* (Paris: Gallimard/La Pléiade, 1967), 402.

Part III. God Incorporate

1. *Le Jeudi-Saint* (Paris: Flammarion, 1931), 17.

2. *Essays of Michel de Montaigne*, ed. William Carew Hazlitt, trans. Charles Cotton (1877; Adelaide, Australia: University of Adelaide/eBooks//ebooks.adelaide.edu.au/m/montaigne/michel/essays /contents.htm l.

3. See Falque, *Le Passeur de Gethsémani* [The guide to Gethsemane] (Paris: Éditions du Cerf, 1999), and *The Metamorphosis of Finitude*, trans. George Hughes (New York: Fordham University Press, 2012).

4. There is a parallel between St Augustine's leitmotif of self-transcendence (elevation of the soul) and transcendence in Husserl's phenomenology. See, for example, the final section of Husserl's *Cartesian Meditations* and St. Augustine's "Do not go outside, return to within yourself; truth dwells in the inner man" (*De vera religione* [On true religion] 39.72), quoted in Benedict XVI, "General Audience," January 30, 2008, *The Holy See*, http://w2.vatican.va/content/benedict-xvi/en/audiences/2008/documents/hf_ben-xvi_aud_20080130.html. Jean-Luc Marion has clearly distinguished two forms of transcendence in the difference between Heidegger and St. Augustine: the first retains nothing but the "burden" that one is to oneself (I am a burden to myself [*oneri mihi sum*]), and the second connects this to the lightness of life with God (but with you my burden is light). See Marion, *Au lieu de soi: L'approche de saint Augustin* (Paris: PUF, 2008), 212–17. See also Falque, "Saint Augustin, le poids de la vie: péché et finitude" (lecture presented at opening of the Institut d'études médiévales, Institut catholique de Paris, June 2010).

5. Maurice Blondel, *Une énigme historique: Le "Vinculum Substantiale" d'après Leibniz et l'ébauche d'un réalisme supérieur*, 2nd ed. (Paris: Éditions Gabriel Beauchesne, 1930), 114–15, accessed November 8, 2015, http://classiques.uqac.ca/classiques/blondel_maurice/vinculum_substantiale/vinculum_substantiale.html. See also Xavier Tilliette, *Philosophies eucharistiques de Descartes à Blondel* (Paris: Éditions du Cerf, 2006), 107–8.

6. See the "Anthologie" of Adrienne von Speyr's work in Hans-Urs von Balthasar, *Adrienne von Speyr, sa vie, sa mission théologique* (Paris: Médiaspaul, 1985), 156; my emphases.

7. For these quotations from St. Augustine and his commentary on them, I am grateful to Jean-Luc Marion's book *In the Self's Place: The Approach of Saint*

Augustine, trans. Jeffrey L. Kosky (Stanford, CA: Stanford University Press, 2012), 266. See also Falque, "Le Haut Lieu du soi: Une disputation théologique et phénoménologique," *Revue de métaphysique et de morale*, no. 3 (July 2009): 362–90.

7. The Passover of Animality

1. Irenaeus, *Against Heresies* 4, preface, in *Ante-Nicene Fathers*, vol. 1, trans. Alexander Roberts and William Rambaut, rev. and ed. Kevin Knight (1885; New Advent, 2009), http://www.newadvent.org/fathers/0103.htm.

2. Augustine, *Enarrationes in Psalmos* 1.33.8, in *Œuvres complètes de Saint Augustin*, vol. 16 (Paris: Vivès, 1871).

3. Maurice Bellet, *La Chose la plus étrange: Manger la chair de Dieu et boire son sang* (Paris: Desclée de Brouwer, 1999). "What is strangest then, in the eucharist (to eat the flesh) is that the believers no longer see the strangeness of what they believe" (p. 14). Bellet's perspective is more exegetical than psychoanalytic, and pastoral rather than philosophical, theological, or metaphysical.

4. John Chrysostom, "Homily 46 on the Gospel of John," in *Ante-Nicene Fathers*, First Series, vol. 14, trans. Charles Marriott, rev. and ed. Kevin Knight (1889; New Advent, 2009), http://www.newadvent.org/fathers/240146.htm.

5. John Chrysostom, "Homilies on the Gospel of Saint Matthew" 83.5, *Documenta Catholica Omnia*, accessed November 4, 2015, http://www.document acatholicaomnia.eu/03d/0345–0407,_Iohannes_Chrysostomus,_Homilies_on _The_Gospel_Of_Matthew,_EN.pdf.

6. On the ban on chewing the Host, the warning not to let it stick to the palate, and the necessity of swallowing it directly (with or without moistening it), see §19 and *Catéchisme de Rome ou Abrégé de la doctrine chrétienne prescrit par Sa Sainteté le pape Pie X* (Paris: Lethielleux, 1906). See also the theological justification in Abbé Ambroise Guillois, *Explication historique, dogmatique, morale, liturgique et canonique du Catéchisme*, vol. 3, 7th ed. (Le Mans: Julien Lanier, 1853), 173.

7. See Thomas Aquinas, *Summa Theologica* 3.75.5, ad. 4, trans. Fathers of the English Dominican Province (1920; New Advent, 2008), http://www .newadvent.org/summa/4075.htm: "Whether the accidents of the bread and wine remain in this sacrament after the change."

8. Ibid. For a discussion of transubstantiation, see Pierre Battifol, *L'Eucharistie: La présence réelle et la transubstantiation* (Paris: Victor Lecoffre, 1913). This book is old—indeed, very old—but it has the merit of retracing the history of the concept and lingering over the thesis of Aquinas.

9. Bonaventure, *Breviloquium*, vol. 9 of *Works of St. Bonaventure*, trans. and ed. Dominic V. Monti (New York: Franciscan Institute, 2005), 242. See also Peter Lombard, *The Sentences—Book 4: On the Doctrine of Signs,* trans. Giulio Silano (Toronto: St. Michael's College Mediaeval Translations, 2010).

10. Bonaventure, *Breviloquium*, 239.

11. [Thomas Aquinas], "*Lauda Sion Salvatorem*" [Praise, O Sion, praise thy savior], in *The Hymns of the Breviary and Missal* (1922), on *Catholic Cornucopia* website, accessed November 4, 2015, http://www.cathcorn.org/hotbam/75.html.

12. The idea of the body of Christ "in the confined space of the consecrated host" was reinforced at the time of the Counter-Reformation. See, for example, Marc-Antoine Charpentier, "O Amor, O Bonitas," first movement of "O Amor," motet for six voices and continuo, H.253, performed by Olivier Vernet Ensemble (In Ore Mel), on *Pour une elevation,* recorded February 18, 2005, Ligia Digital, 202150, compact disc: "Oh love, oh goodness, oh charity! Not only is he born man, he who is God, and he dies, though not a criminal, but he lives amongst us, present in the confined space of the consecrated host so that each of us lives the unfailing memory of so many blessings!"

13. Thomas Hobbes, *Leviathan* (1651; London: Penguin Classics, 1985), 633–34; emphases in original.

14. André Green, "Cannibalisme: réalité ou fantasme agi?" in *Nouvelle Revue de Psychanalyse,* no. 6 (Autumn 1972): pp. 34–35. Jacques Attali also brings up Christianity, in *Cannibalism and Civilization: Life and Death in the History of Medicine* (London: Continuum, 1984). Claude Lévi-Strauss discusses the eucharist among the many possible mythological narratives in *The Raw and the Cooked,* vol. 1 of *Mythologiques,* trans. John Weightman and Doreen Weightman (Harper & Row, 1969). On the revival of interest in "the act of devouring," see artists such as André Masson, Oswald de Andrade, and Lygia Clark.

15. René Girard, *Evolution and Conversion: Dialogues on the Origin of Culture* (London: Continuum, 2007), 217.

16. See Falque, "Manger la chair: la querelle eucharistique comme querelle sacrificielle," in *Archivio di Filosofia (Il sacrificio)* 26, no. 1 (2008): 151–64.

17. Marcel Jousse, *La Manducation de la parole* (Paris: Gallimard, 1975), 262n9.

18. Ibid., 24n1.

19. Ibid., 34n1: "The history—Palestinian history of man is the history of his mouth. It is by the mouth that temporal death enters into mankind. It is by the mouth that eternal life enters into mankind." See also p. 257: "In truth, this young Galilean Rabbi was truly the good shepherd, in the gestural and analogic sense of the Palestinian verbal root: 'He who makes eat,' 'He who teaches mouth-to-mouth.'" We might recall Jesus to Simon Peter: "Feed my sheep" (John 21:17).

20. Ibid., 263.

21. An interpretation recalled in Bellet, *La Chose la plus étrange,* 18. (The book's title suggests that the book concerns "the thing that is most strange," but Bellet risks making the thing not very strange from the start of his book!)

22. Edmond Ortigues, *Le Discours et le Symbole* (1962; Paris: Aubier, 1977), 65.

23. The symbolism of the meal, once a necessary topic, has had its day. Still, traces remain in André Manaranche, *Ceci est mon corps* (Paris: Éditions du Seuil, 1975), 122–40; and Ghislain Lafont, *Eucharistie: Le repas et la parole* (Paris: Éditions du Cerf, 2001), chap. 1.

24. Bonaventure, *Itinerarium Mentis in Deum* [Journey of the mind into God], vol. 2 of *Works of St. Bonaventure*, ed. Philotheus Boehner and Zachary Hayes (New York: Franciscan Institute, 2003) 42.

25. Maurice Blanchot, *The Book to Come*, trans. Charlotte Mandell (Stanford, CA: Stanford University Press, 2003), 87.

26. See the interlinear literal translation—"who *consumes* me"—in the translation of the New Testament by Sister Jeanne d'Arc: *Les Évangiles: Évangile selon Jean* (Paris: Les Belles-Lettres/Desclée de Brouwer, 1990).

27. See the posthumously published text by Charles Péguy, "Note conjointe sur M. Descartes et la philosophie cartésienne" in *Œuvres en prose complètes*, vol. 3, ed. Robert Burac (1914; Paris: Gallimard/La Pléiade, 1992), 1307.

28. François Mauriac, *Le Jeudi-Saint* (Paris: Flammarion, 1931), 99–100, 97. See also Péguy, "Note conjointe sur M. Descartes," 1307–12: "There is something worse than having a wicked [perverse] soul; it is having a tepid soul. It is having an habituated soul (according to a formula that counts also in my opinion and par excellence for the eucharistic communion). . . . One has not seen that which was varnished become soaked, one has not seen that which was impermeable passed through, one has not seen the habituated soul become involved. The moral skin (of these righteous people) is constantly intact."

29. Gilles Deleuze, *Francis Bacon: The Logic of Sensation*, trans. Daniel W. Smith (London: Continuum, 2003), 24.

30. [*Sensualisme* in French; sometimes also translated as "sensationalism." I follow the lead of Etienne Gilson, Thomas Langan, and Armand A. Maurer, *Recent Philosophy: Hegel to the Present* (1966; Eugene OR: Wipf & Stock, 2015), 171: "What the French here call *sensualisme*, an ill-chosen word on account of unfavourable ethical connotations, and which we propose to replace by the ethically neutral designation of '*sensism*.'" —Trans.]

31. These terms are used by F. J. Leenhardt and Edward Schillebeeckx but had already been questioned by Pope Paul VI: "It is not permissible . . . to discuss the mystery of transubstantiation without mentioning . . . the marvelous conversion of the whole substance of the bread into the Body and the whole substance of the wine into the Blood of Christ, as if they involve nothing more than 'transignification,' or 'transfinalization.'" *Mysterium Fidei*, encyclical of Pope Paul VI on the Holy Eucharist, September 3, 1965, §11, *The Holy See*, http://w2.vatican.va/content/paul-vi/en/encyclicals/documents/hf_p-vi_enc_03091965_mysterium.html.

32. Ratramne de Corbie, *Liber de corpore et sanguine*, PL 121, quoted and translated in *L'Eucharistie, le sens du sacrement*, ed. J.-P. Bouhot (Lyon: Profac, Faculté de théologie, 1971), 127. "Your majesty asks if the body and blood of Christ, that which believers receive in their mouths in the church, is present as a mystery or in truth." See also Ratramne de Corbie, *Histoire littéraire et controverses doctrinales* (Paris: Études augustiniennes, 1976), 120–24.

33. Henri de Lubac, *Corpus Mysticum: The Eucharist and the Church in the Middle Ages*, trans. Gemma Simmonds, Richard Price, and Christopher Stephens

(Notre Dame, IN: University of Notre Dame Press, 2007): "In the thinking of the whole of Christian antiquity, the Eucharist and the Chruch are linked. . . . *Spiritual flesh, mystical flesh, mystical body* [*caro spiritualis, caro mystica, corpus mysticum*]: these three expressions formed a chain and, with the passage of time, became practically equivalent" (pp. 13, 123).

34. Ibid., 305.

35. Lanfranc, "De corpore et sanguine Domini," PL 150, 421 D 2–5, in Jean de Montclos, *Lanfranc et Bérenger: La controverse eucharistique du XIème siècle* (Leuven: Université Catholique de Louvain, 1971), 361; my emphases.

36. Ibid., 347.

37. See Berengarius, "Rescriptum contra Lanfranum" 2, in De Montclos, *Lanfranc et Bérenger*, 532. The quarrel is made particularly clear and accessible in two articles: Jean de Montclos, "Lanfranc et Béranger: les origines de la doctrine de la Transubstantiation," in *Lanfranc di Pavia e l'Europa del secolo XI*, ed. Giulio d'Onofrio (Rome: Libraria Editrice Vaticana, 1993), 297–326; and Christian Brouwer, "Les condamnations de Bérenger de Tours (XIe siècle)," in *Le Penseur, la violence, la religion*, ed. Alain Dierkens (Brussels: Éditions de l'Université Libre de Brussels, 1996), 9–23.

38. The Sixth Council of Rome, 1079 (The Oath of Berengarius of Tours), trans. John F. Clarkson in *The Church Teaches: Documents of the Church in English Translation* (Charlotte NC: Tan, 2009), 712. It is common today, particularly in contemporary philosophy, to try to "save Berengarius from Lanfranc"—often by taking, erroneously, the side of the condemned as if in this case he were not open to condemnation. This view goes along with a perspective that is unilaterally logical and semiotic, reducing (quite mistakenly, as I see it) the eucharistic *disputatio* to a simple question of language and not of body. See, for example—and despite their lively analyses—Kurt Flasch, *Introduction à la philosophie médiévale* (Paris: Éditions du Cerf, 1992) 43–56; and Irène Rosier-Catach, *La Parole efficace* (Paris: Éditions de Seuil, 2004), 353–469. For a stronger siding with Berengarius against Lanfranc, from a theological point of view, see (along with the article by Jean de Montclos cited above) Gustave Martelet, *Résurrection, eucharistie et genèse de l'homme* (Paris: Desclée de Brouwer, 1972), 138–49, which contains an excellent discussion of what is at stake, even for us today, in the doctrine. And for a precise commentary on documents concerning the sacrament, see Damarius Van den Eynde, "Les définitions des sacrements pendant la première période de la théologie scolastique (1050–1235)," *Antonianum*, vol. 24 (1949): 186.

39. Berengarius, "Lettre à Adelman de Liège," in De Montclos, *Lanfranc et Béranger*, 132.

40. Lanfranc, *De corpore et sanguine Domini*, 416 C.8–11. I have developed this argument drawing on current research in two brilliant doctoral theses by students at the Institut Catholique de Paris: Philippe Richard, "La vision de Dieu à l'époque carolingienne," and Pascaline Turpin, "La querelle eucharistique à

l'époque carolingienne." I congratulate both authors on their researches and look forward to the submission of their completed theses.

41. Paul Claudel, "Hymne du Saint-Sacrament," in *Œuvres poètiques* (Paris: Gallimard/La Pléiade, 1967), 398. See also Claudel, "La physique de l'eucharistie" (1910), in *Positions et propositions*, vol. 2 (Paris: Gallimard, 1934), and "Le sentiment de présence de Dieu" (1933), in *Le Poète et la Bible*, vol. 1, *1910–1946* (Paris: Gallimard, 1988), 389–421. "It is by the frequent reception of the sacrament in the Holy eucharist that we become *accustomed to God*, that we become familiar with his *way of doing things*, that we learn to recognize his touch, to wait for the sound of His voice, His impulses, His inhibitions. . . . It is the spirit that speaks to spirit, but also *flesh* that *speaks to flesh*, blood that joins blood and develops our circulation. Our flesh has ceased to be an obstacle, it becomes a *means, a vehicle*, it has ceased to be a veil, it becomes an apprehension" ("Le sentiment de présence," p. 391; my emphases).

42. "Eucharistic Prayer IV," *The Roman Missal: English Translation according to the Third Typical Edition* (Chicago: Liturgy Training, 2011), §117, 657.

43. [Hominization is a term used by Pierre Teilhard de Chardin to mean the evolutionary process of becoming human. —Trans.]

44. Pierre Teilhard de Chardin, *Hymn of the Universe* (1961), trans. Simon Bartholomew, on *Religion Online* website, accessed November 5, 2015, http://www.religion-online.org/showbook.asp?title=1621.

45. Hans-Urs von Balthasar, *The Glory of the Lord: A Theological Aesthetics*, vol. 1, trans. Erasmo Leiva-Merikakis (San Francisco: Ignatius, 2009), 355. For an implacable demonstration of the Trinitarian dimension of the eucharistic mystery, from this perspective, see Vincent Holzer, "La christologie trinitaire de l'eucharistie," *La Maison Dieu*, no. 210 (1997), 7–28. "The Holy Spirit is not simply the agent of the *conversio eucharistica*, it shows here its inalienable character. . . . Balthasar affirms that the eucharistic action is more than a sacrament [*mehr ist als nur ein Sakrament*]" (pp. 16–17).

46. *See* Martelet, Résurrection, eucharistie et genèse de l'homme, 26–60. I owe an important debt to this work, though the different aims (philosophical and metaphysical) of this present book lead me in another direction to that of Martelet.

47. François Varillon, *Joie de croire, Joie de vivre* (Paris: Le Centurion, 1981), 286; my emphases.

48. "Ordo Missae of the Missale Romanum 1962," *Sancta Missa*, accessed November 5, 2015, http://www.sanctamissa.org/en/tutorial/ordo-missae-0.html.

8. "This Is My Body"

1. In particular, by way of a vast synthesis and an appropriate examination of the status of the sacraments, see Louis-Marie Chauvet, *Symbole et sacrement: Une relecture sacramentelle de l'existence chrétienne* (Paris: Éditions du Cerf, 1987), 392–418.

2. See discussion of Jean-Luc Nancy's view in Chapter 2, §8.

3. Marcel Jousse, *La Manducation de la parole* (Paris: Gallimard, 1975), 258, 263. The distinction between "presence" and "object" in the context of the eucharist has been developed at length by Jean-Yves Lacoste in *Présence et parousie* (Geneva: Ad Solem, 2006), 78: "What is transubstantiation, if it is not where the visible remains intact while the invisible takes over, to make it the site of its presence? What does that mean, if not the transgression of all the phenomenology of *thing-ness*? The liturgy does not deal with objects, and even less with *things*, but it is well and truly directed toward a *beyond the thing*, toward a *personal presence* under the visibility of things" (my emphases).

4. Joseph Ratzinger, "Das Problem der Transubstantiation und die Frage nach dem Sinn der Eucharistie," *Theologische Quartalschrift*, no. 147 (1967): 129–59, quoted and translated in Gustave Martelet, *Résurrection, eucharistie et genèse de l'homme* (Paris: Desclée de Brouwer, 1972), 129n77; my emphasis.

5. Council of Trent (Thirteenth Session), "Decree Concerning the Most Holy Sacrament of the Eucharist," chaps. 3–4, trans. James Waterworth (1848; Hanover Historical Texts Project, 1995), accessed November 5, 2015: https://history.hanover.edu/texts/trent/ct13.html.

6. Thomas Aquinas, *Summa Theologica* 3.75.1, ad.3; 3.75, co.4, trans. Fathers of the English Dominican Province, ed. and rev. Kevin Knight (1920; New Advent, 2008), http://www.newadvent.org/summa/4075.htm.

7. Aquinas, *Summa Theologica* 3.75, co.5.

8. René Descartes, *The Philosophical Writings of Descartes*, vol. 1, trans. J. Cottingham, Robert Stoothoff, and Dugald Murdoch (Cambridge: Cambridge University Press, 1985), 99.

9. Friedrich Nietzsche, *Thus Spoke Zarathustra*, Part I: 4, trans. Graham Parkes (Oxford: Oxford University Press, 2005), 30; my emphasis.

10. See Falque, *Passeur de Gethsémani* (Paris: Éditions du Cerf, 1999), part 3.

11. "Eucharistic Prayer II," *The Roman Missal: English Translation according to the Third Typical Edition* (Chicago: Liturgy Training, 2011), §102, 646.

12. Édouard Pousset, "Il leur dit 'Ceci est mon corps,'" supplement to *Vie Chrétienne*, no. 245 (1981): 71; my emphasis.

13. See Maurice Merleau-Ponty, "Eye and Mind," trans. Carleton Dallery, in *The Primacy of Perception: And Other Essays on Phenomenal Psychology*, ed. James Edie (Evanston, IL: Northwestern University Press, 1964). "It is by lending his body to the world that the artist changes the world into painting. To understand these transubstantiations we must go back to the working, actual body" (p. 162).

14. Aquinas, *Summa Theologica* 1.3.4, ad.2.

15. Aquinas, *Summa Theologica* 3.75.8, ad.4.

16. Lacoste, *Présence et parousie*, 78.

17. See G. W. Leibniz, "Principles of Nature and Grace, Based on Reason" (1714), accessed November 5, 2015, http://www.earlymoderntexts.com/assets/pdfs/leibniz1714a.pdf. Maurice Blondel, *Une énigme historique: Le "Vinculum Substantiale" d'après Leibniz et l'ébauche d'un réalisme supérieur*, 2nd ed. (Paris:

Éditions Gabriel Beauchesne, 1930), 114, accessed November 5, 2015, http://classiques.uqac.ca/classiques/blondel_maurice/vinculum_substantiale/vinculum_substantiale.html. For a commentary on this topic, see Xavier Tilliette, *Philosophies eucharistiques de Descartes à Blondel* (Paris: Éditions du Cerf, 2006), 37–62, 101–6.

18. "Eucharistic Prayer I," *Roman Missal*, §22, 307.

19. Hans-Urs von Balthasar, *The Glory of the Lord: A Theological Aesthetic*, vol. 1, trans. Erasmo Leiva-Merikakis (San Francisco: Ignatius, 2009), 554–55.

20. Irenaeus, *Against Heresies* 5.2.3, in *Ante-Nicene Fathers*, vol. 1, trans. Alexander Roberts and William Rambaut, rev. and ed. Kevin Knight (1885; New Advent, 2009), http://www.newadvent.org/fathers/0103.htm.

21. Irenaeus, *Against Heresies* 4.18.5.

22. Simone Weil, *Gravity and Grace*, trans. Arthur Wills (Lincoln: University of Nebraska Press, 1997), 80.

23. Quoted by Simone Weil in *Cahiers*, vol. 1 (Paris: Plon, 1951), 126. See comments in Tilliette, *Philosophies eucharistique de Descartes à Blondel.*

24. Jean-Paul Sartre, "Intentionality: A Fundamental Idea of Husserl's Phenomenology" (January 1939), trans. Joseph P. Fell, *Journal of the British Society for Phenomenology* 1, no. 2 (1970): 4–5.

25. Ibid.

26. Paschasius Radbertus, *De corpore et sanguine Domine*, quoted and translated in Martelet, *Résurrection, eucharistie et genèse de l'homme*, 141; my emphases.

27. Paul VI, "*Lumen Gentium*," dogmatic constitution on the Church, November 21, 1964," §11, *The Holy See*, http://www.vatican.va/archive/hist_councils/ii_vatican_council/documents/vat-ii_const_19641121_lumen-gentium_en.html.

28. Bonaventure, *Breviloquium*, vol. 9 of *Works of St. Bonaventure*, trans. and ed. Dominic V. Monti (New York: Franciscan Institute, 2005), 241.

29. Thérèse de Lisieux, "Derniers entretiens," in *Œuvres complètes de Thérèse de Lisieux* (Paris: Desclée de Brouwer, 1992), ms B, 2v–3v.

30. *Catechism of the Catholic Church* (Vatican City: Libreria Editrice Vaticana, 2003), 1104, http://www.vatican.va/archive/ENG0015/__P2X.HTM; my emphases.

31. For a discussion of an immemorial past based on the originary mode of the Apocalypse, we can of course go back to René Girard, *Things Hidden since the Foundation of the World*, trans. Stephen Barn (London: Continuum, 2003): "On each occasion the Vulgate uses the translation *a constitutione mundi*. But *katabolês* really seems to imply the foundation of the world in so far as it results from a violent crisis" (p. 160).

32. Friedrich Nietzsche, *Fragments posthumes* (1880–1881), reprinted in *La Volonté de puissance*, vol. 1 (Paris: Gallimard, 1942), §246.

33. See Henri Bergson, *Creative Evolution*, trans. Arthur Mitchell (1911; Project Gutenberg, 2008), accessed November 6, 2105, http://www.gutenberg.org/files/26163/26163-h/26163-h.htm: "Intelligence has even more need of instinct than instinct has of intelligence" (p. 142).

34. Tertullian, *On Prayer* [*De Oratione*], in *Ante-Nicene Fathers*, vol. 3, trans. S. Thelwall, rev. and ed. Kevin Knight (1885: New Advent, 2009), chap. 6, http://www.newadvent.org/fathers/0322.htm; my emphasis. A freer translation might read as follows: "Moreover, in the bread of the eucharist, his body is also present ('This is my body' [Luke 22:19]). That is why, in the Lord's Prayer, when we ask for our daily bread, we ask to live *always united with Christ* and to be *a single body with him.*"

35. See Paul Ricœur, *Memory, History, Forgetting*, trans. Kathleen Blarney and David Pellauer (Chicago: University of Chicago Press, 2004): "Finally, there would come what I have ventured to call the *immemorial*: that which was never an event for me and which we have never even actually learned, and which is less formal than ontological. At the very bottom, we would have the *forgetting of foundations*, of their original provisions, life force, creative force of history, *Ursprung*, 'origin,' irreducible to the beginning, and origin always already there, like the Creation" (p. 346; my emphases).

36. *Roman Missal*, §24, 529.

37. Pierre de Bérulle, "De l'eucharistie," in *Conférences et fragments (Oeuvres de piété, 1–165)*, vol. 3 of *Œuvres complètes de Pierre de Bérulle* (Paris: Éditions du Cerf, 1995), 328, fragment 119.

38. See Josef Andreas Jungmann, *Missarum Sollemnia: Explication génétique de la messe romaine*, vol. 1 (Paris: Aubier, 1972), 159: "Contemplation of the blessed sacrament at the moment of consecration becomes thereafter, for many believers, the essential part of worship in the mass. It was enough to have seen the Body of the Lord at the consecration to find peace. In the towns, people chased from one Church to another to see as often as possible the elevated host, and this was thought to lead to the greatest of benefits." The historic debut of the practice of adoration of the Blessed Sacrament during the "worship of forty hours," was a form of continuous adoration starting in Milan in the middle of the sixteenth century, and then extended and codified by Clement VII in 1592 (the constitution *Graves et Diuturnas*), several decades after the Council of Trent, 1563. See also Édouard Dumontet, *Le Désir de voir l'hostie et la dévotion au Saint-Sacrement* (Paris: Beauchesne, 1926), 67.

39. Bonaventure, *Breviloquium*, 190; my emphases.

40. On the conversion of the sense in the eucharistic Adoration according to Bonaventure, see Falque, *God, the Flesh, and the Other*, trans. W. C. Hackett (Evanston, IL: Northwestern University Press, 2015).

41. Jérôme de Gramont, "Le monde muet et la patrie de la phénoménologie," *Transversalités*, no. 110 (April 2009): 177–95. "God is certainly present in a thing, and a thing now entirely given up to our view, but not only him: God is present in the bread and the wine, the *Eucharist*. . . . God observed (in the morning of experience) becomes God clearly there, given to see but only for the eyes of faith, entirely present for the *eucharistic adoration* which knows how to welcome him, but God obscured still in that he overflows all presence and does not allow himself to be brought back to that which we can see. It needs to be said that God makes

himself present in the eucharistic adoration, but it needs also to be said that our experience does not give us any power over his presence" (p. 187). See also, by way of complement, Jérôme de Gramont, "Une expérience du quatrième type: la liturgie," *Theophilyon* 15, no. 1 (2010): 51–76. I share with this author not only a deep friendship but also a conviction in our faith, and indeed the practice of the Adoration of the Blessed Sacrament. It is, I hope, the moment to underline this, with all due modesty demanded by the silence of the presence in the Adoration.

42. Levinas says that "consciousness is challenged [*mise en question*] by the face. The challenge does not come from awareness of that challenge. . . . The visitation is the upset of the very egoism of the Ego that upholds that conversion. *The face disorients the intentionality that sights it. This is a challenge of consciousness, not a consciousness of the challenge.*" Emmanuel Levinas, *Humanism of the Other*, trans. Nidra Poller (Urbana: University of Illinois Press, 2003), 32–33; my emphasis.

43. The expression "inverse intentionality" comes from Merleau-Ponty. I refer here to the sense employed by John Llewelyn in "L'intentionalité inverse," in "Dossier: Art et phénoménologie," ed. Eliane Escoubas, special issue, *La Part de l'Œil*, no. 7 (1991): 93–101. This dossier "makes us see" phenomenology in unusual depth.

44. "Eucharistic Prayer IV" and "Eucharistic Prayer III," *Roman Missal*, §118, 658; §113, 653.

45. [Cyprian of Carthage], Epistle 57.2.2, in *Saint Cyprien: Correspondance*, ed. L. Bayard (Paris: Le Belles Lettres, 1961), 156 [translation slightly modified].

9. Plunging Bodily

1. Jean-Luc Marion, "Esquisse d'un concept phénoménologique de don," in *Filosofia della Revelazione: Actes du colloque Enrico Castelli*, ed. Marco M. Olivetti (Rome: Archivo di filosofia, 1994), 78n1–3.

2. Henri de Lubac, *Corpus mysticum: L'eucharistie et l'Église au Moyen Âge* (Paris: Aubier, 1949), 279–80.

3. For the neologism "encharnement," see Charles Péguy, *Le Porche du mystère de la deuxième vertu* (1929; Paris: Gallimard, 1986), 74: "His incarnation, which is really his assumption of the flesh [*encharnement*], His making one of the flesh and of the carnal, his taking on of man and his taking on of the cross and his taking on of the tomb. His in-carnal-ment [*encharnellement*] and his ordeal, His life as a man and his life as a worker and his life as priest and his life as saint and his life as martyr, His life as a believer. His life as Jesus."

4. Augustine, "On the Nature of the Sacrament of the Eucharist," Sermon 272, *Early Church Texts*, accessed November 6, 2015, http://www.earlychurch texts.com/public/augustine_sermon_272_eucharist.htm.

5. Charles Péguy, "Victor-Marie, Comte Hugo," in *Œuvres en prose complètes*, vol. 3 (Paris: Gallimard/La Pléiade, 1992), 235. See also Péguy, "Le dialogue de l'histoire et de l'âme charnelle," in *Œuvres en prose complètes*, vol. 3, 753.

6. I have previously discussed the relationship between the episode of the washing of the feet and that of the woman with the issue of blood, in terms of the

toucher-touched; see *Le Passeur de Gethsémani* (Paris: Éditions du Cerf, 1999), 148–52, and *God, the Flesh, and the Other*, trans. W. C. Hackett (Evanston, IL: Northwestern University Press, 2015), §45 (with reference to Origen).

7. Marcel Jousse, *La Manducation de la parole* (Paris: Gallimard, 1975), 33n1.

8. *Catechism of the Catholic Church* (Vatican City: Libreria Editrice Vaticana, 2003), 1104, http://www.vatican.va/archive/ENG0015/__P4O.HTM. "The Church offers those who are about to leave this life the Eucharist as viaticum. . . . The sacrament of Christ once dead and now risen, the Eucharist is here the sacrament of passing over from death to life, from this world to the Father" (art. 1524).

9. Pierre Teilhard de Chardin, *The Divine Milieu*, trans. B. J. Wall (New York: Perennial, 2001), 57; emphases in original.

10. [*Transitus*: an annual Franciscan ritual that celebrates the passing of St. Francis to eternal life. —Trans.]

11. Benedict XVI, *Sacramentum Caritatis*, post-synodal apostolic exhortation, February 22, 2007, sec. 72, *The Holy See*, http://w2.vatican.va/content/benedict-xvi/en/apost_exhortations/documents/hf_ben-xvi_exh_20070222_sacramentum-caritatis.html.

12. See Edith Stein, "Husserl and Aquinas: A Comparison," in *Knowledge and Faith*, trans. Walter Redmond (Washington, DC: Institute of Carmelite Studies, 2010), 13.

13. On the *via* as *status viae* (state of earthly pilgrimage) (Aquinas) rather than *Itinerarium* (itinerary) (Bonaventure), see Falque, "Limite théologique et finitude phénoménologique chez Thomas d'Aquin," *Revue des Sciences philosophiques et théologiques* 93, no. 3 (2008): 532–34.

14. See Nietzsche's notebooks of 1888 (Dionysos vs. the Crucified One), in *Writings from the Late Notebooks*, ed. Rüdiger Bittner, trans. Kate Sturge (Cambridge: Cambridge University Press, 2003), §89, 249–50; emphases in original.

15. Friedrich Nietzsche, *The Birth of Tragedy*, trans. W. A. Haussmann (London: George Allen & Unwin, 1909), 34, 26–27.

16. Friedrich Nietzsche, *Writings from the Early Notebooks*, trans. Ladislaus Löb (Cambridge: Cambridge University Press, 2009), 7[13], p. 33. Quoted and commented upon in Barbara Stiegler, *Nietzsche et la critique de la chair* (Paris: PUF, 2005), 281. Stiegler clearly and sharply establishes a comparison between Nietzsche's view of life, on the one hand, and St. John's, on the other (pp. 280–88). The parallel is also found, though not developed, in François Gachoud, *Par-delà l'athéisme* (Paris: Éditions du Cerf, 2007), 153–59.

17. See, for example, the proposal of this parallel (between Dionysus and St. John) in Rudolf Bultmann, *Das Evangelium des Johannes* (Göttingen: Dandenhoed & Ruprecht, 1959), 78, and its refutation in Heinz Noetzel, *Christus und Dionysos* (Stuttgart: Calwer Verlag, 1960), both cited in Stiegler, *Nietzsche et la critique de la chair*, 282n3.

18. Friedrich Hölderlin, "Bread and Wine," st. 8, in *Poems of* Friedrich Hölderlin, trans. James Mitchell (San Francisco: Ithuriel's Spear, 2004), 14; Novalis, "Spiritual Songs of Novalis," trans. George MacDonald (London: Strahan, 1876), VII. See the citations and commentary by Manfred Frank (disciple of Hans-Georg Gadamer) in *Le Dieu à venir [Der kommende Gott]* (1982; Arles: Actes Sud, 1989), 16–17, 26–27.

19. Tertullian, *On Fasting: In Opposition to the Psychics*, chap. 16, in *Ante-Nicene Fathers*, vol. 4, trans. S. Thelwall, rev. and ed. Kevin Knight (1885; New Advent, 2009), http://www.newadvent.org/fathers/0408.htm.

20. Paul Valadier, *Jésus-Christ ou Dionysos: La foi chrétienne en confrontation avec Nietzsche*, rev. ed. (Paris: Desclée, 2004), 184.

21. Nietzsche, *Writings from the Late Notebooks*, §14, 250. See Valadier, *Jésus-Christ ou Dionysos*, 150. The opposition between "resurrection" and "over-resurrection" is established in Didier Franck, *Nietzsche and the Shadow of God*, trans. Bettina Bergo and Philippe Farah (Evanston, IL: Northwestern University Press, 2012): "it is very clearly against the resurrectional power of God that the power unfolded by eternal recurrence must be measured" (p. 337). On this point, see also Falque, *Metamorphosis of Finitude*, trans. George Hughes (New York: Fordham University Press, 2012), chap. 4.

22. Didier Franck, in *Nietzsche and the Shadow of God*, quotes a brief note by Nietzsche "from the summer of 1881": "A wholly other eternalization—glory moves in a false dimension [in Christianity]. We must introduce into it eternal depth, eternal repeatability" (p.68). Franck comments further, "The resurrection of the carnal body as a spiritual one, or the resurrection of an earthly body as a celestial one, fails to grant the body its true power, that it is a *false resurrection*, or a resurrection unto a *false life*" (p. 69; my emphases).

23. Valadier, *Jésus-Christ ou Dionysos*, 187.

24. Stanislas Breton, *Le Vivant Miroir de l'univers* (Paris: Éditions du Cerf, 2006), 42.

25. Thus, there is an explicit link in him between eucharistic sacrifice and the communion of spouses. See *Catechism of the Catholic Church* (Vatican City: Libreria Editrice Vaticana, 1993), 1621 ("The Celebration of marriage"): "It is therefore fitting that the spouses should seal their consent to give themselves to each other through the offering of their own lives by uniting it to the offering of Christ for his Church in the Eucharistic Sacrifice, and receiving the Eucharist so that, communicating in the same Body and the same Blood of Christ they may form but 'one body' in Christ."

26. Origen, *Homélies sur Jérémie* 14.7.81 (Paris: Éditions du Cerf, 1997), and *Homélies sur le Lévitique* 7.2.317 (Paris: Éditions du Cerf, 1981). See the citations and commentary in Falque, *God, the Flesh, and the Other*.

27. See Falque, *Metamorphosis*, chap. 7, §24.

28. [Sitting at a desk to keep an office open during "office hours" is referred to in French as doing the "permanence." —Trans.]

29. Jean-Yves Lacoste, "Petite phénoménologie de la fatigue," in *Présence et parousie* (Geneva: Ad Solem, 2006), 315–16.

30. Jean-Louis Chrétien, *De la fatigue* (Paris: Éditions de Minuit, 1996), 67–74. "God becomes tired, he made for himself the possibility of becoming fatigued in becoming man, in becoming incarnate" (p. 71).

31. Bernard of Clairvaux, "Sermons on the Song of Songs" 74, in *Œuvres complètes*, vol. 4 (Paris: Vivès, 1878–1887), 522 [not included in Sources Chrétiennes]. On this point, see Falque, "Expérience et empathie chez Bernard de Clairvaux," *Revue des Sciences philosophiques et théologiques* 89 (October–December 2005): 655–96.

Conclusion. The Flesh in Common

1. [The French proverbial expression for "the Mass is ended" (*la messe est dite*) is widely used, even in a secular context, to conclude events. It is sometimes translated as "the die has been cast." —Trans.]

2. See Henri Bergson, *The Two Sources of Religion and Morality* (Paris: PUF, 1958), 330. "The mechanical calls up a mystique"—which I apply here to the dimension of the eucharistic body. "We don't limit ourselves to saying, as we were saying above, that the mystical calls up the mechanical. Let us add that this enlarged body awaits a *supplement of soul*, the *mechanical demands the mystical*" (Ibid., my emphasis).

3. John Chrysostom, Homily 24 (on the first Epistle to the Corinthians), quoted in Henri de Lubac, *Catholicism: Christ and the Common Destiny of Man*, trans. L. Sheppard and E. Englund (San Francisco: Ignatius, 1988), 89, 89n21, 69.

4. Irenaeus, *Against Heresies* 3.20.2, in *Ante-Nicene Fathers*, vol. 1, trans. Alexander Roberts and William Rambaut, rev. and ed. Kevin Knight (1885; New Advent, 2009), http://www.newadvent.org/fathers/0103.htm.

5. In addition to the triptych that this book completes (death-birth-body: anguish-resurrection-eucharist; *Le Passeur de Gethsémani* [The guide to Gethsemane]–*Metamorphosis of Finitude*–*The Wedding Feast of the Lamb*), a further volume is projected: *The Disquiet of the Created: A Philosophical Essay on the Mystery of Iniquity*.

6. See Jean-Louis Vieillard-Baron, "Quel avenir pour le christianisme dans la démocratie moderne?" *Cités* 12, no. 4 (2002): 33–45. This article deserves careful consideration, in particular for its theologico-political approach and for its claim of a "quality that is interior" both for the future of Christianity and for democracy.

7. Gabriel Marcel, *Homo Viator: Introduction to a Metaphysic of Hope*, trans. Emma Craufurd (Chicago: Henry Regnery, 1951), 132. See the commentary in Pierre Colin, *Gabriel Marcel: Philosophe de l'espérance* (Paris: Éditions du Cerf, 2009), 66–68.

Index

Kühn, Rolf, 259
Küng, Hans, 184

Perspectives in
Continental Philosophy

John D. Caputo, series editor

John D. Caputo, ed., *Deconstruction in a Nutshell: A Conversation with Jacques Derrida.*

Michael Strawser, *Both/And: Reading Kierkegaard—From Irony to Edification.*

Michael D. Barber, *Ethical Hermeneutics: Rationality in Enrique Dussel's Philosophy of Liberation.*

James H. Olthuis, ed., *Knowing Other-wise: Philosophy at the Threshold of Spirituality.*

James Swindal, *Reflection Revisited: Jürgen Habermas's Discursive Theory of Truth.*

Richard Kearney, *Poetics of Imagining: Modern and Postmodern.* Second edition.

Thomas W. Busch, *Circulating Being: From Embodiment to Incorporation—Essays on Late Existentialism.*

Edith Wyschogrod, *Emmanuel Levinas: The Problem of Ethical Metaphysics.* Second edition.

Francis J. Ambrosio, ed., *The Question of Christian Philosophy Today.*

Jeffrey Bloechl, ed., *The Face of the Other and the Trace of God: Essays on the Philosophy of Emmanuel Levinas.*

Ilse N. Bulhof and Laurens ten Kate, eds., *Flight of the Gods: Philosophical Perspectives on Negative Theology.*

Trish Glazebrook, *Heidegger's Philosophy of Science.*

Kevin Hart, *The Trespass of the Sign: Deconstruction, Theology, and Philosophy.*

Mark C. Taylor, *Journeys to Selfhood: Hegel and Kierkegaard.* Second edition.

Dominique Janicaud, Jean-François Courtine, Jean-Louis Chrétien, Michel Henry, Jean-Luc Marion, and Paul Ricoeur, *Phenomenology and the "Theological Turn": The French Debate.*

Karl Jaspers, *The Question of German Guilt*. Introduction by Joseph W. Koterski, S.J.

Jean-Luc Marion, *The Idol and Distance: Five Studies*. Translated with an introduction by Thomas A. Carlson.

Jeffrey Dudiak, *The Intrigue of Ethics: A Reading of the Idea of Discourse in the Thought of Emmanuel Levinas*.

Robyn Horner, *Rethinking God as Gift: Marion, Derrida, and the Limits of Phenomenology*.

Mark Dooley, *The Politics of Exodus: Søren Kierkegaard's Ethics of Responsibility*.

Merold Westphal, *Overcoming Onto-Theology: Toward a Postmodern Christian Faith*.

Edith Wyschogrod, Jean-Joseph Goux, and Eric Boynton, eds., *The Enigma of Gift and Sacrifice*.

Stanislas Breton, *The Word and the Cross*. Translated with an introduction by Jacquelyn Porter.

Jean-Luc Marion, *Prolegomena to Charity*. Translated by Stephen E. Lewis.

Peter H. Spader, *Scheler's Ethical Personalism: Its Logic, Development, and Promise*.

Jean-Louis Chrétien, *The Unforgettable and the Unhoped For*. Translated by Jeffrey Bloechl.

Don Cupitt, *Is Nothing Sacred? The Non-Realist Philosophy of Religion: Selected Essays*.

Jean-Luc Marion, *In Excess: Studies of Saturated Phenomena*. Translated by Robyn Horner and Vincent Berraud.

Phillip Goodchild, *Rethinking Philosophy of Religion: Approaches from Continental Philosophy*.

William J. Richardson, S.J., *Heidegger: Through Phenomenology to Thought*.

Jeffrey Andrew Barash, *Martin Heidegger and the Problem of Historical Meaning*.

Jean-Louis Chrétien, *Hand to Hand: Listening to the Work of Art*. Translated by Stephen E. Lewis.

Jean-Louis Chrétien, *The Call and the Response*. Translated with an introduction by Anne Davenport.

D. C. Schindler, *Han Urs von Balthasar and the Dramatic Structure of Truth: A Philosophical Investigation*.

Julian Wolfreys, ed., *Thinking Difference: Critics in Conversation*.

Allen Scult, *Being Jewish/Reading Heidegger: An Ontological Encounter*.

Richard Kearney, *Debates in Continental Philosophy: Conversations with Contemporary Thinkers*.

Jennifer Anna Gosetti-Ferencei, *Heidegger, Hölderlin, and the Subject of Poetic Language: Toward a New Poetics of Dasein*.

Jolita Pons, *Stealing a Gift: Kierkegaard's Pseudonyms and the Bible*.

Jean-Yves Lacoste, *Experience and the Absolute: Disputed Questions on the Humanity of Man*. Translated by Mark Raftery-Skehan.

Charles P. Bigger, *Between Chora and the Good: Metaphor's Metaphysical Neighborhood*.

Dominique Janicaud, *Phenomenology "Wide Open": After the French Debate.* Translated by Charles N. Cabral.

Ian Leask and Eoin Cassidy, eds., *Givenness and God: Questions of Jean-Luc Marion.*

Jacques Derrida, *Sovereignties in Question: The Poetics of Paul Celan.* Edited by Thomas Dutoit and Outi Pasanen.

William Desmond, *Is There a Sabbath for Thought? Between Religion and Philosophy.*

Bruce Ellis Benson and Norman Wirzba, eds., *The Phenomenology of Prayer.*

S. Clark Buckner and Matthew Statler, eds., *Styles of Piety: Practicing Philosophy after the Death of God.*

Kevin Hart and Barbara Wall, eds., *The Experience of God: A Postmodern Response.*

John Panteleimon Manoussakis, *After God: Richard Kearney and the Religious Turn in Continental Philosophy.*

John Martis, *Philippe Lacoue-Labarthe: Representation and the Loss of the Subject.*

Jean-Luc Nancy, *The Ground of the Image.*

Edith Wyschogrod, *Crossover Queries: Dwelling with Negatives, Embodying Philosophy's Others.*

Gerald Bruns, *On the Anarchy of Poetry and Philosophy: A Guide for the Unruly.*

Brian Treanor, *Aspects of Alterity: Levinas, Marcel, and the Contemporary Debate.*

Simon Morgan Wortham, *Counter-Institutions: Jacques Derrida and the Question of the University.*

Leonard Lawlor, *The Implications of Immanence: Toward a New Concept of Life.*

Clayton Crockett, *Interstices of the Sublime: Theology and Psychoanalytic Theory.*

Bettina Bergo, Joseph Cohen, and Raphael Zagury-Orly, eds., *Judeities: Questions for Jacques Derrida.* Translated by Bettina Bergo and Michael B. Smith.

Jean-Luc Marion, *On the Ego and on God: Further Cartesian Questions.* Translated by Christina M. Gschwandtner.

Jean-Luc Nancy, *Philosophical Chronicles.* Translated by Franson Manjali.

Jean-Luc Nancy, *Dis-Enclosure: The Deconstruction of Christianity.* Translated by Bettina Bergo, Gabriel Malenfant, and Michael B. Smith.

Andrea Hurst, *Derrida Vis-à-vis Lacan: Interweaving Deconstruction and Psychoanalysis.*

Jean-Luc Nancy, *Noli me tangere: On the Raising of the Body.* Translated by Sarah Clift, Pascale-Anne Brault, and Michael Naas.

Jacques Derrida, *The Animal That Therefore I Am.* Edited by Marie-Louise Mallet, translated by David Wills.

Jean-Luc Marion, *The Visible and the Revealed.* Translated by Christina M. Gschwandtner and others.

Michel Henry, *Material Phenomenology.* Translated by Scott Davidson.

Jean-Luc Nancy, *Corpus.* Translated by Richard A. Rand.

Joshua Kates, *Fielding Derrida.*

Michael Naas, *Derrida From Now On.*

Shannon Sullivan and Dennis J. Schmidt, eds., *Difficulties of Ethical Life.*

Catherine Malabou, *What Should We Do with Our Brain?* Translated by Sebastian Rand, Introduction by Marc Jeannerod.

Claude Romano, *Event and World*. Translated by Shane Mackinlay.

Vanessa Lemm, *Nietzsche's Animal Philosophy: Culture, Politics, and the Animality of the Human Being*.

B. Keith Putt, ed., *Gazing Through a Prism Darkly: Reflections on Merold West-phal's Hermeneutical Epistemology*.

Eric Boynton and Martin Kavka, eds., *Saintly Influence: Edith Wyschogrod and the Possibilities of Philosophy of Religion*.

Shane Mackinlay, *Interpreting Excess: Jean-Luc Marion, Saturated Phenomena, and Hermeneutics*.

Kevin Hart and Michael A. Signer, eds., *The Exorbitant: Emmanuel Levinas Between Jews and Christians*.

Bruce Ellis Benson and Norman Wirzba, eds., *Words of Life: New Theological Turns in French Phenomenology*.

William Robert, *Trials: Of Antigone and Jesus*.

Brian Treanor and Henry Isaac Venema, eds., *A Passion for the Possible: Thinking with Paul Ricoeur*.

Kas Saghafi, *Apparitions—Of Derrida's Other*.

Nick Mansfield, *The God Who Deconstructs Himself: Sovereignty and Subjectivity Between Freud, Bataille, and Derrida*.

Don Ihde, *Heidegger's Technologies: Postphenomenological Perspectives*.

Suzi Adams, *Castoriadis's Ontology: Being and Creation*.

Richard Kearney and Kascha Semonovitch, eds., *Phenomenologies of the Stranger: Between Hostility and Hospitality*.

Michael Naas, *Miracle and Machine: Jacques Derrida and the Two Sources of Reli-gion, Science, and the Media*.

Alena Alexandrova, Ignaas Devisch, Laurens ten Kate, and Aukje van Rooden, *Re-treating Religion: Deconstructing Christianity with Jean-Luc Nancy*. Pre-amble by Jean-Luc Nancy.

Emmanuel Falque, *The Metamorphosis of Finitude: An Essay on Birth and Resur-rection*. Translated by George Hughes.

Scott M. Campbell, *The Early Heidegger's Philosophy of Life: Facticity, Being, and Language*.

Françoise Dastur, *How Are We to Confront Death? An Introduction to Philosophy*. Translated by Robert Vallier. Foreword by David Farrell Krell.

Christina M. Gschwandtner, *Postmodern Apologetics? Arguments for God in Con-temporary Philosophy*.

Ben Morgan, *On Becoming God: Late Medieval Mysticism and the Modern Western Self*.

Neal DeRoo, *Futurity in Phenomenology: Promise and Method in Husserl, Levinas, and Derrida*.

Sarah LaChance Adams and Caroline R. Lundquist, eds., *Coming to Life: Philos-ophies of Pregnancy, Childbirth, and Mothering*.

Thomas Claviez, ed., *The Conditions of Hospitality: Ethics, Politics, and Aesthetics on the Threshold of the Possible*.

Roland Faber and Jeremy Fackenthal, eds., *Theopoetic Folds: Philosophizing Multifariousness.*

Jean-Luc Marion, *The Essential Writings.* Edited by Kevin Hart.

Adam S. Miller, *Speculative Grace: Bruno Latour and Object-Oriented Theology.* Foreword by Levi R. Bryant.

Jean-Luc Nancy, *Corpus II: Writings on Sexuality.*

David Nowell Smith, *Sounding/Silence: Martin Heidegger at the Limits of Poetics.*

Gregory C. Stallings, Manuel Asensi, and Carl Good, eds., *Material Spirit: Religion and Literature Intranscendent.*

Claude Romano, *Event and Time.* Translated by Stephen E. Lewis.

Frank Chouraqui, *Ambiguity and the Absolute: Nietzsche and Merleau-Ponty on the Question of Truth.*

Noëlle Vahanian, *The Rebellious No: Variations on a Secular Theology of Language.*

Michael Naas, *The End of the World and Other Teachable Moments: Jacques Derrida's Final Seminar.*

Jean-Louis Chrétien, *Under the Gaze of the Bible.* Translated by John Marson Dunaway.

Edward Baring and Peter E. Gordon, eds., *The Trace of God: Derrida and Religion.*

Vanessa Lemm, ed., *Nietzsche and the Becoming of Life.*

Aaron T. Looney, *Vladimir Jankélévitch: The Time of Forgiveness.*

Richard Kearney and Brian Treanor, eds., *Carnal Hermeneutics.*

Tarek R. Dika and W. Chris Hackett, *Quiet Powers of the Possible: Interviews in Contemporary French Phenomenology.* Foreword by Richard Kearney.

Jeremy Biles and Kent L. Brintnall, eds., *Georges Bataille and the Study of Religion.*

William S. Allen, *Aesthetics of Negativity: Blanchot, Adorno, and Autonomy.*

Don Ihde, *Husserl's Missing Technologies.*

Colby Dickinson and Stéphane Symons (eds.), *Walter Benjamin and Theology.*

Emmanuel Falque, *Crossing the Rubicon: The Borderlands of Philosophy and Theology.* Translated by Reuben Shank. Introduction by Matthew Farley.

Emmanuel Falque, *The Wedding Feast of the Lamb: Eros, the Body, and the Eucharist.* Translated by George Hughes.

Colby Dickinson, *Words Fail: Theology, Poetry, and the Challenge of Representation.*

Jean Wahl, *Transcendence and the Concrete: Selected Writings.* Edited and with an Introduction by Alan D. Schrift and Ian Alexander Moore.

An Yountae, *The Decolonial Abyss: Mysticism and Cosmopolitics from the Ruins.*

CPSIA information can be obtained
at www.ICGtesting.com
Printed in the USA
JSHW080959080323
38650JS00001B/61

9 780823 270415